PSYCHOLOGY OF ADJUSTMENT

Personal Growth in a Changing World

EASTWOOD ATWATER

PRENTICE-HALL, INC., Englewood Cliffs, N.J. 07632

Library of Congress Cataloging-in-Publication Data

ATWATER, EASTWOOD, [date]
   Psychology of adjustment.

   Bibliography: p. 387
   Includes indexes.
   1. Adjustment (Psychology) 2. Adulthood.
3. Interpersonal relations. 4. Self-actualization
(Psychology) I. Title. [DNLM: 1. Adaptation,
Psychological. 2. Human Development.
3. Interpersonal Relations. 4. Self Assessment
(Psychology) BF 335 A887p]
BF335.A88 1987   158   86-16907
ISBN 0-13-734864-9

Editorial/production supervision and interior design: Virginia Rubens
Cover design: Karen C. Stephens
Cover photo by Fred Burrell
Photo Research: Page Poore
Manufacturing buyer: Barbara Kittle
Photo Editor: Lorinda Morris

Printed in the United States of America

10 9 8 7 6 5 4 3 2 1

ISBN 0-13-734864-9 01

PRENTICE-HALL INTERNATIONAL (UK) LIMITED, *London*
PRENTICE-HALL OF AUSTRALIA PTY. LIMITED, *Sydney*
PRENTICE-HALL OF CANADA, INC., *Toronto*
PRENTICE-HALL HISPANOAMERICANA, S.A., *Mexico*
PRENTICE-HALL OF INDIA PRIVATE LIMITED, *New Delhi*
PRENTICE-HALL OF JAPAN, INC., *Tokyo*
PRENTICE-HALL OF SOUTHEAST ASIA PTE. LTD., *Singapore*
EDITORA PRENTICE-HALL DO BRASIL, LTDA., *Rio de Janeiro*

Contents

7

8

9

10

11

WORK AND LEISURE   245

12

FREEDOM AND DECISION MAKING   270

13

PSYCHOLOGICAL DISORDERS   294

14

THERAPY 319

15

ADULT LIFE STAGES 342

16

DEATH AND BEREAVEMENT 364

Preface

This book is intended for those who are interested in applying psychological insights and principles to their own lives as a way of better understanding themselves and others and of living more effectively. To this end I've included topics that are relevant to the three recurrent themes of the book—personal adjustment, interpersonal relationships, and personal growth. Since a well-rounded text on adjustment and growth cuts across several branches of psychology, I've included contributions from clinical, personality, social, and developmental psychology, as well as from the rapidly expanding fields of cognitive psychology, health psychology, and neuroscience.

This third edition of *Psychology of Adjustment* offers three new chapters. One of these covers the three major approaches to adjustment and growth—the psychodynamic, social learning, and humanistic perspectives. A new chapter on the body and health reflects the growing interest in health psychology and the vital relationship between our mental and emotional outlook and bodily health. The chapter on psychological disorders deals with difficulties such as anxiety disorders, depression, suicide, and schizophrenia.

As a means of updating the material throughout the rest of the book, I have added new topics, findings, and examples. Six chapters have been completely rewritten: Adjustment and Growth; Meeting People, Making Friends; Sexuality; Love and Marriage; Work and Leisure; and Therapy.

Several new features have been provided to help you study more effectively. First, there is a section on studying techniques (How to Study) that immediately follows this preface. Second, the chapter summaries are in greater detail and are arranged by the major sections of the chapter. Third, there is a self-test at the end of every chapter. Each self-test contains ten multiple-choice questions to help you check how well you understand what you've read. The items in the self-tests are also included in the test bank provided for the instructor (although there they are worded differently). Thus, mastering the self-test items is an excellent way to prepare for the classroom tests, especially if your instructor uses the test items in the Instructor's Manual, as most of them do.

Throughout the book the reader is encouraged to apply the concepts and findings to his or her own experience. Accordingly, I've included many examples and boxed items of personal interest to readers. Also, at the end of each chapter there are exercises, questions for self-reflection, and recommended readings. The exercises are especially valuable as a way of heightening your involvement in the material.

I am grateful for the suggestions received from faculty colleagues, especially Emory Holland, Martin Gelman, Carol Rae Hoffman, Elmer Ritzman, and Cynthia Love. I've also benefited from the critiques and suggestions of reviewers, including Patricia A. Cote, Community College of Rhode Island; Charles G. Frederickson, Centenary College; and Kenneth J. Sher, University of Missouri–Columbia.

I'm thankful for the help of my wife Kay, who taught me how to use the computer without which this revision would not have been completed on time.

Finally, it is my hope that each of you will find this book helpful and rewarding.

Eastwood Atwater

How to Study

Like many teachers, I hear hundreds of excuses why students haven't done well on a test. Occasionally, students will admit outright, "I just didn't study." But more often, they will say, "I really *studied* for that test. I can't understand why I did so poorly on it." A common problem is waiting until the last minute to study for a test. But in many instances, students just don't know *how to study*. Whether you fall into this category or not, chances are you could improve your studying habits by applying one of the time-honored methods of studying explained below.

THE PQ4R METHOD

The PQ4R method gets its name from the six overlapping stages for studying material such as a textbook chapter—preview, question, read, reflect, recite, and review.[1] Extensive experience has shown that this method can improve your understanding and memory, and thus your test performance.

Preview

It's a good idea to look over the chapter as a whole before you begin it. When you read a novel, you usually start at the beginning and read straight through so as not to spoil the surprise ending. But with concepts and factual material, it's just the opposite. Here, it's important to get an idea of the material as a whole so you can put the details in context as you read.

First, look over the table of contents.

Next, skim through the chapter, looking at the headings and subheadings.

Then, read the chapter summary.

Finally, decide how much you want to read at a sitting.

[1] E. L. Thomas and H. A. Robinson, *Improving Memory in Every Class: A Sourcebook for Teachers* (Boston: Allyn and Bacon, 1972).

Question

Once you've looked over the chapter, you may be curious about the material. A helpful technique is to ask yourself questions about the material. Then read the chapter with the aim of finding the answers to your questions. One way to do this is to turn each bold-faced heading and subheading into a question. For example, the first major heading and subheading in Chapter 5, Stress, are shown below.

SOURCES OF STRESS

Meaning of Stress

Common Stressors

Personal, Situational Factors

Now use these headings and subheadings to think up some questions. Here are some examples. What does the term "stress" mean? Does stress refer to external forces or to something within? What are the most stressful events in our lives? Why do some individuals find the same event more stressful than others? Your use of such questions may prove even more effective if you jot them down, and then, as you read, write down your answers.

Read

Make it a point to understand what you're reading, digesting the material in one section before proceding to the next. Skimming through material without comprehending it leads to superficial understanding at best, but more often, to downright confusion. In contrast, when you take the time to understand what you read, you'll also retain it better. If you're not clear about the meaning of a word, look it up in the glossary in the back of the book. If you can't find the word in the glossary, look it up in one of the better dictionaries such as *Webster's New World Dictionary*. Also, feel free to make explanatory notes to yourself in the margins of the pages of your textbook.

Reflect

A good way to improve your understanding of something is to pause periodically and reflect on it. Ask yourself: Do I really understand this material? Could I explain it to someone else? If the answer is no, reread the material.

It's also helpful to mark or underline key passages in the chapter. This makes you an active participant in reading and provides you with key passages to review for tests. Some students prefer to mark or underline as they read. Others prefer to read through the material, and then to go back and highlight the most important points. I prefer the latter approach, because I usually have a better idea of the key passages after I've read through the material. Here are some suggestions for marking or underlining:

Read through each section before marking or underlining.

Mark only key passages or ideas.

Use a marker or pen. Pencil often smears.

Recite

Perhaps you've had this experience: you look up someone's telephone number, but no sooner have you closed the phone book than you've forgotten the number. You reopen the book and find the number again. But this time as you close the book, you repeat the number to yourself, either silently or audibly. You're improving your memory through *recitation*—the act of repeating or speaking aloud.

Recitation improves your memory in several ways. First, by focusing your attention on the page a bit longer, you can encode the material better, thereby ensuring accurate storage of the material. Repeated practice may also help you to retrieve the material when you need it.

There are several ways to use recitation. First, the act of reflection, or asking questions about the material, mentioned above, is itself a form of recitation. Second, you may also recite by closing the book and mentally rehearsing what you've just read. A third way is to recite aloud, either by discussing the material with a classmate, or by sharing your reactions or asking questions about it in class. A fourth way is to make a written outline of what you've read. I highly recommend this method because it forces you to select the main ideas in the material. Occasionally, students attempt to escape the thinking process by simply copying down the headings and subheadings, including little else. Others include too much detail, which becomes distracting. Instead, be selective. You should be able to outline an entire chapter of this book in just several written pages, depending, of course, on how large you write. The entire process of selecting the major ideas and writing them down is an excellent form of recitation. It also provides you with a handy guide to review for the test.

The amount of time spent on recitation depends on the material covered. When you're trying to remember isolated bits of information, like names or numbers, up to 80 percent of your time should be spent in recitation. But when you're learning ideas or concepts that are highly meaningful and well-organized, perhaps you would spend only 20 percent of your time in recitation. Personal experience will help you to determine which method of recitation works best for you.

Review

When you're ready to review, reread the summary at the end of the chapter to give yourself a sense of the material as a whole. Then look back over the material in the chapter, paying special attention to the key ideas you've marked or underlined under each heading and subheading. If you've made a written outline of the chapter, review this too. Ideally, you should review the material periodically, to offset the rapid decline in retention once you've learned something. It's recommended that you review the material within twenty-four hours of the initial reading, and then again seventy-two hours later. After this, it's a good idea to review the material about once a week until you're tested on it.

When you're ready, do the self-test at the end of the chapter. Then check your responses against the list of correct answers provided in the book. When you miss a question, it's important to go back and look up the correct answer. Otherwise, you may make the same mistake again. You may observe that the order of test items parallels the sequence of material in the chapter, thus facilitating your use of the self-test for study purposes. Also, you might be interested to know that all the items in the self-tests are included in the test bank provided for the instructor, but are worded differently. Consequently, mastering the self-test items is a good way of preparing for the classroom tests, provided, of course, that your instructor uses the test items in the instructor's manual, as most instructors do.

WHERE AND WHEN TO STUDY

Once the semester is underway, you're ready to plan your study schedule. Consider your class schedule, the workload in each course, and other commitments, such as a part-time job or family responsibilities. Be realistic. Don't try to study too much material at one time.

First, it's important to find a place to study which is free from distractions. Then use this place only for studying. In this way, you'll develop a set of associations that will strengthen your study habits. When you find yourself daydreaming or worrying about something else, take a short break, and return when you're ready to study. When you finish studying, leave this place. By consistently doing this, you'll associate this place with studying and feel more like studying there.

It's also important to set aside particular times for study. You may wish to study for a given block of time and quit at the end of this period regardless of how much you've read. Or, you may want to study until you've covered a certain amount of material. Either way, it's best to study in reasonable blocks of time, about one to three hours. After a long stretch you may have difficulty concentrating on the material at hand. That's why it's a good idea to take a short break at least once an hour, or even on the half-hour when you're covering very difficult material. Also, you might select other things you enjoy doing, and make them contingent on completing your study goal for a given time slot. For instance, if you'd like to call up a friend or watch television, do your studying first. Then make your call or watch TV as a reward to yourself.

Above all, don't procrastinate. Distribute your study times realistically so you don't try to absorb too much material at a time. For instance, if you must cover four chapters in this book for a test, plan to read no more than one chapter in a given time slot. Spacing out your study time cuts down on boredom and fatigue. Also, your mind may continue absorbing the material in the intervals between study periods. This is especially important to keep in mind when you're learning complex or difficult material.

Finally, you can improve your study methods by learning from your test results. If your instructor goes over the test in class, make it a point to attend that day. Find out what you missed, and, equally important, why. Were the questions different from what you expected, requiring, say, factual information rather than an understanding of concepts? If you didn't do well on an essay test, ask your instructor how you can do better next time. Try not to waste time making excuses or blaming your instructor or yourself. Find out what you need to do in order to improve your test performance next time. Then modify your study methods accordingly.

1 Adjustment and Growth

A familiar drama is being enacted in millions of homes. Karen, recently graduated from college, arrives home late for dinner. She has spent the day looking for a job, and is discouraged. Flinging down the want-ads, she complains that the nine-to-five job is a sham and that starting salaries are an insult.

Enter the parents. The father, who arrived home earlier from his nine-to-five job, is depressed from paying the latest bunch of bills. The mother, tired from a day at the office herself, is busy starting dinner. They've all been through this scene before.

Karen's parents point out that young people tend to be unrealistic about the job market. They suggest that despite the initial difficulties in getting employment, she might be happier with a secure job in a large corporation. But Karen objects, saying she prefers the freedom of a small company, or, better still, being on her own. She has also thought of getting an advanced degree, but now she considers this a waste of time and money. Frustrated from seeing their suggestions dismissed one after another, the parents finally say, "Karen, when are you going to face the real world?"

CHANGE

Is Karen's problem with her parents just another conflict between the generations? Or is there something else involved? Could it be that Karen and her parents are not talking about the same "real world"? The tensions in this family may be due to changes in the ground rules governing everyday behavior that have been brought about by important social changes in recent years. Many of the new rules challenge much of what people have been taught in the past, such as the importance of punctuality, the need for conformity, and the notion that bigger is better. Nor are such scenes limited to homes in the United States. Japanese parents also complain about the decline of the work ethic and corporate loyalty among the young. And even middle-class parents in the Soviet Union are confronting similar problems with their youth (Toffler, 1980).

Social Change

One of the major characteristics of our time is the accelerated rate of social change and its far-reaching effects on our lives. For instance, technological innovations such as air travel, space technology, television, and computers have made the world a smaller place. A terrorist attack in the Middle East or an earthquake in South America affects the entire world. In the past, it took days or weeks to learn of such an important event, much less respond to it. Today, we are bombarded around the clock with information from the mass media, making it almost impossible to be oblivious to national and world events. Furthermore, pictures of earth sent back from travelers in outer space have provided us with a new symbol of our age—the planet earth.

We're also more aware of transience or impermanence in society. Because of the pervasive effects of social change, we soon learn that everything is temporary. The combination of technology and competition has produced planned obsolescence—designing things not to last. We often find it's cheaper to buy a new watch than to repair our old one, giving rise to a throwaway culture. In the same way, we expect ideas and organizations to change. We take it for granted that we will change jobs and move more frequently than our parents did. As a result, we make fewer lasting ties to institutions, political parties, or products. Although we come into contact with more people during a given month than was the case in the past, we form fewer close relationships with them. Instead, there's a tendency to form relationships on the basis of shared interests and satisfactions rather than deep emotional ties. Although this enables us to develop a wider range of interests and relationships, it also calls for greater flexibility and less emotional investment on our part. Consequently, there is increased loneliness and widespread lack of a sense of community.

Although most people recognize that things are changing, they often disagree on the direction in which we're headed. Many people assume that the world as we know it will last indefinitely and that all the changes around us will

View of earth from the moon. (NASA)

not shake the familiar social, economic, and political structures which hold our society together. They may reminisce about the "good old days," unaware that people in past eras may not have considered themselves so happy at the time. Others, fed by a steady diet of bad news about crime, economic problems, world crises, and the threat of nuclear destruction, have adopted a bleaker view. They feel that no one is really in control and that society is falling apart. The more cynical of this group feel that the earth is heading inevitably toward its final collapse. However, like travelers on the ill-fated *Titanic*, they want to go down first-class, in deck chairs with the best view of the sinking horizon.

Tomorrow's Society

In his book *The Third Wave* (1980), Alvin Toffler presents another, more optimistic view of where our society is heading. He holds that many of the technological and social changes we're experiencing are neither isolated nor random. Instead, they are part of a larger pattern of an emerging civilization. Viewing history as a succession of rolling waves of change, Toffler sees a major new wave of change sweeping over our society. The First Wave era began with the development of agriculture about 10,000 years ago. Until that time, people survived primarily through fishing, hunting, food-gathering, and raising animals. But gradually, the sowing and harvesting of grains and other crops provided a more reliable food supply, which in turn advanced civilization. Such changes made possible an increase in the population and set the stage for the rise of cities. The Second Wave of major change began with the Industrial Revolution in the seventeenth century. The knowledge of mechanical causation led to inventions such as the steam engine, which made possible our urban, industrial society based on the technological conquest of nature. As Toffler sees it, our industrial society peaked in the late 1950s, when white-collar and service workers outnumbered blue-collar workers for the first time. Yet this was the same era that saw the introduction of the computer, commercial jet travel, the birth control pill, and many other technological innovations that have brought about the present state of society.

Today, Toffler believes we are in the midst of a Third Wave of major social change that is radically altering the way we live. We are moving into a postindustrial society, with new ground rules for almost everything. Although the pattern of social change is complex and continues evolving, certain characteristics are already evident.

First, we are moving toward a more diversified economy, and away from the domination of the giant industrial hierarchies, such as the large steel and automobile corporations. A major result is a shift from a manufacturing-oriented to a service-oriented economy, with the prediction that nine out of ten of the new jobs in the American economy between now and 1995 will be in the service-producing industries (U.S. Department of Labor, 1985). The increasing role of high technology and information throughout the world is also aiding in the proliferation of smaller companies.

Second, the growth of separatist movements, together with pressing human rights issues throughout the world, is giving rise to new political structures that more nearly reflect the realities in a given society. The ruling parties are having to share their power with the minorities in order to achieve stability in a heterogeneous society.

A major characteristic of the emerging social pattern is an increased role for the individual in society. This is already evident in the greater insistence on individual rights and individual participation in various social institutions. Such changes are leading to new, less polarized relationships between political leaders and their constituents, between managers and workers, and between men and women. Mass communication and the availability of information is also assuming a major role in society. The rise in personal and social freedoms has also resulted in greater acceptance of nonconforming lifestyles. Yet at the same time, the more individualized we are, the more difficult it becomes to select a job or a mate with matching interests and values. The result is ill-matched relationships or the lack of relationships altogether. Therefore, while the breakup of mass society holds out the promise of greater personal fulfillment, it also results in more loneliness and lack of community.

Still another characteristic of tomorrow's society is the increased importance of change, with change occurring at an accelerated pace and having more far-reaching effects on our lives. The influence of change is amplified by the ripple effect, with a given change producing changes in other parts of society as well. For example, the greater variety of living arrangements, including the increased number of single adults living alone, cohabiting couples, and single-parent families, has led to extensive changes in housing, food packaging, and child care; to more flexible work arrangements such as flextime; and to young people assuming more responsibility at an earlier age. Consequently, society is changing more rapidly than in the past. For instance, while the agricultural revolution was preceded by millions of years of human development, it took less than 10,000 years to produce the Industrial Revolution. Toffler speculates that the increasing rate of social change may well bring in the Third Wave civilization in a matter of decades.

Values, Lifestyles, and Change

How people respond to social change varies widely among individuals, depending on their attitudes, needs, and values. In an attempt to analyze and organize Americans' values and how they are affected by social change, Arnold Mitchell developed a values and lifestyles typology (VALS). The VALS typology includes nine American lifestyles clustered in four major groups: (1) The *need-driven*, made up of America's poor, includes two lifestyles—the "survivors," characterized by extreme poverty, and the "sustainers," the least satisfied of any group who hope to improve their situation. (2) The *outer-directed*, making up the vast majority of Americans, includes the "achievers," the "belongers," and the "emulators." The achievers are the hard-working, successful leaders of the major institutions such as the giant corporations and government. The belongers typify what is usually regarded as middle-class America. The emulators are intensely ambitious people who are in transition between the belongers and the achievers. All of these people tend to be traditional, conservative, and opposed to radical change. (3) The *inner-directed* group comprises a smaller proportion of the population that is actively engaged in personal or social change. Included here are the "I-Am-Me's," the "experientials," and the "societally conscious" lifestyles. The I-Am-Me's are younger adults in transition from the outer-directed upbringing of their parents to a more inner-directed way of life involving new interests and life goals. The experientials are older, highly educated individuals in well-paying , professional jobs. They have little faith in institutional leaders and are open to change and experimentation. The societally conscious are successful, influential, and mature individuals who are concerned about social issues and work for social change. (4) The *combined outer- and inner-directed group* make up the "integrated" lifestyle, which includes only 2 percent of the population. Yet these are the people who have a truly integrated outlook on life. They have the decisiveness of the outer-directed lifestyle and the insight and penetration of the inner-directed. Accordingly, they combine great stability and achievement with openness to change, and see things in global perspective. They are generally the most adaptive to change.

Figure 1–1. NINE AMERICAN LIFESTYLES.

Inner-directed			Combined
I-AM-ME	*EXPERIENTIAL*	*SOCIETALLY CONSCIOUS*	*INTEGRATED*
Youthful, impulsive, and experimental; in transition from outer-directed to inner-directed lifestyle.	Highly educated professionals; person-centered; intensely oriented toward inner growth.	Successful individuals concerned about social issues; often active in single-issue groups.	Mature, tolerant individuals with large field of vision; combine great stability with openness to change.

Need-driven		Outer-directed		
SURVIVOR	*SUSTAINER*	*BELONGER*	*EMULATOR*	*ACHIEVER*
Old, very poor, fearful, and depressed; removed from mainstream society.	Living on the edge of poverty; angry and streetwise; often involved in the underground economy.	Mainstream majority, traditional, and conventional; very stable and intensely patriotic.	Youthful, intensely ambitious; individuals trying to make it big by breaking into the system.	Middle-aged, successful, and prosperous; leaders of the major institutions in society.

Adapted from Arnold Mitchell, *The Nine American Lifestyles: Who We Are and Where We Are Going* (New York: Warner Books, 1984).

How well individuals from each of these lifestyles will fare in society depends partly on the social and economic directions in which the country moves. Marked prosperity not only strengthens the role of outer-directed individuals, but also provides the necessary affluence for inner-directed individuals to pursue their own interests and goals. By contrast, hard times tend to bring greater traditionalism, conformity, and a concern for law and order, thereby strengthening the position of outer-directed individuals and putting inner-directed ones on the defensive. However, if we are moving in the direction of a postindustrial society with a more decentralized government and economy, as Toffler and others claim, then there could be a massive shift in the values of Americans, resulting in a greater proportion of inner-directed, simpler lifestyles, greatly increasing the number of inner-directed individuals. In this scenario, the openness to change so characteristic of inner-directed indiviuals will be a definite asset in adapting to social change.

Change—Challenge or Threat?

The ability to cope with change is also closely linked with one's tolerance for stress. Perhaps you're familiar with the pressures facing people in jobs such as air-traffic controller who must make split-second decisions affecting many lives; such workers can develop stress-related illnesses at several times the rate

Middle-class Americans tend to hold traditional values. (Teri Leigh Stratford)

of people in other jobs. Despite this, some people work night and day at high-powered jobs without becoming ill, while others in easier jobs develop ulcers and hypertension. Researchers (Pines, 1980) say the difference depends on a greater degree of psychological "hardiness." Such hardiness consists of a specific set of attitudes toward life, including an openness to change, a feeling of personal involvement in whatever one is doing, and a sense of control over events. The most important factor is the attitude toward change, with stress-resistant individuals generally regarding change as a challenge rather than a threat. Individuals were rated on the challenge dimension by statements such as "A satisfying life involves a series of problems, such that when one is solved, you move on to the next," and "I would be willing to give up some financial security if I found a more interesting job." People who strongly agreed with such statements rated high on challenge and were much more likely to use change and unexpected events constructively. For example, when one is fired at work, this can be seen either as a catastrophe that precedes one's inevitable downfall, or as a challenge that if accepted, may become an opportunity to find an even more suitable career. A great deal depends on the individual's attitude toward change and the willingness to use change to his or her advantage.

ADJUSTMENT

Regardless of our attitude toward social change, we face a considerable amount of change in our everyday lives. Our bodies continue to change throughout life, reminding us of our mortality. Our understanding and values change, making it difficult to choose wisely in regard to our life's work and marriage partners. What seemed important to us at 25 is no longer that important at 45. Leaders and organizations change, confronting us with new roles and responsibilities. Our marriage partners change and grow, making marriage itself an ever-changing relationship. Old friends move on. Loved ones die. The only thing we know for sure is that tomorrow will not be like today; next year will not be like this one.

The process of coping with such changes is called adjustment. Essentially, *adjustment* refers to the changes we make in ourselves and in our environment in order to achieve satisfying relationships with others and with our surroundings. Often we must modify our own attitudes or behavior in order to adapt to inevitable changes, such as getting older. In other instances, we can get a fresh start by altering something in our surroundings, such as courses or schools, our living arrangements, or our jobs. More often than not, successful adjustment requires a combination of these changes, such as adopting a better attitude toward work while getting used to a new job. Most important of all is knowing which type of adjustment is the most appropriate at the moment, as expressed in the following prayer:

> God grant us the *courage* to change what can be changed, the *serenity* to accept what cannot be changed, and the *wisdom* to know the difference.

Adapt or Else

Originally, the meaning of adjustment was borrowed from the concept of adaptation in biology. At the biological level, *adaptation* refers to changes in an organism's structure or function that facilitates the survival of the species. Adaptation is considered successful as long as the species is able to survive, regardless of whether individual organisms fail to adapt. At the psychological level, however, adjustment refers to the *individual's* struggle to survive in his or her surroundings. Here, the emphasis is on the learned, functional changes—rather than biological ones—that we must make in order to cope successfully with our environment. Yet it may be helpful to realize that our distinctively human abilities for coping are themselves the result of a long evolutionary process.

According to Charles Darwin's principle of natural selection, expressed in the familiar phrase "survival of the fittest," the organisms "selected" to survive are those best able to adapt to their environment. For example, fish with a darker coloring may be more likely to survive in some environments because their coloring provides camouflage against predators. In such an environment, the darker-colored fish are more apt to survive into adulthood and reproduce fish with darker coloring. Similarly, humans have evolved through a long process of natural selection that has favored those of our ancestors who were best adapted to survive their environment. Our ancestors gradually developed a bone structure enabling them to walk upright on two feet; they developed other advantages such as stereoscopic vision and versatile hands with opposable thumbs. Most important of all has been the evolution of the human brain, especially the cerebral cortex, which makes up 80 percent of the volume of the brain. The cortex is the seat of reasoned behavior, memory, and abstract thought. The cortex is also the part of the brain where sensory impressions and memories are stored, to be called forth when needed. Therefore, while animal behavior usually occurs automatically or through previous conditioning, much of human behavior is performed consciously. Homo sapiens is "thinking man." It is largely because of superior mental abilities that humans have developed language, speech, self-awareness, and culture. When humans needed food, they didn't develop claws or fangs; they made weapons of wood and stone for hunting and gathering, and later for growing crops. Their ability to speak enabled them to communicate verbally in planning a hunt or improving their methods of agriculture. The development of culture made it possible for elders to pass along their knowledge to the next generation.

The superior cognitive abilities and culture of humans also play a significant role in our individual efforts at coping with the environment. Our mental capacity gives us greater resourcefulness and flexibility in dealing with problems. We can learn new ways of seeing things, entertain alternate solutions, and proceed in a rational manner toward problem-solving. We can also learn from past experience, including our mistakes. Then too, through culture and communication, we may benefit from other people's experience—through reading, observing, talking, and listening to others. All of this enables us to cope more effectively with our environment. But perhaps the most astonishing thing about humans is not our superior mental capabilities themselves, but our laziness in using them. At the turn of the century William James hypothesized that the average person functioned at only 10 percent of capacity. More recent observers estimate we use only about 4 percent of our potential (Otto, 1980). Perhaps the precise figure varies, depending on the individual and the situation, as well as the particular aspect of ourselves in question.

John, an engineer in his early 30s, has worked for an established firm for 5 years. Recently, as a result of a takeover by a larger corporation, John faces a new job description and a new superior. Confronted with these changes, various individuals would respond differently. Some people are so rigid in their thinking that they cannot make the necessary changes that will allow them to adapt to such a situation. Or they may be so stubborn that they are unwilling to do so. Such people tend to become casualties. Either they quit their jobs, or they are eventually fired or transferred. Others may be so unresourceful or submissive that they readily conform to the required changes, mainly to keep their jobs. Yet many of these people survive at the price of considerable insecurity and resentment. Still other individuals might be called the true "survivors." They have that valuable quality of psychological hardiness mentioned earlier. That is, they have the will to survive plus the willingness to make the necessary changes to adapt without surrendering their integrity. Let's say John falls into this category. Instead of reacting blindly to the situation, he thinks things through in a problem-solving manner. Perhaps he'll talk things over with his spouse, colleagues, and friends. John considers his own needs, his abilities, his future, along with the demands and potential of the situation at work. If John decides to stay, he'll probably make some changes in his own way of doing things he wouldn't have made otherwise, learning a lot more in the process. At the same time, if John's superiors are reasonable, they may also make certain allowances that will help John to make a satisfying adjustment.

Adapting to a new situation by modifiying ourselves may be functional up to a point. Beyond that, the price may be excessive. I recall a man who, because he had never completed high school, felt he was fortunate to have a job reading water meters. Yet it was not a congenial job for him. He hated the job so intensely that each day when he returned from work he took to his bed, physically ill. When I suggested that he look for another job, he protested, "I'd rather have a job I hate than risk having no job at all."

Changing Our Environment

Sometimes, as the situation of the unhappy meter reader above would suggest, it may be wiser to adapt through changing our environment. In the case of disagreeable work, adapting might just mean a simple request for a new assignment for another job in the same company. If this isn't feasibile, then it might be better to look for work elsewhere. A change of surroundings may be helpful in a variety of other situations. For instance, students who have failed a course often enroll again in the same course with the same teacher. But in many cases, it might be wiser to get another teacher who uses a different approach, thereby

---

What Was Your Most Difficult Adjustment?

If you were to name the most difficult adjustment you've had to make, what would it be? Was it overcoming a physical handicap or illness? Did it involve coming to terms with disappointment or failure in school? Or was it the breakup of a close relationship?

Some people say their most difficult experience was overcoming a drug or drinking problem, partly because it posed a test of willpower, and partly because it required a change of lifestyle. Others say that their most difficult time was going through a divorce or getting over the death of a parent, spouse, or child. The loss of someone who has meant so much to us is like losing a part of ourselves, evoking deep emotions that are not easily resolved.

Interestingly, what people say was their most difficult adjustment varies widely from one person to another. Can you explain why your experience was the most difficult for you? What did you learn about yourself from it?

providing a new start. Recent high school and college graduates living at home who are constantly at odds with their parents might create a more tolerable living arrangement by moving into a place of their own. Individuals going through a divorce, getting over problems with alcohol or drug abuse, or coping with the death of a loved one, often get a fresh start in a new setting. At the same time, there is always the temptation to escape one's problems solely through a change of surroundings. A former client of mine with a variety of serious personal problems was obsessed with the idea that she could solve her problems by moving to California. I suggested that while a new setting might give her a fresh start, such a move in itself would not solve her problems.

Humans have a long history of surviving not only through their ability to make adaptive changes in their own makeup, but also because of their unique capacity to shape their surroundings. For instance, when Charles Darwin first arrived in Tierra del Fuego at the southernmost tip of South America aboard the *Beagle* in 1832, he was amazed at how people had adapted to this barren land. During the day, stark-naked Indians plied their canoes through the rough seas in freezing weather. At night, they lay naked on the wet, near-frozen ground. Darwin reasoned that their long-standing habits had made it possible for them to adapt to such miserable conditions. He was partly right, in the sense that the Fuegians' rate of metabolism is higher than average for the human species. Such is the marvelous capacity for adaptation at the biological level. Yet, in the long run, humans are more distinguished by *cultural* adaptation. Today, if you and I were to move to that part of the world, we would take a more aggressive role in shaping our surroundings to our needs. We would take thermal clothing. We would build houses with special insulation and warm our buildings with artificial heat. We would also develop industries, preferably using natural resources from the immediate region, that would yield products we could sell to people elsewhere. This would give us the money to buy things we couldn't grow or produce at home.

At the same time, there's a price to be paid for shaping the environment to meet our needs. For each time we change the world around us, we're modifying the environment to which we then have to adapt. Thus, at the level of individual adjustment, the person who changes jobs too frequently may get a reputation for instability, which can alienate employers, making it all the more difficult to achieve satisfaction at work. Similarly, the person who marries and divorces repeatedly as in the case of some celebrities, may acquire a tangled web of relationships and financial problems that makes domestic happiness even more unattainable. In each case, the cumulative effect of the attempted solutions becomes worse than the original problem. This is also true at the social and cultural level. Today, the most pressing problems we face are of our own making—namely, an increasingly polluted environment; ever-more-powerful chemicals and drugs whose consequences we cannot fully control; a way of life that has become unduly stressful for creatures better adapted to a life of hunting and fishing than to modern urban civilization; and finally, the threat of nuclear

Domed stadiums allow games to be played rain or shine. (Houston Tourist and Convention Center)

destruction of the entire earth. Bernard Campbell (1985) points out that we now find ourselves in a vicious circle of ever-increasing instability. Each new cultural adaptation leads to a larger population, which in turn uses more of the world's resources. This tends to increase the destruction of the natural environment, which leads to the development of new technology as a compensation, which in turn leads to increases in the world's population, thus completing the circle. It is essential that we make an all-out attempt to break this accelerating vicious circle and bring about a new stability by controlling the size of the world's population, using technology to preserve rather than destroy the natural environment, and adopting lifestyles with more realistic patterns of consumption. But the outlook is not at all certain.

The Person of Tomorrow

So far we've seen that adjustment is a dynamic *process*, involving changes in ourselves as well as in our environment. The rapid rate of social change makes adjustment all the more difficult by increasing the changes we need to make in ourselves in order to adapt. Yet as humans we have the distinctive qualities of intelligence and resourcefulness to shape our environment to meet our needs. Successful adjustment involves a constant give and take between ourselves and our surroundings in order to achieve a satisfying relationship with our environment.

Adjustment can also be seen as an *end state*, or a set of desirable personal qualities achieved by the well-adjusted personality. In earlier decades, when society was somewhat more static and adjustment implied a greater degree of social conformity, mental health professionals spoke of the well-adjusted personality. Such a person—always more of an ideal than an actuality—was assumed to have his or her emotions well under control, be relatively free from anxiety and problems, be happily married, and get along harmoniously with others at work and in the community. It was also assumed that such personal qualities were equally desirable for everyone and that conventional society was a conducive setting in which to become this type of person. But what does it mean to be well-adjusted today, in a world characterized by rapid and pervasive social change? Should we continue to assume that social conformity is automatically good for us, when society itself is "sick" in many ways? And how realistic is it to strive for the same set of personal qualities in the light of what we know about individual differences? Questions like these have led many people to abandon the notion of adjustment. Others, including the author, believe we should focus our energies all the more on *adjusting* or on the *process* of adjustment rather than on the passive state of "being adjusted," and on those personal qualities that are especially adaptive in a complex, rapidly changing society.

I once had the pleasure of hearing Isaac Asimov, the well-known author, speak on science fiction. Asimov kept his audience enthralled with the possibilities of people traveling to far-off planets and settling space colonies. Then, during the question period, one girl asked, "How do you know what it's going to be like 50 years from now?" Asimov readily admitted that we can't know exactly what the future will be like. We can only imagine what it might be like, in science fiction, for example. The only thing we can be certain of is that life in the future will be *different*. In a similar way, scientists and social planners talk about the "person of tomorrow." Usually, there's the implied notion that such a personality profile most aptly fits those who are not only surviving but also thriving in their world. At the same time, such accounts are speculative. We don't know what people will be like in the future. We can only imagine. The only thing we know for sure is that people will be somewhat different from, as well as similar to, people today. Yet such accounts may be helpful because they suggest personal qualities we may need to accept the challenge of living with uncertainty.

Drawing on his knowledge of long-term social trends, Alvin Toffler (1980) suggests that people of tomorrow will grow up differently from the way we grew up. They will most likely live in a less child-centered society than ours, take on responsibility at an earlier age, and grow up sooner than young people today. They will be more likely than their parents to question authority, and to value individuality in themselves and others. They will realize the value of money but, except under conditions of extreme poverty, they will resist working primarily for money. Instead, they will strive for more balance in their lives—

between work and play, producing and consuming, and headwork and hand-work. Above all, they will be even more adaptable to change than we are.

Carl Rogers (1984) also recognizes that people in future generations will need to be different in order to thrive in their respective environments. He suggests that those who thrive will possess certain personal qualities, though no one person will have all of them. Rogers suggests that people of tomorrow will resist the blind use of technology to control people and destroy nature, while eagerly supporting those changes that may enhance self-awareness and a humane life. They will also put a greater value on closeness, in their communi-cations and in intimate relationships. They will resist living in a compartmental-ized world, but will instead strive for greater wholeness in such areas as intellect and feeling, work and play, and the indiviual and the group. Above all, they will be "process persons." That is, "they are keenly aware that the one certainty of life is change—that they are always in process, always changing" (Rogers, 1984, p. 351).

PERSONAL GROWTH

The upheaval in social values during the past few decades has also shifted the emphasis from adjustment to growth and fulfillment. Generally, this has resulted in less concern for adapting to things as they are, and a greater interest in controlling the environment to accomplish one's personal goals. In his book *New Rules*, Daniel Yankelovich points out that changes in social values are modi-fying the basic giving/getting contract between ourselves and the environment—the unwritten rules governing what we give in our personal relationships, work, and community, and what we expect in return. The old giving/getting contract was based on self-denial, and it might be paraphrased this way: "I'll work hard and be loyal to my boss and spouse. I'll suppress what I like and do what is expected of me. And in return I'll get a stable family, a secure job, and a protec-tive government." In recent years, however, more people have grown wary of demands for sacrifices that they believe are no longer warranted. They feel that the old rules needlessly restrict the individual at the expense of large institu-tions, especially the government and big business, which use their power to advance their own interests. Consequently, millions of people are engaged in correcting the imbalance. They want more in return for their efforts.

The Search for Personal Fulfillment

Drawing on in-depth interviews and national surveys, Yankelovich (1981) and his colleagues have found that 80 percent of Americans are now engaged in the search for self-fulfillment in some way. About 17 percent of them are com-mitted to the "strong form" of self-fulfillment; the other 63 percent endorse the "weak form" of self-fulfillment.

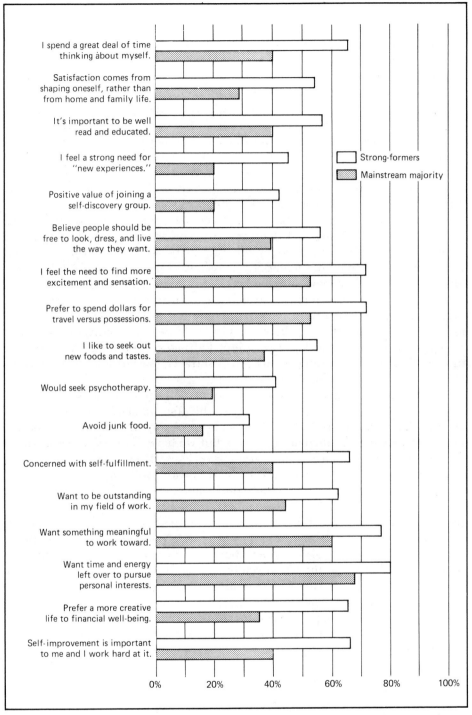

Figure 1-2. PREFERENCES FOR SELF-FULFILLMENT VALUES. Preferences of the strong-formers versus the mainstream majority.

Adapted from Daniel Yankelovich, "New Rules in American Life: Searching for Fulfillment in a World Turned Upside Down," *Psychology Today*, April 1981, p. 52.

Although the strong-formers are in the mainstream of Americans who strive for self-improvement, they pursue different goals. The strong-formers tend to be younger and better educated than the general population. Many of them are unmarried. They want more from life than money and material possessions, important as these things are. They are primarily interested in actualizing themselves as persons. They also feel that they have a much greater freedom of choice than their parents did and that they can control their lives to a considerable extent through the decisions they make.

Mark and Kathy, a couple in their 30s, are typical of the strong-formers when it comes to self-fulfillment. Mark, a lawyer, prefers to practice in a small office rather than in a big law firm. He also gives some of his time to a legal aid clinic for the poor. Kathy is a buyer in a large department store. Both feel that their jobs are challenging and that they are good at what they do. Mark and Kathy prefer to spend their money for travel, education, and leisure pursuits, rather than acquiring more material possessions to "keep up with the Joneses." Mark and Kathy also have a good marriage, though at times each of them would like to have an even more satisfying relationship. They want to have children, but Kathy doesn't want to take the time out of her career just yet. Like many other couples sharing the same values, Mark and Kathy presuppose a favorable environment, including continued affluence, abundant career opportunities, flexible work arrangements, low-cost travel, low burdens of responsibility, and diverse outlets for personal growth.

A much larger proportion of the population pursues the weak form of self-fulfillment. That is, they have many of the same values as the strong-formers, but to a lesser degree. Most of us would probably fit in here. We find the notion of personal fulfillment appealing, but we have many other concerns in our lives as well. We have to deal with the realities of our jobs, health, getting along with others, our marriages, and children with problems at school. Yet we too are questioning many of the traditional values. We are reluctant to make an all-out effort at work, especially when our employers take us for granted and put their own interests first. Likewise, we wonder if we should invest so much of ourselves in our marriage and family when these relationships are not always mutually satisfying. We also wonder about the future—where the economy is headed and what shape the world will be in 5 or 10 years from now. We question the old rules of working hard, sacrificing for our kids, and defining happiness and success in materialistic terms. This is not to imply that people are saying, "To hell with the job, forget the family, I couldn't care less about money and respectability." The weak-formers want to keep many of the traditional values. But they are struggling mightily to make room for greater personal choice and fulfillment.

Seeking Fulfillment in a Topsy-turvy World

At the same time, serious obstacles to the pursuit of personal fulfillment have surfaced in recent years. In the first place, the emphasis on self-actualiza-

Those who strongly endorse self-fulfillment values tend to be younger and better educated than the general population. (Ken Karp)

tion presupposes continued economic prosperity. Yet we've been weathering one of the most prolonged periods of economic and social uncertainty in our history. We've had to struggle with inflation, a tight job market, and financial instability, along with political unrest in many parts of the world—all of which threaten our survival rather than encourage growth. Young people reared with heightened expectations about the quality of life now face a world of diminished resources, increased competition, and an uncertain future. Even though they may not talk much about the threat of nuclear war, they have a deep concern about the coming years; they fear not being able to achieve their goals and not fulfilling their parents' expectations of them. Many of them feel they may be the first generation of Americans to face the real possibility of downward mobility—that is, to be less well off as adults than their parents were (Sifford, 1985).

The economic pressures have only intensified one of rhe chronic flaws in the search for fulfillment—the impact of spiraling expectations on our lives. Ordinarily, the greater our hopes for accomplishing a goal, the harder we strive to achieve it. However, when our expectations are constantly being raised, as they are in a consumer-oriented, growth-oriented society, they may have the opposite effect. Then we feel frustrated out of all proportion to the social realities involved. We're suffering from "relative deprivation"—the discontent generated largely by one's excessively high expectations in relation to the overall objective situation. It is this "relative" rather than absolute deprivation that accounts for much of the unhappiness today. We all know successful individuals who are unhappy mostly because they haven't met their personal goals, and couples who are getting divorced for reasons that would not have led to divorce in the past. Exaggerated expectations are especially apt to occur when it comes to the realization of our human potential. Up to a point, such a notion may energize us. Yet there comes a point, varying from one person to another, when the attempt to translate our potential into reality becomes damaging. From then on, we may saddle ourselves and others with unrealistic expectations as well as guilt for our supposed shortcomings, thereby increasing our unhappiness (Lichtenberg, 1984).

Still another obstacle to the pursuit of personal fulfillment is the attempt to satisfy one's psychological needs on an indivdiual basis, often at the expense of one's relationships or social involvement. Some critics hasten to point out that this merely reflects the narcissism or selfishness inherent in the search for self-fulfillment. But in their book *The Inner American* (1981), Joseph Veroff and his colleagues provide a more plausible explanation. They report that in the past several decades Americans have shifted their orientation to well-being from a socially integrated approach to a more personal one, an adaptive response—or adjustment—to the increasing complexity, impersonality, and uncertainty of society. Having lost faith in the worth of institutions such as government and big business, and feeling powerless to do anything about it, individuals are retreating to the realm of personal fulfillment. As a result, while individuals may be optimistic about their personal futures, they tend to be pessimistic about the outlook for their country and the rest of the world. But how realistic is this?

Commitment and Community

Fortunately, there has been a major reassessment of the human potential movement in recent years, which has resulted in a more realistic view of personal fulfillment. Daniel Yankelovich (1981) reports that millions of people are discovering, often by painful experience, that preoccupation with their inner needs is not a direct path to fulfillment. But their life experiments are not leading them back toward a stifling of the self, as in the past; nor are they retreating to the cultivation of their own gardens without regard for the rest of the world. Instead , Yankelovich suggests we are in the midst of developing new rules for living, which involve a realignment of the claims of self and society. The heart of this new outlook is the realization that personal fulfillment can be realized only in relation to others —through a web of shared meanings that transcend the isolated individual. Personal fulfillment in the deeper sense of the term requires commitments that endure over long periods of time. These commitments may be to people, projects, ideas, beliefs, experiences, nature, places, or adventures—depending on the individual and his or her values. The term "commitment" shifts the focus away from the self, either self-*denial* or self-*fulfillment*, and toward our connectedness with others. Two kinds of commitments are becoming especially important—one to closer, more satisfying relationships with others, and the other to expressive values.

The desire for closer, more satisfying relationships with others probably reflects in large part a growing dissatisfaction with superficial, fleeting relationships in our mobile, impersonal society. In our daily routine we make contacts with a larger number of people than our parents or grandparents ever did. Yet we form fewer lasting ties with them. More than two-thirds of Americans admit they have many acquaintances but few close friends. Two out of five report having fewer friends now than in the past. As a result, more individuals are engaged in the search for closer, more satisfying relationships with others. Yankelovich, who labels this trend the "search for community," periodically measures its strength in the population. In the early 1970s, about one-third of the population was engaged in the search for community. By the 1980s, almost half of Americans (47 percent) were seeking closer relationships with others. In some cases, individuals form intimate relationships on the basis of shared interests and personal values. In other instances, they may establish closer ties on the basis of common backgrounds, ethnic bonds, or religious values. In both cases, there is a realization that satisfying relationships don't just happen in our fast-moving society. They have to be nurtured, as we'll discuss in the chapters on friendship, sexuality, and love and marriage. Yet there seems to be a growing awareness that the mutual give and take of satisfying relationships with others is an integral part of personal fulfillment.

Another important trend is the shift from instrumental to expressive values. Generally this means putting less emphasis on such rewards as money, status, or security in exchange for a more satisfying way of life. Steve, in his early 40s, gave up a promising career with an established stockbroker's firm to open his own business—making plastic pouches for surgical supplies. He enjoys the freedom of being his own boss and having more time for his family and avocational pursuits. Cheryl, still in her late 20s, turned down a chance to work as a flight attendant for one of the major airlines in favor of a small, fledgling airline. Although she receives lower pay and has a more generalized job description—such as rotating to other positions when needed—she is enthusiastic about her job because of the variety of people she meets as well as the chance to share in the company's profits. Individuals such as Steve and Cheryl are not forsaking traditional values. What they seek is a better balance of the older and new values. Like most Americans they want to preserve traditional values: political freedom, the opportunity to achieve material well-being through one's own efforts, a place of respectability in the community, and pride in America's unique role in the world. But they also wish to pursue the emerging values, such as the freedom to pursue one's own lifestyle, greater autonomy for men and women, enjoyment of life as an adventure as well as an economic chore, a more caring attitude toward others, and the sense that one is engaged in a deeply meaning-ful and satisfying life—not just existing. In short, they identify with many of the personal qualities ascribed to the "person of tomorrow."

Yankelovich's analysis of the social changes in American life illustrates the dynamic process of personal adjustment and growth. Looking back, it seems that the traditional rules of living put an undue burden on the individual, sup-pressing personal desires for the sake of social adjustment. In time, as a social reaction to this, greater importance was given to the individual and to the fulfill-ment of inner psychological needs. However, as we've seen, people are discover-ing that human fulfillment is more complex than ordinarily portrayed and requires a better balance between the claims of self and society. Hans Selye (1978), the noted authority on stress, once observed that people suffering from stress-linked illnesses also have a warped code of behavior—one that emphasizes either too much selfishness or too much sacrifice. A one-sided approach to life won't do. One of the greatest challenges each of us faces is to integrate these two aspects of life. Throughout this book we'll explore some of the major areas of adjustment and growth, such as motivation, stress, sexuality, intimate relation-ships, careers, and coping with loss. But in every realm of life, we must con-stantly strive to achieve that level of give and take between ourselves and others which makes for mutually satisfying relationships.

Summary

Change

1. A major characteristic of our era is the accelerating rate of social change and the far-reaching effect it is producing in our lives.

2. Alvin Toffler suggests we are in the midst of a Third Wave of major social change, comparable to that in the earlier Agricultural and Industrial Revolutions.

3. The emerging pattern of society may be characterized by a more diversified economy, more heterogeneous political structures, a greater role for the individual, and the increased importance of social change.

4. How people are affected by social change varies widely depending on their attitudes, needs, and values, with people who adopt inner-directed lifestyles generally more receptive to personal and social changes.

5. The ability to cope with change is also closely related to one's tolerance for stress, with individuals who have greater openness to change being more resistant to stress-related illnesses.

Adjustment

6. *Adjustment* refers to the changes we must make in ourselves and our environment in order to achieve a satisfying relationship with others and with our surroundings.

7. The meaning of adjustment was borrowed, with modifications, from the concept of adaptation in biology; at the psychological level, adjustment refers to the *individual's* struggles to survive in his or her surroundings.

8. Humans have survived largely because of their superior adaptability, including advantages such as an upright posture, versatile hands, superior intelligence, and culture.

9. The superior cognitive abilities of humans play a significant role in individual adjustment, affording us potentially greater resourcefulness and flexibility in dealing with our problems.

10. Humans have also survived because of their unique abilities for cultural adaptation, or the shaping of the environment to meet their needs. Similarly, it is sometimes wiser for individuals to adapt through changing their environments.

11. Yet each time we change the world around us, we also modify the environment to which we have to adapt, thus creating a vicious circle of ever-increasing instability

12. Various descriptions of the "person of tomorrow" indicate that, among other things, those who thrive in the emerging society will be "process persons"—people especially adept at coping with personal and social change in their lives.

Personal Growth

13. The upheaval in social values in the past few decades has resulted in a shift of emphasis from adjustment to personal growth. This has also led to a revision in the giving/getting contract between ourselves and society, with people now expecting more from life in return for their efforts.

14. As a result, the majority of Americans are now engaged in the search for personal fulfillment to some degree, with most of them endorsing the weak form of self-fulfillment.

15. At the same time, serious obstacles to the pursuit of fulfillment have surfaced in recent years, including economic reversals, the discontent born of rising expectations, and a trend toward social disengagement.

16. Such changes are fostering a more realistic understanding of personal fulfillment, involving a realignment of the claims of self and society.

17. The heart of the new outlook is the realization that personal fulfillment can only be realized in a web of shared meanings that transcend the isolated individual, including more commitment to close relationships and expressive values in our lives.

Self-test

1. The accelerated rate of social change has resulted in a greater awareness of:

    a. world events   **c.** fleeting relationships

    b. impermanence   **d.** all of the above

2. According to Toffler's notion of the Third Wave of social change, we are moving toward:

    a. a return to traditional values   **c.** a postindustrial society

    b. an industrial revolution   **d.** world destruction

3. Which lifestyle among the following includes highly educated, well-paid professionals who are open to change and experimentation?

a. inner-directed
b. need-driven
c. outer-directed
d. sustainers

4. Psychological hardiness consists of a set of attitudes that includes:

a. relative indifference to others
b. an openness to change
c. a low desire to control one's environment
d. all of the above

5. Which term below refers to the changes we must make in ourselves and our environment in order to achieve a satisfying relationship with others and our surroundings?

a. self-actualization
b. cultural adaptation
c. adjustment
d. personal growth

6. Humans have a long history of survival because of their:

a. adaptable bodies with upright posture
b. capacity for cultural adaptation
c. greater resourcefulness and intelligence
d. all of the above

7. The "person of tomorrow" will be keenly aware that the one certainty of life is:

a. society
b. change
c. continuity
d. human survival

8. Compared to the general population, people who endorse the strong form of self-fulfillment tend to be:

a. more materialistic in their values
b. younger and better educated
c. less in control of their lives
d. cynical about our political leaders

9. Peope who suffer from "relative deprivation" are unhappy largely because of their:

a. financial limitations
b. exaggerated expectations
c. social deprivation
d. lack of ambition

10. According to Daniel Yankelovich, there is an increasing awareness that personal fulfillment involves:

a. a return to traditional values
b. a commitment to one's growth needs
c. greater self-denial than in the past
d. a commitment to close relationships

Exercises

1. *Social contacts.* Count the number of people you come into contact with during the course of one week. How many of these people do you have a close relationship with? Would you agree that many of our daily contacts involve fleeting or superficial relationships?

2. *Identifying your lifestyle.* Reread the section in this chapter titled "Values, Lifestyles, and Change." Which group of lifestyles most resembles your own? What does this say about your attitude toward social change?

3. *Change as a challenge or threat.* Select some change that has occurred in your life recently, such as a new boss at work or a new course you're taking. Then write a paragraph or two describing how you feel about this change, especially the degree to which you see it as a challenge or threat. To what extent would you say you are open to change? Which types of change do you find the most threatening?

4. *What was your most difficult adjustment?* Reread the boxed item on this subject. Then write a page or so describing your experience.

5. *How important is personal fulfillment to you?* Look over the items in Figure 1-2 on the importance of self-fulfillment as a lifestyle. Which do you most resemble: the profile of the strong-formers, those who strongly endorse self-fulfillment? or the values of the weak-formers, the mainstream majority?

6. *Personal fulfillment and relationships.* To what extent does one's personal fulfillment depend on having satisfying relationships? Write a paragraph or two describing your views on this, providing some specific examples in your own life supporting and challenging this idea. How much does one's happiness depend on others?

Questions for Self-reflection

1. Would you agree that many of the ground rules for everyday living are changing?
2. In what ways has your life been most affected by these changes?
3. Which types of change do you find most threatening?
4. What has been the most difficult personal adjustment for you?
5. Looking back, do you ever regret putting up with a difficult situation as long as you did?
6. Do you sometimes seek new surroundings or relationships to get a fresh start?
7. How many of the qualities ascribed to the "person of tomorrow" apply to you?
8. Do you expect more in return for your efforts at work than your parents did?
9. How important is personal growth and fulfillment to you?
10. Would you agree that ultimately, personal fulfillment can only be realized in a relationship with others?

Recommended Readings

Lazarus, A., and A. Fay. *I Can If I Want To.* New York: Warner Books, 1977 (paperback). A guide to personal growth and self-actualization.

Mitchell, Arnold. *The Nine American Lifestyles.* New York: Warner Books, 1984. Describes various American lifestyles and how these may be affected by social change.

Peck, M. Scott, M.D. *The Road Less Travelled.* New York: Simon & Schuster, 1978 (paperback). A psychiatrist discusses the ways people avoid facing and solving life's problems and the less well-travelled road of heathy personal growth.

Rogers, Carl. *On Becoming a Person.* Boston: Houghton Mifflin Company, 1961 (paperback). Carl Rogers shares his personal and professional experience as a therapist to explain what it means to become a person.

Toffler, Alvin. *The Third Wave.* New York: William Morrow and Company, Inc. , 1980. Describes the far-reaching effects of social change associated with the emergence of postindustrial society.

Yankelovich, Daniel. *New Rules.* New York: Bantam Books, 1982 (paperback). A clear explanation of the social trends that are changing the ground rules for living in today's society.

2 Perspectives on Adjustment and Growth

It was six men of Indostan
    To learning much inclined
Who went to see the Elephant
    (Though all of them were blind),
That each by observation
    Might satisfy his mind.

The First approached the Elephant
    And happening to fall
Against his broad sturdy side
    At once began to bawl:
"Bless me! but the Elephant
    Is very like a wall."

The Second, feeling of the tusk,
    Cried, "Ho! What have we here,
So very round and smooth and sharp?
    To me 'tis mighty clear
This wonder of an Elephant
    Is very like a spear."

The Third approached the animal,
    And happening to take
The squirming trunk in his hands
    Thus boldly up and spake:
"I see," quoth he, "the Elephant
    Is very like a snake."

The Fourth reached out his eager hand
    And felt about the knee.
"What most this wondrous beast is like
    Is mighty plain," quoth he;
"'Tis clear enough the Elephant
    Is very like a tree."

The Fifth, who chanced to touch the ear,
    Said, "E'en the blindest man
Can tell what this resembles most;
    Deny the fact who can,
This marvel of an Elephant
    Is very like a fan."

The Sixth no sooner had begun
    About the beast to grope
Then, seizing on the swinging tail
    That fell within his scope,
"I see," quoth he, "the Elephant
    Is very like a rope."

And so these men of Indostan
    Disputed loud and long.
Each in his own opinion
    Exceeding stiff and strong,
Though each was partly in the right,
    And all were in the wrong.

James Godfrey Saxe

Like the six blind men of India, psychologists approach the understanding of human behavior from different angles. We can divide these different viewpoints into three broad perspectives that focus, respectively, on the psychodynamic, social learning, and humanistic theories of adjustment and growth. The psychodynamic perspective focuses on how we manage the inherently conflicting forces of life—both within and without. The social learning perspective stresses the crucial role of learning in the environment. And the humanistic perspective emphasizes the importance of perceived reality—especially how we see ourselves and others—as well as the process of self-actualization. By calling attention to particular aspects of behavior that tend to be neglected by others, each perspective is "partly in the right." But none of them envisions the whole "elephant." Instead of wasting energy trying to prove which view is more correct—especially on issues that admit to no simple test of truth, such as motivation—it may be more helpful to regard each perspective as offering an optimal range of explanation of some aspects of human behavior. That is, each of them explains some aspects of adjustment and growth especially well, while admittedly minimizing, if not neglecting, other aspects. By examining the distinctive viewpoints of each of the three perspectives, we may arrive at a better understanding of adjustment and growth than we might have by studying only one.

THE PSYCHODYNAMIC PERSPECTIVE

The psychodynamic approach consists of a group of related theories and therapies that view human behavior in terms of the dynamics, or interaction, of the driving forces of personality—such as desires, anxieties, conflicts, and defenses. According to this viewpoint, individuals are inevitably caught in the clash between the conflicting forces of life, such as between impulses and inhibitions or between individuals and society. Although different psychodynamic theorists emphasize different aspects of personality, most agree that the basic dynamics of personality include conflict between two opposing forces: *anxiety* (which results from the clash of desire and inhibitions) and *defenses* against the desires that arouse anxiety. Since Freud's thought provides the core concepts for this perspective, we'll devote much of our discussion to his ideas. But we'll also indicate some of the ways in which later psychodynamic theorists modified and expanded Freud's views.

Freud (1965) compared personality to an iceberg in which only the surface shows: most of the psychic activity remains unconscious. Since behavior originates in unconscious impulses, psychology in its search for the causes of behavior cannot simply rely on observations of the individual, much less the person's self-reports. Instead, the psychologist must interpret the individual's behavior, revealing its intrapsychic motives. Thus, every aspect of behavior, whether humor, dreams, or works of art, can be interpreted in terms of its surface meaning or of its true, unconscious meaning. Throughout his writings,

Freud characteristically interpreted various human behaviors in terms of their deeper, unconscious meanings. And the goal of his therapy was to help patients, through the same approach, to gain insight and mastery of their unconscious motives. In order to understand the psychodynamic point of view, we'll describe several aspects of Freud's thought, including the structure of the mind or personality, the dynamics of personality, and the development of personality.

Structure of Personality

Freud held that the personality consists of three interacting processes: the id, the ego, and the superego. Since each has different goals, their interaction often takes the form of conflict. The *id* is the unconscious reservoir of psychic energy for the overall personality and the source of its later development—the ego and superego. All the drives that make up the id are derived from the two primal instincts: the "life" or sex instinct, and the "death" or aggressive instinct. Freud regarded the sex drive as the major source of psychic energy, affecting the entire personality, including the need for affection, love of family and friends, the urge toward creativity, as well as erotic behavior. The id operates entirely on the *pleasure principle*, taking no account of reason, reality, or morality.

The *ego* is a direct outgrowth of the id and functions as a manager of personality, enabling the individual to cope with the conflicting demands of the id, the superego, and society. Accordingly, the ego operates on the basis of the *reality principle*, with the primary concern for the individual's well-being. When a desire from the id bids for expression, the ego looks for a potential means of gratifying the desire in a socially satisfying way. The ego anticipates the consequences of such action, and then either acts accordingly or delays gratification, as the case may be.

The *superego* is that part of the personality which has been shaped by the moral standards of society as transmitted by the parents. It is roughly equivalent to "conscience," though much of it remains unconscious. As such, the superego takes no more account of reality than does the id and, instead, operates in accordance with the principle of *perfection*. Thus, the effects of the superego on personality tend to be harsh and punitive, or hypermoral. Much of the repression of unacceptable impulses is carried out by the superego directly or by the ego at the urging of the superego.

The id, ego, and superego are not entities or even parts of the mind. They are best seen as metaphors or names that Freud gave to highly complex psychological processes which make up our mental life.

Personality Dynamics

As we've already seen, the ego, id, and superego are often in *conflict* with each other, such that individuals commonly experience *ambivalence*—being pulled in opposing directions simultaneously. Ordinarily, the ego keeps the conflict at a manageable level, giving the id and superego their due consideration. But at times, the urges of the id or the judgments of the superego threaten to usurp the ego's control, resulting in unacceptable feelings or behavior. When this happens, the ego experiences anxiety.

Anxiety is an alarm signal, analogous to the sense of pain in the body, that warns the ego of danger. Freud distinguished three types of anxiety according to the source of danger. In *reality anxiety* the individual (1) is threatened by something that occurs in the external world, (2) experiences the appropriate anxiety, and (3) acts accordingly. In *neurotic anxiety* the ego senses that some impulses of the id are threatening to get out of control, tempting the individual to do something he or she will be punished for. In *moral anxiety* the person feels guilty about something he or she has done—either real or imagined. Sometimes the ego handles anxiety in a direct, realistic way, such as studying to reduce one's anxiety about an important exam. However, the most common response to anxiety is avoidance, covering it up through reliance on the ego defenses.

Defense mechanisms are unconscious reactions that automatically reduce the level of anxiety, thereby helping the individual to cope with the situation at hand. Repression, or the blocking of unacceptable desires or memories from awareness, is the fundamental defense underlying all others. We'll identify some of the other ego defense mechanisms in a later chapter on stress. But here, it is important to point out that the defense mechanisms in themselves are neither good nor bad. Up to a point, they are adaptive mechanisms, helping us to cope with psychological threat. Beyond that, defenses become self-defeating, as in the case of people who habitually make excuses or blame others for their own failures, rather than correcting their own inadequacies.

A major characteristic of personality dynamics is the constant shift or displacement of psychic energy from one aspect of personality to another. Freud thought there is only a certain amount of energy available to the organism, but it may be focused or displaced onto different objects. For example, a man who is angry at his boss but fearful of saying so may displace his anger onto a safer object by banging his fist on the desk. Thus, much of the adaptibility of personality consists in the transformation of motives through the redistribution of psychic energy.

Development of Personality

Since Freud regarded the *libido*, the psychic energy of the sex drive, as fundamental to the entire personality, he interpreted the development of personality on the basis of the sequential process of psychosexual stages. In each stage, the child seeks to gratify the drive for pleasure in the various bodily zones, the mouth, the anus, and the genitals. The manner in which children handle the conflict between their impulses and environmental restrictions are decisive for adult personality. Too little or too much gratification may result in fixation, by which the personality becomes emotionally fixed at a particular anxiety-ridden stage and continues to act out symbolically the wishes that were overly inhibited or indulged.

The *oral stage* occurs during the first year of life, during which the mouth becomes the primary means of gratifying the desires of the id. Although infants must suck milk from the breast (or bottle) to survive, their mouths soon become a means to satisfying sucking pleasure and, to some extent, aggressive impulses. Thus the various ways infants achieve gratification through sucking or holding on lay the foundations for later adult personality traits such as acquisitiveness and tenacity. Fixation at this stage may result in the passive personality associated with addictive eating, smoking, or drinking, or the sarcastic person who is always criticizing everyone else's ideas without offering any of his or her own.

The *anal stage* occurs during the second year of life when the child's major source of physical pleasure becomes the releasing or retaining of feces. Caught between the pleasurable urges of the id and parental demands, the child may experience considerable anxiety and conflict. Fixation in the early phase of this stage may result in adult tendencies toward disorderly, messy behavior. By contrast, fixation in the later phase of this stage would give rise to the stubborn, compulsively orderly personality.

The *phallic stage*, which extends from the third to the fifth or sixth year, is the period which the child experiences sensual pleasure through handling of his or her genitals. Again, too little or too much gratification sets the stage for later difficulties, such as the individual who feels guilty about her sexuality or engages in sex to reduce anxiety. The phallic stage is especially important because of the occurrence of the Oedipus complex for boys and the Electra complex for girls during this period. In the Greek legend, King Oedipus unwittingly killed a man who turned out to be his father and married a woman he later discovered was his mother. And Electra, the legendary daughter of King Agamemnon, longed for him after his death and plotted the revenge of his killers—her mother and her mother's lover. Similarly, children during the phallic stage are sexually attracted to the opposite-sex parent and envy the same-sex parent. The unconscious conflict arouses considerable anxiety in children of both sexes, though, in due time in most cases, it is resolved as spontaneously as it emerged. Instead of trying to possess the opposite-sex parent and risk losing the love of the same-sex parent, the child settles for identification with the same-sex parent. In so doing, children incorporate that parent's sexual orientation, mannerisms, and values. Furthermore, the resolution of the Oedipus conflict results in the formation of the superego. Examples of people who suffer from unresolved oedipal conflicts would be the male Don Juan who "loves 'em and leaves 'em" without ever getting close to his partners, and the actively seductive female who continues to feel guilty about sex.

The *latency* period takes place between about 5 years and 12 years of age. During this time the child's interests turn away from erogenous satisfactions, with early sexual feelings being forgotten and sexual urges lying relatively dormant.

Sigmund Freud—the founder of psychoanalysis.
(Austrian National Tourist Office)

The *genital stage* begins with the onset of puberty and sexual maturation, from about 12 years of age on. In this period the individual's sexual interests are reawakened and focus on gratification through genital or sexual activity. In the well-adjusted adult the experiences of the oral, anal, and phallic stages have become incorporated into genital strivings so that he or she is capable of genuine love and adult sexual satisfaction. However, most adult problems with sex derive from fixations at the earlier oral, anal, or phallic stages. Some examples of such fixations would be people who are cynical about sex and enter into lustful relationships as ends in themselves or those who withdraw from all sexual relationships.

Modifications

Many of Freud's followers were original thinkers in their own right who revised and expanded his views. Although post-Freudian thought developed in many different directions, two trends are especially significant. First, there has been a greater emphasis on the ego. Many of the later psychodynamic thinkers deemphasized sex, the unconscious, and the deterministic aspects of Freud's views. Instead, they stressed the goals and self-directed aspects of development.

Carl Jung held that the purpose of insight is not simply to gain rational control over the id and the source of psychic energy. It is also to help the individual discover and develop his or her wholeness and individuation. Heinz Hartman stressed that the ego develops independently of the id and has its own autonomous functions. He held that many of the cognitive functions, such as memory, perception, and learning are "conflict-free." Accordingly, the psychodynamic approach to behavior should focus on the ego and the relationship between the conflict-free functions as well as the conflict-resolving functions, such as the defenses.

A second trend in the revision of Freud has been a more positive emphasis on the individual's social interactions. Freud had interpreted the child's social interactions in relation to the forces of the id. Later thinkers, especially Harry Stack Sullivan and Karen Horney, emphasized the importance of social relationships in their own right. Erik Erikson also succeeded in transforming Freud's psychosexual stages into a sequence of psycho*social* stages of normal, lifespan development, thus widening the potential applications of Freudian concepts to include normal behavior. These revisions of Freud's thought have enriched the psychodynamic perspective and brought it closer to the other branches of psychology, with their current emphasis on cognitive functions and social influences.

Evaluation

Many of Freud's ideas remained controversial during his lifetime. Later, during the heyday of Freud's popularity, his views were often reified and accepted without question. With the critical assessment of Freud's views in recent years, people have sometimes gone to the opposite extreme, dismissing Freud prematurely without ever understanding him. Freud's thought is not something, however, that must be accepted or rejected as a whole. Instead, it is a complex structure with many parts, some of which deserve to be accepted, some rejected, and still others are in need of revision (Greenberg and Fisher, 1977).

A major criticism of Freud is that many of his ideas are vague and speculative, and thus hard to test. How do you prove or disprove the notion that sex is instinctive? Most theorists have abandoned the idea of instincts and tend to regard the sex drive as a complex blend of biological, psychological, and social components that function in relation to many other motives. A related criticism is that Freud's views were derived from clinical experience and lacked experimental support, and were based on inferences and interpretations of selected cases that involved disturbed people. In contrast, the field of psychology today includes both experimental and clinical approaches, with a concern for representative sampling and empirical methods of verification. Lab experiments have shown that dreams serve a variety of functions other than wish fulfillment, such as serving memory, problem solving, and neurological discharge. Still another criticism of Freud's approach is that it amounts to a reductionistic interpretation of human behavior. Every aspect of behavior is interpreted on the basis of animal instincts, childhood experience, and deterministic forces. As we've seen, many of these latter criticisms have been taken to heart and corrected by Freud's followers.

It should also be pointed out that Freud's ideas and those of the psychodynamic perspective in general have made substantial contributions to our understanding of behavior. First, such an approach has directed our attention to the inner life, to our memories, dreams, fantasies, and self-deceptions. It has helped to bring about the "psychological age," in which we take for granted the adaptive value of insight and self-knowledge. Second, Freud helped to remove the mystique of abnormal behavior by showing that disturbed behaviors stem from the same impulses and developmental processes as normal behavior. The big difference is the lopsided distribution of psychic energy, with the ego being overwhelmed by the id or superego in abnormal behavior. Third, Freud's use of insight in the helping process has spawned, in addition to orthodox psychoanalysis, a vast array of insight therapies that now include group therapy, marital therapy, and family therapy. Finally, the impact of Freud's thought has been felt far beyond professional psychology, such that terms like repression, unconscious, ego, and rationalization have become part of everyday usage.

Erikson's Eight Stages of Psychosocial Development

Erik Erikson has widened the potential application of psychodynamic theory by transforming Freud's psychosexual theory of development into a more inclusive view of personality development. Whereas Freud focused on the child's psychosexual development with the family, Erikson takes into account the individual's psychosocial relationships within the larger society. And while Freud's stages covered only the years between birth and puberty, Erikson's stages extend throughout adulthood into old age. Each of the eight psychosocial stages is presented as a polarity, with a positive ability to be achieved along with a related threat or vulnerability. Personality development is sequential, with one's overall personality composed of the strengths and weaknesses acquired during each of the following stages.

1. *Trust versus mistrust.* If children's physical and emotional needs are met in the first year of life, they learn to trust people around them. If not, they become anxious and mistrustful of their environment.

2. *Autonomy versus doubt and shame.* As parents encourage children to walk, talk and do things for themselves through the second and third years of life, the children will develop age-appropriate autonomy. But if the parents are coercive or overprotective, children will experience self-doubt and feel ashamed of themselves.

3. *Initiative versus guilt.* During the fourth and fifth years of development, children readily roam about and make new friends. If such efforts are supported by the parents, children will enjoy exploring their environment. However, if such actions are unduly restricted or punished, children may become passive and guilt-ridden about taking the initiative.

Adjustment and Growth

According to the psychodynamic perspective, clinical judgments about adjustment revolve around the issue of how well people are managing the conflicting forces in their lives. Driven by unconscious desires and motives, how adequate are their defenses for coping with the resulting conflicts? Also, considering the inevitable tension between the primitive impulses of the unconscious and social restraint, how well are people adjusting to their everday environment? Yet, at best, adjustment is a matter of compromises, mostly because of the inherent conflict in the individual's makeup.

Maladjustment usually results from a lopsided distribution of psychic energy within the individual's psychic makeup, so that the ego's managerial role is threatened. In some instances, intense asocial desires of sex and aggression threaten to break through, making the individual anxious and ambivalent. The individual may engage in behavior that is impulsive, addictive, or socially punished. In other instances, the individual may suffer from an excessively harsh superego, such that one is overly inhibited, obsessive, or guilt-ridden. Although

4. *Industry versus inferiority.* From about 6 to 11 years of age, children enjoy developing various abilities at home, school, and play. The more competent they become in dealing with their environment, the better they feel about themselves as persons. Undue frustration and failure evokes the sense of inferiority or worthlessness.

5. *Identity versus role confusion.* Throughout adolescence, roughly 12 to 18 years of age, individuals are busily redefining their identities in ways that incorporate the various changes occurring in their bodies, minds, and sexual development. The more successful they are in this task, the stronger their sense of personal identity. The more difficulty experienced, the more confusion adolescents feel about who they are and what they may become.

6. *Intimacy versus isolation.* As family ties are loosened during early adulthood, individuals need to form satisfying, close relationships with peers of both sexes. The inability to establish satisfying relationships with friends, including a lover or spouse, results in a painful sense of isolation or loneliness.

7. *Generativity versus stagnation.* By middle age, individuals are especially ready to develop generativity—the ability to look beyond one's self, family, and job, and to contribute to the welfare of others. The person who succeeds in doing so may continue being productive and happy. The person who doesn't tends to become self-absorbed.

8. *Integrity versus despair.* In late adulthood, individuals tend to look back upon their lives as a whole. To the extent they have achieved a satisfying life, they will feel happy with themselves in old age. But if they feel that their life has been disappointing and a failure, despair will be the result.

Source: Erik H. Erikson, Childhood and Society, 2nd ed. (New York: Norton, 1963). By permission of Chatto & Windus.

there are a variety of symptoms of maladjustment, they share a common feature: the individual's ego and coping defenses are weakened—making the person vulnerable to maladjustment. In extreme cases, the individual's defenses break down, overwhelming the ego with archaic impulses and with anxiety. This can lead to a major psychological disorder.

Optimal adjustment comes from strengthening the ego and the attendant reality orientation. Essentially this consists of increasing the individual's self-mastery, so that one can manage meaningful accommodations between one's desires and social demands. The goal of adjustment and growth would be to maximize instinctual gratification while minimizing punishment and guilt. But at best, this involves a series of practical concessions through the successful management of the inherently conflicting forces in life.

THE SOCIAL LEARNING PERSPECTIVE

While Freud's thought was still gaining in popularity, another approach to personality and behavior was in the making, one based more on scientific laboratory methods. Turning away from introspective clinical approaches that inferred motives, some psychologists used laboratory methods to observe behavior. As such, they focused on how behavior is learned—hence the term "learning theory" is often associated with their approach. Some, like Dollard and Miller, sought to integrate Freud's basic ideas with the laboratory approach. But most learning theorists have pursued the study of behavior apart from psychodynamic theory. Social learning theorists in particular focus directly on people's behavior and are less concerned with underlying motives or traits.

Social Learning Theories

As behavioral research has shifted to complex human behavior, the possibility of social learning without any apparent direct reinforcement has been recognized. As a result, learning concepts are being expanded and integrated with ideas and findings from other areas of psychology, and are increasingly being applied to real-life problems (Mischel, 1986).

One of the major mechanisms of social learning is *observational learning*, the process in which people learn by observing other persons and events without any direct reward or reinforcement. What people know and how they behave depends on what they see and hear, and not merely from the direct consequences of what they do. This type of learning has been labeled "observational, modeling, vicarious, or cognitive." But all these terms refer to the individual's acqusition of new knowledge and potential behavior without receiving direct reinforcement, though observational learning is sometimes combined with other techniques, such as direct reinforcement, to enhance learning.

Albert Bandura, a leading social learning theorist. (Courtesy of Albert Bandura)

One area of learning, fear of snakes, has received a great deal of attention because of the symbolic sexual significance of snakes in the psychodynamic perspective. If such a phobia is symbolic of a deep, underlying problem, as psychodynamic theorists contend, then it can't be cured without dealing with the unconscious conflicts involved. Yet it has been repeatedly demonstrated that such fears can be modified directly without exploring their possible unconscious meanings. In a classic experiment, Bandura (1971) and his colleagues studied how various treatment approaches affect the severe fear of snakes. Intensely phobic adults were randomly assigned to a group that received either systematic desensitization, symbolic modeling in the form of a film, live modeling with guided participation, or a no-treatment control group. Those seeing a film observed people of all ages handling snakes. They were also taught how to relax throughout their exposure to the film. In the group undergoing live modeling with guide participation, people first safely observed live models handling snakes and then were led by the models to handle the snakes themselves, first with gloves and then with bare hands. The results showed that people who received live modeling and guided participation experienced the greatest reduction in fear and were most receptive to approaching snakes.

By focusing on what people *do* rather than on the underlying motives and traits they *have*, social learning theorists have emphasized the importance of the situation in which behavior occurs. Accordingly, they have called into question much of the emphasis on the consistency of the individual's behavior as interpreted by psychodynamic and trait theorists. For instance, after reviewing hundreds of studies of traits such as dependency, assertiveness, and self-control, Walter Mischel (1986) concludes that our behavior is more often shaped by the requirements of the particular situation we happen to be in than by some inner trait. Consequently, rather than simply describing people in terms of global personality characteristics, it makes more sense to show how their behavior varies according to their interaction with particular events and situations. The same individual may act rebelliously at home, compliantly in the classroom, and yet autonomously and democratically among peers.

Cognition and Behavior

In recent years, psychologists have begun exploring the impact of cognition on behavior. Essentially, cognition has to do with the processing of information, and it includes a variety of processes such as selective attention, information gathering, memory, and motivation. Psychologists are studying cognition as a means of understanding those processes that mediate between the environmental stimulus and the individual's response. They believe that the impact of a stimulus depends on more than its objective physical characteristics. It also depends on contextual clues such as how it is presented and the meaning it has for the individual. In other words, many learning theorists recognize that behavior is influenced by the total stimulus complex, not just some single stimulus acting in isolation.

Walter Mischel (1979) suggests that there are five basic categories of cognitive variables that influence our response to a given stimulus:

1. *Competencies.* Each of us has a different combination of abilities and skills that shape our responses to events. When a car battery doesn't work, one person takes the bus to work; another person, with a different set of skills, borrows battery-jumper cables to get the car started.

2. *Encodings.* We also have different ways of perceiving and categorizing experiences that shape our responses. For example, when looking at a teenager's messy room, one mother fusses and fumes with no results. But another calmly takes it in stride with the realization that people at this age are preoccupied with other matters.

3. *Expectancies.* Learning experiences lead each of us to form different expectations that help to determine our reactions to events. One person buys state lottery tickets hoping to win a million dollars; another person, realizing the

overwhelming odds against winning such a fortune, is content to buy tickets occasionally for "fun"—or doesn't buy them at all.

4. *Plans.* We also formulate goals and plans that influence our actions. For instance, one student may regard foreign languages as a monumental waste of time, while another student finds such knowledge useful for future travel.

5. *Values.* Our sense of priorities and values also shapes our decisions and actions. Thus, when office politics at work become intolerable, one worker quits the job—but another worker takes it in stride by sticking to her work.

The recognition of cognitive variables between the environment and an individual's behavior means that people are seen as active, complex organisms and that behavior is affected by a host of complicating factors. Such a view gives us a richer, more realistic view of human existence than the earlier learning theories.

Evaluation

A primary objection to learning theorists, especially those who adhere strictly to the principles of classical and operant conditioning, is that they over-simplify human life. By reducing human experience to bits of measurable behavior, they portray us as mechanistic and passive, thereby excluding much of what makes people human. However, much of the criticism of learning theory has been blunted by the development of the social learning approach, especially with its emphasis on cognitive variables. In fact, cognitive psychologists have been criticized by strict behaviorists for compromising the empirical method. In response, cognitive psychologists contend that a distinction should be made between methodological behaviorism (which may investigate any type of behavior that is measurable) and the commitment to a philosophical behaviorism that automatically rules out the study of inner experience. Furthermore, by recognizing the complexity of our cognitive life and the importance of interpersonal, real-life settings, social-learning psychologists have expanded the behavioral approach to include more of the richness of human life, including the possibilities of human freedom.

One of the major contributions of learning theory has been to advance psychology as a science. By insisting on a method of investigation that focuses on actual, measurable behavior that is subject to being retested, learning theorists have given new credibility to the scientific study of human behavior. They have also produced many effective treatment strategies that are less time-consuming and expensive than traditional methods, such as systematic desensitization. Finally, the social-learning view reminds us of the importance of situational factors, and that behavior usually results from an interaction of inner dispositions and environmental influences.

Adjustment and Growth

Advocates of the social learning perspective tend to view adjustment and maladjustment in terms of the learning process and the interaction of individuals with their environment. They hold that, with proper understanding and guidance, many of the same mechanisms that are involved in maladaptive behavior can be used to improve adjustment. For example, an individual's drinking problem is more apt to be viewed as a tension-reducing habit maintained by a complex set of antecedent cues and consequent reinforcers than as the symptom of some deep, intrapsychic conflict. Efforts to help alcoholics overcome their problem usually aim at breaking up the acquired association between tension reduction and alcohol, on the one hand, and teaching them more adequate skills for reducing tension, such as deep muscle relaxation, stress management techniques, and social skills for achieving greater satisfaction with people.

Optimal adjustment and growth, according to the social learning perspective, consist of maximizing the competencies and coping skills of individuals, along with improving interactions with their environment. Conflict, whether intrapsychic or interpersonal, is not considered inevitable and is dealt with in terms of its behavioral and, thus, learned aspects. Change is not only possible but actually occurs fairly continuously, especially in an environment conducive to growth. Humans are seen as active organisms with tremendous capacity to learn, especially with the wide range of cognitive variables at their disposal, such as their problem-solving skills and the power of self-reinforcement.

THE HUMANISTIC PERSPECTIVE

Although the psychodynamic and social learning perspectives differ in many respects, they agree on one point, namely in breaking down human behavior into separate components. More specifically, both approaches seek to identify the causal relationships in human behavior in a manner similar to the natural sciences. For instance, if we are having difficulty getting along with our boss at work, both psychodynamic and behavioral theorists would reduce the problem to special causal factors, such as sexual conflicts or learning experiences. In contrast, the humanistic psychologists claim that such an approach leaves out much of what makes human existence distinctive, such as the meaning and richness of subjective experience, the holistic characteristics of experience, and the capacity to choose and determine ourselves.

During the 1950s and 1960s, when many thinkers became concerned over modern technology's threat to human values, humanistic psychology achieved national prominence as the Third Force in psychology, an alternative to the deterministic outlook of psychodynamic and behavioral psychology. Humanistic psychology consists of a group of related theories and therapies that emphasize the values of human freedom and the individual. We'll describe three main ideas in the humanistic perspective: the phenomenal self, inner freedom, and self-actualization.

The Phenomenal Self

The term *phenomenon* refers to that which is apparent to or perceived by the senses; in short, reality as experienced by the individual. Carl Rogers (1980), a leading humanistic psychologist, emphasizes that it is this "perceived reality," rather than absolute reality, that is the basis of behavior. Essentially, human behavior is the goal-directed attempt by the organism to satisfy its needs as it experiences or perceives them. In other words, how we see and interpret events in our environment determines how we react to them.

Two key concepts in Rogers' phenomenological theory of personality are the organismic actualizing tendency and the self-system. Rogers assumes the existence of an actualizing tendency at the biological level—the human organism's tendency to develop and fulfill itself. In the course of actualizing itself, the organism engages in a valuing process. Experiences that are perceived as enhancing are valued positively and sought after; those that are perceived as blocking fulfillment are valued negatively and avoided. The degree to which individuals trust this valuing process depends in a large measure on their self-concept. Self-concept is the self-image derived from one's experience with significant others during the formative years of childhood. As children become aware of themselves, they automatically develop a need for positive regard or acceptance. However, parental acceptance tends to come with strings attached, and the child incorporates these "conditions of worth" into his or her self-concept. From now on, this extraneous valuing process competes with the organismic valuing process. If the conditions of worth are few and reasonable, the self engages in a variety of experiences and, in cooperation with the organismic valuing process, can judge independently which are enhancing and which are not. However, if the conditions of self-worth are many and severely limiting, they serve to screen out much of the organism's experience, such that the self distorts and denies much of its overall experience.

The resulting tension between the self-concept and the organismic valuing tendency is the major source of maladjustment. The basic problem is the discrepancy between the organism's tendency to value experiences on the basis of what is good or desirable to fulfill its basic needs, and the self's tendency to value experiences selectively, screening out experiences that don't conform to these conditions of worth.

For example, a woman grew up feeling she had to be docile to be accepted by her parents. As a result, she spent many years denying her anger toward her parents as well as the need to be herself. After she had discovered her buried anger in therapy, she said: *"So much hurt and anger came out of me that I never really knew existed. I went home and it seems that an alien had taken over. . . . I continued to feel this way until one night I was sitting and thinking and I real-*

ized that this alien was the *me* that I had been trying to find" (Rogers, 1980, p. 210). Here, the women's denial of her own thoughts and feelings had become so strong that the self-alienation was thwarting her own growth.

Rogers developed person-centered therapy as a way of bringing about a more harmonious interaction between the self and the inherent actualizing tendency of the organism. In this approach, the therapist adopts the attitude of unconditional positive regard toward clients and, through empathetic listening, helps them get in touch with their own thoughts, feelings, and needs. In the climate of acceptance, clients can relax the defenses of the self and explore their thoughts and feelings more freely, thereby bringing their self-perceptions more in line with the basic actualizing tendency of the organism. In the process, clients become more trusting of their own experiences, more self-directed, and more fully functioning personalities.

Human Freedom

Another major characteristic of the humanistic perspective is the insistence on human freedom as opposed to the deterministic viewpoint prevalent in psychology. Seeing free will from an existential viewpoint, Rollo May says, "The existentialist point is that self-consciousness itself—the person's potential awareness that the vast, complex, protean flow of experiences is *his* experience—brings in inseparably the element of decision at every moment" (1974, p. 346). That is, given the high level of self-awareness and capability for symbolic thinking, we already have at our disposal the capacity to transcend blind obedience to impulses or environmental stimuli. The failure to accept this inner freedom results in the denial of our true selves. We experience a kind of spiritual death in which life becomes meaningless and we surrender our lives to the claims of institutions, materialistic comforts, and technological control. On the other hand, when we affirm our inner freedom we begin to live authentically. This means living in the here and now, making basic choices in a less than perfect world, accepting ourselves as a process of becoming, and being responsible for our lives. We cannot blame our problems on our childhood, past misfortune, or restrictive circumstances.

Carl Rogers adds, "My experience in therapy and in groups makes it impossible for me to deny the reality and significance of human choice. To me it is not an illusion that man is to some degree the architect of himself" (1974, p. 119).

Self-actualization

The term self-actualization, a central concept in the humanistic perspective, is usually associated with Abraham Maslow, who gave it its fullest explanation. Maslow, like Rogers, assumes the existence of an actualizing tendency in the organism at the biological level. Accordingly, each person has an inherent need to actualize his or her potentialities. However, the core of such growth needs functions in relation to a hierarchy of needs. Only as the individual's most basic needs are met do the higher growth needs become a potent force in motivation. As long as the individual's needs of hunger, safety, and human companionship remain unsatisfied, the person's existence is governed mostly by deficiency motivation. But once these needs are relatively satisfied, the individual becomes more aware of his or her growth motivation and of the need to fulfill needs such as autonomy and creativity. It may take an entire life for

Terry Fox, minus a leg lost to bone cancer, ran 3,339 miles across Canada. (AP/Wide World Photos)

growth needs to unfold, so that self-actualization is more of a lifelong process than a readily attainable goal.

Maslow (1970) held that some people have reached a healthier, more optimal level of functioning than the average person. He called them self-actualizing people, and held that the study of such people may teach us much about our potential for growth. Such people are relatively free from major psychological problems and have made the best possible use of their talents and strengths. Compared to the average person, self-actualizing people have certain characteristics in common, such as a continued freshness of appreciation of everyday realities, greater acceptance of themselves and others, high creativity, though not necessarily in the arts—and high resistance to conformity.

People with an incomplete understanding of Maslow often have misconceptions of self-actualization. For instance, in one survey students were asked, "Would you like to be self-actualizing? Why or why not?" Three-fourths of the students said yes. But the answers of both groups reflected mistaken but widely held notions about self-actualization. Some of the affirmative respondents explained that being actualized would bring them peace of mind, give them control over their own minds, and make them powerful people. Some of those who responded "no" felt that self-actualizing people, having met all their goals, would have nothing to live for. As one person said, "No, not anytime soon, but yes before I die. I have so much to live for and I want to have a good time before I reach self-actualization" (Feist, 1985). However, Maslow made it clear that self-actualizing people are not perfect. They remain vulnerable to the existential concerns and problems that plague everyone. At times they can be boring, irritating, or depressed. Essentially, self-actualizing people are like the rest of us but without the inhibited capabilities so characteristic of the average person (Lowry, 1973).

According to Maslow (1971), each of us may facilitate the process of self-actualization by observing the following suggestions:

1. Experience life fully in the present moment, rather than dwelling on the past or worrying about the future.

2. Make choices that will enhance growth, by taking reasonable risks that will develop one's potentials rather than by sticking with the safe and secure.

3. Actualize your self, in the sense of listening to your own needs and reactions and trusting your own experience.

4. Be honest in your relationships. When in doubt, be honest with yourself and with others.

5. Be assertive in expressing your own needs, ideas, and values.

6. Strive to do your best in achieving the tangible goals of life because, as Maslow puts it, "Self-actualization is a matter of degree, of little accessions accumulated one by one" (1971, p. 50).

7. Recognize and live by the inspiration of special moments or peak experiences in which one feels especially close to fulfilling one's potentials.

8. Be open to new experiences. Identify your defenses and be willing to put them aside in order to revise your expectations, ideas, and values.

In sum, Maslow made it clear that self-actualization is a continual process; it is never fully achieved. We should commit ourselves to concerns and causes outside ourselves, since self-actualization comes more as a by-product of developing our full capacities than from the egocentric pursuit of growth itself.

A major criticism of Maslow's views is often voiced this way: "If each of has an inborn actualizing tendency, why aren't more people self-actualized?" Maslow (1971) himself pondered this question and offered several possible explanations. First, one factor that blocks growth is the Jonah complex, or the fear of becoming one's best self. Just as the biblical Jonah tried to escape his destiny, so each of us tends to fear success, partly because such experiences can be overwhelming and because of the demands that come with them. Second, our inner core of growth needs is relatively weak and undeveloped, making it hard to discover and easily stifled by discouraging circumstances. Many people fail to actualize themselves due to the lack of supportive circumstances. Yet, on the other hand, countless people have been significantly creative despite deprived circumstances, and Maslow acknowledged that it is something of a mystery why affluence releases some people for growth while stunting others. As a result, Maslow suggested that a favorable environment is not enough to insure growth. Individuals must also have an intense *desire* to grow, to offset the apathy and resistance to growth. All things considered, Maslow envisioned personal development as a struggle between growth-fostering forces and growth-discouraging forces, such as fear of the unfamiliar. He felt that our society discourages growth by overvaluing safety. Instead, he suggested that we should minimize the attractions of security and maximize its dangers, such as boredom and stagnation. At the same time he felt we should emphasize the attractiveness of growth while minimizing its dangers. Maslow repeatedly emphasized that "growth is, *in itself*, a rewarding and exciting process, thereby overcoming much of our resistance to self-actualization" (1968, p. 30).

Evaluation

The primary criticism of the humanistic perspective is that it is unscientific. Critics contend that much of the information is gained from humanistic therapy and from studies based on self-reports, resulting in formulations that are incomplete, lacking scientific precision and a comprehensive analysis of the causes of behavior. A related criticism is that the phenomenological position with its emphasis on the individual's freedom removes the perceiver from the causal chain, and therefore from scientific scrutiny.

To such charges, humanistic psychologists would reply that as long as the scientific method is restricted to methods borrowed from the natural sciences, the fault lies more in the use of the wrong tools than in the subjects investigated. Leading psychologists, such as Maslow and Rogers, have long argued that the study of the individual and of personal relationships calls for a more comprehensive and flexible view of the scientific method. Speaking on this topic, Carl Rogers (1985) described some of the recent developments in many fields of science that are bringing about a broader view of science, a view which recognizes that there is no *one* scientific method that is always best. The linear, cause-effect, behavioristic model is not being thrown out. But it is being viewed as a method that, while adequate for investigating some questions, is clearly inappropriate for others. Similarly, the phenomenological approach is increasingly recognized as an excellent way of investigating issues that have to do with the living, acting, whole human being.

Humanistic psychologists have made a tremendous contribution to the larger field of psychology and society by tackling issues of urgent concern to all human beings, such as individual freedom, autonomy, love, and personal growth and values. They have also called our attention to the constructive side of psychology. Individuals are now being viewed in the light of their potentials for health and fulfillment as well as in terms of their vulnerabilities and maladjustments.

Adjustment and Growth

Humanistic psychologists tend to view adjustment in relation to the organism's inherent growth tendency, with no sharp separation between adjustment and growth. But they are more concerned with the individual's growth or self-actualization than with sheer survival. Tension and conflict are neither necessary nor inevitable. When they occur, it's apt to be because of the social context of behavior. For instance, the individual's restrictive self-image may derive from growing up in a home with unloving or domineering parents. Yet these shortcomings may be overcome in an environment conducive to growth, such as a love relationship or therapy. Similarly, there is no necessary conflict between the individual's successful living and a satisfying interpersonal life.

Adjustment from the humanistic viewpoint is rarely interpreted in terms of conventional conformity because of the high value placed on the individual. Maladjustment tends to occur when individuals live as if there were no inherent growth tendency. In terms of Rogers' phenomenal self, the maladjusted accept their limited, defensive self as their inevitable state of existence. In terms of May's human freedom, they've made a decision, if only by default, to deny a considerable part of themselves and life. And in terms of Maslow's concept of self-actualization, maladjusted people have settled for the conventional life based on security and boredom rather than on the more challenging choice to actualize themselves.

The humanistic approach views optimal adjustment in relation to the process of self-actualization, i.e., in terms of a progressively greater differentiation and integration of one's capabilities. The more fully individuals are actualizing themselves, the better their adjustment. Yet, self-actualization is highly individual, such that growth-oriented people may well experience a *positive* tension between themselves and their environments. Self-actualization is a lifelong process that is only imperfectly realized in any person's experience. As a result, the less actualized people are, the more they will experience conflict and tension as well as the defensive coping that accompanies such experience. Yet, as we've seen, conflict and defense tend to come from one's environment rather than from the individual's makeup. The more individuals actualize themselves, the more they tend to transcend, rather than conform to the imperfections of their society.

Summary

The Psychodynamic Perspective

1. Psychodynamic psychologists view individuals as inevitably caught between the conflicting forces of life, such as incompatible impulses and the tension between the individual and society.

2. The ego is the part of the psyche that manages personality, thereby enabling the individual to cope with the conflicting demands of the id, supergo, and society.

3. Since the ego, id, and superego are often in conflict, individuals commonly experience anxiety and rely on various psychological defenses to reduce anxiety.

4. Personality develops through a sequence of stages, with the manner in which the child handles the characteristic intrapsychic conflicts being decisive for his or her adult personality.

5. Many of Freud's followers have deemphasized sex and given greater emphasis to the ego functions and positive potential of the individual's social interactions.

6. Psychodynamic concepts of adjustment place great emphasis on the adequacy of one's ego functions and attendant reality orientation in managing the conflicting forces of life.

The Social Learning Perspective

7. Learning theorists focus on how behavior is learned through interaction with the environment.

8. Social learning theories include more complex behaviors that may be learned without direct reinforcement, such as observational learning.

9. The recognition of cognitive variables between the environment and behavior suggests that learning is affected by a host of complicating factors rather than an isolated stimulus.

10. The social learning perspective views both adjustment and maladjustment in terms of the individual's interaction with the environment, with people having great potential for modifying their behavior.

The Humanistic Perspective

11. Humanistic psychologists stress the holistic characteristics of human experience; that is, people are to be regarded as more than the sum of their parts.

12. According to this perspective, people act on the basis of perceived reality—how they see themselves and their surroundings.

13. Humanistic psychologists affirm the importance of our inner freedom but regard it as something that complements rather than contradicts the cause-and-effect understanding of human behavior.

14. Self-actualization, a lifelong process of developing one's potentials, is rarely ever fully achieved, even among self-actualizing people.

15. In the humanistic psychological perspective, adjustment is interpreted in terms of the organism's growth tendency, with no sharp separation between adjustment and growth.

Self-test

1. In the psychodynamic perspective, the part of the psyche that manages personality according to the reality principle is the:

a. id
b. ego

c. superego
d. ego ideal

2. When the ego senses that some impulses of the id are threatening to get out of control, one experiences:

a. reality anxiety
b. moral anxiety

c. neurotic anxiety
d. existential anxiety

3. Oedipal conflicts arise in what stage of personaltiy development?

a. oral
b. latency

c. anal
d. phallic

4. Psychodynamic conceptions of adjustment and growth tend to emphasize the individual's management of:

a. intrapsychic conflicts
b. learned behaviors

c. self-actualization
d. conditioned responses

5. The process in which people may acquire new behaviors without any direct reinforcement is called:

a. the conditioned response
b. operant conditioning

c. observational learning
d. aversive conditioning

6. Which of the following has to do with the processing of information, including functions such as expectancy and selective attention?

a. reinforcement
b. self-actualization

c. ego defense
d. cognition

7. Theorists from which psychological perspective tend to view adjustment and maladjustment in terms of the individual's learned behavior and environment?

a. social learning
b. psychodynamic

c. humanistic
d. all of the above

8. According to humanistic psychologists like Carl Rogers, human behavior is determined largely by:

a. perceived reality
b. reinforcement

c. ego defenses
d. unconscious instincts

9. Maslow holds that self-actualization:

a. occurs only in self-actualizing people
b. is achieved by middle age or not at all

c. is a lifelong process that is rarely fully achieved.
d. occurs in about one-third of the population

10. The humanistic psychological perspective views the individual's tension and conflict as:

a. inherent in one's makeup
b. a function of the social context of behavior

c. inevitable in everyone's life
d. all of the above

Exercises

1. *Which of Erikson's stages are you in?* Write approximately a page explaining how well you're mastering the appropriate developmental task for your stage, according to Erikson's theory. How important do you regard this task for someone at your stage of life? If possible, comment on how your past development affects your experience in the present stage of development.

2. *The important people in your life.* Describe several of the important people, including your parents, who have most influenced your past development. What are these people like? What effect did they have on your development? To what extent has your personality been learned?

3. *Self-actualization.* Reread Maslow's eight suggestions for actualizing yourself more fully. Then apply them to your present personality and behavior. Make an honest assessment of yourself in each of these eight areas. In which area are you the most fully actualized? In which area is further growth most needed?

4. *Barriers to personal growth.* Each of the three major perspectives covered in this chapter offers a different view of the barriers to personal growth. The psychodynamic view stresses unconscious conflicts and fixations; the social-learning view emphasizes faulty models, environments, and maladaptive behavior; and the humanistic view highlights the importance of restricted self-concepts and self-actualization. Write a paragraph or so explaining how each of these views may help to account for the barriers to your personal growth.

5. *Which major perspective most reflects your views?* Select one of the three major perspectives that is the most compatible with your own thoughts on adjustment and growth. Then write a page or so explaining why you prefer this viewpoint. To what extent are you receptive to viewpoints different from your own? Would you agree that no one perspective possesses the whole truth?

6. *Read an article or a book favoring a different psychological perspective from your own.* This might be a journal article in the college library, a section from another textbook, or an entire book on some aspects of adjustment and growth of special interest to you. Do you find that the more fully informed you become regarding other psychological perspectives, the more likely you are to acknowledge the truth inherent in each?

Questions for Self-reflection

1. Do you agree that the human mind is like a submerged iceberg—with only the tip surfacing in awareness?

2. Would you agree that Freud's theory is too complex to be accepted or rejected as a whole?

3. Do you sometimes experience ambivalence—being pulled in opposite ways simultaneously?

4. Do you believe that much of the inconsistency in people's behavior can be explained by situational factors?

5. When psychologists label their perspective "cognitive-behavioral," what does this mean to you?

6. How would you explain the difference between Bandura's social learning view and Rogers' humanistic view?

7. Are you as convinced as Carl Rogers that we have within ourselves vast resources for self-understanding and growth?

8. Would you agree that self-actualization is always "in process" rather than complete?

9. Why do you think people aren't more fully self-actualized?

10. Would you agree that no single psychological perspective has a monopoly on truth?

Recommended Readings

Bandura, Albert. *Social Foundations of Thought and Action.* Englewood Cliffs, NJ: Prentice-Hall, 1986. Major ideas and applications of the social learning approach by one of the leaders in the field.

Erikson, Erik H. *Childhood and Society,* 2nd ed. New York: W. W. Norton & Company, 1963. An explanation of Erikson's eight developmental stages in the individual's life cycle.

Freud, Sigmund. *New Introductory Lectures on Psychoanalysis.* Trans. and ed. by James Strachey. New York: W. W. Norton & Company, 1964. A lucid overview of Freud's major ideas about personality and therapy.

Lowry, R. (ed.). *Dominance, Self-esteem, Self-actualization: Germinal Papers of A. H. Maslow.* Monterey, CA: Brooks/Cole, 1973. A collection of Maslow's writings that summarizes his understanding of self-actualization.

Nye, R. D. *Three Psychologies: Perspectives from Freud, Skinner, and Rogers,* 2nd ed. Monterey, CA: Brooks/Cole, 1981. A concise comparison of the basic ideas of psychoanalysis, behaviorism, and humanistic psychology.

Rogers, Carl. *A Way of Being.* Boston: Houghton and Mifflin Company, 1980 (paperback). Rogers describes his personal development and major ideas associated with his person-centered approach to therapy and life.

Motivation

Mr. Johnson constantly complained to his wife about how lazy Alex, their teenage son, was. It seemed that Alex studied very little and hardly ever did anything useful around the house. Out of curiosity, Mrs. Johnson decided to observe Alex's behavior for a couple of days. She duly noted his frequent trips to the kitchen for snacks. She also recorded Alex's lengthy telephone calls to his girlfriend each evening. She observed that he had spent most of one evening working on his car out in the garage. In response to questioning, Alex told her that he spent several hours each afternoon practicing with the basketball team and a couple of hours studying each evening. Since Alex kept the door to his room closed a lot, she wasn't sure how much time he spent studying. But as she looked over her notes one thing became clear: Alex wasn't lazy—Alex was a very active person. Yet Mrs. Johnson realized that her husband might continue to regard their son as lazy because Alex wasn't doing those things his father considered important—like studying and performing chores around the house.

UNDERSTANDING MOTIVATION

Like Alex, most of us are busy doing something most of the time. Yet we may not be accomplishing the things we really want to accomplish. We procrastinate a lot. We may wait until we "feel" like studying. We also waste a lot of time, especially talking with our friends. We may feel little or no enthusiasm for the task at hand. In short, we're often lacking in motivation. Not surprisingly, parents, teachers, and managers in the workplace want to know how to "motivate" people.

Essentially, motivation ("to move") has to do with what causes us to act. It involves the initiation of a course of action, as well as the direction and intensity of the ensuing behavior. We'll begin by explaining the concept of motivation and how our behavior is affected by both inner and outer influences. Then we'll discuss the basic survival motives such as the desire for food and sleep. In a later section we'll examine several of the common motives that are shaped mostly by learning, such as achievement motivation. Finally, in the last part of the chapter, we'll look at some of the factors that affect our personal motivation.

Push and Pull Motives

When we say someone is "highly motivated," we usually mean that person acts in a purposeful, goal-related way. An example would be the basketball player who practices hard before an important game. Yet experts themselves differ as to which are the most important causes of behavior. Do we act mostly from inner forces? Or is our behavior affected more by environmental forces that attract us from without? Such forces are labeled "push" or "pull" motives, respectively.

Traditionally, psychologists have explained behavior in terms of push motives. That is, our behavior is energized by certain inner tension states, called needs or motives. A need may be defined as a state of biological or psychological deprivation, and thus a state of tension, whose gratification is felt to be vital for the maintenance of the organism. The tension of these unmet needs, in turn, arouses and energizes us to seek the appropriate gratification. This goal-directed behavior is known as a motive. The feeling of satisfaction that follows the gratification of our motives serves to further reinforce them, leading us to engage in a similar sequence of behavior in the future. Thus, according to the drive-reduction model of motivation, our behavior is energized by the inner tension of unmet needs.

At the same time, perhaps you've had the experience of watching a mouth-watering food ad on television and then feeling hungry when you really aren't hungry. Or think of the times when you've done something you don't like, mostly because of the money you'll be paid for it. Such instances remind us that our behavior is also shaped by incentives—objects or conditions in the envi-

Athletes competing in the Olympics tend to be highly motivated. (AP/Wide World Photos)

ronment that attract or repel us. Deadlines, the fear of failure, or the threatened loss of a job are all negative incentives that may motivate us to work harder. Positive incentives include recognition, success, and money. In both cases, our motivation is strengthened by forces outside ourselves.

Psychologists disagree as to which type of motive plays the more important role in our behavior—the push or pull motive. Actually, a lot depends on the particular person and situation. When you've been driving all night without sleep you're not too particular where you sleep. You might even go to sleep curled up on the car seat. Here, the inner need for sleep predominates. On the other hand, a group of football players dejected over a losing score at half time may become either resigned to failure or challenged to play their best, depending on how well their coach motivates them through the qualities of leadership. In the latter case, incentives may make a crucial difference in the players' behavior.

A Hierarchy of Needs

In Chapter 2 we mentioned Maslow's "hierarchy of needs" in passing. Our understanding of motivation may be enhanced by a more detailed look at Maslow's growth model of motivation. Maslow (1970) suggests that our needs and motives function in a hierarchical manner, as shown in Figure 3–1. He describes five levels of needs as follows: (1) *physiological needs* include the need for food, sleep, and sex; (2) *safety needs* include the need for protection from bodily harm, security from threat, as well as the need for order and stability; (3) *love and belongingness needs* include the need for acceptance, affection, and approval; (4) *esteem needs* refer to the need for self-respect and the sense of achievement; and (5) *self-actualization needs* include a variety of needs such as the need for autonomy, uniqueness, aliveness, beauty, and justice in our lives.

Figure 3-1. MASLOW'S HIERARCHY OF NEEDS. The needs are arranged hierarchically from the bottom up according to how crucial the need is for survival. The higher needs are experienced only to the degree that the more basic ones have been relatively satisfied.

Diagram based on "A Theory of Human Motivation" in *Motivation and Personality,* 2nd edition, by Abraham H. Maslow. Copyright © 1971 by Abraham H. Maslow. Reprinted with permission of Harper & Row, Publishers, Inc.

Maslow holds that the lowest level of unmet needs remains the most urgent, commanding our attention and efforts. Once a given level of need is satisfied, we become motivated more by the unmet needs at the next higher level. Thus, as we satisfy our needs for food and shelter we become more concerned about things like job security. At the same time Maslow points out that our needs are only relatively satisfied. He once estimated that the average person is only 85 percent satisfied in terms of physiological needs, 70 percent in safety needs, 50 percent in love needs, 40 percent in esteem needs, and only 10 percent in self-growth needs.

An important implication of Maslow's growth model of motivation is that we aren't content to achieve a stable, harmonious state. Instead, once we've reached a relative level of satisfaction, biologically and psychologically, we're increasingly motivated by growth needs. This helps to explain why successful people are rarely satisfied to rest on their accomplishments. They're constantly striving to attain something better. Likewise, people who are happily retired seldom sit around doing nothing; they're forever developing new interests and deepening their relationships with others. It seems we're happiest when we're growing and actualizing ourselves.

Individual Differences

Although each of us desires the creature comforts of food and sleep, as well as higher goals such as success in our jobs, the relative strengths of such motives differs from one person to another. Accordingly, we need to think in terms of the individual's personal hierarchy of motives as well as Maslow's generalized pattern. Which motives have top priority in a given person will depend on factors such as inborn disposition, personal values, sex-role identity, and past experiences. For example, firstborn individuals tend to have a more intensive achievement motivation than their brothers and sisters, mostly because of the greater attention they received from their parents while growing up. On the other hand, individuals who have been deprived of love and affection as children may be more motivated by the desire for approval than achievement. We'll return to the importance of individual differences in our discussion of personal motivation at the end of the chapter.

Our motives also change over time depending on the "motive targets" around us—people toward whom our motives are directed. For example, at work you have a strong motive to compete with your associates. Yet in your leisure hours you may be more concerned about being accepted by your friends. Then again, at home you may feel inclined toward intimacy and sexual involvement with your lover or spouse. As a result, our motives are constantly changing throughout the day, as we move from one situation to another.

In the rest of this chapter, we'll explain the workings of several of the more common motives. But keep in mind that each of us has a unique hierarchy of motives. Furthermore, the particular combination of motives that commands our immediate attention not only changes with the satisfaction of motives but also with the motive targets around us.

SURVIVAL MOTIVES

Like all other organisms, we must eat, drink, and avoid extreme pain and injury if we are to survive. Although sex is not essential to our personal survival, it is necessary for the survival of the species. All these motives, though shaped by learning in varying degrees, have a clear physiological basis. As a result, they are usually labeled as drives or survival motives.

Hunger and Thirst

When you go without food or water for half a day, you feel hungry and thirsty—right? If you were deprived of food even longer, the effects would be more marked. People who are deprived of food for a long period of time become less efficient in their thinking and behavior. They become apathetic, irritable, and depressed. The desire for food dominates their daytime activities as well as their daydreams. Fortunately, most of us never experience this extreme state. But we realize how important food is. Water is even more crucial to our survival. Although we can survive for weeks on minimal food, we can live only a few days without water.

Food intake is so important to our survival that nature has provided some automatic controls. Most of these controls are regulated by the brain, especially the hypothalamus. Because the hypothalamus is more richly endowed with blood vessels than other parts of the brain, it is readily influenced by several bodily processes. One is the glucose level in the blood, called blood sugar level. When our blood sugar level becomes low, we feel weak and hungry. Yet the conversion of food into blood sugar is a slow process. A more immediate signal to the brain is sent by the receptors in the walls of the stomach. At the same

People eat for a variety of reasons whether they are hungry or not.
(Teri Leigh Stratford)

time, it is important to realize that there is a delay between the time you've eaten and when the stomach modifies the brain. Thus, you may eat quickly, say in 5 or 10 minutes, and still feel hungry. But if you wait 20 minutes, or until your food has had time to be digested, you'll feel less hungry. Accordingly, when we eat or drink quickly we may consume more than we need. Still another way the hypothalamus regulates eating behavior is through monitoring the fat content of the body, as indicated by substances in the blood. When the fat content falls below a certain level, called the *set point*, the hypothalamus increases our desire to eat; when the fat content rises above this level, it decreases our desire to eat.

Our eating behavior is also affected by a variety of learned, social influences. Some of the more common ones are; the smell, sight, and taste of food; emotional stress; and self-control (over our eating habits).

Much of the felt need for food results from our eating and exercise habits. People who sit at a desk all day and don't exercise much soon become fat. Conversely, those who exercise regularly not only burn up more calories but increase their rate of metabolism, so that even when they are not exercising, calories are being burned faster. Unfortunately, as people reach middle age, they tend to continue the same eating habits but exercise less. As a result, more excess calories are converted into fat. Ideally, we should modify our eating and exercise habits to fit our lifestyle, especially as we get older.

The aroma, sight, and taste of food also affect how much we eat. Some people inclined toward obesity are especially affected by such external cues, paying less attention to the inner promptings of the hypothalamus. At the same time, all of us are affected by external cues to some extent. Perhaps you've noticed that you eat more on special occasions like Thanksgiving, mostly because the greater variety of food stimulates the senses of smell and taste. Also, because eating is a social custom, we tend to eat more and linger longer when socializing at the table.

Sometimes we eat more when we're tense or anxious. This is especially true of individuals prone to obesity. On the other hand, many normal-weight individuals say they *lose* their appetites when under stress. They tend to eat more in low-stress situations. Which is true for you? When under stress, do you snack and overeat? Or do you eat less?

Probably the most important factor of all is the awareness and self-control you have over your eating behavior. Are you aware of how many calories you consume on a typical day? Do you eat balanced meals, combining the various essentials of good nutrition? Do you leave the table feeling just a bit hungry? Or do you stuff yourself, only to regret it later? One final thought. People who are long-lived tend to exercise regularly, have a low-calorie intake, and don't eat between meals. Think about it.

Sleep and Dreams

Have you ever stayed up all night? Perhaps you've missed several consecutive nights of sleep. If so, how well did you get along the next day? Although the effects of sleep deprivation vary from one person to another, they are not as drastic as we once thought. Deprived of sleep, most people make greater errors on routine tasks and experience increased drowsiness, a strong desire to sleep, and a tendency to fall asleep easily. When they finally fall asleep, chances are they'll sleep a few hours longer than usual. But extra hours of sleep won't make up the total sleep-time lost. Our sleep/wake cycles follow a biochemical clock in our makeup designed to help us conserve energy. Reestablishing our natural sleep cycle is more important than trying to "make up" all the hours of lost sleep. We can accommodate ourselves to a variety of changes such as shift work, jet lag, and all-night study sessions. But these adjustments take a toll on our bodies as well as our sense of well-being.

How much sleep do you need? Although the average person sleeps about 7 hours each night, the need for sleep varies from one person to another. You're probably getting enough sleep if you (1) wake up spontaneously, (2) feel well rested, and (3) don't have to struggle through periods of sleepiness during the day. If you are not sure, try this regimen. One night during the first week go to bed at 5 A.M. and get up at 7 A.M. Observe yourself all day to recognize the symptoms of not getting enough sleep. One night during the next week, go to bed at 3 A.M. and get up at 7 A.M. and see how you feel. Then let yourself sleep 2 hours longer one night each successive week, until you wake up spontaneously and don't feel tired during the day. That is your natural sleep length (Goleman, 1982).

We also need to dream, though the amount of dream time diminishes as we get older. Newborns spend about half their sleep time in dreams; young adults only about one-fourth. This means that most of us dream about one and a half hours each night. Each person's sleeping pattern alternates between various stages of sleep, with the deepest, most restful sleep—Stage 4 sleep—occurring within the first hour or so after falling asleep. During the night sleep alternates between REM (rapid eye movement) sleep, in which our muscles twitch, and our hearts beat faster, and various stages of non-REM sleep. (See

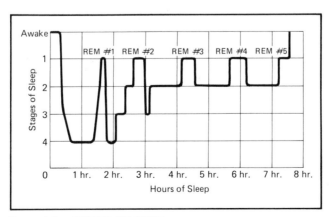

Figure 3-2. STAGES OF SLEEP.

Can't Get to Sleep?

Most of us have trouble falling asleep occasionally. For some, especially older adults, it's a recurring problem. Although there is no magical solution to this age-old complaint, here are some suggestions.

- Go to bed and get up at about the same time each day. Make sure you're allowing enough time for sleep.

- Relax before bedtime. Listen to music or practice yoga. But avoid strenuous exercise.

- Keep your bedroom conducive to sleep. Make sure it's quiet and dark and at a suitable temperature.

- Avoid alcohol and sleeping pills. Although these may put you to sleep sooner, they interfere with the normal sleep cycle.

- Take a lukewarm bath before bed. Hot or cold showers tend to be too stimulating.

- When you're having trouble falling asleep, count sheep or think of something pleasant that will distract you from worrying.

- If you can't get to sleep after a reasonable time, get up and have a glass of warm milk; heated milk contains tryptophan, a natural sleep inducer.

- Don't fret that sleeplessness will harm your health or impair your performance the next day. We usually accomplish more than we realize after a bad night's sleep.

- If your home remedies don't work, seek professional help.

Figure 3–2.) Dreams occur more frequently, and in greater vividness and detail (including color), in REM sleep. Because the stages of REM sleep and dreaming grow progressively longer toward the end of our sleep, we often awake in the morning toward the end of a dream. We may remember that last dream, but we will likely have forgotten the others unless we've learned how to recall our dreams.

Do all dreams have meaning? The experts disagree on this. Most of us are familiar with Freud's wish-fulfillment theory, in which dreams are regarded as an expression of our repressed impulses or conflicts. Sure enough, our dreams are more likely to reflect themes of aggression, failure, and misfortune than friendliness, success, and luck. Yet, more recent and controversial neurological theories hold that dreams are mostly the result of spontaneous activity of neurons in the pons area of the brain; that, in fact, dreams have little or no psychological meaning. Then there is the cognitive theory, which holds that dreams are related to the process of thinking, learning, and memory. According to this theory, the more we learn during the day, the more we need to dream at night, which may help to explain the student's familiar complaint of not having enough sleep. Dreams may also aid in problem solving. In one study, students in a sleep laboratory were presented just before bedtime with problem stories dealing with common concerns of young adults, such as leaving home. Then some students were allowed to dream while others were awakened during REM sleep or were not allowed to sleep at all. Those who were allowed to dream proposed more creative solutions to the stories. This suggests that dreams may serve a positive purpose, helping us to solve problems and repair self-esteem (Cartwright, 1978). Perhaps this is why we should delay making an important decision until we can "sleep on it."

Sex

Imagine that you read the following in the obituary column:

John D. Suggs, 37, died last night at Riverview Hospital of complications following acute sexual deprivation. A hospital spokesman said, "John was a high-risk individual who suffered from intense headaches, high blood pressure, and outbursts of rage when denied sexual gratification. The recent hospitalization was apparently brought on by a marital separation. The grieving widow could not be reached for comment."

Sound ridiculous? You bet, because nobody dies from the lack of sex. As we explained earlier, sex is a "survival" motive only in the sense of preserving the species. Some people, especially young males, worry they could "die" from too little sex. Yet, even Sigmund Freud, who held that sex was a basic instinct, abstained from having sex with his wife for lengthy periods of time after mid-life, mostly as their preferred method of birth control. And Freud lived to the ripe old age of 83.

At the same time, since sexuality plays such a vital role in human behavior, we're devoting an entire chapter later to the subject. At this point, we'll simply look at some of the most distinctive aspects of human sexual motivation.

Human sexuality differs from that of lower animals in the greater role of psychological and social influences in relation to hormonal secretions. For example, castration or removal of the testes in the adult male rat results in a swift decrease and eventual disappearance of sexual activity. Yet, in human males, the effect of castration is much less consistent. For example, some men whose testicles were obliterated through land-mine injuries during war did in fact lose their sex life; others retained the desire and ability for sexual inter-course. One explanation is that our sex drive depends on a variety of hormones, including those produced by the adrenal and pituitary glands, that are situated elsewhere in the body. Also, emotional and social factors often make a decisive difference. Among females, the cessation of ovarian functioning at menopause is often followed by an *in*creased interest in sex, largely because of the diminished fear of pregnancy. In short, human sexuality depends on a variety of influences, including psychological and social factors. Having good health, keeping physically fit, having a zest for life, and being sexually attracted to one's partner—all influence our ability to keep sexually active long after our sex hormones have decreased.

Variety also enriches sexuality. Partners may enhance their sexual satisfaction by varying their lovemaking techniques. Divorced people who marry later in life become more active with a new partner. The enrichment of sex through variety has been referred to as the "Coolidge Effect," after the following anecdote. It seems that during a farm tour, Mrs. Coolidge reached the hen yard ahead of her husband. Noticing the vigor with which the rooster mounted one hen after another, she asked the tour guide to make sure her husband took note. When President Coolidge arrived in the hen yard, he was duly told about the rooster's exploits. After a few moments thought, he replied, "Tell Mrs. Coolidge that there is more than one hen" (Walster and Walster, 1978).

PSYCHOSOCIAL MOTIVES

The psychosocial motives have less to do with physical survival and more to do with our sense of well-being and psychological competence in dealing with our environment. Some—such as the motive for stimulation, curiosity, and exploration—seem to be largely inborn and are sometimes labeled "stimulus needs." Others, like the achievement motive, are shaped more extensively by psychological and social influences. Because of the complexity of human behavior, there is no one authoritative list of our psychological and social motives. Some of these motives will be covered in other chapters, such as our sexual motives, affiliative motives, and the need for personal freedom and control. Here, we'll focus on several of the basic motives not covered elsewhere, namely, stimulation, security, and achievement.

Stimulation

With age and experience, many things become less interesting. Life may become routine and too predictable. We become bored and indifferent. Soon we experience a new motivation—the desire to escape from boredom. In one small town where few emergencies occurred, several firefighters went around setting fires in fields and vacant buildings; they would then return to the firehouse, get their equipment, and rush to put out the fire. This went on for several months until they were finally caught. When asked why they engaged in such outrageous behavior the firefighters admitted, "We were bored."

We need both sensory and social stimulation. People deprived of both—for instance, prisoners in solitary confinement and subjects in sensory deprivation experiments—display symptoms of stress, including distorted perceptions.

People who score high in sensation-seeking often seek out exciting, risky sports. (Kawasaki News Bureau)

They see and hear strange things, they hallucinate, have delusions, and fear losing their sanity. Military personnel in lonely outposts have shown similar reactions, though to a lesser degree. Most of us are rarely placed in a situation where we suffer from extreme sensory or social isolation. But even after several hours of studying alone, you may feel a need to listen to the radio, call someone on the phone, or talk to your roommate, mostly for the stimulation involved.

You may have also noticed how you're sometimes attracted to novel experiences. You may feel a need to try a new game, go somewhere different, or meet new people. Marvin Zuckerman (1979) has examined people's differences in this area by measuring their sensation-seeking motive. People who score high on measures of sensation seeking are more likely to experiment with drugs, engage in a variety of sexual practices, and seek excitement in risky sports like sky diving or mountain climbing. Those who score low prefer more comfortable and peaceful activities, like stamp collecting or reading. Zuckerman believes that our sensation-seeking motive may be partly determined by biological factors, including the levels of certain neurotransmitters in the brain related to mood and arousal. But they are also shaped by many psychological and social influences. In any event, the sensation motive tends to get weaker after the college years.

Security

At times we may feel a stronger desire for security than for new experience. The need for security develops early in life. Young children feel especially secure with their own parents, their own beds, and familiar routines. As they get older, they like to know the rules, what they're permitted to do and not do. The prospects of uncertainty, whether sleeping in a strange bed or having a new babysitter, can be upsetting for them.

As we grow up, our need for security takes different forms. We develop habitual ways of doing things, such as habits of eating and sleeping. We also like to know where we stand at work and in our close relationships with others. We like to know where we'll be tomorrow and what we'll be doing. An undue need for security may keep us in a rut, doing the same old things day in and day out. Yet, within bounds, the desire for order and security helps to keep our lives on an even keel.

Each of us, whether we realize it or not, also has a need for cognitive consistency. That is, we need to believe that our attitudes, motives, and behaviors are consistent with one another. When we feel our attitudes or behaviors are psychologically inconsistent, though not necessarily logically incompatible, the resulting tension is unpleasant and we're motivated to do something about it. For example, suppose you smoke a pack of cigarettes a day. You may well become worried about the increased risk of getting lung or mouth cancer. You could resolve this tension by giving up the smoking habit. But there are easier ways to reduce the tension. You could minimize the danger of smoking, pointing out to your critics that it hasn't yet been proven conclusively that smoking actually causes cancer. Or, you could emphasize the positive reasons you smoke, such as the taste or how much it calms your nerves. The main point here is that we have an intense dislike for cognitive *in*consistency and the anxiety it arouses, and we're constantly resorting to a variety of self-justifying mechanisms in order to feel more at ease within ourselves. However, dissonance reduction does not always make for effective dealings with our environment, especially when it leads us to rationalize away real dangers, such as cigarette smoking.

Achievement

Perhaps you've noticed how your friends differ in achievement motivation. Some relish taking on a challenge. No matter what the task, they strive to do their best. Others seem to be happy just getting the job over and done with.

Actually, achievement motivation is a complex combination of factors. Two keys are the desire for success and the counteracting fear of failure. Each of us has a different mixture of these two tendencies, mostly because of our personal makeup and past experiences. As a result, people differ in the difficulties of the tasks they choose. For example, someone who has a strong desire for success and a low fear of failure is more apt to choose moderately difficult but realistic tasks, thus maximizing the chances of success. But another person with

Astronaut Sally Ride. (NASA)

an intense desire for success coupled with a high fear of failure will set a much lower goal. Those motivated primarily by the wish to avoid failure may behave in either of two ways. They can aim at very easy tasks, with a low reward but a low risk of failure as well. Or they may pursue an elusive, high-pay-off task where failure is so likely they won't be blamed if it happens. At the same time, situational factors also influence our choices. The way options are presented to us determines to a large extent whether we'll take a chance or play it safe.

Another important factor in achievement motivation is the fear of success. Matina Horner (1972) found that many women were haunted by such a fear, often due to the way they had been reared: that is, women were taught that success in all but a few careers was unfeminine. Interestingly, at least one study found that a woman's fear of success disappeared when the job involved a typically female role such as nursing. In this case, men expressed greater fears about succeeding (Feather, 1975). Actually, many men are also plagued by the fear of success because of the responsibility that goes with it and the pressure to stay successful.

Although our achievement motive remains fairly stable over time, it may vary according to several factors. First, there is the sheer desire to succeed. When you really want to accomplish something, notice how it usually gets done? Second, the amount of satisfaction you derive from what you're doing counts a lot. Third, the degree of responsibility you feel for what you're doing influences your motivation to achieve. When you have a personal stake in something, you work harder at it. Fourth, self-confidence greatly strengthens achievement motivation. A fifth factor is being familiar with the means to accomplish your goals. Talking with experienced people, getting the necessary training and feedback, are all realistic ways to increase your achievement motives. Finally, how much you're willing to risk to reach your goals depends on the strength of your achievement motive in relation to your other needs. If you have a strong need for approval and acceptance, you may shy away from competing with others. Or if you're driven by a need for power, you may take high risks to get attention and recognition. However, when your achievement motives are uppermost, you're more likely to choose tasks of medium risk, ones that give you the best chance of overall success.

Must High Achievers Be Competitive?

The cliché "Nice guys finish last" implies that you must be a highly competitive person to get ahead in our society. But is this always so?

Recent studies suggest not. In their research, Janet Spence and Robert Helmreich distinguished between three separate motives: *work orientation*—the desire to do a good job; *mastery*—the preference for challenging tasks; and *competitiveness*—the desire to win over others. They found that the highest achievers were those who were high in the work and mastery motives but low in the competitiveness motive. This pattern held true among college students who made the highest grades, scientists who made the greatest contributions, and business executives who made the highest salaries. They speculated that competitiveness may interfere with achievement because the desire to outdo our peers in prestige or money may diminish our interest in the task itself.

Janet Spence and Robert Helmreich, *Masculinity and Femininity* (Austin: University of Texas Press, 1978).

PERSONAL MOTIVATION

The relative strength of the various personal motives differs in each person, as explained earlier. As a result, the motivational pattern is somewhat unique for each of us. One person is so strongly achievement-oriented that she will risk health and security in order to complete important work. Another individual may be so needy of love and approval that he will avoid competition at all costs. Still others seem to be driven by little more than the need for sensual pleasure, whether that of gourmet eating, excessive drinking or drug-taking, or sexual experimentation. It is rarely clear, even to ourselves, what motivates us in a particular situation. How much awareness we have of our needs and priorities is an important factor. So are our past experiences of success and failure. Personal values are often a crucial influence. Yet, there are many other factors that help to shape our motivation. In this section, we'll discuss several of these: the importance of incentive, self-direction, and personal goals.

Incentives

An incentive is any external influence that stimulates us to take action or work harder, usually through the anticipation of receiving the incentive. Almost anything can serve as an incentive. Status, honor, and power are familiar incentives. Attention is a powerful incentive. Having our accomplishments recognized or praised, as in a promotion at work, is a very important incentive in the workplace. The anticipation of success is a strong incentive. When the promise of success exceeds the risk of failure, we're apt to try hard at a task. But when the fear of failure becomes too strong, we may only try half-heartedly, thereby lessening the likelihood of success. At the same time, experiences of disappointment and failure sometimes strengthen our incentive to work harder to succeed.

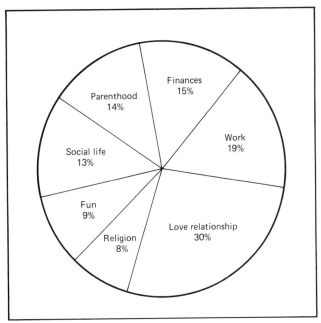

Figure 3-3. HOW IMPORTANT IS MONEY? This question was asked in the *Psychology Today* survey on money. Most of the respondents were in their 20s and 30s, college educated, with about half of them married. Respondents rated the importance of money and other aspects of life by imagining them as slices. The numbers are averages of the percentages they gave.

Carin Rubenstein, "Survey Report: Money and Self-esteem, Relationships, Secrecy, Envy, Satisfaction," *Psychology Today*, May 1981, p. 31. Reprinted with permission from *Psychology Today* Magazine. Copyright © 1981 American Psychological Association.

Money has become a major incentive, especially in the workplace. One reason is that money serves as a means of satisfying other values. People who want to buy a better car or house value money as a means of achieving these things. Similarly, those who value security will see money as a means to that end. Since money is a tangible way of measuring performance, salary is commonly used as a way of evaluating our success at work. People also use money as a way of "keeping score" in their overall success in life. According to a *Psychology Today* survey on the subject, people have become even more money-conscious in recent years, mostly because of factors such as inflation and a tight job market. Yet, some people are more money-conscious than others. An important factor is the frustration of one's materialistic aspirations. Money-conscious people admit, "I always seem to be wanting things I can't have." But many people who are money-troubled also lack a secure sense of self and are more dissatisfied in their relationships with others at work and home. As a result, simply making more money won't necessarily make these people happy (Rubinstein, 1981).

As long as we feel we're being paid unfairly or our work is uninteresting, money will continue to be a powerful incentive for us. Once we're adequately paid or find our jobs interesting or rewarding in other ways, money will probably become less of an incentive for us. This is especially true when we feel good about ourselves, when we feel proud of our work, and when we are happy in our close relationships. Yet, for the majority of people in the middle and working classes, caught between materialistic aspirations and economic pressures, money continues to be an important incentive.

Self-direction

So often we lack motivation because we're not acting out of our own needs, desires, or aspirations. We're trying to do something we feel we "ought" to do or that someone else "expects" us to do. But our hearts aren't in it. Perhaps it's something our parents suggested we do, or maybe a teacher or employer advised us. In any case, we're not fully convinced. And it shows. We can usually strengthen our motivation by becoming more self-directed.

Karen, a young woman of 19, came to me at the suggestion of her parents. Concerned about Karen's lack of motivation to do anything, they feared she might be mentally retarded. She had made poor grades throughout high school. Visits to the school psychologist and counselors had not resulted in any improvement. Following graduation, Karen hadn't been able to hold down a steady job. She was moody and hard to live with at home. After a thorough evaluation, including a battery of tests, I discovered that Karen was a very bright but depressed young woman. I soon discovered why she was so down on herself. Karen's parents were overly critical and demanding. She also suffered from constant comparison with an older sister who was a high achiever. Her self-esteem was at rock bottom. When I asked Karen if she wanted to attend college, she replied, "Yes, but I'll never get into a decent college with my grades." I suggested she begin by taking one course in a subject that interested her at a nearby community college. She liked the idea but had no notion of what course to take. When asked, "What do you enjoy doing?" Karen cautiously said, "I like to write, but my high school grades in English were just average." With a little encouragement, Karen decided to take a course in English composition. She completed the course with a "B." More importantly, she gained confidence, the belief that she could do college-level work. The next semester she took two courses, making an A and a B. The following fall she took a full load. Later, she transferred to a 4-year college and eventually received her bachelor's degree with honors. At this point in life, Karen had become a highly motivated young woman, largely because she was acting out of her own desires and self-confidence.

Personal Goals

Another secret of being an active, motivated person is setting personal goals and then striving hard to reach them. In one sense, goal setting comes naturally in that we are all future-oriented. We are more concerned about today and tomorrow than yesterday. Yet it takes some thought and soul-searching to set personal goals or objectives, which is why a lot of people don't bother to do it. But the risk of not doing so can be costly in terms of wasted time and energy. This idea is expressed succinctly in the title of David Campbell's book *If You Don't Know Where You're Going, You'll Probably End Up Somewhere Else* (1974).

Campbell suggests setting several different types of goals as follows:

Long-range goals are concerned with the kind of life you want to live in regard to your career, marriage, and lifestyle. It's wise to keep these broad and flexible, especially during your college years.

Medium-range goals cover the next 5 years or so, and include the type of education you're seeking or the next step in your career or family life. You have more control over these goals, so you can tell how well you're progressing toward them and modify them accordingly.

Short-range goals apply from the next month or so up to one year from now. You can set these goals quite realistically and should try hard to achieve them.

Mini-goals cover anything from one day to a month. You have a lot of control over these goals and should make them specific.

Micro-goals cover the next 15 minutes to few hours. Realistically, these are the only goals you have direct control over.

As you can see, the shorter the time span covered, the more control you have over your goals. Yet, it is only through achieving the modest, short-range goals that you'll ever attain your medium and long-range goals. Too often, people make the mistake of setting grandiose goals and then quickly becoming disillusioned because they're making so little progress toward achieving them. It's far better to set realistic but desirable goals; then concentrate on achieving your day-to-day goals, which will make it more possible to reach your "dream" goals.

Once you've achieved a goal, it's important to set new ones. This is what Maria has been doing. Following high school graduation, Maria worked as a secretary for several years. Then she married Tom and had two children. Although she was happily married, she became increasingly restless as the children spent more time in school. At first, Maria began taking courses in a nearby community college on a part-time basis. She was surprised to discover that she was a much better student than she had been in high school. Eventually, as she acquired more self-confidence, she enrolled full-time in the nursing program. After graduation she worked in a nearby medical clinic for 4 years. Recently, she began a master's degree program in one of the area universities, with the aim of specializing in pediatric nursing. For Maria, the experience of achieving goals and setting new ones has not only strengthened the desire to excel in her career but has also given her a new zest for life in her marriage and family as well.

Summary

Understanding Motivation

1. Motivation has to do with what causes us to initiate a course of action, as well as the direction and intensity of the ensuing behavior.

2. Much of our behavior results from the combination of inner forces and environmental influences—labeled "push" and "pull" motives respectively.

3. Our needs and motives tend to function in a hierarchical manner; once a given level of need is relatively satisfied, we become motivated more by the unmet needs at the next higher level.

4. At the same time, individual motive hierarchies differ from one person to another, and from one situation to another within the same person.

Survival Motives

5. Survival motives like hunger have a physiological basis and are necessary for our survival to some degree.

6. Hunger is a function of several inner forces such as the hypothalamus, blood sugar level, receptors in the walls of the stomach, and the fat content of the body, though it is also influenced by learned, social influences such as the aroma, sight, and taste of food.

7. Each of us has an inborn need for sleep and dreaming, though this varies considerably among individuals and depending on one's habits.

8. Human sexuality differs from that of lower animals in the greater role of psychological and social influences in relation to hormonal secretions.

Psychosocial Motives

9. Psychosocial motives have to do with our sense of well-being and psychological competence in dealing with our environment.

10. Although we need both sensory and social stimulation, individuals differ in such things as their sensation-seeking motives.

11. Our need for security takes many different forms, ranging from our preference for habitual ways of doing things to the need for cognitive consistency.

12. Achievement motivation is usually a complex mixture of forces, including the desire for success, fear of failure, and fear of success.

Personal Motivation

13. The relative strength of motives differs in each person, thus producing a motivational pattern that is somewhat unique for each of us.

14. Incentives—external influences that stimulate us to work harder—like status, honor, power, and money have a significant impact on our behavior.

15. Increasing our motivation often involves becoming more self-directed and acting out of our own needs, desires, and aspirations.

16. Another secret of being an active, motivated person is the use of personal goals, setting our own goals and then striving to reach them.

Self-test

1. Specific, goal-directed behaviors are known as:
- **a.** motive targets
- **b.** motives
- **c.** motivations
- **d.** needs

2. According to Maslow, the most urgent need in the hierarchy of needs is:
- **a.** self-actualization
- **b.** a physiological need
- **c.** the lowest level of unmet needs
- **d.** belongingness

3. Our eating behavior is definitely affected by our:
- **a.** hypothalamus
- **b.** blood sugar level
- **c.** exercise habits
- **d.** all of the above

4. Which of the following is a true statement?
- **a.** The average person sleeps about 5 hours a night.
- **b.** Most dreams occur in REM sleep.
- **c.** The more we learn by day, the less sleep we need at night.
- **d.** All dreams occur in black and white.

5. The sensation-seeking motive:
- **a.** is rarely related to drug abuse
- **b.** becomes stronger after the college years
- **c.** is entirely learned
- **d.** may be partly biological

6. You could reduce the cognitive dissonance or tension brought on through smoking by:

a. minimizing the dangers of smoking

b. giving up smoking

c. emphasizing the positive reasons for smoking

d. all of the above

7. People with strong achievement needs tend to choose tasks with:

a. low risks

b. medium risks

c. high risks

d. maximum rewards

8. Which of the following would be classified as an incentive?

a. attention

b. hunger

c. lack of sleep

d. all of the above

9. When someone lacks motivation, the problem often turns out to be:

a. too little outside pressure

b. too many things to do

c. lack of self-direction

d. excessive ambition

10. What kind of goals, according to David Campbell, cover the next 5 years or so?

a. medium-range

b. long-range

c. short-range

d. mini-range

Exercises

1. *Examine your eating habits.* How healthy are your eating habits? Do you know how many calories a day you consume? How does this compare with others of your age and lifestyle? Good nutrition requires eating food from the basic food groups—milk, meat, bread–cereal, and fruit–vegetables. Are your meals well-balanced? Do you have any bad eating habits, such as overeating at mealtimes, snacking between meals, or frequently dining in fast-food restaurants? Describe your eating habits in a page or so, including your responses to the above questions.

2. *How much sleep do you need?* To find out, reread the directions for discovering your natural sleep pattern described in this chapter. Then apply them to your own sleeping behavior. Did you find that your natural sleep length corresponds to your regular sleeping habits? Or is it shorter or longer than you are accustomed to sleeping?

3. *Seek out new experiences.* Sometimes the stimulation from new experiences helps to revitalize your motivation and zest for life. You might try several of the following suggestions: Taste a food you've never tried. Take up a new sport or hobby. Invite someone out socially you would like to know better. Attend a workshop or a special course you're interested in. Perhaps you can add other ideas. Try several of these suggestions, and write up your reactions in a page or so. Would you agree that variety is the spice of life?

4. *Assessing your achievement motivation.* Take a look at your achievement motivation in a specific area of your life. This could be a course you're taking, your motivation in school as a whole, your job, or progress toward your career goals. Then answer the following questions:

How strongly do you want to succeed?

Do you believe your ability is crucial, or is success mostly a matter of luck?

How much do you enjoy what you're doing?

Do you have the needed skills to succeed?

If not, what are you doing about this?

Honest responses to such questions may help you to understand the strength of your achievement motivation and what's needed to increase it.

5. *Money as an incentive.* To what extent has money been an incentive in the choice of your career or job? Would you agree that money is a major incentive because it is a means of satisfying other values, such as buying a car or measuring your success at work? Would you consider taking a less satisfying career or job for a 30-percent increase in salary? Write a paragraph or so explaining the importance of money as an incentive in your life.

6. *Personal goals.* Do you set goals for yourself? If so, describe some of your long-range, medium-range, and short-range goals in a page or so. Even if you don't usually formulate personal goals, try writing out some of your important goals as explained in the chapter. You might find goal setting especially helpful in the areas of career, marriage, and family life.

Questions for Self-reflection

1. What are some of the dominant motives in your life?
2. How important are incentives like money and success?
3. Has overeating or snacking between meals become a problem for you?
4. Do you ever remember your dreams?
5. How strong is your sensation-seeking motive?
6. To what extent is competitiveness essential for success?
7. How strong is your achievement motive in school?
8. Do you often have trouble explaining why you've acted a certain way?
9. Are you a self-starter? Or do you work better "under pressure"?
10. What are your personal goals for the next year? What about the next 5 years?

Recommended Readings

Arkes, H. R., and J. P. Garske. *Psychological Theories of Motivation*, 2nd ed. Monterey, CA: Brooks/Cole, 1982. An overview of the various theories of motivation.

Bennett, W., and J. Gurin. *The Dieter's Dilemma.* New York: Basic Books, 1982. Covers the various aspects of our eating behavior and weight management.

Bolles, R. C. *Theory of Motivation,* 2nd ed. New York: Harper & Row, 1975. One of the classics in the field.

Spence, Janet, and R. Helmreich. *Masculinity and Femininity.* Austin: University of Texas Press, 1979 (paperback). An informed view of sex differences, including the impact of sex roles on human motivation and behavior.

Webb, W. B. *Sleep.* Englewood Cliffs, NJ: Prentice-Hall, 1976 (paperback). A concise explanation of sleep patterns by one of the leading researchers in the field.

Zuckerman, M. *Sensation Seeking.* New York: Halstead Press, 1979. Deals with individual differences in the sensation-seeking motive, including drug use, sports, and sexual behavior.

Emotions

Have you ever stopped to think how often we explain our motivation in terms of emotions?

Why didn't you come to class yesterday? *I didn't feel up to it.*
Why did you leave the meeting early last night? *I was upset and angry.*
I'm surprised you're still working with her. *I feel guilty about not doing my part.*
Why are you and Tom breaking up? *I'm not in love with him anymore.*

Our *motives* and *emotions* are closely associated for a good reason: both terms have the same Latin origin referring to movement or activity. The "motivated" person usually moves actively toward some goal or, in some instances, away from an unrewarding situation. The "emotional" person tends to be stirred up internally by a situation that has special meaning for him or her; in due time, however, an emotionally "moving" experience leads to changes in outward activities and relationships as well. Positive emotions such as affection and love move us to form meaningful relationships with others, as with friends, lovers, and married couples. When things are going well, the emotions of acceptance, joy, and happiness add zest and meaning to our lives. At the same time, negative emotions of anxiety and anger interfere with our thinking and tempt us to act in irrational, self-defeating ways. Furthermore, feelings of hurt and jealousy disrupt relationships and make our lives miserable.

UNDERSTANDING EMOTIONS

Sometimes when we are emotionally aroused, we act in childish, self-defeating ways, causing us to wonder if we might be better off in a world without emotions. At the same time, the emotions of caring and grief are among our most distinctive human qualities. They set us apart from the most sophisticated thinking machines, such as computers and robots—as well as those unfeeling alien creatures from outer space we see in the movies. Even animals have emotions, as seen in the sulking dog or the enraged chimpanzee. Surprisingly, the higher we go up the evolutionary scale, the *greater* the capacity for emotional awareness, implying that emotions have a positive survival value. Yet understanding emotions continues to be a difficult matter, both for researchers and for the average person. Today, we still lack a single, unifying theory of emotions.

What Are Emotions?

Despite the disagreement among authorities, most psychologists would agree that an emotion is a complex pattern of changes involving our minds and bodies, rather than a simplistic, self-contained reaction, visceral or otherwise. Accordingly, an emotion has four components, including: (1) physiological arousal, (2) subjective feelings, (3) cognitive processes, and (4) behavioral reactions in response to a situation the individual perceives to be personally significant in some way (Kleinginna and Kleinginna, 1981).

1. *Physiological arousal.* Emotions involve the brain, nervous system, and hormones. Sometimes the bodily changes can be dramatic. When we become very angry or fearful, our breathing becomes rapid or uneven, our heartbeat may accelerate from the normal rate of about 72 beats a minute to as many as 180 beats a minute, and our blood pressure may rise to alarming levels.

2. *Subjective feelings.* An emotion also includes a subjective awareness or "feeling" that involves elements of pleasure or displeasure or liking or disliking. Such feelings are the emotionally colored meanings that an experience has for us. This is why in studying emotion, we must rely on people's self-reports, despite the wide variations in describing feelings.

3. *Cognitive processes.* Emotions also involve cognitive processes, such as our memories, perceptions, expectations, and interpretations. Accordingly, our cognitive appraisal of an event plays a significant role in the meaning it has for us, and it helps to create our emotional reaction, as we'll explain throughout this chapter.

4. *Behavioral reactions.* Emotions also involve behavioral reactions, both expressive and instrumental. Facial expressions—smiles, frowns, and pouts— as well as bodily postures, gestures, and tones of voice all serve to communicate

our feelings to others. Cries of distress, screams for help, and running for our lives are also adaptive responses that may enhance our chances for survival.

The various theories of emotion differ mostly in regard to which of these various components is given greater priority. In much the same way, authorities differ as to how our emotions are activated or triggered.

How Emotions Are Activated

Charles Darwin held that emotions are innate, spontaneous responses through which the organism reacts appropriately to emergencies, thus enhancing its chances for survival. Emotions also served as the primary mode of communication before the development of language. For example, in a situation of threat the emotion of anger led our ancestors to scowl and bare their teeth, thereby deterring their enemies. According to this view, emotions are largely inborn responses that motivate us to act in adaptive ways. Partial support for this idea can be seen in studies showing that infants are capable of displaying the distinctive expressions of anger, disgust, contempt, happiness, surprise, or sadness at 8 or 9 months of age, long before these can be learned (Izard, et al. 1980). Similarly, photographs of facial expressions demonstrating these basic emotions have been recognized by college students in different countries around the world, including non-Western countries (Ekman, 1975). At the same time, what triggers a particular emotion varies somewhat from one culture to another. For example, although the emotion of fear is innate, people fear different things depending to a large extent on their development and surroundings.

William James also regarded emotions as instinctive responses to recurring survival situations. But he reversed the commonsense notion that we feel first and then act. Instead, James believed that we see a tiger and instinctively run for our lives, with the physiological arousal accompanying this behavior being perceived as an emotion. A modern version of emotion produced by behavioral responses is the facial feedback hypothesis. Paul Ekman (1984) asked professional actors to move sets of facial muscles in ways that are characteristic of certain emotions. The actors were not asked to assume the emotional expressions, just to move the appropriate muscles. At the same time, the actors' physiological reactions were monitored. Results showed that a distinct pattern of physiological changes accompanied some of the facial expressions. The heart rate rose with anger, fear, and sadness, and decreased with happiness, surprise, and disgust. According to this view, there's some truth to the adage—frown and you'll feel sad, smile and you'll feel happy.

Still another view holds that cognitive appraisal plays the primary role in triggering emotions. Sensory experiences lead to feelings only when we judge the stimuli as being meaningful or significant to us. According to this view, cognitive appraisal precedes and in large part creates much of our emotions. Usually it is when stimuli are recognized as being related to our life concerns, goals,

Basic emotions like fear are recognized by people around the world. (Laimute E. Druskis)

and values that we experience an emotion. Because of cognitive appraisal, what is exciting for you may be a source of fear for me.

The role of cognitive appraisal has important implications for health and illness, as we'll explain in the chapters on stress and the body and health. Apparently, it isn't simply stressful events that get us down. The critical factor is *how* we react emotionally to such events. Some people respond to life stresses, even severely stressful events, with little or no emotional upheaval. Others with less adequate coping skills react to the same stresses with a great deal of anxiety and depression. In turn, the emotional stress lowers their bodily resistance, thus setting the stage for a greater incidence of physical illness (Maier and Laudenslager, 1985).

These different explanations of how emotions are activated are not mutually exclusive. Each clarifies a part of the overall process of emotions, thus helping us to understand our emotional life as a whole. Thus, in line with Darwin's approach, it is natural to become emotional in the face of danger or mistreatment. At the same time, taking into account the role of cognitive appraisal, it's important to understand our present situation at any particular time and then respond in a way that will best accomplish our goals, rather than simply acting on our initial feelings. In other words, we have more control over our feelings than popularly understood, as we'll explain in the section on handling troublesome emotions.

Primary and Mixed Emotions

Emotions are a kind of barometer of our inner world, providing us with an intuitive knowledge about ourselves and others at the moment. Perhaps that's why we're constantly asking each other, "How do you feel about this?" or "What's your gut reaction to that?" Unfortunately, it's not always easy to say, is it? A major reason is that we often have trouble recognizing just what it is we're feeling, much less finding the right word to express our feelings. The truth of the matter is that our emotions are in a state of constant flux or change, and defy easy labels. As a result the language of feelings is, at best, imprecise.

Emotions, like colors, vary in intensity, as reflected in the distinctions we make between annoyance and anger on the one hand or sadness and grief on the other. Intense emotions tell us our lives are strongly affected by some person or event and prompt us to act accordingly. On the other hand, when we feel little or no emotion in a given situation, chances are our needs, goals, or values are not affected. We're not "emotionally involved."

Emotions also vary in their personal meaning or significance for us. In order to determine the meaning of various emotions, Robert Plutchik (1980) and his colleagues asked a group of people to rate the relative similarity of more than 140 words expressing emotion to three other words—accepting, angry, and sad. Thus, people were asked how similar they considered, say, surprise and disgust to each of the three reference words. From these correlations the researchers plotted the location of every emotion on a circular emotion-wheel chart shown in Figure 4–1. The emotion wheel shows the eight primary emotions, which are made up of four pairs of opposites, such as joy and sadness. Each adjacent pair of the eight primary emotions, such as disgust-sadness, are called primary dyads, combinations of the basic emotions most closely related to each other. The emotions that fall outside the circle are mixtures of these primary dyads. Thus, love consists of joy plus acceptance; remorse is a mixture of disgust and sadness. We can also imagine mixing emotions that are somewhat further apart on the circle, such as acceptance and sadness. These combinations are called secondary or tertiary dyads.

Occasionally, we may experience a "pure" emotion, such as joy. But more frequently we experience a mixed emotion such as love, which is a mixture of joy and acceptance. Most of the time our feelings are composed of even more impure mixtures of emotions that reflect the complexities of our lives. For example, suppose you're having an argument with your lover or spouse about that person's attraction to someone else. You may be aware of intense anger at the moment. But some reflection may reveal you're also feeling hurt, jealousy, fear, guilt, and sadness. Ventilating one aspect of your feelings, such as anger,

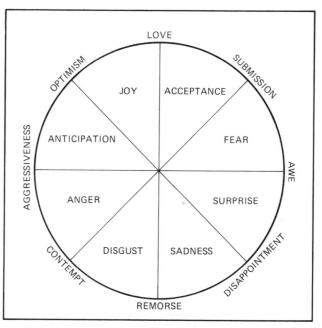

Figure 4-1. PRIMARY AND MIXED EMOTIONS.

From Robert Plutchik, "A Language for the Emotions," *Psychology Today*, February 1980, p. 75. Reprinted with permission from *Psychology Today* Magazine. Copyright © 1980 American Psychological Association.

to the exclusion of your overall feelings distorts your inner experience and misrepresents your feelings to others. It may be more helpful to acknowledge the other emotions as well as the ambivalence of your feelings at the moment, better reflecting the complexity of the problem or your relationship with this person.

EXPRESSING OUR EMOTIONS

Emotions not only move us to do things or to avoid situations, they're also a primary way of communicating with others. Perhaps this is the rationale behind the ritualistic greeting, "How are you?" According to folklore, this is a shortened version of an old saying "How are your bowels?" based on the ancients' belief that the bowels were the seat of emotions. With the advent of Ex-lax and Kaopectate, we're less concerned about the state of one's bowels. But we still want to know how others feel. Knowing feelings gives us clues to what people care about as well as why they act as they do.

At the same time, it's not always safe to share our intimate feelings, much less while casually greeting a friend in the hall or on the street. Sharing our feelings is risky and makes us vulnerable to the judgment of others. Some people are so afraid of their inner feelings, they're unable to experience, much less express, their deeper emotions in times of joy or sorrow. Others, who are more in touch with their emotions, share their feelings more readily, whether in anger or love. Whichever way we're inclined, the most important thing is to find that balance of expression and control of feelings we feel most comfortable with.

Expression and Control

When you hear an infant screaming in distress or cooing with satisfaction after a meal, you realize babies have little trouble expressing their emotions. The baby's uninhibited display of feelings attracts the attention of those who can relieve its discomfort. At the same time, taking care of infants, or children for that matter, can be nerve-wracking. Consequently, as the baby's nervous and glandular systems mature, it is gradually taught better control. The child continues to experience intense emotions, but often refrains from showing them openly. In so doing, the child risks adopting the hyprocrisy and characteristic masks of adult society. As a result, many people grow up overcontrolling their emotions.

People often keep a tight rein on their feelings through repression—the automatic, unconscious blocking of an emotion that, if consciously admitted, would be threatening. In this way they are shielded from threatening feelings, but not from the detrimental effects of repressed emotions. For example, in discussing a disappointing test grade with his teacher, Burt raises his voice and absentmindedly crushes a paper cup in his hands while denying he's angry. Yet he has a sullen look on his face and at several points in the conversation stares at the teacher without saying anything. The instructor also points out that Burt habitually comes to class late and missed the review session before the test. Also, Burt's written papers are done carelessly and submitted late. In short, Burt exhibits many of the tell-tale signs of anger and resentment, with little or no awareness of his feelings. Yet as long as Burt is oblivious to his own anger, he will remain his own worst enemy and continue to act in a self-defeating manner.

It's more desirable to manage our feelings through suppression—the conscious and deliberate control of emotion. In this way, we remain in touch with our feelings and, upon appropriate reflection, can decide when and how to best express them. This is especially important in regard to troublesome feelings such as anger, guilt, and jealousy. But suppression is only a stopgap: chronic or habitual suppression of one's feelings may lead to many of the same undesirable effects as repression.

Learning to express our feelings effectively—the best solution to the problem—involves a suitable balance between spontaneous expression and deliberate, rational control. The areas needing improvement vary somewhat from one person to another. People who are overly emotional and impulsive may blurt out their feelings without much thought; they need to develop better control. On the other hand, those who keep their emotions under tight control may need to loosen up, become more aware of their feelings and more comfortable expressing them. Most of us fall into this category.

Emotional Crying

Women cry three times more often than men, the typical crying episode lasts about 6 minutes, and tears are usually shed between the hours of 7 and 10 p.m. These are some of the findings from a pioneering study of adult crying behavior by William H. Frey and his colleagues.

Frey, a biochemist, claims that emotional tears may be nature's way of releasing bodily chemicals built up through stress. To demonstrate that tears from emotional crying were different from those brought on by eye irritation, the researchers paid volunteers to sit through a tear-jerker movie and later to cry over chopped onions. The results showed the emotional tears contained a significantly greater amount of protein, though the link between this and emotional stress is less clear. The researchers also had 286 women and 45 men (men volunteered much less often than women) volunteer to keep records for 30 days of all emotional-crying and irritant-crying episodes. Less detailed information about crying was also gathered from 201 women and 124 men. The results showed:

Women cried about 5.3 times in the month-long test; men cried about 1.4 times. Almost half the men, but very few of the women, reported no crying episodes.

Most men's crying episodes (71 percent) consisted of only watery eyes, while nearly half the women's crying episodes included flowing tears.

The most frequent stimuli for crying in both men and women involved interpersonal relationships (arguments, weddings, and other such emotional events) and media presentations (movies and TV programs).

Nearly 75 percent of the women felt "generally positive" about crying, compared to only 58 percent of the men. At the same time, more than three-fourths of both sexes said they usually felt better after emotional crying.

There was no significant relationship between the frequency of emotional crying and age.

Reprinted by permission of the publisher from "Crying behavior in the human adult," by W.H. Frey, II, C. Hoffman-Ahern, R.A. Johnson, D.T. Lydden, and V.B. Tuason, *Integrative Psychiatry*, September 1983, 94–98. Copyright 1983 by Elsevier Science Publishing Co., Inc.

We can become more adept in expressing our emotions by sharing our everyday feelings more readily. Many times we may feel pleased about something a person has done for us. Why not share this feeling? As you become accustomed to sharing your safe emotions, you'll get in better touch with your feeling life. Then when you experience an intense emotion, like anger or disgust, you may find it easier to recognize your feelings and be more willing to express them. More often than not, it's a risk worth taking. When you express your feelings openly and in a constructive manner, this helps to clear the air and facilitate communication. Sharing your feelings with an attentive person may also help us to clarify them. All too often, we're not certain what we're feeling until we've expressed it and hear how others respond to what we have said. Even negative feedback may help to test the strength of our emotional convictions. Frequently all we need is more experience in sharing our feelings to become more articulate about our emotions. This comes more naturally when we're talking with someone we trust, such as a close friend, lover, or spouse, or in some instances, a counselor or therapist.

"I" Messages

Many times when we experience an intense emotion such as anger, we hesitate to express it because of the mistaken notion that if we're honest with our feelings we'll alienate others. Yet this isn't necessarily true. A lot depends on *how* we express our feelings. All too often we fail to acknowledge our emotions. Instead we express ourselves judgmentally, attributing our feelings to others. We say things such as "that was a stupid thing to do" instead of "I resent what you did." Such "you" messages tend to put others on the defensive and provoke an argument, rather than encouraging them to listen to us.

A more effective way of expressing intense negative emotions is the use of an "I" message, as explained by Tom Gordon (Gordon and Sands, 1978). Essentially, this is saying what you honestly feel in a way that encourages others to listen and cooperate. "I" messages are especially helpful in expressing your feelings about someone whose behavior has become a problem for you. An "I" message consists of four components: (1) an objective, nonjudgmental description of the person's behavior; (2) the tangible effects on yourself; (3) your feelings about this; and (4) what you'd prefer the person do instead. (See Table 4–1.)

Table 4–1. EXAMPLES OF "I" MESSAGES.

Nonjudgmental Description of Person's Behavior	Concrete Effects on Me	My Feelings About It	What I'd Prefer the Person To Do
1. If you don't complete what you promised to do	then I have to do it in addition to my other tasks	and I feel annoyed.	I wish you would do what you've promised.
2. Each time you criticize my work without telling me what I'm doing wrong	I don't know how to improve it	and I feel frustrated and resentful.	Tell me what I'm doing wrong so I can correct it.
3. When you change your mind at the last minute	it's too late to make other plans	and I feel angry and disappointed.	Give me more advance notice when you think things may not work out.

Let's break down the "I" message point by point, in more detail. First, describe the other person's objectionable behavior in specific but nonjudgmental terms. For instance, you might use the phrase, "when you fail to return my book on time," instead of "you're irresponsible." Avoid using fuzzy and accusatory responses or guessing the person's motives. Such communication only intensifies the person's resistance to changing his or her behavior.

Second, point out the specific ways in which that person's behavior affects us. In most instances, people are not deliberately trying to make life miserable for us; they simply aren't aware of the consequences of their actions. Once they become more aware of how their behavior has become a problem for us, they're usually willing to modify it.

Third, tell the person how you feel about their behavior in a way that "owns" your emotions. Say "I feel hurt" instead of "you hurt me." Avoid projecting your emotions onto the other person.

Finally, tell the person what you want him or her to do. For example, if you object to the casual way telephone messages are left for you, you might say something like, "When you don't write down my telephone messages, I don't have the information I need and I feel frustrated. I'd appreciate your writing down my telephone messages."

Initially, "I" messages may seem a bit contrived or stiff to you. But as you become more experienced using them you'll feel more comfortable expressing your feelings in this way. In due time you will learn how best to incorporate the four components of an "I" message in a way that suits your own personality and style of communication.

Nonverbal Cues

Much of our emotional life is expressed nonverbally. We speak of people "frozen with fear," "trembling with rage," or "bursting with pride." Facial expressions are especially revealing, with tightly squeezed lips and staring a ready sign of anger. Part of the reason may be that words alone fail to convey the full meaning of strong feelings. Suppose someone says, "That's wonderful!" How do you decide whether the remark is sincere or sarcastic? Dane Archer (1979) points out that there is a specific nonverbal "script" for sarcasm, as with other emotions. When people in North American societies express sarcasm, they tend to raise both eyebrows to an exaggerated degree, say the words slowly, and change the tone of voice as they say "wonderful." We're so impressed with nonverbal cues that whenever people are sending mixed messages—that is, saying one thing and expressing another in their face and gestures—we tend to judge more by the nonverbal cues.

Chances are you know people who have clear facial expressions, use gestures freely, and engage in a great deal of body language. Do you find it's easier to understand what these people are saying than those who make little use of nonverbal cues? People from the first group are said to have a great deal of

Facial expressions tell us a lot about a person's emotions at the moment.
(Laimute E. Druskis)

expressiveness. Research has shown that people who are very expressive are more successful in sending nonverbal messages than those with less of this quality. In one study, college students were administered a questionnaire designed to measure differences in expressiveness. (Sample item: "I show that I like someone by hugging or touching that person.") The results showed that expressiveness is closely linked to important aspects of social behavior. For instance, people who scored high on expressiveness were more likely to have had experience in public speaking, been elected to an office in an organization, or held a major part in a play. The researchers also found that expressiveness is related to success in various careers. For example, physicians who were popular with their patients were more expressive than their less popular colleagues. And people who were successful in sales scored higher on expressiveness than unsuccessful ones (Friedman, et al., 1980).

Perhaps you've heard that women, because of "feminine intuition," can read and express unspoken messages more effectively than men. But is there any truth to this notion? Apparently so, although it may have more to do with sex roles than with one's biological sex. Zuckerman (1982) and his colleagues showed there is a significant relationship between standard measures of masculinity and femininity and success in transmitting nonverbal messages. Generally, the higher individuals scored in masculinity, the poorer they were in this respect. And this held true both for facial expressions and nonverbal cues for the voice. Most important of all, these findings held true regardless of whether the subjects happened to be female or male. That is, the important differences between men and women in sending nonverbal messages have more to do with what society views as appropriate *behavior* for each sex than with their biological sex. Thus, men who work in nurturing roles (psychologists, family therapists) as well as those who are sensitive to people's emotional preferences (artists, interior decorators) often become·skilled at interpreting nonverbal cues. And, with the movement toward more flexible sex roles and greater emphasis on men expressing their feelings more openly, we may see fewer differences between the sexes in regard to nonverbal communication. In any event, Archer (1980) believes that all of us can train ourselves to become more effective in reading nonverbal cues by recognizing their importance and paying greater attention to them.

Can You Tell if Someone Is Lying?

Most of us think we can distinguish lies from the truth. But, after extensive studies on this subject, researchers have concluded that detecting a lie is more difficult than we think (DePaulo, Zuckerman, and Rosenthal, 1980). There's no foolproof strategy in detecting lies, but there are some helpful cues.

The face is often regarded as the best source of nonverbal cues because of its versatile channels of communication, like the mouth and eyes. Yet facial expressions are relatively easy to control, so that *by itself*, the face provides the least reliable cues for lying, especially premeditated lies. The body, with its slower, less controllable movements, is more revealing of our hidden emotions. Fleeting body movements and gestures, such as fidgeting of the hands, convey nervousness and often deceit. The voice is even more revealing of hidden emotions, especially on the telephone when there are fewer distractions to the listener. Because of the acoustics of the human skull, our speaking voices don't sound the same to us as to others, as people who have listened to their recorded voices know. Hence the voice is more revealing than the face, especially inflection and tonal qualities, which are controlled by the more "emotional" right hemisphere of the brain. When people are lying, they usually raise the pitch of their voices. By far the most reliable sign of lying is the discrepancy between two channels of communication, such as a smiling face and an angry voice. Perhaps this explains our preference for face-to-face conversations, despite the risk of being distracted by the wealth of stimuli (Zuckerman, DePaulo, and Rosenthal, 1981).

But remember this caution: All these cues reveal hidden emotions, but not necessarily lying, unless supported by other evidence. Furthermore, the listener's own attitudes and personality make a difference. People who are the most adept at detecting lies tend to be friendly, outgoing, and somewhat anxious in social situations. Their unease around people alerts them to the tell-tale signs of lying in others. Yet they tend to be poor at telling lies, partly because of their fear about being caught in a lie (Goleman, 1982).

HANDLING TROUBLESOME EMOTIONS

There are times, even for the best of us, when because of one thing or another life becomes temporarily miserable. We may become so emotionally upset that we don't act like our usual selves. Generally, the more complex our situation, the more emotions interfere with our lives. For example, suppose you're preparing for an important exam at school the next day. Midway through your studying you get a call informing you that a 2-year relationship with your lover is over. You're hurt. You can think of nothing else the rest of the evening. You sleep badly that night. Next day you manage to get up and make it to school on time. Once in class, however, you may find yourself dwelling on your feelings of hurt and anger instead of on the exam before you. In times like these, it's very important that you know how to cope with troublesome emotions.

Almost any emotion can become troublesome. Even excessive anticipation and happiness over an approaching wedding day can become stressful, though negative emotions such as anger are more likely to be the culprit. Elsewhere in the book we'll discuss the emotions of love, sadness, depression, and grief. Here, we'll focus on several other potential troublemakers, including anxiety and fear, anger, guilt, and loneliness.

Anxiety and Fear

You have an uneasy feeling that something bad is about to happen. Your heart is pounding, your breathing becomes rapid, and your muscles are tense. You have the classic symptoms of anxiety—a vague, subjective awareness of threat or danger. Fear, a related emotion, refers to a more specific and objective danger. Both are potential troublemakers for all of us.

Adults exhibit a wide variety of fears, depending on their personalities and experiences. According to one survey, the five most common adult fears are: the death of a loved one, a serious illness, financial worries, nuclear war, and being the victim of a crime. Such supposedly commonplace fears as natural disaster, the dark, flying, heights, public speaking, and going to the dentist scored very low. But the most surprising finding was that many respondents were more afraid of spiders and snakes than of losing their jobs (Stark, 1985). What are some of your worst fears? Are you doing anything about them?

Anxiety serves as an emotional alarm signal, warning us of threat or danger. When the threat is real and can be pinpointed, such as the risk of losing our job, anxiety may motivate us to take the necessary steps to avoid such a misfortune. Unfortunately we often feel anxious when there is little real danger. Furthermore, chronic anxiety leads us to overreact to stressful situations, thereby making them worse. High levels of anxiety also distort our thinking and perception. Anxiety also siphons off energy by keeping us mobilized for action when none is needed. It makes us tense and tired, thereby robbing us of much of the enjoyment of life.

Test anxiety is a familiar problem for most college students. Does test anxiety help us to learn better? Or does it interfere with our performance? A lot depends on the person and test situation. Generally, the relationship between anxiety and test performance takes the form of an inverted U curve. That is, at low levels of anxiety, we remain unmotivated and perform well only on easy tasks. More moderate levels tend to enhance performance, at least up to a point. But at high levels of anxiety many people become distracted and overwhelmed, thereby performing more poorly on tests. At the same time, people differ widely on their optimal level of anxiety—the degree of anxiety at which they do their best. People with relatively low levels of anxiety often do their best only when challenged, as in a highly competitive situation. But those with characteristically high levels of anxiety tend to better, at least on difficult tasks, under conditions of less pressure (Sarason, 1978). Which of these two patterns do you most resemble? Do you find it depends somewhat on the situation as well as your own mastery of appropriate skills and motivation?

If your academic performance is hindered by test anxiety, you may benefit from a number of anxiety-reducing strategies, including the techniques of desensitization and thought control, explained in the chapter on stress. For instance, when you find yourself getting anxious on the test, you employ anxiety-reducing statements such as "I know I can do it" and "I'll just take one question at a time."

One of the most effective anxiety-reducing strategies is learning more effective study techniques. In an experimental study, it was found that students in an advanced psychology course who were anxious about tests did relatively well on multiple-choice questions. Most of the difficulty they encountered was on short-answer questions, essay questions, and take-home exams—all of which call for a more comprehensive understanding of the subject matter. The students also reported problems in learning new material and learning how to pick out the most important points. In short, the researchers found that much of the students' anxiety resulted from their inadequate grasp of the subject matter (Benjamin, et al., 1981). Best of all is a combined strategy, including effective methods of study, relaxation techniques, and thought control.

Anger

A basketball coach yells profanities at the referee after a controversial call. A teenage girl screams, *"No, no, no"* at her mother. A red-faced worker slams his fist on the table to make his point during labor-management negotiations. All these people are ventilating anger—feelings of displeasure or resentment over mistreatment. Most of us have grown up with the idea that when you're angry it's healthy to "get it off your chest" or "let it all hang out." Holding anger in, goes the popular notion, leads to all kinds of problems—high blood pressure, increased risk of heart attacks, depression, and suicide. But is this always so?

Not according to recent thinking on the subject. Carol Tavris (1983), in her book *Anger: The Misunderstood Emotion*, says that there's little evidence that suppressing anger is necessarily dangerous to your health. In fact, "blowing off steam" often makes you angrier and aggravates the situation. Tavris points out that much of our understanding of anger has been influenced by the "catharsis" view of anger, which assumes that inside each tranquil soul is a furious one screaming to get out. The assumption is that anger is an inborn, fixed amount of energy that must be released or it will fester and cause harm. But Tavris points out that, as with other emotions, anger also involves our cognitive processes and is best dealt with through cognitive appraisal. Even though the capacity for anger is part of the inborn response pattern to stress, it is important to know what we're angry about and how to express that anger best—all of which requires cognitive appraisal. For example, during an argument between friends, the free expression of anger may help to clear the air. Yet getting angry and making insulting remarks to your boss may only make matters worse. In the second situation, where there is greater danger of retaliation, it may pay to engage in more reflection.

> I was angry with my friend:
> I told my wrath, my wrath did end.
> I was angry with my foe:
> I told it not, my wrath did grow.
>
>   William Blake, from "A Poison Tree'

To know whether ventilating your anger will get rid of it you need to know *what* you're angry about and *how* to respond to the situation. This involves what Tavris calls the reappraisal method—engaging in sufficient reflection to know what we're angry about and what to do about it. Anger is rarely a "pure" emotion. Frequently we feel angry when we're actually frustrated, scared, or jealous. Ventilating the anger to the exclusion of the other aspects of our emotional state distorts our communication and aggravates the situation. Expressing your anger is usually more effective when it makes known your grievance and helps to restore your sense of control. All too often, when people get angry they rant and rave so that the intended targets of anger may be baffled. "What's this all about?" they wonder. Slow down and ask yourself, "How should I behave in this situation to convince the person I'm angry and get her to do something about it?" Usually, it's most effective to express yourself in a calm, nonaggressive way, as in the "I" messages explained earlier. At the same time there are no simple guidelines to determine when talking is better than yelling. A lot depends on your personality, your style of communication, and the situation. For example, the wife of a construction worker claims that the only way to convince her husband she is really angry is to go into a fit of "abusive rage." Yet she readily admits that both of them feel worse afterwards. In contrast, people who are

Body language helps to express strong emotions. (Laimute E. Druskis)

exposed to constant provocations as part of their jobs, such as police officers and bus drivers, are finding the reappraisal method especially helpful. By reflecting on their feelings and how best to deal with the situation, they can avoid needless stress. For example, a bus driver who took reappraisal training said afterwards, "Before I got this training, if a passenger rang the bell five or six times, I'd take him several blocks further to get even. Now I'll say maybe this person didn't think I heard the bell the first time, or he isn't sure where the bus stop is." With the reappraisal method, the bus driver feels less aggravation and performs more effectively.

Guilt

We experience guilt whenever we violate the moral principles or values of our conscience, either by doing something we consider wrong or failing to do what we feel is right. The sense of guilt is often a complex mixture of remorse, self-reproach, and apprehension (anxiety) over the fear of punishment. Guilt is potentially a useful emotion in the sense that it awakens us to our sense of responsibility when we have done something wrong. As such, it is an essential part of autonomy or self-direction. Yet we should also keep in mind that our conscience originates in childhood, so guilt feelings may be associated mistakenly with anger toward authority and shame about our bodies and sexuality. Since the values of the adult conscience tend to supersede rather than entirely displace the dictates of our childhood conscience, our sense of guilt sometimes reflects the vestiges of this harsh, punitive childhood conscience. Accordingly, we may feel guilty when we haven't done anything wrong. For example, a student who was angry about the grade he had received on a test asked me to reconsider the grade. I agreed to do so. Then I noticed he was absent from the next couple of classes. When I returned the test, with the modified grade, I remarked that he hadn't been in class that week. He replied, "I felt badly about the way I spoke to you. I'm sorry." I explained that he had acted civilly and had done nothing wrong, and that he was being too hard on himself. He was suffering from what Maslow once called "silly guilt."

When people are motivated by childish, usually unconscious guilt feelings, they tend to act in a self-punitive and self-defeating way. One manifestation of such guilt is the habitual tendency to apologize ("I'm sorry") or to be unduly critical of one's self. When something goes wrong, guilt-prone individuals are quick to blame someone, either themselves or others. They may act in a self-righteous manner, scapegoating others for what went wrong. Those who can't live with their guilt may refuse to accept responsibility for their part in the wrongdoing or seek the protection of groups that provide a "sanction for evil." Some of history's most aggressive acts have been accompanied by a sense of righteousness. Many Nazis felt they were saving their country from the "greedy exploitation of the Jews" when they exterminated over 6 million people. Guilt-ridden people may also be accident-prone or keep hurting themselves in unexplained ways. For example, a woman reported that her husband, who had been reared by a harsh father, was always hurting himself on his power saw at home. Other times, guilty people may act in a manner that tests the limits of acceptability, such as engaging in senseless vandalism, making insulting remarks to authority figures, or engaging in provocative sexual behavior that invites cen-

---

The Conscience Fund

Each year, guilt-ridden Americans voluntarily sent the government thousands of dollars to absolve themselves of thefts once committed against the country. The money is frequently accompanied by explanations of the misdeeds, though most letters are unsigned. One person wrote, "Enclosed is $5 to pay for a 'borrowed' government item." Another said, "My conscience has been bothering me and I feel better now." Still another person said, "I want to be ready to meet God."

Many such letters come from men and women who have been in the armed services and who stole articles from the bases where they were stationed. A large number of letters come from people who have cheated on their income tax returns.

All the money goes into a "Conscience Fund," which was begun in 1811 when someone anonymously sent in $5 with an explanation that he had defrauded the government. Since then, the fund has accumulated over 4 million dollars.

In a day when many Americans are complaining of oppressive taxes and fraud in the government, what would you say about such acts of conscience?

Are they signs of a sensitive, adult conscience? Or are they manifestations of a childish, authoritarian conscience? How would you tell the difference?

Marlene Cimons, *Los Angeles Times-Washington Post* News Service, 1975.

sure. When corrected, such individuals may protest loudly, but they may inwardly feel a sense of relief—their exaggerated sense of guilt makes them long to be caught and "punished." Yet, such self-defeating behavior will continue until these people become more aware of their guilt and take appropriate steps to resolve it.

By contrast, a healthy sense of guilt leads to self-correction and constructive behavior. Individuals with high self-esteem and a healthy conscience—and these two go together—become aware of their guilt in a direct, intuitive way and take steps to modify their behavior accordingly. For instance, a husband who feels bad about the way he has mistreated his wife may change his behavior, rather than repeating lame excuses. Individuals with high self-esteem can readily admit their wrongdoings and take the appropriate steps to make amends. Healthy guilt serves to maintain the integrity of our relationships with others as well as our self-respect. As with anxiety, it is self-injurious to have too much guilt, especially childish, punitive guilt. But worse still is to lack any capacity for guilt at all.

Loneliness

Each of us is familiar with loneliness—the feeling of unhappiness at being alone accompanied by a longing for companionship. Yet loneliness involves more than the absence of people. Occasionally we may choose to be alone without being *lonely*, such as when we're tired, embarrassed, busy, or after an extended period of socializing with others. We may also seek solitude for periods of personal thought and reflection, to sort out what's happening in our lives. At other times we want to be with others, especially when we're in a new situation, happy, or in a good mood. (See Table 4–2.) Even then we may sometimes feel lonely while surrounded by people. The truth of the matter is that loneliness has more to do with the lack of satisfying relationships than the absence of people.

Loneliness is partly a state of mind. That is, loneliness often results from the gap between our desire for closeness and the failure to find it. This can be seen in a survey of loneliness that, surprisingly, showed that 18- to 25-year-olds suffer the most from loneliness. Having loosened the ties with their parents, people this age are actively seeking intimacy with their peers, especially those of the opposite sex. The idealism of youth, plus the desire for self-fulfillment and happy marriages, makes them especially sensitive to the discrepancy that exists between their expectations of intimacy and their actual relationships. Each successive age group, however, reports diminishing levels of loneliness. People over 70 suffer the least of all from loneliness. Although old people spend much of their time alone, they've also learned how to take it in stride. Older people seem to be able to put their need for companionship in better perspective (Rubinstein, Shaver, and Peplau, 1982).

Table 4–2.   WHEN COLLEGE STUDENTS MOST WANT TO BE ALONE OR WITH OTHERS.   Situations in which 70 percent or more of the students wished to be with others or alone are listed separately from those situations in which there was no such level of consensus.

	PERCENTAGE OF STUDENTS WHO:		
	Wished To Be With Others	Wished To Be Alone	Had No Preference
Situations in which most want to be with others			
When very happy	88	2	10
When in a good mood	89	0	11
On Saturday night	85	1	14
When you are in a strange situation or doing something you've never done before	77	13	10
Situations in which most want to be alone			
When physically tired	6	85	9
When embarrassed	16	76	8
When you want to cry	8	88	4
When busy	12	70	18
After an extensive period of social contact—after being with others for a long time	12	75	13
Situations in which there was no consensus			
When depressed	42	48	10
When worried about a serious personal problem	52	44	4
When mildly ill (e.g., with a cold)	32	49	19
When feeling very guilty about something you have done	45	43	12

Source: Patricia Niles Middlebrook, *Social Psychology and Modern Life*, 2nd ed. Copyright © 1980, 1973 by Alfred A. Knopf, Inc. Reprinted by permission of Alfred A. Knopf, Inc.

How we interpret our state of loneliness affects our feelings and, in turn, how we cope with the situation. People who blame their loneliness on their personal inadequacies ("I'm lonely because I'm unlovable") or bad luck ("My lover and I have split up, but that's the way my relationships go") make themselves even more lonely and depressed. In contrast, people are more likely to overcome their loneliness when they focus on their own efforts ("I'll stop working so much and get out and meet more people") and on the specific situation ("People aren't intentionally cold, they're just busy"). Similarly, people who react to loneliness in passive ways—watching television, crying, sleeping—feel all the more lonely. Those who adopt more active strategies—reading, writing a letter, calling up a friend—are more likely to alleviate their loneliness (Rubinstein, Shaver, and Peplau, 1982).

How do you cope with loneliness? Do you blame yourself and feel there's nothing you can do about it? Or do you take more active steps to overcome your loneliness, such as calling up a friend? In the final analysis, successfully coping with loneliness, as with other emotions, involves understanding why we're feeling this way and then taking the appropriate steps to remedy the situation.

Summary

Understanding Emotions

1. We began the chapter by explaining that an emotion is a complex pattern of changes, which includes physiological arousal, subjective feelings, cognitive processes, and behavioral reactions, usually in response to a situation we perceive to be significant.

2. Our emotions may be triggered by our thought and behavior as well as by bodily arousal, and thus we help to shape our feelings to a considerable extent.

3. Also, emotions, like colors, vary in intensity and meaning, such that our feeling life often includes a mixture of the primary emotions.

Expressing Emotions

4. To express our emotions effectively each of us must find a suitable balance, varying somewhat from one person to another, between spontaneous expression and deliberate, rational control of our feelings.

5. A helpful way of expressing negative feelings is the "I" message, which includes: a nonjudgmental description of the other person's behavior, the tangible effects on yourself, your feelings about it, and what you'd prefer the person to do instead.

6. Much of our emotional life is expressed in nonverbal cues. So when we're getting mixed messages from others, we're apt to judge more by the nonverbal expressions of emotion.

Handling Troublesome Emotions

7. We may cope with disruptive anxiety, such as a debilitating test-anxiety, by a variety of anxiety-reducing strategies, including desensitization, thought control, and more effective methods of study and test taking.

8. To know whether ventilating your anger will get rid of it, you need to know what you're angry about and how to respond to the situation in a way which will make your grievance known and help to restore your sense of control.

9. Guilt is a useful emotion in awakening us to our responsibility when we have violated our conscience, though the sense of guilt often includes childish, irrational feelings that can lead to self-defeating behavior.

10. Successful ways of coping with loneliness include focusing more on our own efforts and the specific situation than on our personal inadequacies, and then taking active steps to overcome loneliness, such as calling up a friend.

Self-test

1. The terms for motives and emotions have the same Latin origin, which refers to:

    a. desire   **c.** attraction

    b. movement   **d.** power

2. An emotion is a complex pattern of changes that includes:

   a. physiological arousal   **c.** subjective feelings

   b. cognitive processes   **d.** all of the above

3. Which emotion below has been identified by Plutchik as one of the eight primary emotions?

   a. anger   **c.** love

   b. remorse   **d.** awe

4. The conscious and deliberate control of emotion is known as:

   a. repression   **c.** suppression

   b. inhibition   **d.** denial

5. When reacting to someone's mistreatment of you, an "I" message would include:

   a. your personal judgment of the person's behavior   **c.** your moral principles and values

   b. how you feel about what this person is doing   **d.** all of the above

6. We are especially likely to understand someone's emotional state when that person is:

   a. masculine   **c.** articulate

   b. charismatic   **d.** expressive

7. What emotion serves as an emotional alarm signal, warning us of psychological danger?

   a. anger   **c.** pain

   b. guilt   **d.** anxiety

8. Ventilating your anger is usually more effective when:

   a. it makes your grievance known   **c.** it helps restore your sense of control

   b. you know what you're angry about   **d.** all of the above

9. A healthy sense of guilt leads to:

   a. guilty behavior   **c.** self-punishment

   b. self-correction   **d.** self-righteousness

10. People in which age group below suffer the most from loneliness?

   a. 14 to 17   **c.** 36 to 45

   b. 18 to 25   **d.** 46 to 60

Exercises

1. *Sharing your everyday feelings.* Do you share your feelings as readily as you'd like? If not, you might try this exercise. A good way to begin sharing your feelings is to share some of the safe, everyday feelings. For example, whenever you're especially pleased by something another person has done for you, tell this person how you feel about it. The practice of sharing these safe feelings may help you to become more aware of and comfortable in sharing your deeper feelings.

2. *Practice sending "I" messages.* Think of several situations in which someone else's behavior has become a problem for you. Then write out the appropriate "I" messages under the respective four headings, as explained and illustrated in this chapter. If you feel comfortable doing so, you might try expressing some of these "I" messages in person.

3. *Exploring the effects of anxiety in your life.* As you may recall, anxiety can have positive and negative effects in our lives. Think of at least two situations in your life, one in which anxiety stimulated you to do your best, and one in which anxiety interfered with your performance. How do you account for the difference?

4. *Handling anger.* Recall a situation in which you became very angry. Did you tend to lose control, saying and doing things you later regretted? Or did you respond to the situation in a way that made known your grievance and helped to restore your sense of control? Looking back, what would you have done differently?

5. *How do you cope with loneliness?* Think of the last time you felt lonely. How did you handle this experience? Did you react passively, sitting around watching television and feeling sorry for yourself? Or did you take more active steps to overcome your loneliness, such as writing a letter or calling up a friend?

Questions for Self-reflection

1. How aware are you of your feelings?
2. Do you often refer to your feelings in explaining your behavior?
3. To what extent can we determine our own emotions?
4. Do others call you a moody person?
5. How easily do you express your feelings?
6. Which emotions are the hardest for you to express?
7. Do you use "I" messages in expressing your feelings?
8. When it comes to anger, do you think before you speak?
9. Which are the most troublesome emotions for you?
10. How do you cope with feelings of loneliness?

Recommended Readings

Friday, Nancy. *Jealousy.* New York: William Morrow, 1985. A thoughtful look at the meaning and impact of jealousy in human relationships.

Gaylin, Willard, M.D. *Feelings.* New York: Ballantine Books, 1979 (paperback). Explains why we feel the way we do and how to manage our emotions more effectively.

May, Rollo. *The Meaning of Anxiety,* rev. ed. New York: Washington Square Press, 1979 (paperback). A classic explaining the various views of anxiety illustrated with numerous case histories.

Phillips, D., and R. Judd. *How To Fall Out of Love.* New York: Popular Library, 1980 (paperback). Contains practical suggestions for overcoming impossible or unsatisfying love affairs.

Rubin, Theodore Isaac, M.D., and Eleanor Rubin, M.D. *Not To Worry.* New York: Pinnacle Books, 1984 (paperback). A noted psychiatrist explains how to handle our worries.

Tavris, Carol. *Anger: The Misunderstood Emotion.* New York: Simon & Schuster, 1983. An innovative approach to understanding and handling anger through the use of cognitive appraisal.

Stress

Steve arrives at the office late, after a harrowing 30-minute delay on the expressway. He is told the boss wants to see him right away. "I wonder what that's about?" Steve muses to himself, as he takes off his coat and heads upstairs. He's ushered inside the boss's office, only to find him pacing back and forth. The boss is furious. The big deal they were counting on with a major corporation has just fallen through. The boss makes it clear that if Steve values his job he'd better have a good explanation. Steve gropes for words. "Frankly, I'm stunned. I can't imagine what happened," he says. "Let me call and talk to the people over there and find out the story." Steve's boss continues making accusations about his incompetence and his uncertain future with the company. Steve feels enraged at being treated this way. He is tempted to punch his boss in the face. Instead, he returns to his office to cool off. He sits down at his desk, his stomach churning, his neck muscles tense, and his blood pressure rising. He reaches for a Maalox and an aspirin.

SOURCES OF STRESS

Steve is discovering that the modern world is no less perilous than the jungle. He feels that extra burst of adrenalin that primes his muscles and steadies his nerves for a fight. Yet the primitive "fight or flight" response used by his Stone Age ancestors is no longer appropriate. It's also dangerous. When people like Steve lash out aggressively with their fists or weapons, they jeopardize the welfare of society itself. Should they try to escape through the use of alcohol or drugs, they only succeed in making their problems worse. Instead they must learn how to manage stress, including the intense emotions aroused, in a more appropriate manner for our times.

Meanwhile, stress is taking a heavy toll on the nation's well-being. Leaders of industry are alarmed about the huge costs of absenteeism, lost productivity, and increasing medical expenses, all of which cost businesses about $75 billion a year. Stress has also become a major contributor, either directly or indirectly, to coronary heart disease, cancer, lung ailments, accidental injuries, cirrhosis of the liver, and suicide—six of the leading causes of death in the United States. In short, it seems as if our modern way of life has become a major source of stress.

Meaning of Stress

Stress is difficult to define partly because it means different things to different people. Some see stress as any external stimulus that causes wear and tear, such as the pressure to perform at work. Competitive pressures, the uncertainties of modern life, job insecurity, the threat of nuclear war, all these factors have made life increasingly stressful. At the same time, people respond to the same stressful event differently. Individuals who constantly complain or panic in the face of job pressures will experience considerably more stress than those who calmly take such things in stride. In this view, stress consists largely of *how* we respond to events, not the events themselves, so that we bring a lot of our stress on ourselves.

Although the experience of stress includes both stimulus and response variables, stress is usually defined in terms of our response to events. Stress has been defined as "the pattern of specific and nonspecific responses an organism makes to stimulus events that disturb its equilibrium and tax or exceed its ability to cope" (Zimbardo, 1985, p. 456). Note that it is when events disrupt our usual level of functioning and require us to make an extra effort to reestablish our equilibrium that we experience stress. Not surprisingly, it is often the combination of events, such as not being able to start our car on the morning we have an important test, that generates stress. In this case stress includes our specific efforts needed to start the car (or get a ride) and to take the test. But stress also involves the nonspecific physiological reactions that occur in response to stresses, such as the increased flow of adrenalin that mobilizes us for an extra effort. We'll discuss this shortly in regard to the general adaptation syndrome.

Hey! Wait for me!
(Jon Huber)

We should be careful not to equate stress with distress. Instead, stress is a many-sided phenomenon that may also have a beneficial effect. Hans Selye (1980), the noted stress researcher, has described four basic variations of stress, each with its own label. When events have a harmful effect on us, stress is correctly labeled "distress." Unfortunately, much of the stress in modern society is distressful. Yet stress may also have a beneficial effect on us. Beginning a new job, getting married, or taking up an exciting sport like sky-diving, all may have a stimulating effect that makes for personal growth. Selye suggests we might call this "eustress," or good stress. He has also described two more variations of stress: hyperstress, or excessive stress, usually occurs when events, including positive ones, pile up and stretch the limits of our adaptability. Hypostress, or insufficient stress, is apt to occur when we're lacking stimulation. As a result, bored people may resort to the sensation-seeking behaviors mentioned earlier, such as experimentation with drugs.

Common Stressors

Stressor is the collective label for the variety of external and internal stimuli that evoke stress. Although almost anything can be a stressor, some conditions are more likely than others to precipitate stress. Catastrophic events like the collapse of a bridge are obviously stressful. For some reason, traumas caused by human actions such as assaults, rapes, fires, construction disasters, and combat tend to bring about more severe stress than natural disasters like earthquakes and floods. Negative events, such as the death of a loved one or the loss of a job, are usually quite stressful. Yet positive events such as starting college or getting married can be stressful too.

There is now widespread recognition that it is often the combined effect of various life changes, positive and negative, that produces stress, and that high levels of stress are closely associated with an increased incidence of illness. Thomas Holmes and his colleagues (Holmes and Rahe, 1967) have constructed a Social Readjustment Rating Scale that measures the stress potential of various life events. (See Table 5–1.) Despite individual differences of age, sex, and race, Holmes and Rahe usually found a high percentage of agreement among the rankings of the various life events. The most important factor is the *total impact* of these life events, which in turn intensifies our need for adaptive responses. A total score of 150 to 199 life-change units (LCU) constitutes a mild life crisis. A score of 200 to 299 LCU constitutes a moderate crisis, and a score of 300 or more, a major crisis. As the number of LCU increases, the risk of illness becomes more certain. Interestingly enough, we continue to suffer from the effects of a stressful event for as long as a year afterwards.

A study of 2,500 officers and enlisted men aboard three U.S. Navy cruisers showed that in the first month of the cruise, men in the high-risk group (300 LCU or more) had nearly 90 percent more first illnesses than men in the low-risk group (150-199 LCU). And, for each month thereafter, the high-risk group continued to report more new illnesses than the other groups. Similar results have been reported for the relation between stress and football injuries, as well as the incidence of such illnesses as heart attacks, respiratory illnesses, skin and colon diseases, schizophrenia, and cancer. The particular kind of illness that strikes as a result of stress, of course, depends on an individual's physical make-up as well as the bacterial and viral agents present. But these studies show that we are more predisposed to becoming sick in some way when we have to cope with an excessive number of rapid changes. It would seem that such vigorous coping activity does tend to lower our resistance to disease (Holmes and Masuda, 1974).

Despite its usefulness, the life-events approach to stress has several limitations. In the first place, the particular selection of events may not be equally relevant for different groups of people, such as college students, blue-collar workers, and the elderly. Second, it does not take into account how individuals perceive and adapt to a given change. Furthermore, since the life-events

Table 5-1. SOCIAL READJUSTMENT RATING SCALE.

Rank	Life Event	Mean Value
1	Death of spouse	100
2	Divorce	73
3	Marital separation	65
4	Jail term	63
5	Death of close family member	63
6	Personal injury or illness	53
7	Marriage	50
8	Fired at work	47
9	Marital reconciliation	45
10	Retirement	45
11	Change in health of family member	44
12	Pregnancy	40
13	Sex difficulties	39
14	Gain of new family member	39
15	Business readjustment	39
16	Change in financial state	38
17	Death of close friend	37
18	Change to different line of work	36
19	Change in number of arguments with spouse	35
20	Mortgage over $10,000	31
21	Foreclosure of mortgage or loan	30
22	Change in responsibilities at work	29
23	Son or daughter leaving home	29
24	Trouble with in-laws	29
25	Outstanding personal achievement	28
26	Wife begins or stops work	26
27	Begin or end school	26
28	Change in living conditions	25
29	Revision of personal habits	24
30	Trouble with boss	23
31	Change in work hours or conditions	20
32	Change in residence	20
33	Change in schools	20
34	Change in recreation	19
35	Change in church activities	19
36	Change in social activities	18
37	Mortgage or loan less than $10,000	17
38	Change in sleeping habits	16
39	Change in number of family get-togethers	15
40	Change in eating habits	15
41	Vacation	13
42	Christmas	12
43	Minor violations of the law	11

Source: T.H. Holmes and R.H. Rahe, "Social Readjustment Rating Scale," *Journal of Psychosomatic Research*, vol. II, p. 216. © 1967, Pergamon Press, Ltd. Reprinted with permission.

Having too many things to do and not enough time to do them is a common source of stress. (Courtesy U.S. Census Bureau)

approach is built around social change, it fails to include a great deal of stress that comes from chronic or repeated conditions, such as a boring job or an incompatible marriage. Finally, the everyday observation that it's the "little things" in life that really get us down has also received empirical support. In their investigation of such stressors, Lazarus and DeLongis (1983) found that people vary widely in the daily hassles that bother them. The most commonly reported hassles among college students were anxiety over wasting time, meeting high standards, and being lonely. Middle-aged people were bothered more by worries over health and money. Professional people felt that they had too much to do and not enough time to do it, as well as difficulty relaxing. The hassles common to all groups were: misplacing or losing things, worries over physical appearance, and too many things to do. Interestingly, these investigators also found a strong link between daily hassles and psychological and physical health, with people who suffer frequent and intense hassles having the poorest health.

Personal, Situational Factors

Our overall experience of stress is affected by a variety of personal and situational factors. Some of the more common ones are described below.

How we perceive a given event may make it more or less stressful. One person may take criticism of her work as a personal attack, become upset, and waste a lot of energy defending herself. Yet another person may take similar criticism as a challenge to improve her work, thereby experiencing less stress. A lot depends on our personal makeup. People plagued by inner doubt, low self-esteem, and suspiciousness may misconstrue even the routine demands of everyday life as stressful. Others, the Type A personality, are more likely to develop stress-related illnesses because of their personal traits. They tend to be highly competitive, judging themselves and others by rigorous standards. They're also impatient. They talk, walk, and eat rapidly, and pride themselves on getting things done in less time than others. As a result they keep themselves

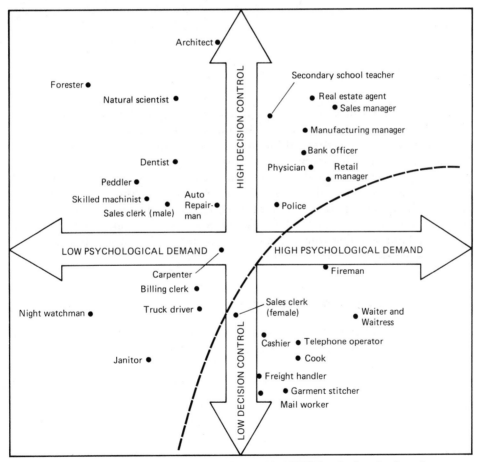

Figure 5-1. SOME JOBS ARE MORE STRESSFUL THAN OTHERS. Studies of male workers suggest that those whose jobs involve high psychological demand but little decision making or control over their work, like cooks, waiters, and assembly-line personnel, are five times more likely to develop coronary heart disease than workers who exercise greater control over their work.

Source: Columbia University Department of Industrial Engineering and Operations Research.

under constant stress and are much more likely to develop heart disease than other people (Friedman and Rosenman, 1974).

Many situational factors may contribute to our experience of stress. Probably the most important of all is the combined effect of various life changes, as explained earlier. Having car troubles, a sick child at home, and a crisis at work generates more stress than any of these events alone. Unpredictable events such as an automobile accident are highly stressful. The threat of bodily harm greatly increases stress, as people taken hostage or military personnel in combat would testify. The constant alertness required of certain workers—such as air-traffic controllers, astronauts, and those working with nuclear reactors—is becoming a more common source of stress. Lack of control or a feeling of futility in a stressful situation are key factors in stress. (See Figure 5–1.) By contrast, successful stress management involves learning what you *can* do in the face of the most difficult situation, as we'll explain in the last part of this chapter.

STRESS REACTIONS

You're under a lot of stress. You have a test coming up this week. A paper is overdue in another course. You're having conflicts with your supervisor at work. You're tense and tired all the time and have just come down with a cold. You also find yourself snapping at friends and loved ones for no reason at all. You're experiencing some of the common emergency responses associated with stress. Certain reactions occur largely automatically, helping us to cope with stressful situations. These reactions may help to alleviate stress temporarily. But if continued, they often make things worse. Such reactions include those of the general adaptation syndrome, defense mechanisms, and other coping devices for minor stress.

General Adaptation Syndrome

There is a characteristic pattern of nonspecific physiological mechanisms that occurs in response to continued threat by almost any stressor. Hans Selye (1974) calls this pattern the general adaptation syndrome. It consists of three progressive stages: the alarm reaction, the stage of resistance, and exhaustion.

The Alarm Reaction. This is our initial emergency response to the stress-provoking agents. At the physiological level of stress, this consists of complicated bodily and biochemical changes that result in similar symptoms regardless of the type of stressor. For this reason people with different illnesses often complain of common symptoms such as a fever, headache, aching muscles and joints, loss of appetite, and a generally tired feeling. When the stress is more directly psychological, the alarm response consists of a heightened sense of anxiety, which arouses and mobilizes our defenses. This usually makes us more apprehensive, unable to concentrate or sleep well, and generally upset. Defense mechanisms like rationalization or denial are frequently used at this stage.

The Stage of Resistance. This occurs when the body successfully adapts to prolonged stress. The symptoms of the alarm stage disappear and the bodily resistance rises above its normal level to cope with the continued stress. The price of this resistance includes increased secretions from various glands and organs of the body, a lowered resistance to infections, and what Selye has termed the "diseases of adaptation," such as ulcers or hypertension. A chronically anxious or neurotic person with a rigid system of defenses or other coping devices is usually in this second stage of psychological stress.

The Stage of Exhaustion. This stage may be reached if the stress continues. Bodily defenses break down, adaptation energy runs out, and the physical signs of the alarm reaction reappear. Since stress accentuates aging, the symptoms at this stage are similar to those of aging, except that the symptoms of exhaustion are more or less reversible with rest. However, continued stress at this stage, like aging, leads to death. When the prolonged stress is felt at the psychological level, there may be hallucinations, delusions, and other bizarre behavior characteristic of severely disturbed people. If this condition remains untreated, the individual tends to regress to the kind of apathetic behavior seen in psychotic patients institutionalized for many years—a kind of psychological death.

Defense Mechanisms

Early in life we demonstrate certain spontaneous reactions to keep ourselves from being overwhelmed by intense doses of psychological stress. These are commonly called defense mechanisms because they are used by the self (or *ego* in psychodynamic terms) for protection from threat. Although these patterns are influenced by learning to some degree, they are largely automatic and spontaneous. Defense mechanisms are triggered by anxiety and generally operate unconsciously, thereby protecting us from sudden or excessive threat. (See Table 5–2.)

Each of us relies on defense mechanisms at one time or another, especially when under intense stress. As emergency reactions, they minimize our awareness of anxiety and help to maintain our sense of adequacy and self-worth in the face of threat. Yet, because these mechanisms involve self-deception and a distortion of reality, habitual reliance on them is maladaptive and prevents personal growth.

Other Coping Devices

There are also a number of other ways we may allay minor stress. We look at these as "coping devices for minor emergencies." Although these responses have been influenced by learning, they tend to operate automatically, though

Table 5–2.   DEFENSE MECHANISMS.

Defense Mechanism	Definition
Repression	Excluding unacceptable ideas or feelings from consciousness
Denial	Misperceiving threatening objects or events as harmless
Fixation	Continuing a kind of gratification after one has passed through the stage at which this was appropriate
Regression	Reverting to a form of behavior that was more appropriate at an earlier stage of development
Rationalization	Justifying our unacceptable behavior through "good" reasons
Intellectualization	Reducing anxiety by analyzing threatening issues in an emotionally detached way
Projection	Attributing our unacceptable ideas or feelings to others
Displacement	Redirecting threatening ideas or impulses onto less threatening objects
Sublimation	Channeling socially unacceptable urges into acceptable behaviors
Acting out	Relieving anxiety or unpleasant tensions through expressing them in overt behavior
Reaction-formation	Developing conscious feelings and behaviors opposite to the unconscious, anxiety-arousing ones

probably at a slightly higher level of awareness than the defense mechanisms. Which of these devices we use in a particular situation depends partly on the circumstances and partly on the suddenness and strength of the disturbance. But mostly the habitual patterns we've acquired in handling past stresses determine how we will react in a particular situation.

The comforts of *touch, food,* and *drink* are so familiar as to be taken for granted. We've all seen how a child will seek increasing physical contact with a parent as a way of gaining reassurance in the face of stress. Adults faced with sadness, sickness, or death also rely more on touching as a way of communicating concern at a time when words are often inadequate. The psychological value of food and drink at times of stress derives from their being substitutes for the primal food, the mother's breast, and their value as symbols of reassurance. When under pressure, some of us nibble or eat more, while others take a drink or a smoke. Still others seek out drugs, especially tranquilizers.

Laughing, crying or *cursing* also have the effect of discharging tension. Have you ever noticed the loud, forced laughter of people just before they take an exam? Laughing at one's troubles can be cathartic, although hostile humor that puts one's self or others down is unhealthy. Crying it out comes naturally to children, who discharge their tensions rather spontaneously. Among adults, though, it has been more permissible for women than men to find release from

Humor is a great way to relieve stress—at least temporarily. (Laimute E. Druskis)

stress through crying. But now more men are discovering that it's normal to cry. Traditionally, men have discharged their tensions more through cursing than crying.

Talking it out and *thinking it through* are probably the most common of all everyday devices for coping with stress. Finding someone who will listen to us is one of the most helpful things we can do when troubled. The more the other person simply listens and responds with empathy, rather than judgment or sympathy, the more we gain perspective on our problems. For we often don't know our own thoughts or feelings fully until we've expressed them. We also need time to think things through in the quietness of our own minds.

Working off tension in work or play affords a release from our pent-up energies, although this does not usually change the situation causing stress. Since our primary activities are moving and doing, it seems natural to use action to afford release from tension. Taking a walk, playing a vigorous game of tennis, or making something that will take our minds off our problems can all be excellent temporary ways to keep our sanity amid stress. Some people also seek out increased sexual activity as a way of displacing tension.

Each of us uses these devices at one time or another, possibly preferring some more than others. Some people are likely to blow off steam through verbal means. Others are more likely to work it off physically in work or play. Some accommodate stress through visceral means by eating, drinking, or emotional expression. Still others seek release through intellectual means, including daydreaming or meditation. You might ask yourself "Which way am I inclined?" Preferably, you should use the way that is most appropriate to you and your situation. The danger is in habitually adopting one of these strategies to the exclusion of the others. In so doing you will tend to rely on one of these devices in and of itself, whether it is appropriate to the external situation or not. In this way, the bottle becomes the alcoholic's best friend. Stress is no longer his problem. His problem now is his response to stress.

How Do You React to Stress?

Each of us spontaneously reacts to stress somewhat differently depending on the type of stress, our personal makeup, and our past experience.

During a stressful time some people are more likely to suffer from respiratory symptoms, such as a cold, while others tend to have gastrointestinal symptoms, such as an ulcer. Some individuals tend to become defensive under stress, complaining a lot and making excuses for their poor performances. Other people may find themselves relying on some of the coping devices for minor stress, such as snacking a lot or overeating at mealtimes, crying easily, or seeking out the company of others to talk things out.

How do you characteristically react to stress? Are you aware of the ways in which your body is especially vulnerable to stress? What steps are you taking to counteract or prevent this?

MANAGING STRESS

Managing stress successfully involves more than the automatic, symptom-reducing reactions to stress, as helpful as these may be. Managing stress means taking charge, directing and controlling our responses to stressors, thereby modifying the overall stress. There are many ways to accomplish this, but most of them fall under two major headings: modifying our environment, and altering ourselves in some way.

Modifying Your Environment

A camera you've had on special order finally arrives. But you discover it's not exactly the model you wanted. What should you do? You could tell the clerk a mistake has been made and then proceed to order the correct model of camera. Or you could simply accept the camera on hand and leave, making sure never to buy anything in that store again. And there's still another option: you could refuse to accept the order and, instead, choose another camera more to your liking from among those already in stock.

These responses illustrate three of the basic ways to modify your environment: assertiveness, withdrawal, or compromise. Let's take a look at each of these strategies.

1. *Assertiveness.* An *assertive approach* is the preferred way to manage stress whenever there is a reasonable possibility of success. Such an approach consists of direct attempts at modifying the stressful situation itself. Common examples would be returning a defective product to a store or manufacturer, or speaking up in response to an unreasonable request.

Frequently, unassertive people let others take advantage of them, building up a lot of resentment in the process. Then in a moment of anger, they may lash out aggressively, often making their situation even more stressful. In contrast, assertiveness has to do with expressing your rights and desires without infringing upon those of others. Assertiveness is a rational and constructive way of handling stress, which in turn tends to alleviate the stress involved. For example, a secretary who experienced a great deal of stress in her job became depressed and took out her frustrations by coming to the office late and putting off deadlines at work. After attending a workshop on assertiveness skills, however, she began to speak up. She told her boss how frustrated she became when he gave conflicting orders, such as wanting two different things typed at the same time. As often happens, her boss was not aware of the inconsistencies in his requests, and he promptly changed his ways, thereby alleviating much of her stress.

2. *Withdrawal* may be an appropriate response to stress, especially when a stressful situation cannot be successfully modified through assertiveness or compromise. Withdrawal is neither good nor bad in itself. Much depends on how it is used. If someone habitually withdraws from stressful situations, that person may drift into a constricted lifestyle that prevents adequate adjustment or personal growth. On the other hand, the use of withdrawal as a *temporary* strategy may be a valuable means of coping with stress that has become overwhelming or detrimental to one's health. Some examples of temporary withdrawal would be students dropping out of school until they can earn more money, or marital partners agreeing to a separation while they seek counseling. When no suitable solution is forthcoming, despite the best efforts of the people involved, a permanent withdrawal may be more appropriate. An example would be the worker who actively looks for another job after getting no satisfaction from his or her supervisor.

3. *Compromise* is still another adaptive response to stress. In contrast to withdrawal, compromise allows us to remain in the stressful situation but in a less active way than with an assertive approach. Compromise is most likely to be

How Assertive Are You?

Assertiveness has to do with expressing your rights, thoughts, and feelings in a direct way without violating the rights of others.

Imagine yourself in each of the following situations. What would you say?

When your parents are giving unwanted advice

When a friend asks you for a loan

When you're being pressured to buy something

When refusing an unreasonable request

When interrupted while you're speaking

In the last situation, simply to keep quiet would be nonassertive. But to blurt out "Shut up!" would be aggressive or hurtful. Instead, an assertive response might be, "Excuse me. I'd like to finish what I was saying."

Ironically, the lack of assertiveness in everyday relationships produces more resentment and alienation in the long run than assertiveness. In contrast, assertive responses not only preserve your self-respect, but they also facilitate good communication, which is essential for mutually satisfying relationships.

used when someone holds a higher rank or authority than you do, or when both participants are at a standstill. The three most common types of compromise are conformity, negotiation, and substitution.

Conformity is one response to stressful situations. Let's say you work as a buyer for a large corporation that has just ordered a more elaborate procedure for purchasing, including much more paperwork and more signatures for approval. At the outset you detest the change. You may comply outwardly by adopting the new procedure even though you dislike it. Or you may conform to the new demands because you like your superiors and co-workers enough to accommodate to the added stress. Since jobs are not easy to get or hold, you may take the new procedures in stride and decide that changing your attitude is the most realistic approach, because endless strife and resentment may be more stressful than accommodation or outright assertion. The key question in any type of conformity response, however, is whether the price of the compromise is worth it.

Negotiation is a more active and promising way to achieve compromise in many situations of stress. Long used in the public areas of labor-management and political disputes, negotiation has now become more widely used at the interpersonal level among co-workers, marriage partners, and friends. Negotiation is preferable to conformity wherever possible because it involves mutual accommodation among the participants.

Substitution is another way to achieve compromise where negotiation or conformity is not appropriate. If a woman desires to resume her college education but has small children and cannot enroll full time, she may decide that the best alternative is to attend part-time at a nearby community college. In this case, a substitute means was found to achieve the same goal. At other times, it may become necessary to choose a substitute goal. For example, the man who after several attempts is not admitted to medical school may choose some related vocational field in which there are more openings, such as pharmacy, physiotherapy, or paramedical training.

Compromise itself is neither good nor bad. Much depends on the relation between the satisfaction achieved and the price paid in the reduction of stress. Habitual compromise may bring more frustration and conflict than a more assertive approach. Too many people suffer in stale jobs or conflict-ridden marriages longer than necessary because compromise has become the easy way out. We need to take into account the long-range effects of compromise as well. A life of passive accommodation to undue stress may be more stressful than an assertive or avoidance approach.

Altering Your Lifestyle

Ultimately, of course, we have more control over ourselves than over our environment. As a result, we may choose to modify something about ourselves or our behavior as a way of better managing stress. The range of possibilities are many and include acquiring greater tolerance for stress, altering our everyday habits, and learning to control distressful thoughts.

First, build up a greater tolerance for stress. Stress tolerance may be defined as the degree of stress you can handle or how long you can put up with a demanding task without acting in an irrational or disorganized way. Many of the competent, successful people we admire are probably under a great deal more stress than we realize; they've simply acquired a high tolerance for it. Greater tolerance for pressure—deadlines, competition, criticism from others— usually comes with greater experience and skill at a given task. People in high-pressure jobs such as police, surgeons, and firefighters have learned how to stay calm in the face of stress through months and years of experience on the job. Our tolerance for frustration may be improved through such means as keeping in good physical shape, selecting reasonable goals to accomplish, and adjusting our expectations to match the realities of the immediate situation. Expecting too much of ourselves is a frequent source of frustration. Each of us experiences disappointment with ourselves from time to time. Rather than wallow in self-pity, it's more helpful to ask what we can do about it and resolve to learn from our experience. Another important aspect of stress tolerance is the ability to function well despite anxiety. There are many instances when it is normal to feel anxious in the face of uncertainty, such as preparing for an important exam or going for a job interview. Competence in these situations means carrying out our responsibilities despite feelings of anxiety. Remember, mild to moderate doses of anxiety may stimulate us to do our best, though too much anxiety may interfere with our performance. In this case, you may need to control your distressful, anxiety-arousing thoughts, as explained later in this section.

Second, change your pace of life. We bring a lot of stress on ourselves by rushing around and trying to accomplish too much in too little time. Frequently, we could lighten the stress by better time management. In other cases, we need to pace ourselves better. The particular adjustments needed vary with each of us. But consider the following suggestions:

- Get up early enough to avoid rushing.
- Set a radio-alarm clock to your favorite station.
- Take time for breakfast.
- Make a list of things to do; put the most important things first.
- Allow enough time to drive to school or work without rushing.
- Avoid scheduling all your classes back-to-back.
- Walk at an unhurried pace. You'll get there just as soon.
- Share at least one meal each day with other people.
- Avoid the excessive use of caffeine, alcohol, or drugs.

Learning to stay calm under pressure comes with experience. (Laimute E. Druskis)

- Take some time to relax each day. Go for a walk, ride your bike, or take a hot bath.

- Avoid procrastination; the sooner you begin a task the less you'll worry about it.

- Concentrate on the task at hand.

- Take time to talk with your friends.

- Set aside regular times for study.

- Schedule some relaxation for the weekends to break the cycle of stress.

- Jot down things you don't get done that you'd like to do the next day.

- Unwind before going to bed. Read or listen to music.

Perhaps there are other changes especially needed in your lifestyle. What are they? Jot these down and add them to your list of suggestions for managing stress.

Third, learn to control distressful thoughts. Perhaps you've had the experience of glancing at the first question on a test and muttering to yourself, "I know I'm going to flunk this test." Ironically, such negative self-monitoring then interferes with your performance, making you do worse on the test.

You can control distressful thoughts by using the following strategy. First, become aware of your negative, catastrophic thinking. You'll probably notice how such thoughts usually assume the worst, such as "I'll never make it," "How did I get into this mess?," or "What can I do?" Second, formulate positive thoughts that are incompatible with your distressful thoughts. Some examples would be, "I can do it, just take it one step at a time, and I'll keep doing my best and see how things turn out." It also helps to relax and practice deep breathing—breathing with your diaphragm. Finally, give yourself a mental pat on the back when you've successfully managed distressful thoughts. Take a few minutes to acknowledge to yourself, "I did it, it worked. I'm pleased with the progress I'm making." Or reward yourself in other ways, such as going to a movie or buying something you've wanted (Meichenbaum, 1977).

Fourth, if needed, seek help for problem-solving skills. Most colleges and communities offer a variety of workshops on topics such as assertiveness training and stress management. The value of this type of training was demonstrated in an experiment involving supportive, problem-solving groups at the University of Kentucky. Initially, researchers identified college students who had reported high levels of stress along with greater-than-average health problems, episodes of new illnesses, and disability days. Thirty-two of the students volunteered to participate. They were randomly assigned to a fall or spring intervention group or a control group. The intervention consisted of ten 90-minute group meetings that focused on problem-solving skills and group support. The

---

Counteracting Stress

There are a variety of methods for lowering the bodily arousal associated with stress. These include biofeedback, meditation, muscle relaxation, and diaphragmatic breathing.

One of the simplest techniques is diaphragmatic breathing. Essentially this consists of breathing more deeply through the diaphragm, the dome-shaped muscular sheet attached to the lower ribs, dividing the chest from the stomach. You may choose to sit in a comfortable chair or lie down. Either way, put one hand on your stomach to see that it rises and falls as you breathe through your diaphragm. Breathe in deeply, through your nose, filling your lungs as full as you can. Hold your breath for a moment. Then exhale slowly, keeping as relaxed as you can. Breathe this way for a half a dozen times or so. Then breathe in the usual way for a few seconds while you think about being relaxed. Now repeat the sequence of diaphragmatic breathing and normal breathing, concentrating on the pleasant feelings of relaxation.

The next time you find yourself getting tense, practice diaphragmatic breathing for a few minutes. See how it helps you to relax.

---

groups were led by professionals and experienced student workers in the mental health field. In the early sessions, common stresses in college life were discussed, along with some of the coping strategies students had found helpful. In later sessions, leaders and students engaged in role playing to demonstrate interpersonal problems and the appropriate coping skills needed. In the final half of the sessions, students were encouraged to bring up additional concerns encountered in college life. Throughout the series, the discussion centered on problem-solving skills, sharing of ideas about managing stress, and group support.

Students who participated in the training groups not only expressed appreciation for the problem-solving skills and group support, they also improved their health-status assessments. In contrast to members of the control group, these students reported fewer health problems, fewer episodes of new illnesses, and fewer disability days when they missed classes (Marx, et al., 1984).

Using Stress for Personal Growth

How you choose to alter your lifestyle or modify your environment is up to you. Stress management, like stress itself, is a personal matter. Each of us faces a different combination of stressful events at work and at home. Each of us has our own strengths and weaknesses, and stress affects each of us differently. The important thing to remember is that you *can* do something to manage stress more effectively. You don't have to be a passive victim to whom things happen. Instead, look at yourself as an active agent who can take charge of your life. No matter how stressful the situation, there's always something you can do to reduce the stress.

Keep in mind that stress can be a valuable means of self-understanding. We don't fully know what we can do until we have to do it. Each time we successfully get through a stressful situation, like a difficult course at school or a trying problem in our love lives, we gain in self-confidence. Even experiences of disappointment and failure are sometimes blessings in disguise. Perhaps we weren't ready for the task at hand, or we were pursuing the wrong goals. Sometimes a minor failure now may save us from a bigger letdown later on.

Finally, make stress work for you. Remember that stress is not synonymous with distress. Too little stress and we become bored and lazy. Too much and we become tense, make mistakes, and get sick more easily. To get the most out of life, each of us needs to find our optimal level of stress and the types of stress we handle best. Properly managed, stress gives zest to life. A stressful situation may challenge us to try harder, evoking our best and bringing personal growth. Managing stress well is a lot like making music with a stringed instrument. Too little pressure and the strings moan and groan. Too much and they snap. But apply just the right pressure and you'll get beautiful music.

Summary

Sources of Stress

1. Stress is taking a heavy toll on the nation's well-being and contributes, either directly or indirectly, to six of the leading causes of death.

2. We've defined stress as the pattern of specific and nonspecific responses an organism makes to stimulus events that disturb its equilibrium and tax its ability to cope. As such, stress may have beneficial as well as harmful effects, depending on the person and situation.

3. Stress usually comes from the combination of various life changes, positive and negative, and includes major life events as well as daily hassles.

4. Our overall experiences of stress is affected by a variety of personal and situational factors, such as how we perceive events and the degree of control we have over them.

Stress Reactions

5. Some reactions to stress occur more or less spontaneously, including certain bodily reactions and defense mechanisms.

6. Many of our bodily reactions to stress can be understood in relation to Selye's general adaptation syndrome, either in the initial alarm reaction or the successive stages of resistance or exhaustion.

7. Defense mechanisms like repression are automatic, unconscious reactions that serve to protect us from sudden or excessive stress.

8. There are also a number of other coping devices for minor stress, such as eating, drinking alcohol, laughing, crying, and talking out or working off tension. All of the above reactions may help us to cope with stress momentarily, but they easily become self-defeating if used to excess.

Stress Management

9. Ultimately, the successful management of stress must deal with the sources of stress, either through modifying our environment or altering our lifestyle.

10. We may modify the situational sources of stress through assertiveness, withdrawal, or compromise, depending on which is most appropriate to the situation.

11. Alleviating stress through changing our lifestyle includes building greater tolerance for stress, altering our pace of life, controlling distressful thoughts, and the use of problem-solving skills.

12. When properly managed, stress may become a means of more effective adjustment as well as personal growth.

Self-test

1. According to Hans Selye, stress that has a harmful effect on us should be called:

    a. distress   **c.** hypostress

    b. hyperstress   **d.** eustress

2. Common everyday hassles include:

    a. misplacing or losing things   **c.** having too many things to do

    b. worries over physical appearance   **d.** all of the above

3. Which of the following tends to be one of the most stressful events for anyone?

    a. sexual difficulties   **c.** the breakup of one's marital

    b. the death of one's spouse   engagement

                                         d. being fired from work

4. What kind of people tend to be highly competitive, impatient, and judge themselves and others by rigorous standards?

    a. low-esteem people   **c.** stress-resistant people

    b. Type A personalities   **d.** Type B personalities

5. In which stage of the general adaptation syndrome are individuals more likely to develop the symptoms of stress-related illnesses such as hypertension?

    a. alarm reaction   **c.** resistance

    b. exhaustion   **d.** anger

6. Which items below are automatic, unconscious ways of coping with the stress of anxiety?

    a. defense mechanisms   **c.** problem-solving approaches to stress

    b. coping devices for minor stress   **d.** all of the above

7. The unconscious blocking from consciousness of a threatening idea or impulse is known as:

    a. suppression   **c.** repression

    b. denial   **d.** rationalization

8. Discharging the emotional tension of one's stress through cursing would be an example of:

    a. defense mechanisms

    b. altering one's lifestyle

    c. a problem-solving approach to stress

    d. a coping device for minor stress

9. In coping with a stressful situation, compromise is:

    a. never an adaptive response to stress

    b. the preferred way to handle stress

    c. neither good nor bad in itself

    d. all of the above

10. Walking at an unhurried pace is a way of managing stress through:

    a. the coping devices for minor stress

    b. altering one's lifestyle

    c. the assertive approach to stress

    d. a problem-solving approach to stress

Exercises

1. *Take an inventory of your stress.* Use the Social Readjustment Rating Scale presented earlier in the chapter to assess the significant changes in your life. Include all the significant events that have occurred in your life during the past twelve months. If you've experienced stressful events not listed in the rating scale, try to assign a numerical value by comparing them to a similar event in the rating scale. Then add up your points to arrive at a total LCU score as explained in the text. When you think back over the past year, does your level of physical health and personal functioning reflect the level of stress indicated by your score?

2. *Daily hassles.* Jot down some of the little things in everyday life that annoy you. How does your list compare with the survey of daily hassles described in the text? Which hassles bother you the most? Select two or three of them and suggest specific ways you could make them less bothersome to you.

3. *Defense mechanisms.* Think of a particular situation in which you reacted defensively. Which defense mechanisms did you rely on? How well did you cope with this situation? If you face a similar situation in the future, how differently would you like to handle it?

4. *Coping devices for minor stress.* Look over the coping devices for minor stress described in the chapter, such as the comforts of touch, food, and drink. Which of these reactions are you most inclined to use? Do you tend to overeat or use alcohol or drugs to excess? Do you curse frequently or cry easily? Have any of these reactions become a problem for you? If so, think of some positive ways you can make such reactions less of a problem for you.

5. *Managing stress assertively.* Recall a stressful situation that you handled in an assertive manner. Describe the situation, how you handled it, and how it turned out. An alternate exercise would be to tell of a similar situation that you wished you had handled in a more assertive manner. How did you react in this situation? What happened as a result? If you're faced with a similar situation in the future, how could you handle it more assertively?

6. *Altering your lifestyle.* Review the suggestions for reducing stress through changing your pace of life. If there are other changes especially needed in your daily habits, what are they? Select two or three of your suggested changes and apply them to your daily life for a week. If you find this helpful, why not continue altering your lifestyle to reduce the stress in your everyday life?

Questions for Self-reflection

1. Can you recall several instances when stress had a beneficial effect?
2. Which situations do you find most distressful?
3. What are some of the "little things" that get you down?
4. Would you agree that having some control over your work activities makes them less stressful?
5. How can you tell when you're under a lot of stress?
6. When you become defensive, how do you behave?
7. Are you inclined to abuse alcohol or drugs when under stress?
8. What are some ways you've modified your environment to decrease stress?
9. Have you tried altering your lifestyle as a way of alleviating stress?
10. All things considered, how well do you manage stress?

Recommended Readings

Dudley, D. L., and E. Welke. *How To Survive Being Alive.* New York: New American Library, 1979 (paperback). Shows how we can use the life-change approach to stress to cope with stress more effectively.

Mascia, M. F., and S. R. Aronson. *The Stress Management Workbook.* Englewood Cliffs, NJ: Prentice-Hall, 1981 (paperback). Contains numerous tests to help you identify and manage stress in your life.

Meichenbaum, Donald. "Stress-inoculation training," In *Cognitive Behavior Modification.* New York: Plenum Press, 1977. A cognitive-behavioral approach to stress management aimed at initiating self-statements and responses that are incompatible with self-defeating behaviors.

Selye, Hans, M.D. *Stress Without Distress.* Philadelphia: J.B. Lippincott, 1974. An authoritative view of the effects of stress by one of the pioneers in stress research.

Tobesing, Donald A. *Kicking Your Stress Habits.* New York: New American Library, 1981 (paperback). Contains practical exercises for improving your management of stress.

Welch, I. D., D. C. Medeiros, and G. A. Tate. *Beyond Burnout.* Englewood Cliffs, NJ: Prentice-Hall, 1981. A discussion of the causes and symptoms of burnout, together with practical suggestions for curing it.

6 The Body and Health

The ancient Greek physician Hippocrates once wrote that the healer must strive "to know what man is in relation to food, drink, occupation, and which effect each of these has on the other," suggesting that our health is potentially affected by everything we think and do. Such a view is implicit in the terms *heal*—to make sound or whole—and *health*—the overall state of wholeness, which includes our mental as well as physical well-being. Like that annoying string of Christmas tree lights that won't work when only one bulb is bad, we are a string of interrelated reactions. A relatively minor body sensation, like a headache, can temporarily undermine our sense of well-being. By contrast, when all the elements are working together, after a vigorous workout or lovemaking, we feel completely happy and together—a Total Person. The notion of wholeness also implies that our overall well-being is affected by practically everything discussed in this book, including stress, emotions, close relationships, work, and bereavement. Here in this chapter we'll focus on the relationship between the body and health, including how we feel about our bodies, the care and abuse of our bodies, the relationship between psychological factors and physical disorders, and how we may promote wellness in our lives.

BODY IMAGE

Body image, in the more inclusive sense of the term, includes not only the concept we have of our bodies but also how satisfied we are with our bodies. The satisfaction with our bodies, in turn, is greatly affected by the particular body ideals prevalent in our culture. Of course every society throughout history has had somewhat different standards of beauty. But at no time in the past has there been such an intense barrage of media attention telling us how we should look. Magazine covers, TV ads and films shower us with images that reflect the standard of beauty for each sex. The ideal man is tall, large, muscular, and energetic. The ideal woman is slim, shapely, smooth-skinned, young and glamorous. The ideal varies somewhat in each era, so that big breasts may be "in" this year, modest breasts the next. Yet the media defines beauty so narrowly that few of us ever feel we have it made. The closer to the ideal body we are, the less pressure we feel to change. But those who are obviously different, the fat, old, and physically disabled, may feel more pressure to change or hide the disliked parts of their bodies. Individuals who don't fit the images may have negative feelings toward themselves, making it difficult to accept themselves as they are.

Body Concept

You'd think we would have a fairly accurate picture of our own bodies. After all, who is more familiar with our own bodies than ourselves? Each day, we spend an unaccountable amount of time receiving messages from our bodies, and touching and grooming ourselves. Naturally, we acquire a great deal of information about our bodies. But we have blind spots as well, so that our body concept only approximates rather than coincides with our bodies.

We have trouble forming a realistic body concept for several reasons. For one thing, our bodies are constantly changing, and there is a time lag in bringing our body images up to date. Perhaps this is why we are always fascinated seeing ourselves in the mirror—though often dismayed when we look closely. The more difficulty we have in accepting the changes in our bodies, the more we resist modifying our body images accordingly. For example, a woman who has had a mastectomy may find that it takes a while to fully accept her altered body contour. In a milder way, each of us may be "holding on" to more-or-less dated body images, like the aging man who still has difficulty recognizing the wrinkles in his face or his sagging waistline. Then too, it is difficult to see one's entire body accurately, even with a mirror. Most of us have only a partial picture of our backs, and rear ends, and even our genitals. And how many times does the average person inspect these parts of the body in the mirror? Our awareness of the insides of our bodies is even less well formed. Most of us have only the vaguest notions of which organs are located within, much less their spatial relations to each other. True, we have many sensations of temperature and pain, but this still doesn't give us the clear image a visual inspection would.

A major barrier in forming an accurate body concept is depersonalization or unembodiment—the sense of not being intimately attached to your body. Extreme examples have been reported by people using hallucinogenic drugs like LSD. Individuals may suddenly feel that parts of their bodies, usually the hands, do not belong to them. Severely disturbed schizophrenic patients sometimes feel so alienated from their bodies that they burn or mutilate themselves as they would a physical object. In less extreme ways, each of us tends to depersonalize our bodies, perhaps in part as a legacy of growing up in Western society, which emphasizes intellectual and technological achievements. Thus, a conscientious student may spend hours sitting at a desk absorbing information from a book while barely moving her body. Similarly, becoming a high achiever in many fields, including medicine, involves long hours of work, and people can become oblivious to their bodies, warding off signs of fatigue with stimulants. Ironically, when the average worker comes home he may be so tired he will spend hours passively watching television, rarely moving his body, except perhaps to shake his foot to keep it from going to sleep or feed his stomach out of boredom. Because of our urban, technological way of life, by the time we've reached college age, about three-fourths of us have some type of physical defect that has resulted from unembodiment and disuse or misuse of our bodies. Conversely, when elderly people are taught how to breathe, sit, stand, and walk properly, many of the "symptoms of aging" disappear (Masters and Houston, 1978).

People who spend long hours at their desks may become oblivious to their bodies. (Irene Springer)

How We Feel about our Bodies

Since our society puts so much emphasis on physical appearance, we might expect that many people would be dissatisfied with their bodies. Apparently, this is the case, as seen in the *Psychology Today* survey on the subject. From the nearly 30,000 people who responded to the body image survey, Thomas Cash, Barbara Winstead, and Louis Janda (1986) did a detailed analysis of a 2,000-person sample that represented the adult population of the United States. However, their sample was somewhat better educated than the population at large, with over half of the respondents having attended college or obtained an undergraduate or graduate degree. Also, because 91 percent of the respondents were white, minorities, especially blacks, were underrepresented.

To determine if there had been any changes in the way people felt about their bodies in the last decade or so, the investigators included a number of items covered in an earlier survey on the subject. According to the results of the recent survey, 47 percent of the men and 43 percent of the women definitely or mostly agreed with the statement "I like my looks just the way they are." But at the other extreme, 34 percent of the men and 38 percent of the women definitely or mostly disagreed with this statement. Furthermore, the percentage of respondents dissatisfied with their bodies had increased significantly since the last survey. (See Table 6-1.) As a result, Thomas Cash and his colleagues conclude that we may be healthier and feel fitter than ever, but we're less satisfied with how we look. As in the earlier survey, women are still less satisfied than men with their appearance, except in regard to their face and height. The most likely reason for such a difference is the greater emphasis on physical appearance for women than for men.

The presence of a physical disfigurement or disability often had a negative impact on how people felt about their appearance, fitness, and health. Among the respondents, 21 percent of the men and 17 percent of the women reported some type of disfigurement or physical disability, ranging from minor nuisances such as a facial mole or slight limp to more serious conditions such as quadriplegia. Compared with people without such conditions, about 12 percent more of the men and 20 percent more of the women with a disfigurement or disability had a generally negative body image.

Weight is a major factor in body image, with 41 percent of the men and 55 percent of the women being dissatisfied with their weight. Men were most dissatisfied with the mid-torso region; women were most dissatisfied with the mid and lower torso, including hips and thighs, the areas most affected by gaining weight. Overweight people, especially women, felt more negatively about their looks, fitness, and health than people with normal weight. Overweight people also were less likely to do anything to improve these aspects of themselves. At the same time, being underweight affected men and women differently. For women, it's a plus, whereas for men it's a minus. Compared to men, women who

Table 6–1. PEOPLE DISSATISFIED WITH BODY AREAS OR DIMENSIONS.

1972 SURVEY	Men	Women	1985 SURVEY	Men	Women
Height	13%	13%	Height	20%	17%
Weight	35	48	Weight	41	55
Muscle tone	25	30	Muscle tone	32	45
Overall face	8	11	Face	20	20
Breast/chest	18	26	Upper torso	28	32
Abdomen	36	50	Mid torso	50	57
Hips and upper thighs	12	49	Lower torso	21	50
Overall appearance	15	25	"Looks as they are"	34	38

Source: Thomas F. Cash, Barbara A. Winstead, and Louis H. Janda. "The Great American Shape-up," *Psychology Today*, April 1986, p. 33. Reprinted with permission from *Psychology Today* Magazine. Copyright © 1986 American Psychological Association.

are underweight are more apt to consider themselves normal while those who have normal weight tend to consider themselves fat. Such findings suggest that women have internalized a more stringent standard of slimness in regard to attractiveness, thereby making themselves more susceptible to dissatisfaction with their looks.

Many of the respondents in the body image survey were trying to do something about their weight problem, whether real or imagined, with 20 percent of the men and 38 percent of the women being on some type of diet or weight loss program. In addition, about one out of four men and one out of three women said they sometimes go on uncontrollable eating binges. A relatively small number of both sexes admitted they sometimes purged by self-induced vomiting. Such actions are characteristic of the eating disorder bulimia, which is especially common among women in their teens and 20s. Yet, the more often men and women dieted, binged, or purged, the more likely they were to dislike their appearance. Interestingly, the great majority of men and women in all weight categories, including overweight people, gave a positive response to such items as "My body is sexually appealing" and "being sexually competent is important to me."

A comparison of the responses from different age groups showed that individuals of both sexes in their teens and 20s were the most concerned about their appearance. After this, there was a steady decline of interest in appearance, with one exception; women over 60 were quite interested in their looks. Although people become less concerned with their appearance with age, they do not report a poorer body image. It may be that as people get older they shift to more appropriate standards of body image for their age. Or possibly the standards of older generations are kinder than those held by the present generation. Either way, a diminished concern with looks helps us adjust to the aging process.

Body Image and Psychological Well-being

In order to see whether people who feel good about their bodies also feel happier about themselves, the investigators who conducted the *Psychology Today* body image survey included several items which tapped people's feelings of self-esteem, life satisfaction, loneliness, depression, and feelings of social acceptance. As expected, they found a positive relationship between body image and psychological well-being. People who like their appearance, fitness, health, and sexual attractiveness also tend to feel happier and more well-adjusted. But it works the other way too. Those who report high self-esteem, life satisfaction, and few feelings of depression also feel good about their bodies.

Men and women who felt positive about their appearance, fitness, health, and sexual attractiveness expressed similar levels of adjustment. But there was a marked difference in psychological adjustment among those who disliked their bodies, with 73 percent of the women but only 63 percent of the men feeling well-adjusted. Perhaps it is more socially acceptable for women than men to think about their appearance and share such concerns with friends. Also, it may be that men's self-esteem is more closely tied than women's to feelings about their bodies. In any case, women receive more emotional and social support from their families and same-sex friends than men do, and this type of support is less dependent on physical appearance than romantic relationships, the main source of men's emotional and social support.

Interestingly, psychological well-being appears to be more closely tied to people's emphasis on fitness and health than their appearance. In the body image survey, people's sense of well-being was unrelated to the importance of appearance for them. But people who cared about their fitness and health were generally happier with their lives than those who were less concerned with such matters. See the responses given by those in the appearance, fitness, and health orientation categories respectively in Table 6-2. The investigators were especially impressed by the finding that people who cared about fitness and health had more positive feelings about their appearance than those who were more concerned with their appearance. Valuing looks and trying to improve them may help us to feel better about ourselves up to a point. But a concern for fitness and health is more closely tied to a satisfying body image. Apparently, people who broaden their perspective about their bodies to include fitness and health are more likely to have a happy body image than those who are preoccupied with their appearance.

CARE AND ABUSE OF THE BODY

Perhaps you've heard the adage, "When you have your health, you have everything." Apparently, more people are convinced of this than ever before, as seen in the physical fitness and health boom in recent years. Americans believe that good health is very important, second only to the importance of a good family

Table 6–2. BODY IMAGE AND PSYCHOLOGICAL WELL-BEING.

	Men	Women
Appearance Evaluation		
Positive	95%	97%
Negative	62	73
Fitness Evaluation		
Positive	92	94
Negative	63	79
Health Evaluation		
Positive	92	94
Negative	45	64
Sexuality Evaluation		
Positive	90	93
Negative	62	76
Appearance Orientation		
High	86	90
Low	91	89
Fitness Orientation		
High	91	94
Low	79	85
Health Orientation		
High	89	94
Low	81	75

Source: Thomas F. Cash, Barbara A. Winstead, and Louis H. Janda, "The Great American Shape-up," *Psychology Today*, April 1986, p. 36. Reprinted with permission from *Psychology Today* Magazine. Copyright © 1986 American Psychological Association.

life. And judging by their own estimates, at least three-fourths of Americans describe their own health as "excellent" or "good." The majority of them believe that diet, exercise, and positive thinking are the keys to good health (Rubenstein, 1982). Yet not all of them follow their own self-prescriptions, as we'll see in this section.

Eating and Exercise Habits

Despite the variety of food available in the United States, some nutritionists think we eat more poorly now than 50 years ago. It is estimated that up to half of middle-class Americans suffer from deficiencies of one or more nutrients. A major reason is the increased consumption of processed foods in which many of the nutrients are lost, such as bread made from white flour rather than whole-wheat. Americans also eat too much fat, salt, and sugar, especially refined sugars (Goodhart and Shils, 1980). Although sugar consumption remains high, partly because of its use in so many foods like cereals and colas, there are some encouraging trends. Americans are eating less red meat and dairy products, and drinking less coffee and tea. And they are eating more fish and poultry as well as more high-fiber foods such as fresh fruits, vegetables, and cereals (Hacker, 1983).

A national survey on health and fitness gives us a glimpse into individuals' eating and exercise habits. The survey was mostly of college-educated people, two-thirds of them under 40 years of age (Rubenstein, 1982). More than half the respondents said they ate breakfast on a regular basis. The same number took vitamins to supplement their meals. About four out of ten of them avoided salt, and three out of ten limited their intake of sugar. One out of ten adhered to a high-fiber diet. Yet nearly half of these people said they ate to excess at least once a month, and 43 percent admitted to being overweight. About 14 percent regarded themselves as compulsive eaters, and 8 percent said they were "junk-food junkies." People who fell into both of the last two categories were the most dissatisfied with themselves and their health.

Over half the respondents exercised regularly, for an average of 6 hours a week. One in four individuals exercised for an hour or more every day. The most popular forms of exercise for men were walking, jogging, and weight-lifting. About one in four rode a bike, swam, or played tennis, squash, handball, or raquetball. The most popular forms of exercise for women were walking, yoga, aerobic dance, jogging, swimming, and biking. The four in ten respondents who didn't exercise regularly claimed it didn't interest them or required

More people are keeping physically fit. (Laimute E. Druskis)

too much discipline. Yet those who exercised less than an hour a week were also more likely to overeat, expected to die sooner, and felt less happy with themselves than those who exercised regularly.

The interest in health and fitness has increased during the 1980s. Even though women are less likely than men to exercise regularly, they are becoming more active in physical activities and sports at a more rapid rate than men, including activities previously considered "for men only." At the same time, only 15 to 20 percent of all adults exercise regularly enough to achieve optimal fitness. And misconceptions about exercise still abound. For instance, over half the adults who don't exercise regularly feel such sports as baseball and bowling provide enough exercise to keep one fit and in good health. But this isn't true. (Corbin and Lindsey, 1985).

Getting Help

From time to time, each of us has minor health complaints, which we usually handle with home remedies like aspirin, antihistamines, and stomach medications. Not surprisingly, most respondents in the survey cited above had been bothered by a congested nose, coughing, sore throat, or flu infections during the past year. A significant number also had experienced symptoms such as upset stomach, lower back pain, and allergies. Many of them admitted that they felt angry and depressed at the same time, confirming the view that psychological stress lowers our bodily resistance, making us more susceptible to illness—and the more psychological symptoms reported, the more physical ones reported as well. Women reported more physical and psychological symptoms than men, and women were more sensitive to changes in their bodies, more troubled about eating habits and diet, and had experienced a greater number of stressful events, such as a new job or the serious illness of a loved one (Rubenstein, 1982).

About three-fourths of American adults see a doctor at least once a year, mostly in a doctor's office or community clinic. Women visit a doctor an average of five times a year, compared to an average of four times for men (NCHS, 1984). Similarly, one out of six women has been hospitalized in the past year, compared to only one out of ten men. But we must keep in mind that many women go to the hospital for the delivery of children (Hacker, 1983).

Surprisingly, as many as half of all adult patients do not follow or complete the doctor's prescribed treatment. Part of the reason has to do with today's diminished confidence in physicians, along with other authorities such as teachers, bankers, politicians, and military leaders. But Howard Leventhal (1982) suggests another reason: patients may want to avoid a confrontation between the doctor's diagnoses and their private theories about what's wrong with them. Throughout the experience with childhood infectious diseases, people create a set of unconscious expectations about the relationship between their symptoms and the nature of their illness that they carry into adulthood. They act as if every illness has a symptom that reflects the severity of the disease, which is not always true. As a result, studies have shown that while patients know *when* something is wrong with them, they are generally poor in recognizing *what* it is. For example, in one study, people were asked to keep track of eighteen symptoms, eleven moods, and to take their own blood pressure at least eight times a day; yet none correctly guessed which of their symptoms was an accurate sign of elevated blood pressure. The same pattern was found among patients with other illnesses, such as diabetes. Leventhal suggests that as medicine moves away from the authoritarian model, it isn't enough for the sophisticated practitioner to dismiss commonsense representations of illness as inaccurate. Physicians also need to recognize that patients have active minds which interpret information about their symptoms partly as a way of coping with them. To ensure that patients will follow a prescribed treatment program, doctors need to take the time to discuss what is known about an illness—both the course of the illness as well as its symptoms—and the aim of the treatment. And most of us would do well to realize that many illnesses are more complex than implied in our commonsense notions.

Health Hazards

There are many potential hazards to our health, ranging from excessive stress to environmental pollutants in the air and water. Workers in certain fields are at increased risk of respiratory diseases; these include miners, asbestos handlers, and metal smelters. Excessive exposure to x-rays during routine medical and dental check-ups can be dangerous. And in an age of nuclear energy, there's the risk of radiation from nuclear reactors, not to mention the horrors of nuclear war. Some of these hazards are more under our control than others. Three major health hazards that are directly associated with our lifestyle, and which *can* be controlled, are obesity, smoking, and alcohol and drug abuse.

Obesity, or an excessive amount of body fat, presents something of a paradox in our society. Nowhere is thinness more desirable than in American society; yet nowhere is obesity more prevalent. Although what constitutes obesity varies somewhat from one culture to another, Americans are usually considered obese if they exceed the desirable weight for their height, build, and age by more than 20 percent as measured by skinfold calipers (Kunz, 1982). In the United States, about 25 percent of all men and over 28 percent of women are overweight. The prevalence of obesity tends to increase with age among both sexes, and is also higher among the lower socioeconomic groups (NCHS, 1984).

Obesity is associated with an increased risk of illness and death from diabetes, high blood pressure, stroke, coronary heart disease, and kidney and gallbladder disorders. The more overweight people are, the greater their risk. For instance, if you're 40 percent overweight you are twice as likely to die from coronary heart disease. Also, diabetes sometimes develops as a consequence of obesity and may disappear when excess weight is lost. Very obese people suffer more surgical and anesthetic complications than leaner people. Finally, childbirth among obese people may be more risky for both mother and child (Kunz, 1982).

Obesity probably results from an interaction of physiological and psychological factors. We all know overweight people who eat moderately but remain fat, and thin people who eat heartily but remain slender. Although apparently some people are born to carry more fat, a lot of obesity results from overeating and insufficient exercise. There are also a variety of psychological and social factors associated with obesity. For instance, obese people tend to be more responsive to external cues, such as the visibility and availability of food, rather than the internal cues of hunger (Herman, Olmsted, and Polivy, 1983).

People who want to lose weight must somehow help their bodies to use up more calories than they consume. The two basic ways to do this are (1) change your diet so that you eat less, and (2) exercise more. The benefits of crash diets are generally short-lived. To make matters worse, strict dieting tends to lower the rate of metabolism so that one can count calories carefully and still not lose weight (Rodin, 1981). Generally it's better to follow a reasonable diet aimed at more modest weight loss—say one pound a week—over a longer period of time, combined with regular exercise. Perhaps you've heard that exercise may be self-defeating because you eat more. But this isn't necessarily true. Furthermore, exercise not only burns up calories but increases the metabolic rate, so that even when people are not exercising, their bodies are burning up calories faster. Many people find it easier to lose weight by joining a weight-loss club, which provides guidance and support for their efforts. Finally, self-mastery plays an important role. In one study, obese individuals followed one of three treatment programs: (1) modification of eating and exercise habits, (2) use of an appetite suppressant only, and (3) a combination of behavior modification and drug therapy. The results showed that people in the first group gained the least weight in the long run. Members of the first group kept daily records of their eating behavior, became more aware of which situations prompted them to eat, rewarded themselves for desired eating behavior, and developed suitable exercise programs. The most probable explanation is that these people acquired a greater sense of self-control, thereby strengthening their efforts to continue managing their weight after the treatment was over (Craighead, Stunkard, and O'Brien, 1981).

Tobacco abuse continues to be a major health hazard. In 1964 the Surgeon General's Report presented compelling evidence that cigarette smoking is a major factor in heart disease, lung cancer, emphysema, and other fatal illnesses. Since then further evidence has indicted smoking in a variety of other diseases, such as bronchitis and many forms of cancer, including cancers of the mouth, larynx, bladder, and pancreas. Smokers who also drink magnify their risks of cancer even more, because alcohol enhances the carcinogenic effect of tobacco

The smoking habit usually begins in the teenage years. (American Cancer Society)

at certain sites of the body, such as the esophagus, mouth, and larynx (*Cancer Facts and Figures*, 1985).

Greater awareness of the hazards of smoking has prompted many people to give up the habit. Today, only 35 percent of men smoke compared to 52 percent in 1965. And only 30 percent of women now smoke, down from 34 percent 20 years earlier. At the same time the proportion of smokers among both sexes is now rising only until the mid-40s, when it decreases, presumably because of increased health concerns. However, the number of women in the 20- to 24-year-old group who smoke has increased, largely because they were teenagers in the 1970s when smoking habits were still increasing (NCHS, 1984). This finding underscores the fact that most people begin smoking in their teen years as they follow parental models and peer pressure. Once they start smoking they are likely to continue because of nicotine addiction and psychological dependence.

There are a variety of techniques to help people stop smoking. In the rapid-smoking method, a variation of the aversive approach, smokers in the lab are asked to smoke continually, puffing every few seconds, until they can't tolerate it any longer. Another technique is stimulus control, in which smokers become aware of the stimuli and the situations that trigger their smoking; then they develop alternative behaviors. For example, if you smoke while drinking coffee during the coffee break at work, you might switch to a soft drink or use the time to take a walk or talk with friends who don't smoke. Unfortunately, about 80 to 85 percent of those who give up smoking resume within 6 months to a year (Lichtenstein, 1982). Once they've stopped smoking, people may be helped to stay off the habit with the support of friends, spouses, or a support group devoted to overcoming smoking. With sufficient motivation, many smokers may give up the habit without any formal program (Schachter, 1982).

Alcohol and drug abuse continue to be major health hazards for many people. Three-fourths of American men and almost two-thirds of women over 18 years of age drink alcoholic beverages. Approximately one-third of both sexes are light drinkers. But at least one out of ten adults are heavy drinkers, with the proportion being higher among men, especially among those in the 18- to 25-year-old group (NCHS, 1984).

Figure 6–1. ARE YOU DRINKING TOO MUCH ALCOHOL?

Yes	No	
____	____	1. Do you often drink alone, either at home or in a bar?
____	____	2. When holding an empty glass at a party, do you always actively look for a refill instead of waiting to be offered one?
____	____	3. Do you feel you *must* have a drink at a particular time every day—such as after work?
____	____	4. Is your drinking ever the direct result of a quarrel, or do quarrels seem to occur when you've had a drink or two?
____	____	5. Do you ever miss work or scheduled meetings because of your drinking?
____	____	6. When questioned, do you ever lie about how much you drink?
____	____	7. Do you feel physically deprived if you cannot have at least one drink every day?
____	____	8. When you're under a lot of stress, do you almost automatically take a drink to "settle your nerves"?
____	____	9. Do you sometimes crave a drink in the morning?
____	____	10. Do you sometimes have "mornings after" when you can't remember what happened the night before?

Every YES answer to the above questions should be taken as a warning sign. Two or more YES answers suggest you're on the way to becoming dependent on alcohol. Three or more YES answers indicate you may have a serious drinking problem that requires professional help.

Source: Jeffrey R. M. Kunz, M.D. (ed.), *The American Medical Association Family Medical Guide.* New York: Random House, 1982, p. 32. Reprinted by permission of Random House, Inc.

Alcohol use constitutes a major health hazard in many ways. Nearly two-thirds of the drivers in fatal traffic accidents have been drinking. Highway accidents involving alcohol are the leading cause of death among young people. At least half of the people who die from falls or drowning have been drinking. And approximately half of all the occupied beds in American hospitals are filled by people with alcohol-related ailments (U.S. Report to Congress, 1981). Furthermore, as mentioned earlier, the heavy use of alcohol together with smoking greatly increases the risk of cancers of the mouth, larynx, esophagus, and liver. Chronic heavy drinking is often accompanied by poor nutrition and results in serious damage to many parts of the body. At least one of every five chronic heavy drinkers develops cirrhosis of the liver (Kunz, 1982).

How much alcohol can we consume before it harms our health? It's hard to say because a great deal depends on the individual, especially his or her weight and susceptibility to alcohol. The rule of thumb for many physicians is about 1.5 ounces of absolute alcohol a day for a 150-pound person. This translates roughly into about 3 ounces of distilled spirits, 3 cans of beer, or 3 glasses of wine, preferably taken with a meal (Whelan, 1978).

The traditional view has been that alcoholism is a disease requiring total abstinence. Critics of the disease model have argued that even though abstinence works well for some people, it's very difficult to achieve and may not be required for everyone. But one study found that a return to controlled social drinking is a realistic goal only for those with few symptoms of alcohol abuse; individuals with six or more alcohol-related problems were more successful in avoiding future problems by becoming abstinent (Vaillant and Milofsky, 1982).

Although alcohol remains the drug of choice for a large segment of the population, the scope of drug use has increased greatly since the 1960s. So much public attention has been focused on the dangers of mood-altering drugs that we tend to overlook the abuse of prescription drugs. Overdose from barbiturates has become a common means of committing suicide. And people who attempt to stop taking barbiturates, or sleeping pills, often experience a rebound effect that disturbs their sleep; as many as half of all insomniacs have drug-induced insomnia as part of their problem (Dement and Zarcone, 1977). An excessive or prolonged use of tranquilizers, especially among the elderly, may damage the respiratory system, kidneys, and liver (Kunz, 1982). Furthermore, combining alcohol with drugs tends to multiply the effect of the drug, sometimes with fatal results.

The use of illegal drugs poses special problems. There is no control over the strength or purity of the drug, who takes them, or the dosage. Thus, individuals may damage their bodies or take a fatal overdose by mistake. Repeated use of most of the mood-altering drugs also increases the user's tolerance so that greater amounts may be needed over time increasing the health hazards of the drug. And since marijuana smoke contains even more carcinogenic hydrocarbons than tobacco smoke does, health authorities are concerned that heavy, prolonged use of marijuana may damage the lungs and perhaps lead to lung cancer.

PSYCHOLOGICAL FACTORS AND PHYSICAL DISORDERS

You're driving home from work on a cold, wintry day. You're feeling more tired than usual. As you wait absent-mindedly for a traffic light, you feel a headache coming on. The more you think about it, the more you're aware that you're not feeling well. Even the prospects of sitting down to dinner are less appealing than usual. You begin to wonder. Am I simply tired? Or am I getting the flu? Perhaps it was the stressful day at work. But you're not certain. As you head for home, you wonder how to treat yourself. Should you do something to unwind, such as having a drink? Or would it be better to go to bed and get some rest?

The Mind-body Unity

There's no easy way to diagnose our condition because of the mind-body unity. Despite the dualistic notion of mind and body that has prevailed in Western society for centuries, most of us have grown up in an era in which the mind and body are increasingly seen as one or, at the most, two aspects of the same thing. There's compelling evidence that organic factors contribute to some of the major psychological disorders such as schizophrenia and severe depression. And it has been demonstrated that physiological functions such as heart rate and blood pressure, once considered completely involuntary, can be controlled partly through biofeedback.

Today, physicians and mental health professionals alike are increasingly skeptical of the traditional separation of mind and body. Consequently, in the authoritative psychiatric reference, *The Diagnostic and Statistical Manual of Mental Disorders,* or the DSM-III, the list of psychophysiological disorders has been replaced by a single category of "Psychological factors affecting physical condition." It is now held that psychological factors can affect *any* condition, not just the so-called "psychosomatic" illnesses. Increasingly, the mind and body are regarded as a mind-body unity. Thus, whatever we experience as a mental event, such as grief or sadness, becomes a physical event whether we realize it or not. And physical events, such as flu, affect our mental and emotional lives as well. It is not so much whether the mind or body influence each other as that these two aspects of our existence cannot be separated.

A Disregulation Model

One of the most important ways of exploring the mind-body unity is the physiological changes associated with emotions. From our discussion of Selye's general adaptation syndrome in the chapter on stress, you may recall that there is a general arousal of the autonomic nervous system in response to any stressful event. But it's not clear why or how individuals react the way they do. Why does one person develop coronary heart disease while another does not? And how does disease develop in response to stress? In an effort to solve this problem, Gary Schwartz (1977, 1982) has proposed a model for understanding the disregulation of the body in response to stress-related physical disorders.

The central idea in Schwartz's model is the concept of negative feedback—the process in which information is returned to a system in order to regulate that system. That is, the turning on of one part of the system leads to the turning off of another part of the system. An everyday example of negative feedback is the way a thermostat regulates a furnace. When an opened window causes the room to cool, the thermostat signals the furnace to turn on. As the room temperature reaches the desired level, say 68 degrees, the thermostat turns the furnace off. The second part of this sequence, in which the crucial information is fed back to the thermostat from the thermometer, is called the negative feedback loop. Negative feedback loops are also critical in regulating the body. When these internal regulatory systems fail to operate properly, disease develops. Disregulation may occur at any of four different stages.

Stage 1. Environmental demands. In some instances, excessive environmental demands may force people to ignore negative feedback from their bodies. Thus, if environmental stress forces us to continually ignore the negative feedback from our bodies, important bodily functions—the heart and circulatory system, the stomach, or the liver—may become overworked and fail.

Stage 2. Information processing in the central nervous system (CNS). Although the environmental demands may not be excessive, the brain may respond inappropriately either because of faulty genes or learning. For instance, when people ignore the signals of a full stomach, they may continue eating until they develop obesity.

Stage 3. The peripheral organ. Even when the environmental demands are reasonable and the CNS is processing information properly, the particular organ of the body may be incapable of responding in an appropriate manner. For example, if some people either through defective inheritance or disease have a vulnerable organ, such as an irregular heartbeat or weak respiratory system, they will be more susceptible to illness in these parts of their bodies in response to stress.

Stage 4. Negative feedback. Even if the environmental demands, CNS information-processing, and the bodily organs are all functioning normally, a problem may develop in the negative feedback loop. Thus, when people do not receive the proper negative feedback from their bodies, either because of inherent limitations or faulty learning, they may continue exerting themselves excessively until disregulation or disease occurs.

Like most systems, this four-part regulatory system is only as strong as its weakest link. If a problem occurs at any one stage, the entire regulatory process is disrupted and disease occurs. The problem may lie either in excessive environmental demands (Stage 1) or in the particular individual's makeup or responses (Stages 2 through 4). Furthermore, when one function is disrupted, disregulation occurs in the entire system to some extent.

Hypertension: An Application

Probably the most common and most dangerous physical disorder associated with psychological stress is hypertension, or chronically high blood pressure. According to the National Center for Health Statistics (1984), 15 percent of all adults in the United States suffer from this disease. It tends to be highest among younger males in the 25- to 44-year-old group and older females in the 65- to 74-year-old group. It is also about twice as high on the average among blacks as whites. Although these figures are based on systolic and diastolic readings of 160/95 respectively, in practice the diagnosis of high blood pressure depends largely on your individual case, including your age. The link between hypertension and other cardiovascular disorders illustrates the principle stated earlier, namely, that disregulation in any part of the system leads to disregulation of the system as a whole. Accordingly, people with high blood pressure are six times more likely to develop heart failure and four times more likely to have a stroke than someone with normal blood pressure. In addition, people who suffer from this disease are more apt to have kidney damage and a significantly shorter life expectancy (Kunz, 1982).

The blood pressure—the pressure that the blood being pumped by the heart exerts on the blood vessels—is a function of several factors. One of the most important is the degree of constriction in the blood vessels. Ordinarily when a person's blood pressure rises too high, the baroreceptors in the blood vessels communicate this information to the brain, which then signals the blood vessels to relax or dilate. However, this regulatory mechanism fails to work among people with hypertension, and the blood vessels remain chronically constricted. In a small number of cases the hypertension is traced to an organic cause, often the kidneys, and labeled secondary hypertension. The remaining cases for which there is no organic cause are known as essential hypertension. The possible contributing factors can be classified according to the stage in which the regulation cycle is disturbed.

Stage 1: Environmental demands. In some instances, hypertension may result from environmental stress, especially situations requiring constant alertness or danger. Thus, people exposed to military combat and certain types of job pressures, such as air-traffic controllers, are more susceptible to high blood pressure (Harrell, 1980).

Stage 2: CNS information processing. Hypertension may also be due partly to the way individuals respond to their environmental stress, whether from genetic vulnerability or faulty learning. For instance, high blood pressure tends to run in families, though this might be explained as the product of learning as well as genetic inheritance. At the same time, studies have shown that anger tends to elevate blood pressure, which remains elevated if the anger is suppressed but returns to normal if the anger is expressed (Diamond, 1982).

Stage 3: Peripheral organ. Chronic hypertension may also lead to structural changes in the blood vessels so that they no longer dilate properly. In this case, the brain is sending the correct instructions, but the blood vessels are no longer capable of obeying them (Schwartz, 1977).

Stage 4: Negative feedback. In due time, chronically high blood pressure may also damage the baroreceptors—the mechanisms in the blood vessels that provide feedback to the brain. Under the pressure of chronically high blood pressure, the baroreceptors may eventually adapt to this stimulus or simply wear down. In either case they cease to send the appropriate signals to the brain.

Although any one of these factors alone might not produce chronic hypertension, a combination of two or more is likely to. That is, a person in a very stressful job who keeps anger to himself runs a higher risk of developing this disease.

Although hypertension may be controlled with medication, there are potential problems—the risk of side-effects, the cost, and difficulties in getting patients to take their medicine regularly. There are also a number of changes in lifestyle that may help, such as losing weight, reducing salt intake, and eliminating smoking. Other strategies consist of helping people to understand and express their anger more effectively, relaxation techniques, and biofeedback. The combined use of relaxation and biofeedback has been especially effective in controlling the long-term effects of high blood pressure (Taylor, 1980).

PROMOTING WELLNESS

Until recently, people in the health care field made little distinction between people who are "not sick" and those who are "healthy." For all practical purposes, wellness was the absence of sickness. For example, think of a person in his 30s who isn't overweight but who eats junk food regularly. Each evening he drinks several beers, though he rarely gets intoxicated. He goes to work regularly but tires easily. He never exercises. He smokes a pack of cigarettes a day but has no symptoms such as high blood pressure or shortness of breath. This man isn't sick. But on the other hand, how well is he? Chances are he could be in much better shape.

It's this distinction between surviving and thriving that has prompted health practitioners to think more in terms of positive health, designated by the terms "well" and "wellness." To be well in this sense means actively pursuing good eating and exercise habits as well as avoiding health hazards like smoking and alcohol abuse. Even the elderly and the handicapped can be considered well in the sense of practicing good health habits and making the best of their present endowments. Realistically, wellness is more of an ideal than something to be fully achieved. But by viewing our everyday well-being in terms of the positive ideal of health, instead of merely the absence of illness, we may function better than we would have otherwise.

Taking Charge of Your Health

A major part of promoting wellness is the individual's taking a greater responsibility for all matters pertaining to one's health. This includes becoming better informed about the working of one's body, the interplay of mind and body, a concern for good nutrition and exercise, monitoring one's health (including medical checkups), keeping one's own medical records, and stress management. As you might expect, some people are more willing than others to assume such responsibility for health. For instance, when patients in a variety of medical settings were surveyed on this topic, the results showed that the greater control people believed they exercised over their health, the more control they preferred over their health care. And the more highly educated people were, the more they wished to exercise such control over their health care (Wallston, et al., 1983).

At the same time, we must guard against emphasizing responsibility for our health to such an extent that people are made to feel guilty when they become sick or fail to get well. For instance, a study of 359 patients with serious cancers showed that patients who had happy, optimistic outlooks were no more likely to survive than those who were unhappy and pessimistic. Such factors as attitude, emotional state, hopefulness, or satisfaction with one's life had no significant effect on the patient's survival rate. Such findings do not deny the importance of psychological factors in health and illness. But they do raise a caution flag against the popular but mistaken notion that one's willpower can override inherent biological factors, especially in an advanced state of serious illness. When we exaggerate the psychological factors in cures, we may be implying that sickness and death can be seen as personal failure. At a time when patients are already struggling against illness, they should not be further burdened by having to take responsibility for the outcome (Cassileth et al., 1985).

Such findings make us wonder whether the desire to control one's health actually results in better health. There's some evidence that it may, up to a point. In the survey on wellness cited earlier (Rubenstein, 1982), the respondents were classified into three types on the basis of how much control they felt they exercise over their health.

Health vigilants included more than a third of all the respondents. They feel that their diet and exercise habits are the keys to good health. When they get sick, they are the most likely to feel it was because they didn't take care of themselves. Typical is the 35-year-old woman who eats a vegetarian diet, takes long daily walks, and gets more than 8 hours of sleep every night. She expects to live into her 90s.

True believers represent about two-fifths of the respondents. They believe that disease can be overcome through positive thinking, prayer or faith, and friendship. They are the most religious, and are inclined to believe that health depends on one's communion with some higher power. They are also the least introspective and the most likely to have a confidant or good friend for support. When these people get sick, they usually think it was because of stress. A 52-year-old man said, "I think you have to stay calm and avoid stress. You don't catch the flu, you *succumb* to it."

Fatalists represent only about one-tenth of respondents. They believe their well-being is in the hands of fate or luck. When they become sick, they are the most likely to think it was due to bacteria or a virus. They are also the most resigned to suffering and sadness in the face of illness. Typical is the 50-year-old woman who feels good health comes from choosing your parents wisely. "I think it's all in the genes," she says. "My father smoked and drank all his life, and lived well into his eighties."

Since the health vigilants feel the most responsible for their well-being, they are also the most vulnerable to feelings of guilt when sick. Yet, it doesn't necessarily follow that such people take responsibility for their health to the extreme, denying the role of viruses and circumstances. Apparently, in many ways, the health vigilants fare better than the other two groups. The health vigilants are the least likely to have a chronic illness; only 15 percent of them reported two or more such illnesses. They also report the fewest physical and psychological symptoms and take the fewest sick days, about five a year. By contrast, the true believers have the most chronic illnesses, with 23 percent of them reporting such illnesses. They also take the most sick days, seven each year. The health of the fatalists falls somewhere in between the other two groups, with about 18 percent of them reporting two or more chronic illnesses a year. Yet the fatalists are the most neurotic and unhappy of all. They tend to be anxious, moody, easily hurt, self-critical, sexually unsatisfied, and least likely to have a friend.

As you read this, you may wonder which of these types you most resemble. To what extent do you believe you control your health? Do you feel that your eating and exercise habits and management of stress make you more resistant to the chronic illnesses? Do you also feel there's a certain amount of luck to having good health?

Psychological Well-being and Health

Given the mind-body unity, it should be apparent that control of one's health involves more than good nutrition, exercise habits, and medical check-ups. It also includes psychological factors, such as positive attitudes, stress management, and a sense of meaning and satisfaction in life. Thus we need a health-promoting personality as well as good health habits. Conversely, it isn't enough to rid ourselves of such habits as overeating, smoking, or the abuse of alcohol or drugs. We must also guard against adopting negative attitudes, overreacting to stress, and becoming demoralized. Otherwise, we make ourselves more susceptible to infectious and chronic diseases. The key word here is susceptible. Stress and negative emotions do not *cause* illness directly as much as they lower our overall resistance, making us more vulnerable to infection. In much the same way, relaxation and positive attitudes do not automatically prevent or cure illness as much as they strengthen our morale and thus our overall resistance to illness. In short, the mind-body unity is more complex than commonsense notions suggest (Maier and Laudenslager, 1985).

Realizing this, we shouldn't be surprised that feeling healthy doesn't necessarily mean you're healthy. Nor does feeling tired or ill mean you're in poor health. In other words, there are two types of health, as was brought out in the survey on wellness. *Subjective* health, or one's feeling of good health, can be measured in terms of self-ratings, as well as by the number of symptoms and psychological stressors reported. *Objective* health can be measured in terms of number of diseases reported as well as sick days, doctors' visits, and time spent in the hospital. Although these two types of health are closely related, they do not completely overlap. Among the top 24 percent of respondents who felt the healthiest, only one in four was actually in good health. It may be more realistic to speak of health optimists who feel healthy despite serious physical ailments or chronic conditions, and of health pessimists—the "worried well"—who are always complaining despite apparent good health (Rubenstein, 1982).

People who habitually complain of unfounded ailments or exhibit an undue fear of illness are often called "hypochondriacs." Paul Costa and Robert McCrae (1985) have shown that the hypochondriac tendency is closely linked with a cluster of personality traits labeled "neuroticism." People high in neuroticism tend to be anxious, self-conscious, hostile, depressed, and impulsive, usually with low self-esteem. Because of their personal makeup these people chronically attend to their internal state, exaggerating their physical symptoms and often imagining illnesses. Yet the researchers found that such individuals do not in fact develop the diseases suggested by their complaints. On the other hand, the tendency to underreport physical symptoms is linked with another cluster of personality traits labeled "extroversion." People high in extroversion tend to be warm and outgoing, and are sufficiently involved in life that they don't have time to complain of their ailments. Costa and McCrae point out that our personality and sense of well-being is a function of both clusters of traits, so that it is the relative strength of each tendency that determines how someone perceives and interprets his or her inner state. Individuals high in neuroticism report two or three times as many symptoms as the better adjusted individuals. Conversely, people high in extroversion and low in neuroticism tend to report relatively few ailments. They may not necessarily *be* any healthier than their neurotic counterparts, but they have a health-*promoting* personality.

Eating Sensibly

An integral part of a health-producing personality is practicing good health habits such as sensible patterns of eating and drinking, keeping physically fit, getting adequate rest, along with regular visits to a physician. Since more people "kill themselves" with a knife and fork than by any other means, one of the best ways to promote good health is to eat sensibly.

Eating sensibly has to do with both the amount and kind of food we eat. The amount of food is often measured in calories—a measurement of energy produced by food when oxidized or "burned" in the body. The number of calories needed each day depends on such functions as our age, sex, size, and rate of metabolism. A woman in her early 20s with a desk job needs about 2000 calories a day; a woman with a more active life needs about 2300 calories. A man with a desk job uses about 2500 calories; one with a fairly active job, such as a carpenter, needs about 2800 calories. Men and women who are in strenuous jobs or in athletic training or sports may need anywhere from 3000 to 4000 calories a day (Kunz, 1982).

A well-balanced diet includes adequate amounts of six groups of substances: proteins, carbohydrates, fats—which contain calories and produce energy—and vitamins, minerals, and fibers, which are also essential to the body but do not provide energy. A balanced diet includes about 55 percent of carbohydrates, 30 percent fat, and 15 percent protein.

Proteins are needed for the repair, replacement, and growth of body tissue. Animal proteins are found in meat, fish, eggs, and cheese. But a wide variety of vegetable protein is also found in beans, peas, nuts, and is present in whole grains.

Carbohydrates, a good source of energy, include sugar, potatoes, pasta, and whole-grain breads and cereals. Most overweight people consume too many carbohydrates in the form of sugar and high-sugar foods. In a balanced diet, lower sugar intake requires the body to use stored fats for energy without depriving the body of essential nutrition.

Fats also provide energy, and in small quantities are used for growth and repair of body tissue. Eccess fat is stored in the body as fatty tissue. Although fatty tissue provides some insulating properties, it can also cause serious health problems. Fats are either saturated or unsaturated. Animal fats, such as those found in red meat, milk, butter, and cheese, are mostly highly saturated and are thought to increase the amount of cholesterol in the blood. In contrast, the fat in chicken, fish, and turkey is largely unsaturated, and most of the fat is in the skin, which you don't have to eat. From a health standpoint these polyunsaturated fats are preferable.

Our bodies also require certain amounts of vitamins and minerals. Many people take daily vitamin supplements along with their meals. Yet anyone who eats a reasonably balanced diet will get the required vitamins and minerals. In the case of salt, too much is harmful, especially if you have high blood pressure. Fortunately, there are an increasing number of low-sodium products on the

Table 6–2. CALORIES PER MINUTE IN VARIOUS ACTIVITIES. To calculate the calories used, multiply the figures in the right column by the time spent in a given activity and your weight. For example, a 120-pound person who plays tennis for 30 minutes would burn .0460 × 30 × 120 = 165 calories.

Activity	Calories Per Minute Per Pound
Daily Activities	
Lying	
Sleeping	.0066
Resting	.0079
Sitting	
Quietly; reading	.0080
Viewing T.V.; conversing; hand sewing; eating	.0116
Writing	.0120
Typing (manual)	.0166
Driving a car	.0150
Playing piano	.0150
Standing	
Dressing; undressing; grooming	.0133
Cooking; dishwashing; ironing	.0150
Household tasks (cleaning, dusting, sweeping, etc.)	.0200
Singing	.0190
Washing clothes	.0190
Showering	.0230
Making bed	.0270
Exercise and Sports	
Archery	.0340
Basketball	.0470
Bicycling (level) 5.5 mph	.0330
(uphill)	.0410
(downhill)	.0180
Bowling	.0440
Calisthenics	.0330
Dancing (moderately)	.0270
(vigorously)	.0460
Football	.0670
Golf	.0360
Squash; racquetball	.0690
Table tennis	.0260
Tennis	.0460
Walking slowly (level)	.0183
(uphill)	.0560

Source: *Nutritive Value of Foods*, U.S. Department of Agriculture, Washington, D.C., Home and Gardens Bulletin, No. 72.

market. You may also be surprised how easily you can become accustomed to food that has not been salted, either during cooking or at the table.

Since the human digestive tract is unable to digest fiber, the presence of fiber in the diet provides bulk to help the large intestine carry away body wastes. In turn, this helps to prevent the difficulties of diverticular disease and may

Individuals may excel in some aspects of fitness without achieving total physical fitness. (Bowling Green State University, Ohio)

help to prevent cancer of the large intestine. Fiber is present in foods such as leafy vegetables, whole-grain cereals, unrefined flour, and legumes like beans and peas.

We also need water. Perhaps you're already aware that our bodies are approximately half water. But did you know that we lose up to four pints of water each day? We lose water through the moisture in our breath and through sweat, urine, and bowel movements. Naturally, this liquid must be replaced; but we do not need to drink four pints of fluids because about 70 percent of our food is water. There is a greater risk of dehydration when we exercise, however, especially if the weather is hot.

Keeping Physically Fit

What comes to mind when you think of physical fitness? Do you imagine some muscular person lifting weights? Or do you think of people jogging or running along the road? Whatever you imagine, chances are that it represents only part of overall physical fitness. Actually, physical fitness is the entire human organism's ability to function efficiently and effectively, and it includes at least eleven different components (Corbin and Lindsey, 1985). There are five *health-related* fitness components (body composition or the ratio of muscle to fat, cardiovascular fitness, flexibility, muscular endurance, and strength) and six *skill-related* fitness components (agility, balance, coordination, power, reaction time, and speed). Each of these components contributes to our overall physical fitness, helping us to work more effectively, enjoy leisure activities, and stay healthy. Although there is some relationship between these components, people may excel in one aspect of fitness without necessarily having the others. For example, John, who lifts weights, possesses exceptional muscular strength and power, but he does not have above-average cardiovascular fitness. On the other hand, Linda, a dance teacher, has good flexibility and coordination but lacks muscular strength in the upper part of her body.

Few of us are likely to achieve the ideal of total physical fitness. Given the limitations of time and our varied responsibilities, most of us must settle for an optimal level of fitness that will promote good health and a sense of well-being. Whatever goal we choose, we must remember that optimal physical fitness is not possible without regular exercise. Even then there is no single exercise program that is best suited for everyone. Each of us has different needs, priorities, and work schedules. In selecting your personal exercise program, you may find it helpful to observe the following points:

1. *Identify your personal physical fitness needs.* A good way to do this is to consult with someone in the physical education department of your college or a specialist in one of the physical fitness centers in your community. There are also books with exercises that help you to assess your fitness; see the book by Corbin and Lindsey (1985) listed in the Recommended Readings at the end of this chapter.

2. *Select personalized physical exercises to make exercise more enjoyable.* Choose physical activities that are related to your interests, needs, and personality. If you are a sociable person, consider a group activity such as volleyball. If you're not inclined toward competitive sports, select an activity that does not require a great deal of physical skill, such as walking, jogging, running, cycling, swimming, or home calisthenics. Finally, choose an activity that feels good to *you*, regardless of what others do.

3. *Vary your activities.* By varying your activities you can include ones that will develop different aspects of physical fitness. This also helps to keep exercise interesting and enjoyable. Usually, changes in the weather and the seasons along with availability of facilities suggest some variation in your exercise program.

4. *Exercise regularly.* It's best to set aside a time and place for your exercise activities, making it a part of your daily routine. It's also important to perform your exercises to a level that will promote optimal fitness. This usually means a minimum of 20 to 30 minutes three times a week at the heart-training pulse rate. To find your own heart-training rate, from the pulse rate of 220 subtract

your age, then multiply by 75 percent. Remember to allow sufficient time to warm up to this level and to wind down gradually.

5. *Periodically evaluate and modify your exercise program.* As time passes your needs and interests change. Shifts in your work schedule and family responsibilities may also dictate a change in your exercise program. Then too, your age and overall level of stress should be kept in mind. Listen to your body. Assess how you feel.

Physical fitness is a vital part of the sense of wholeness mentioned earlier. But from all that we've said, it should also be clear that our overall well-being includes other considerations, such as our eating habits, work schedules, lifestyle, awareness of health hazards and stress, personal attitudes, and morale. We've also stressed the importance of each person taking responsibility for his or her own health, while recognizing the limits of our control over illness. Most important of all is the realization that the pursuit of wellness, though this is never fully achieved, may enable each of us to function better than we would have otherwise.

Summary

Body Image

1. We began the chapter by pointing out that body image generally refers to the concepts we have of our bodies and how we feel about them, with the body concept approximating rather than coinciding with our bodies.

2. Many people are dissatisfied with their bodies, especially overweight people whose bodies are at odds with the prevailing ideals of slimness in our society.

3. There is a mutual relationship between body image and well-being, such that satisfaction with our bodies helps us to feel good about ourselves and vice versa.

Care and Abuse of the Body

4. Greater public awareness of health and fitness has brought about some improvement in eating and exercise habits, though many people eat too much on occasion and do not exercise regularly.

5. As many as half the people who visit doctors don't follow the prescribed treatment, partly because of the conflict between the physician's diagnosis and their own private, and often erroneous, views of what's wrong with themselves.

6. Obesity, smoking, and alcohol and drug abuse continue to be major health hazards for many people.

Psychological Factors and Physical Disorders

7. Growing acceptance of the mind-body unity suggests that psychological factors may play a significant role in any physical ailment, not just in the traditional psychosomatic disorders.

8. According to Schwartz's disregulation model, physical disorders develop when internal regulatory systems, including psychological factors, fail to operate properly.

9. As an example, essential hypertension may develop in response to a variety of factors, such as environmental stress and the way individuals cope with it.

Promoting Wellness

10. An important factor in promoting wellness is the individual's taking greater responsibility in all matters pertaining to his or her health.

11. Although positive psychological well-being may promote good health, subjective feelings of health are not synonymous with good health.

12. Sensible eating habits include a balanced diet that provides the needed calories for someone of your age, size, and lifestyle.

13. Physical fitness in the form of a personalized exercise program especially suited to one's interests and needs is an integral part of promoting wellness.

Self-test

1. We have difficulty forming a realistic body image because:

   a. our bodies are constantly changing
   b. of depersonalization
   c. of the dated images of our bodies
   d. all of the above

2. Both sexes feel the most satisfied about their:

   a. teeth
   b. hands
   c. faces
   d. noses

3. Body image tends to be strongly related to:

   a. intelligence
   b. self-esteem
   c. height
   d. sex

4. Three-fourths of Americans judge their own health to be:

   a. average
   b. poor
   c. better than average
   d. superior

5. Up to half of the adult patients who consult physicians do not:

   a. consult medical doctors
   b. follow the prescribed treatment
   c. return for a second visit
   d. all of the above

6. Obesity is associated with an increased risk of death from:

   a. diabetes
   b. high blood pressure
   c. gallbladder disorder
   d. all of the above

7. The central idea in Schwartz's disregulation model of physical disorders is:

a. negative feedback

b. stress tolerance

c. environmental stress

d. thought control

8. What condition is especially apt to develop among people who keep anger to themselves?

a. alcoholism

b. diabetes

c. obesity

d. essential hypertension

9. In the survey on wellness, the respondents who reported the least number of chronic diseases were known as the:

a. fatalists

b. true believers

c. health vigilants

d. hypochondriacs

10. Individuals who chronically attend to their internal state of feelings and sensations tend to:

a. have fewer then average chronic diseases

b. exaggerate their bodily symptoms

c. enjoy better than average health

d. rate higher in extroversion

Exercises

1. *Examine yourself in a mirror.* Stand naked in front of a full-length mirror. First, move up to the mirror and examine your face closely. What do you most notice about your face? Then step back and examine your entire body. Turn around slowly, looking at yourself from each side, and then at your rear. Which aspects of your body do you like the most? Are there parts of your body you have difficulty accepting? All things considered, how satisfied are you with your body?

2. *Do you practice good eating habits?* Describe your eating habits in terms of the calories consumed each day and a balanced diet. If you're not sure how many calories you consume, keep a daily count for at least three days and take an average. How does your calorie count compare to the average for someone like yourself as indicated in the text? Do you also choose foods from each of the major food areas as described in the chapter?

3. *Describe your personal exercise habits.* How much exercise do you get in the course of your daily activities? Would you agree that everyone needs to be physically active on a regular basis? If you have a personalized exercise program, describe it in a paragraph or two. Indicate whether or not you exercise your heart to the optimal training rate for at least 20 minutes three times a week.

4. *Identify your biggest health hazard.* Are you guilty of one of the common health hazards, such as overeating, eating unbalanced meals, smoking, drinking, or drug abuse? If so, what are you doing about it? Try eliminating this hazard for five consecutive days and see if you feel better about yourself and your health.

5. *Do you suffer from a chronic ailment?* Do you have to cope with some type of chronic or recurring condition, such as an allergy, asthma, arthritis, hypertension, diabetes, hypertension, migraine headaches, or ulcers? How well are you managing such ailments? Are you aware of the psychosocial factors that may influence your ailments, such as environmental stress and your emotions? What are you doing to improve your condition?

6. *How much control do you exercise over your health?* Do you believe you can minimize your chances of getting sick by practicing good nutrition, regular exercise, positive attitudes, and stress management? Or do you feel that coming down with a cold or the flu is mostly a matter of luck? To what extent would you classify yourself as a "health vigilant" as described in this chapter?

Questions for Self-reflection

1. Which part of your body or face has been the most difficult for you to accept?

2. Do you take care of your body?

3. What aspect of your eating habits would you most like to change?

4. Do you enjoy regular, vigorous physical exercise?

5. What is your worst health hazard?

6. If you're a smoker, how many times have you tried to quit?

7. Are you aware that the use of alcohol easily becomes a health hazard?

8. Do you often find that a cold or flu you get was preceded by a period of intense emotional stress?

9. Would you agree that a healthy body and a sound mind go together?

10. To what extent do you believe you control your health?

Recommended Readings

Brown, Barbara B. *Between Health and Illness.* New York: Bantam Books, 1984 (paperback). Explores the relationship between stress and illness.

Cooper, Cary L. (ed.). *Psychosocial Stress and Cancer.* New York: John Wiley & Sons, 1985. A state-of-the-art report on how life events, personality, and the body's defenses interact in the development of cancer and management of cancer patients.

Corbin, Charles B., and Ruth Lindsey. *Concepts of Physical Fitness with Laboratories,* 5th ed. Dubuque, Iowa: Wm. C. Brown, Publishers, 1985 (paperback). Provides a succinct, factual presentation of the why, how, and what of exercise and physical fitness, with practical exercises.

Eisenberg, Howard, M.D., and Keith W. Sehnert, M.D. *How To Be Your Own Doctor Sometimes,* 10th ed. New York: Putnam, 1986 (paperback). This is a classic in the field, providing guidelines and useful information for self-care.

Hamburg, D. A., G. R. Elliott, and D. L. Parron (eds.). *Health and Behavior.* Washington, D.C.: National Academy Press, 1982. Contains an expert assessment of the relationship between behavior and health, with chapters on heart disease, alcoholism, smoking, and coping with stress.

The New Our Bodies, Ourselves. The Boston Women's Health Book Collective. New York: Simon & Schuster, 1984 (paperback). A comprehensive, down-to-earth health book for women of all ages.

Self-concept

You're shopping with a friend. You stop to admire the clothes in a shop window. "Let's go in," suggests your friend. You enter the store and browse around for a few minutes. Then you try on a pair of jeans. Looking at yourself in the mirror, you notice your hair is in disarray. You instinctively straighten it so that you'll appear more the way you want to look. But suppose you notice that you've gained 10 or 15 pounds and that the usual size jeans are too tight? Since you can't lose that much weight in a few minutes, you'll probably try various ways of reconciling your appearance in the mirror with your self-image. You might ask your friend how you look in the jeans, and your friend might reply, "Not bad, but they may be a little tight around your rear end." You could try on a larger size. But the very idea bothers you. Perhaps you could put off buying new clothes to avoid looking at yourself in the mirror. Or you may be inspired to resume your weight-loss program. Whatever you decide, one thing is clear. The discrepancy between your self-concept and the image of yourself in the mirror has a powerful influence on your behavior.

WHAT IS THE SELF-CONCEPT?

Essentially, the self-concept is the overall image or awareness we have of ourselves. It includes all those perceptions of "I" and "me," together with the feelings, beliefs, and values associated with them. As such, the self-concept is actually a cluster of selves, even though we habitually refer to it in the singular. Ordinarily we take the self-concept for granted, as when we are engaged in an activity at work or play. At other times we are very much aware of our selves, such as when we're making an important decision or taking on a heavy responsibility. We may become acutely self-conscious whenever we experience a discrepancy between our self-image and the way we appear to others. In all of these instances, the self-concept exerts a powerful influence on our experience, affecting the way we perceive, judge, and behave.

The self-concept provides us with our personal identity or sense of who we are. Even though situations and people around us change, the self-concept reassures us that we are basically the same person we were yesterday. Our self-image is more real to us than our bodies, and it governs the way we experience our bodies. Our sense of identity is so important to us that we resist anyone or anything that threatens it. Even the fear of death itself may not be a fear of suffering or of the unknown so much as it is the deep fear that our personal identity will be dissolved—which is inconceivable.

It is somewhat arbitrary how many selves we care to distinguish within our overall self-concept. At a general level, however, it is common to identify the *body image*, the awareness of my body: the *subjective self*, the self I see myself to be; the *ideal self*, the self I'd like to be; and my *social selves*, the way I feel others see me. Since we've already discussed the body image in the last chapter, let's begin by taking a look at the subjective self and the ideal self. We'll examine the importance of our social selves in a later section of this chapter.

The Subjective Self

This is the way I see myself. It is the self I think I am. It is composed of highly personal self-images. Since it is so private, each of us is an expert on our subjective self—however realistic or unrealistic our perception may be.

Our subjective self is made up of the many self-perceptions we have acquired growing up, especially in our formative years. It is mostly influenced by the way we are seen and treated by significant others, especially by our parents. When we are young and impressionable, we tend to internalize what they think of us, their judgments and expectations, and regard ourselves accordingly. For example, I knew a mother who resented having to take care of her children and was constantly yelling at them, "Don't do that, stupid!" "What's wrong with you?" "You're going to be the death of me yet." Can you imagine how her children felt about themselves after years of repeated exposure to such remarks? Are you surprised that they were troublemakers at home and at school?

Fortunately, we tend to revise our self-images through later experience with others, especially with our friends, teachers, and spouses. One girl who suffered from a low opinion of herself, partly because of overly critical parents, began seeing herself in a new way at adolescence. Through doing more things on her own and sharing with her friends, she began appreciating her good points and acquired a more positive view of herself. She even got to the point of being able to shrug off her parents' sarcastic remarks, much to her parents' amazement.

The Ideal Self

This is the self I'd like to be, including my aspirations, moral ideals, and values.

According to the psychoanalytic view, we are not fully aware of our ideal self because we have acquired much of it through identifying with parental demands and prohibitions during the formative years of childhood. Accordingly, many of the "shoulds" and "should nots" of our conscience represent unconscious and unrealistic demands that may keep us from growing up. An example would be the perfectionist student who feels he must make all As or he will not be a worthwhile person. I once knew a very competent but rigid graduate student who told all his friends that he would kill himself if he ever received a B in any of his courses. When he eventually made a B, he stopped short of taking his life, but he managed to make himself and everyone else around him miserable for months after that. Interestingly, many students who succeed in taking their lives make better than average grades but suffer from unrealistically high expectations of themselves.

Ordinarily, we think of having to change our self-image and behavior to conform more to our ideal self. Indeed, our ideal self remains more consistent across time than our subjective self. But when our aspirations prove to be excessive or unrealistic, it may be more appropriate for us to modify our ideal self as a way of furthering our growth and self-esteem. Fortunately, we tend to modify many of the dictates of our ideal self with experience so that they represent self-chosen values that express in a healthy, adult way what we expect of ourselves. Accordingly, our ideal self may serve as an incentive for us to do our best, as with the student who puts forth his or her best effort in hopes of entering medical school. But when we fail to live up to our ideal self, it is healthy to feel we have a choice either to redouble our efforts to achieve our aspirations or to modify them in the direction of more fruitful incentives.

What Does It Mean To "Be Yourself"?

We are constantly being told, "Be yourself." And almost everyone would agree this is necessary. But what does it mean?

People speak of "peeling off the layers" or "shedding the masks," as if there were some underlying "real self" waiting to be discovered. The unspoken assumption seems to be that there is some sort of "true self" that was given at birth or for all eternity, and if uncovered it will simply emerge and guide your every thought and action. In this sense, "be yourself" implies abandoning all responsibility for your actions on the grounds that whatever you do spontaneously comes from the demands of this hidden self. Such a view of an intrinsic self is not far from the Greek view of fate.

If, on the contrary, "be yourself" means "live authentically," then the aim is both more understandable and challenging. Here the focus is on just "plain ole' me"—the only self I have. It consists of all my past experience, my physical and mental limitations, and, most important, my past decisions. But this self is never finished. It is always in the process of self-creation. At each moment I am creating the self I choose to be, I can choose to explore more of my own potential through trial and error, or I can simply persist in the way I am. Either way, being myself means being thrown on my own responsibility. My fate consists in the self I create with every new decision I make. At every moment it is I who decides what sort of person I shall be.

Adapted from James W. Felt, "How to Be Yourself," *America*, May 25, 1968, p. 705.

Multiple Selves

Actually the overall self-concept, as indicated earlier, is an organized cluster of selves, so it would be more accurate to speak of our multiple selves. As such, the self-concept includes hundreds, perhaps thousands, of self-perceptions in varying degrees of clarity and intensity that we have acquired in growing up. Much of the diversity of the self reflects our social roles, so that even the normal happy person wears "many masks," as we'll discuss later in this chapter. At the same time there are many other self-perceptions that are less clearly associated with social roles. Some self-images arise from the experience of our own bodies, as explained in the last chapter. Others reflect needs, interests, traits, and habit patterns acquired through experience, and these self-images may be integrated within our overall self-concept in varying degrees. For instance, suppose you are ordinarily an easy-going person. Then one day you discover a friend has misrepresented your intentions. You become angry and tell your friend how you feel. A couple of hours later, after an apology from your friend, you appear calm again. Your friend might think, "You certainly have changed!" But when you stop and think, it's not that you changed so much as that you have expressed different *aspects* of yourself at different times.

We seldom like to think of ourselves as made up of different parts or selves. Even if we acknowledge this in theory, we tend to forget it in practice.

Yet making due allowance for the diversity of selves, both in ourselves and others, may help to account for some of the inconsistency in human behavior. It may also help to avoid the endless circle of blame and guilt that undermines good relationships.

Because our various selves exhibit a certain consistency or organizing pattern as a whole, we refer to them collectively as a self-concept. But it should be clear that the self-concept is more of a hypothesis or theory we use to explain how these selves function in our experience. People with a fragmented, incoherent view of themselves—such as the severely emotionally disturbed—are often unsure of who they are and may behave in a highly inconsistent manner. In extreme cases, as with multiple personality disorders, individuals alternate between two or more distinct personalities, each with its own name, habits, memories, and behaviors. In contrast, those of us who have achieved a more desirable integration of our various selves may feel a clearer sense of personal identity and behave in a somewhat more consistent manner. I say "somewhat" because, as we've described above, even the healthiest person's psychic makeup includes a considerable degree of inconsistency.

CHARACTERISTICS OF THE SELF-CONCEPT

Once established, the core of the self has a high degree of stability. Peripheral aspects of the self can, and often do, change rather quickly. But the core of the self, which comprises those aspects of ourselves we regard as very important to us, tends to perpetuate itself. Essentially, the self-concept functions as a filter through which everything we see or hear passes. It thereby exerts a selective, circular influence on our experience, so that we tend to perceive, judge, and act in ways that are consistent with our self-concept.

Self-consistency

This characteristic tendency toward self-consistency is best understood in relation to Carl Rogers's (1980) view of the phenomenal self, as visualized in Figure 7–1. The circle on the right represents the total experience of the organism, including sensory and bodily experience. The circle on the left represents the self-concept, which has been acquired through interaction with significant others, mainly parents, throughout the formative years of development. It is fully available to awareness. These two circles, representing the typical or "normal" person, do not fully coincide because the self-concept develops in response to what Rogers calls "conditions of worth." That is, instead of growing up in an atmosphere of unconditional acceptance, most of us feel we are loved and accepted only if we meet certain expectations and approvals. Whatever is acceptable to our parents, and other significant persons in our lives, becomes incorporated into our self-concept. In turn, our self-concept functions as a filter through which everything we see or hear passes.

Experiences that are consistent with both our sensory reactions (Circle B) and our self-concept (Circle A), tend to be labeled or "symbolized" accurately and admitted fully into our conscious awareness. These self-perceptions comprise the core of our self-concept and are visualized by the shaded area where the two circles overlap in Figure 7–1. Experiences that are *not* consistent with both our sensory experience and our self-concept are perceived more selectively. Such experiences are either distorted or denied to awareness.

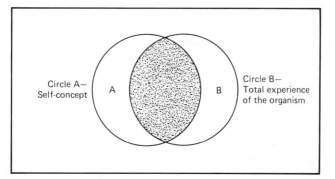

Figure 7–1. THE INTERACTION OF THE SELF-CONCEPT AND THE ENVIRONMENT.
From Carl R. Rogers, *Client-centered Therapy* (Boston: Houghton Mifflin, 1951), p. 526. Reprinted by permission of the publishers.

When we experience something that is consistent with our self-concept but is not confirmed by our own sensory reactions, we perceive and label such experiences in a distorted fashion, as if they were part of us. Such experiences are visualized by the area in Circle A outside the shaded area. They are part of our learned self-concept. For example, suppose a woman influenced by the stereotyped sex-roles in our society believes herself to be inept in math. Each time she works with numbers, she indeed does poorly. But she readily assimilates such experiences of failure because they are consistent with her existing self-concept. Here the self-concept distorts her actual experience, so that she actually believes she is no good in math, even though that distorted perception of herself is not valid.

Experiences that are not consistent with our learned self-concept are perceived as too threatening and are not even recognized as self-experiences. Consequently, they are not accurately perceived or labeled, but are denied to awareness, either in part or in whole. Here, denial is roughly comparable to the concept of repression in Freudian terms and refers to an unconscious exclusion of experience because of the threat associated with it. Such experiences are visualized in the diagram by the area in Circle B outside the shaded area.

Suppose a woman who believes she is no good at math is required to take two semesters of math as a part of her major studies. She may begin the course with a determination to do well, accompanied by a vague fear that she won't. At first she works hard and even discovers to her surprise that she enjoys the precision of mathematical thinking. Then she receives the grade on her first test. It's a 96! "Me doing well in math? How can this be? Maybe the instructor made a mistake in grading the papers. Maybe he likes me or feels sorry for me. It's probably dumb luck. It won't happen again." Like the rest of us, she will probably rely on a variety of such self-justifying mechanisms to make this experience acceptable to her existing self-concept. In doing so she also denies her actual experience of success, and thereby fails to discover her personal potential for math. On the other hand, suppose this woman completes both semesters of math with As and gets a job working with computers. Chances are she will gradually revise her self-concept in a way that reflects her real ability in math, thereby incorporating aspects of herself previously denied to awareness.

Self-esteem

The tendency to think and act in a self-consistent manner is also strengthened by our self-esteem—the personal judgment we make about our own worth. Such self-evaluation is built up through repeated experiences of success and failure, other people's impressions and treatment of us, and the self-appraisals in relation to our ideal selves. From late adolescence on, when the self-concept becomes more stable, we tend to have a characteristic level of self-worth, sometimes called global self-esteem, which remains fairly consistent. Yet our self-esteem also varies from one situation to another, depending on the experiences of the moment. An important achievement or a satisfying experience with a friend or lover often raises our self-confidence as well. But an experience of failure or disappointment at the hands of another usually evokes self-doubt and temporarily lowers our self-confidence.

Fortunately, most people enjoy moderately high self-esteem. They are generally pleased with themselves and make inferences about themselves that are slightly more positive than might be expected. There is a sizeable minority, however, who suffer from low self-esteem. These people are usually haunted by anxiety and self-doubt and report lower levels of happiness. In both cases, self-esteem exerts a powerful influence on people's expectations, their judgments about themselves and others, and their behavior. People with high self-esteem are willing to test the validity of their inferences about themselves. Having a high level of self-acceptance, they tend to be accepting of others, including those with different opinions than themselves, and enjoy satisfying relationships with other people. They also expect to do well in their accomplishments, try hard, and tend to be successful in their careers. They are also inclined to attribute their success to their abilities, and to make due allowance for circumstances in interpreting their failures. As a result, people with high self-esteem generally enjoy a great deal of self-confidence and have a realistic assessment of their strengths and weaknesses. By contrast, people with low self-esteem are generally less willing to put their ideas about themselves to the test and are never really convinced of their own self-assessment. Furthermore, low-esteem people tend to expect the worst, exert less effort on their tasks—especially challenging, demanding ones—and achieve less success in their careers and relationships with others (Wegner and Vallacher, 1977). Of course, there are exceptions to this pattern. But even when low-esteem people achieve success, they are less apt to attribute their success to their abilities or enjoy it. For example, people sometimes compensate for an insecure sense of self by making a lot of money or achieving considerable power over others. But they continue to be dissatisfied in their relationships with others at work and at home.

Self-efficacy

Self-efficacy, or the sense of personal mastery, is similar to but not the same as self-esteem. According to Bandura (1977), who originated the concept, self-efficacy refers to our belief or expectation that we can perform adequately in a particular situation. In contrast to the ideas of self-concept and self-esteem, self-efficacy depends primarily on specific situations. That is, you may have a great deal of confidence that you can play a good game of tennis this afternoon, but you may harbor considerable doubts about your ability to do well on that math test at school tomorrow. Once established, positive expectations about your abilities may generalize somewhat to new situations. Yet, our sense of self-efficacy is best thought of as a collection of *specific* self-evaluations.

Bandura suggests that our sense of self-efficacy may be enhanced through any one or a combination of the following ways. A major source of self-efficacy is our performance accomplishments, with success generally raising our sense of personal mastery and failure lowering it. Whether success raises our self-efficacy or not depends on several factors: the difficulty of the task, whether we perform it ourselves, and whether we put forth our best effort. Easy accomplishment—especially with the help of others—or failure after only half-hearted efforts have little influence on our sense of self-efficacy. On the other hand, when you put your reputation on the line in a given task, try your best and succeed, you'll probably increase your sense of self-efficacy. Another source of efficacy is observing successful performances by competent people, or models, especially those who are similar to ourselves. For example, if a friend of yours gives up smoking, you may be inspired to try it again yourself, with more self-confidence than before. A third source of efficacy is through verbal persuasion, especially people you look up to. Examples would be positive feedback and encouragement from teachers, coaches, counselors, and mentors at your job.

Self-confidence comes with the experience of mastery in particular situations. (Official U.S. Coast Guard Photo)

Just a simple matter like writing a helpful suggestion on a student's test paper may encourage that person to try harder next time. Still another source of efficacy is the management of emotional arousal. We tend to use emotional arousal as a cue to judge how well we'll do in a situation. For example, an actor may know his lines well in rehearsal, but an intense fear of opening night may block his recall at the crucial performance. Enhancing his self-efficacy in this situation would include not only mastering his lines, but also learning how to relax and manage his anxiety as well.

The concept of self-efficacy helps to demystify the notion of self-esteem and highlights the relationship between self-esteem and competence. For instance, educators have long realized that self-esteem plays a crucial role in learning; students with high esteem forge ahead academically while those with low esteem fall behind. But, as Barbara Lerner (1985) points out, the practice of teachers giving priority to raising the student's esteem, especially since the 1960s, has often been at the expense of self-esteem based on competence. Teachers have been trained to accept students as they are, to provide ample encouragement and praise, and, above all, to protect students' self-esteem from injury through criticism or failure. An unintended result has been the awarding of good grades for mediocre accomplishments, sometimes accompanied by a lack of basic competence. Furthermore, an undue emphasis on "feel-good-now" esteem has fostered an orientation toward instant success and a constant hunger to get more for less, which ultimately leads to restlessness and dissatisfaction with one's life. In contrast, an emphasis on the development of competence, as reflected in the striving for excellence in the 1980s, tends to build self-esteem of another, more durable sort. "Earned self-esteem" is based on success in measuring up to standards at home, school, and work. It is necessarily hard-won and develops slowly, with the cumulative development of competence in one area of life after another. Standards, and the demand on students to keep working until they really succeed in meeting them, are critical steps in acquiring this type of self-esteem. Individuals must learn to persist in the face of momentary unhappiness, self-criticism, and occasional failure. But in the long run, this earned self-esteem provides us with a stable and lasting foundation for further growth.

SELF AND PERSONAL GROWTH

Suppose someone asked, "Are you the same person now you were five years ago, or ten years ago?" What would you say? Most of us would probably acknowledge that we're different in many ways. Much of the change in ourselves has to do with the maturity and mellowing that comes with age and experience. But a lot of it comes through adapting to different people and situations. New jobs, new acquaintances and friends, and new responsibilities like marriage and parenting, all affect the way we see ourselves. Although we retain a stable core of self, as described above, the many self-perceptions that make up our overall self-concept are in a state of flux or change, and they are readily influenced by our current experience. In this section, we'll examine how our self-concepts tend to change, or can be changed, through our changing social selves, personal criticism, and the warmth and acceptance of a therapeutic relationship.

Our Changing Social Selves

The term "social selves" is used to describe the impression we think other people have of us. It is the way we *think* they view us, which may or may not be an accurate reflection of their views. Our perception of how others view us heavily influences the way we see ourselves. If someone admires us and compliments us, we'll find it easier to think of ourselves accordingly. On the other hand, if someone is very critical of us, we begin doubting ourselves and become very guarded around that person.

"A man has as many different social selves as there are distinct groups of persons about whose opinion he cares," observed William James. As a result, we are somewhat different with each person we meet. With close friends and loved ones we may be relaxed and informal, readily disclosing information about ourselves. But with strangers we may be guarded, at least until we know what kind of people we're dealing with. Then again, to our employers we may be conscientious and ambitious. It's not that we're being two-faced or untrue to ourselves. Instead, each of these people brings out a different side of ourselves. The concept of multiple social selves reminds us that we have many potential selves, with the social conditions around us helping to determine which of these selves we express at the moment.

Some of us are more aware of and influenced by our social selves than others. This was brought out in a study showing how people differ in their characteristic self-awareness, especially whether they exhibited a private or a public self-consciousness. People who scored high on the public self-consciousness were generally concerned about the way they appeared to people and what others thought of them. Those who scored high on the private self-consciousness paid more attention to their inner feelings and were more apt to figure things out for themselves. These two aspects of self-consciousness, which are present in all of us in varying degrees, are related to our tendency either to look

Meeting new people makes us aware of how others see us. (Stan Wakefield)

toward the immediate situation to guide our actions or to look inwardly to our own standards. For example, suppose two people are invited to a party. The person who looks more to the situation for behavioral cues might think, "A lot of my friends will be there. It's a good time to be sociable and forget about my problems for a while." But someone less attuned to the social self might decide, "I think I'll pass. I'm just not in the mood for all the small talk at the party" (Snyder, 1979).

The Changeable Self

There is some evidence that rapid technological and social change affects the fundamental way we perceive and understand ourselves. At least this is what Louis Zurcher found in his study using the Kuhn and McPartland Twenty Statements test. In this open-ended, relatively unstructured procedure, each student is asked to answer the question "Who am I?" twenty times. The answers are then scored according to several basic categories.

During the 1950s, Zurcher found that students gave answers that predominantly identified their selves with a social role or institutional status. For example, students tended to define themselves by saying, "I am a student," "I am a female," or "I am an American." Such responses indicated that their personal identity was largely a social identity, closely linked with existing social roles and institutions. The prevalence of such statements in the 1950s reflected the relatively stable and widely accepted social order of that time.

Since the 1970s, however, Zurcher discovered that students tended to give a different type of response. Now the prevalent responses reflected a self-concept *not* closely identified with social roles or institutions. For example, students tended to describe themselves in more personal statements, such as "I am happy," "I am searching," or "I am a frustrated person." Such statements reflected a self-concept based more on personal characteristics and relatively "situation-free," compared to the typical self-concept of the 1950s. The prevalence of such statements has been interpreted as a sign that contemporary students are more at home with constant change and may sometimes deliberately seek change.

Zurcher suggests that such a changeable or mutable self may be a more functional mode of self-concept for coping with the accelerated change in our contemporary society.

Louis A. Zurcher, Jr., *The Mutable Self* (Beverly Hills, CA: Sage Publications, 1977), chap. 2.

The relative ease with which our social selves may be influenced by others was demonstrated in a series of experiments. In one study, a woman interviewed eighteen women undergraduate students. Half the students had been assigned to an experimental group; the other half to a control group. Before the interview, students in the experimental group were instructed to do their best to gain the liking of the interviewer. They could say or do anything to achieve this goal. These students generally described themselves in glowing terms. They told how they were intelligent, successful, hard-working, and socially popular. Students in the control group who had not been instructed to seek the interviewer's approval showed no such change of masks. After the interview, each student made a private self-evaluation, which was then compared to tests each had taken a month earlier. The investigators found that in trying to convince the interviewer of their favorable qualities, the students also succeeded in convincing themselves. These students felt more positively about themselves than before. No such change in self-esteem was found in the control group (Gergen, 1980).

The realization that our self-concept is affected by social influences heightens the importance of our relationships with others. Once we have chosen to associate with certain friends, select a marriage partner, or attend a given school or job, the people involved in turn help to shape the way we see ourselves. Are there highly critical people who put us down and discourage us? We should avoid them whenever possible. Are there others who bring out the best in us and make us feel good about ourselves? Perhaps we should seek them out more often. In both instances, we can change the way we see ourselves by modifying the social influences on our lives. It would be foolish to think we can change everything about ourselves this way. But the notion of fluid, changing social selves reminds us that we have more possibilities for change and growth than we may be using.

Learning from Criticism

How do you feel when you are criticized? Do you feel angry and rejected? Do you feel resentful, even when you're in the wrong? For most people, the answer to these questions is yes. When people have been asked to finish the statement "When I am criticized . . .," typical responses include: "I get upset." "I resent it." "I feel she doesn't love me anymore." "I wonder when the ax will fall." Sound familiar? All too often, as these comments suggest, people feel that criticism is a personal attack that they must defend themselves against at all costs. As a result, they waste a lot of energy worrying about criticism, justifying themselves, and going to great lengths to avoid it.

By contrast, accepting criticism can become a valuable means of personal growth. For example, when asked to complete the same statement cited above, some people make more positive responses. One woman said, "Criticism tells me where the other person is coming from, how he sees me, what he expects of me." An experienced executive said, "Your critics can tell you where you're going wrong before your friends can." A woman said, "When I'm criticized, I try to figure out what the other person is trying to tell me, especially how I can improve my performance." All these people have learned the valuable art of taking criticism constructively.

In the bestseller *Nobody's Perfect*, Hendrie Weisinger and Norman Lobsenz (1981) suggest many ways we can use criticism for personal growth. Each major strategy centers around the three familiar aspects of personality—our thoughts, feelings, and behavior.

First, view criticism as a valuable source of new information to be evaluated objectively. Each time you're criticized, you don't necessarily have to rush out and change something about yourself. Instead, criticism should be taken as a cue that *may* require action. Even then, you must look beyond the surface of the criticism and ask yourself, "What is this person trying to tell me?" Ask yourself too, "How important is this criticism?" The more important the information is to you, the more likely you'll need to do something about it. Consider also how many times a specific criticism is offered. If you're frequently criticized for the same behavior by different people, there's a good chance that the criticism is valid and should be acted upon. Then too, you must assess the source of criticism. People often feel they're being criticized unfairly, especially if the other person is under a lot of stress. The more qualified the person is to judge your work, the more you should take criticism to heart. Yet even criticism spoken in frustration or anger many need to be heeded, taking into account the exaggerated emotion because of stress. Finally, weigh the pros and cons of acting on a criticism. You should decide whether the benefits that come from acting on the criticism balance or outweigh the effort involved. For example, a student who does poorly on her tests may wonder whether it's worthwhile following the teacher's suggestion that she get help in comprehension and note-taking skills.

The more qualified someone is to judge our work, the more we should take the criticism to heart.
(Marc P. Anderson)

Yet if she continues to get low grades, her entire career goal may be in jeopardy.

Second, put the emotional energy aroused by criticism to work for you, not against you. As mentioned earlier, emotional arousal tends to interfere with our ability to perform well, lowering our self-confidence as well. Instead, when criticized try to stay calm. Relax physically. Remind yourself that nobody is trying to hurt you. What this person is saying probably will be helpful. Then use your emotions as a source of energy to make the necessary changes. For example, whenever Julie did something her husband Brad disliked, he would yell, "That's stupid. How dumb can you be?" Julie became upset and ignored his accusations as a way of justifying her actions. Gradually Julie learned to remain calm in the face of Brad's emotional outbursts. She would ask, "What is it you're objecting to?" or "How would you suggest handling this?" Responding in kind, Brad learned to give more specific criticisms, which Julie found more helpful.

Third, take positive steps to put the needed changes into action. Don't waste energy defending yourself. Instead, listen carefully to what is being said. Ask for more information. Ask the person for suggested solutions to the criticism. You might ask for this indirectly, such as, "If you were in my place, what would you do?" Or you might ask, more directly, "What would you like me to do?" People usually criticize something we're doing. But it often comes across as a personal attack because many people do not know how to give criticism constructively. So if someone says, "You're rude and inconsiderate," ask them, "In what ways have I been inconsiderate?" In this way, you'll focus on something tangible that you can do, which in due time may lead to the desired changes in your self-image and reputation.

How Well Do You Take Criticism?

Recall a recent instance in which you were criticized for something. How well did you take it? Did you react defensively, as if you were being attacked personally? Or did you try to look beyond the surface of the criticism to what the other person was trying to tell you?

All things considered, to what extent was this a positive learning experience for you? If you feel secure enough, ask some of your friends, "How well do I take criticism?" You might want to keep a diary of personal criticism, including the date and setting, who criticized you, a summary of the criticism, and some of your thoughts and feelings in response to it.

Toward Greater Self-direction

Although we must possess a reasonable degree of maturity to learn from criticism, most of us readily benefit from love and acceptance. When someone is warm and accepting toward us, listens to us, and genuinely tries to understand our feelings, we feel freer to explore ourselves and become open to change. Such conditions are present in varying degrees in any satisfying relationship such as a close friendship or a good marriage. But they play a more critical role in the insight therapies that foster self-discovery. As Carl Rogers says, "When someone understands how it feels and seems to be me, without wanting to analyze or judge me, then I can blossom and grow in that climate" (Rogers, 1971, p. 90).

Rogers (1980) has found that the client's experience of personal growth and self-revision in psychotherapy tends to follow a general pattern. The early stages of self-revision are usually characterized by a movement away from the "other-directedness" and distorted self-perceptions acquired while growing up. Individuals are busily sorting out aspects of themselves acquired under social pressure or the desire to be accepted. Some self-perceptions are affirmed and strengthened; others are modified or rejected. This may explain the typical negativism of adolescents as well as youth in the process of leaving home. It also accounts for the prevalence of complaints and self-disparagement so often seen in the early phases of psychotherapy.

For example, Pam, a woman in her early 30s, told her therapist how she had tried to be a good wife by giving in to her husband, and how discouraging it had been. Although she had tried to meet his demands, each time he would make another, until it became an endless series of demands. In the process Pam had become overly submissive and resentful toward her husband. She had also built up a great deal of self-hatred. "I don't like myself this way," Pam said. "How can you have any self-respect when you're always giving in to someone? Yet I've always felt this is the way you have to be if you want to be loved. But I just can't live this way any longer." The disdain in her voice made it clear that Pam had already begun moving away from a self-image designed to please other people.

The later stages of self-actualization are characterized by greater self-direction and self-acceptance. Individuals become more open to and trusting of their own experience. As they come to accept themselves more fully, they are more accepting of others. And most importantly, as individuals strive to discover themselves, they become more willing to accept themselves as a process of becoming.

First, individuals become more open to their own experience. They become more aware of and comfortable with the complexity of their feelings. They may feel love and hatred toward the same person. Or they may feel excited and fearful about their new job. In both instances, they become more trusting of their own experience and find it a suitable source for discovering the most satisfying behavior in each immediate situation. For example, a young woman considering marriage may ask herself, "Is this the man I want as my partner in love?" As long as she feels she must justify the decision of marriage, she may see only the good qualities in her prospective mate. Greater openness

Mothers returning to school tend to be self-directed people. (Laimute E. Druskis)

to her experience would indicate that he has faults as well. The more open the young woman is to the full range of her feelings, the more she can weigh all the pros and cons of such a choice. A mistaken choice might be made. But because there is greater openness to her experience, a quicker correction can also be made. The important point is that she is choosing out of the richness of her own experience rather than out of a sense of obligation or from seeking the approval of others.

Second, as individuals accept themselves more fully they become more accepting of others. This is a reversal of self-alienation. That is, when we fail to acknowledge or accept certain aspects of ourselves, we feel these qualities are foreign to us and we project them onto others whom we then dislike. Thus, the man who appears to be strong and self-sufficient, while denying his own dependency needs, will feel contempt for men who allow themselves to be taken care of when weak. In contrast, a man who, through therapy or a loving relationship, recognizes within himself the existence of dependency needs alongside those of adequacy and self-confidence, may be more accepting of men who exhibit their need for others. Affirming the complexity of feelings and needs within himself, he can appreciate a wider variety of people as well as the inconsistency they display in different situations.

Finally, there is a greater willingness to affirm one's self as a process of becoming. People enter therapy hoping to achieve some fixed state in which their problems will be resolved, they will be more successful in their careers, or their marriages will be more satisfying. It is usually a sign of progress when clients drop such fixed goals and accept a more satisfying realization that they are not a fixed entity but a process of becoming. They come to appreciate that change is the one true constant in life, and that the good life is more of a direction than a destination. People who are actualizing themselves to a high degree learn to live more in the present moment. They enjoy the richness and complexity, even the inconsistency, of life as it is, using their aspirations more as guideposts than as fixed points.

Summary

What Is the Self-concept?

1. The self-concept is the overall image or awareness we have of ourselves. It includes all those perceptions of "I" and "me," together with the feelings, beliefs, and values associated with them.

2. The subjective self is the self I see myself to be.

3. The ideal self is composed of our aspirations, moral ideals, and values.

4. Because these various selves exhibit a certain consistency or organizing pattern as a whole, we refer to them collectively as the self-concept.

Characteristics of the Self-concept

5. Once formed, our self-concepts tend to perpetuate themselves as they are. Experiences that are not consistent with the self-concept tend to be distorted or denied to awareness.

6. The tendency to think and act in a self-consistent manner is also strengthened by our self-esteem—the personal judgment we make about our own worth.

7. Self-efficacy, or the sense of personal mastery, is a collection of self-evaluations not unlike self-esteem, but it depends primarily on specific situations and thus may be enhanced through learning and improved performance.

Self and Personal Growth

8. Since the many selves that make up our self-concept are in a state of flux or change, they are influenced by our current experience, so that we continue to grow in our understanding of ourselves.

9. We may improve our social selves—the impressions we think others have of us—by changing the type of people we associate with, especially seeking out those who accept and affirm what we like about ourselves.

10. We may use personal criticism for growth by taking it as an opportunity to learn about ourselves and take positive steps to put the needed changes into action.

11. Ultimately, personal growth entails becoming a more self-directed person so that we are more open to our own experience and values. And the more we accept ourselves, the more accepting we become of others.

Self-test

1. Which "self" includes all those perceptions of "I" and "me" together with the feelings, beliefs, and values associated with them?

a. ideal self

b. self-concept

c. the super ego

d. unconscious self

2. The subjective self is:

a. the way I see myself

b. entirely unconscious

c. unaffected by experience

d. all of the above

3. Our ideal self:

a. should be unattainable

b. is easier to change than our subjective self

c. should be modified when unrealistically high

d. does not affect our self-esteem

4. Experiences that are not consistent with our self-concept tend to be:

a. distorted

b. denied to awareness

c. inaccurately labeled

d. all of the above

5. What kind of people tend to expect the worst, exert less effort in their jobs, and achieve less success in their careers?

a. perfectionist

b. happy

c. low-esteem

d. introverted

6. Self-efficacy is best thought of as a:

a. global self-esteem

b. collection of specific self-evaluations

c. defense mechanism

d. cluster of personal goals

7. People who score high on measures of public self-consciousness are generally:

a. concerned about what others think of them

b. more neurotic than the average person

c. very much aware of their personal feelings

d. afraid to speak in public

8. A good way of handling personal criticism is to regard it as a:

a. need for immediate change on your part

b. signal for defending yourself

c. cue that may require action

d. reflection of another person's shortcomings

9. During the early stages of psychotherapy, clients generally express feelings of:

a. greater self-direction

b. self-disparagement

c. greater self-acceptance

d. self-reliance

10. When we fail to acknowledge certain qualities within ourselves, we:

   a. feel they are foreign to us

   b. project them onto others whom we then dislike

   c. become alienated from ourselves

   d. all of the above

Exercises

1. *Who am I?* Write down twenty answers to this question as spontaneously and quickly as you can. Then go back and examine your responses. How many of them reflect a social identity, such as "I am a student." How many describe yourself in a more personal way, such as "I'm a loving person?" You might reread the boxed item describing Zurcher's studies of the mutable self in order to better understand your responses.

2. *Self-esteem.* Our sense of personal worth fluctuates somewhat from one situation to another. Think of several situations or occasions in which you usually feel good about yourself and exhibit a lot of self-confidence. Then think of several situations in which you feel unsure of yourself or inferior. Can you identify the people or demands that make you feel good or bad about yourself? What are some practical steps you can take to improve your self-esteem?

3. *Identifying your social selves.* We have as many social selves, as William James observed, as there are people whose opinion we care about. Select five or six people you associate with regularly. Then identify which aspects of yourself are most readily expressed when you're with these people. Jot down some of the shared interests, typical activities, and your feelings and attitudes toward that person. Would you agree that you feel and behave somewhat differently with different people?

4. *How well do you take criticism?* Select an instance when someone criticized you and describe your experience in a page or so. Did you interpret the person's remarks as a personal attack? Or did you try to look beyond the surface of the criticism to what the person was trying to tell you? Looking back, to what extent was this a positive learning experience for you? Jot down some suggestions that will help you to benefit from personal criticism in the future.

5. *Self and ideal.* This is a exercise to measure the correspondence between your subjective self and your ideal self.

   Reproduce the items on the next page on a separate sheet, and cut out the sixteen cards or rectangles as indicated by the lines. Shuffle the cards. Then put them on a table or desk in random order.

   First, get a profile of your subjective self or the self you see yourself to be. To do this, arrange the cards in a line, either from top to bottom or left to right. At one end, place the statement that you think describes you best. At the other end, place the statement that you think is the least like you. Arrange the remaining cards in between, ranging from the most true to the least true. Write down the order of the cards as you have arranged them—for example, 1 (C), 2 (A), etc.

   Next, get a profile of your ideal self. Reshuffle the cards and place them in front of you again. But this time arrange the cards in the order that describes the self you'd like to be. Put the statement that you wish were most true of you at one end, and the one you wish were the least true of you at the other end. Arrange the remaining cards in between as described above. When you've completed the pattern, record the order of the cards as you did earlier.

I'm a likable person **A**	I have sex appeal **I**
I'm rather self-centered at times **B**	I'm an anxious person **J**
I'm physically attractive **C**	I have above-average intelligence **K**
I have a strong need for approval **D**	I'm shy in groups **L**
I'm usually a hard worker **E**	I have a good sense of humor **M**
I daydream too much **F**	I'm sometimes dishonest **N**
I can be assertive when necessary **G**	I have a good disposition **O**
I often feel discouraged **H**	I gossip a lot **P**

To find the correspondence between your self-image and your ideal self, note the difference in the rank of each card. For example, if the card A was ranked 8 on your self-image and 2 on your ideal self, the difference would be 6. Do this for each card. Then total the differences. A score in the range of 50 would be about average. A difference lower than 30 indicates a high correspondence between your self-image and your ideal self. A score of more than 80 indicates a rather low correspondence between your self and ideal. However, a high score doesn't necessarily mean you have problems in this area. Remember, this is an exercise, not a test.

Write a page or so commenting on the items on which you scored the highest discrepancies between your self and your ideal. What would you conclude about your self-concept?

Questions for Self-reflection

1. How would you describe your self-image?

2. Which aspects of your self-concept would you like to change?

3. Do you basically like yourself?

4. Are you more self-confident in some situations than others?

5. Are you aware of how others see you?

6. When you've accepted some quality within yourself, are you more accepting of this in others?

7. How well do you take personal criticism?

8. What do you say when complimented by others?

9. Are you aware that self-actualization is a direction rather than a destination?

10. Do you tend to trust your own experience?

Recommended Readings

Branden, Nathaniel. *Honoring the Self.* Los Angeles: Jeremy P. Tarcher, Inc., 1984. A psychologist explains how we achieve self-esteem, why it's so often lost, and how it may be recovered.

Smedes, Lewis B. *Forgive and Forget.* New York: Harper & Row, 1984. A reflective book aimed at facilitating the process of self-forgiveness.

Snyder, C. F., R. L. Higgins, and R. J. Stucky. *Excuses.* New York: John Wlley, 1983. An in-depth view of excuse making, including its pros and cons.

Snyder, C. R., and Howard Fromkin. *Uniqueness.* New York: Plenum Press, 1980. A description of the myriad ways in which individuals strive for the optimal balance between uniqueness and sameness in relation to others.

Snyder, Mark. "Self-monitoring processes." In *Advances in Experimental Social Psychology,* vol. 12, Leonard Berkowitz, ed. New York: Academic Press, 1979. A view of self-awareness and impression management, relating the self-concept and social roles.

Weisinger, Hendrie, and Norman Lobsenz. *Nobody's Perfect.* New York: Warner Books, 1981 (paperback). Guidelines for giving and receiving criticism constructively.

8 Meeting People, Making Friends

Suppose you're a single man sitting at a bar. You see an attractive woman seated nearby with a female friend. You'd like to meet her. But how? If you wait for a suitable occasion, it might never happen. Instead, if you're like a growing number of people in our mobile society, you're likely to take the initiative and introduce yourself.

Some men who fear being rejected use flippant lines, such as "Your place or mine?" or clichés such as "Haven't we met somewhere before?" Yet most women are put off by these opening lines. When both sexes are questioned on the subject, they overwhelmingly prefer a more tactful but straightforward approach, such as "I don't think I've had the pleasure of meeting you," or "Hi, my name is so-and-so."

Women are also more willing to take the initiative in meeting men than in the past. In some cases, women may introduce themselves first, especially while socializing in a mixed group. In other cases, they may arrange for an introduction through a mutual friend.

MEETING PEOPLE

Singles have a special interest in meeting new people, especially those of the opposite sex. Today, there are over 50 million single adults over 18 years of age, most of them under 40. As a result, a variety of new organizations are springing up to help these people meet each other. The primary purpose of some of these endeavors is to introduce singles; these organizations include singles magazines, matchmaking agencies, and singles bars. Other agencies focus more on a common interest or activity with the side benefit of meeting new people; these agencies often include single and married people alike. Examples are adult education classes, physical fitness centers, and organizations for single parents. Most singles prefer the latter type of setting in which they can get to know each other in a more relaxed fashion while they learn something of special interest.

Even before people meet personally, they begin forming impressions of each other, often on the basis of physical stereotypes. So we'll begin by taking a look at how people perceive others, and by exploring some of the reasons for their mistaken impressions. In subsequent sections, we'll discuss the factors that attract people to each other, the importance of friendship, and why friends stay together or break up.

First Impressions

You're seated in your car, waiting for the traffic light to change. Two young women are crossing the street. As they walk by you can't help but wonder about them. Who are they? What are they like? Where are they going? The light changes, and you drive off. You've seen these two people for about 20 seconds; you know nothing about them but what you've seen. But notice how you've already formed a definite impression of them. All of us do this. But why?

Perhaps we're curious. We're intrigued by the unknown. Another reason has to do with anxiety and the need for understanding people around us, especially if we think we may have to respond to them. Furthermore, the more fearful we are about people, the more likely we are to misjudge them. Whatever the reasons, the basic principle of person perception is this: we tend to form extensive impressions of others on the basis of very little information.

A person's physical appearance makes a strong impression on us. Someone's height, weight, sex, facial features, and dress all affect our senses and feelings. We're influenced a lot by a person's physical attractiveness. The more physically attractive someone is, the more positively we judge that person. When people have been asked to give their impressions of others, they attribute all sorts of positive qualities to attractive people. Many of these qualities have little or nothing to do with a person's physical appearance. Attractive people are judged to be more interesting, intelligent, compassionate, and sociable than less attractive people. They are regarded as more successful in their careers and

A person's physical appearance makes a strong impression on us. (Laimute E. Druskis)

happy in their personal lives. Physical attractiveness is also associated with such diverse accomplishments as getting good grades, better jobs, and faster promotions, as well as having less serious psychological disorders than others. But, we're not always so favorably impressed. Handsome men and beautiful women are apt to be viewed as more egotistical and less sincere and concerned about others. As a result, they are often rejected by their same-sex peers, partly because of jealousy.

On the other hand, people we regard as physically unattractive may be judged unfavorably. Like beauty, ugliness is mostly in the eye of the beholder. For some, fatness or homely facial features may qualify. For others, irregular features such as a large nose, discolored skin, or a physical handicap makes for ugliness. Whatever the reason, unattractive people may be discriminated against for no good reason. One young man who was confined to a wheelchair since an automobile accident, observed, "Even when people hold the door open for me, they avoid touching me or looking me in the eye." Yet, those who've gotten to know this man look past his handicap at the person himself.

Someone's reputation also affects our impression of that person. A friend says, "I can't wait for you to meet Ann." Chances are you will like her. Even before you meet Ann, you'll probably find yourself forming a positive image of her based on what your friend tells you. Should you later discover Ann has some unfavorable qualities your friend didn't tell you, chances are you'll give her the benefit of the doubt. Of course, it works the other way too. If someone says, "I hear Professor Johnson is a terrible teacher," you may find yourself forming a negative impression of that teacher, rightly or wrongly. Such is the power of reputation.

Once we begin interacting with people, what they say and do affects our judgment of them. Do they act the way we expect them to? Is this consistent with their past behavior in similar situations? What do others think about them? All these factors influence our impressions of others. We also pay a lot of attention to how they express themselves. People who are confident and well-spoken make a more favorable impression on us than those who are unsure of themselves and less articulate. People who talk a lot are more apt to be chosen as leaders in a group, especially if they know what they're talking about. Otherwise, they may appear domineering or rude. We tend to like people who are friendly and talkative, at least up to a point. Women who talk up to three-fourths of the time in a conversation may be seen as more friendly, intelligent, and outgoing than less talkative women. Yet, men who talk this much don't usually fare so well. Men who talk a lot may be regarded as inconsiderate and domineering. Perhaps talkative men also contradict the stereotype of the "strong silent male." (Kleinke, 1975).

People who smile and look us in the eye make a favorable impression on us. (A.T.&T. Co. Photo Center)

Our impressions of others are also shaped by a variety of nonverbal signals. A person's posture, facial expressions, and gestures definitely affect our impressions. Those who sit or stand erect while talking to us make a more favorable impression than those who slouch in their chairs. Also, people who point, glare, and interrupt a lot make a more negative impression than those who are attentive to what we say. Generally, we are more favorably impressed with people who smile and look us in the eye. People who make eye contact with us are apt to be seen as more trustworthy and likable. Those who avoid our gaze may strike us less favorably, whether from shyness or deceit.

Mistaken Impressions

The biggest single reason we misjudge others is the lack of sufficient information about them. Nor should this be surprising, given our tendency to "size up" people so hastily. We often get the wrong impression of others because of false cues, stereotypes, global judgments, and by underestimating the importance of their circumstances.

False cues consist of various signals and indirect suggestions that unconsciously trigger certain associations in our minds. Signs of money and status are often misleading, especially to the unsuspecting. Because people who are successful and financially well-off often live in large, impressive houses and drive expensive cars, we may assume, mistakenly, that anyone who indulges in expensive cars and clothes is rich. Realizing this, some unscrupulous individuals deliberately take prestigious addresses and entertain at lavish parties to impress others. One man and his wife, who were living on Social Security at the time, transformed themselves into jet-setters by displaying the signs of wealth. They let it be known that they were soon to inherit millions from a rich uncle. Then they ran up huge charge accounts against their anticipated fortune. In due time, however, their unpaid creditors became suspicious and the couple was brought to justice. Because this couple *acted* rich, most people assumed they were.

We also misjudge people because of stereotypes—widespread generalizations that have little, if any, basis in fact. Whenever people begin statements with such phrases as "all teachers" or "all women drivers," they're slipping into stereotypic thinking. A similiar stereotype is that people who wear glasses are smarter than those who don't. The unspoken assumption is that such people need glasses because they've strained their eyes so much from reading. The truth of the matter is that the need for glasses depends more on hereditary weakness than it does on one's study habits. Here are some other stereotypes. Men with beards, mustaches, and an abundance of body hair are regarded as more masculine and virile than those with less hair. Brunette women are seen as being more intelligent and responsible than blondes—the latter as being more fun and sexier than brunettes. Redheads of both sexes are seen as being more "hot-tempered" than people with other hair colors. Do you sometimes feel misunderstood because of stereotypes? If so, which ones?

We also tend to label people good or bad because they possess a few good or bad characteristics. This is called the *halo* or *devil effect*. In the former case, it's as if the person we like wears a halo (ring of light) over his or her head, like an angel, and can do no wrong. We're especially likely to do this in regard to such

---

Personal Ads

Personal ads are no longer relegated to underground newspapers and sex magazines. Today, they are a booming business and run in over 100 newspapers and magazines. Personal ads have become a popular and reputable way of meeting people in our mobile, urban society.

Composing an ad with one's self as the product is itself an interesting exercise, requiring a blend of self-confidence and humor. Interpreting these ads is equally demanding. One must first decipher the codes used, such as DWF (divorced white female) and SBM (single black male). Then too, one must make due allowance for exaggeration. For instance, "slim" and "attractive" are not taken literally. Similarly, "sensuous" is likely to mean sexual; "discrete" often implies a married person seeking an affair. Humor almost always helps. On the other hand, words like "sincere" are often counterproductive. If you write "Sincere young woman 32 would like to meet sincere man," you're apt to receive a dozen boring letters (Foxman, 1983).

The more responses the ad draws, the more choices the advertiser has of various types of people to meet. Thus, the greater the ad's success. In one simple study, Jeff Rubin (Raven and Rubin, 1983) found that the most successful ads generally highlighted the author's needs and trust of the reader, did not stress the importance of the reader's qualities, and/or were placed by women. One of the most successful ads was the following:

> Lonely WF, 22, seeks WM 22–28 for companionship, dating, fun times, and possible love making. No promises of deep involvement. Sincerity necessary. Please write. I need you.

In contrast, most unsuccessful ads imposed various demands or restrictions on the reader and emphasized the services that the author would provide rather than what the author needed. The following ad yielded no response at all:

> Complete satisfaction and gratification guaranteed by experienced WM. Discretion assured! By appointment only, of course, because of the tremendous demand for my services. Big, medium to heavy, strong sexy women preferred, and all of their demands will be completely met.

Perhaps the biggest surprise of all is that many of the ads reflect traditional values. It seems that many people are seeking romance, love, and long-term relationships, rather than sex (Morrow, 1985).

important qualities as warmth and sociableness. When we regard people as warm and outgoing, we're apt to attribute all sorts of other positive qualities to them, such as intelligence and industriousness. Conversely, if we see others as cold and withdrawn we tend to attribute other negative qualities to them as well. In reality, of course, few individuals are all good or all bad. Instead, it's well to bear in mind that each of us is a complex mixture of traits, some desirable and others not so desirable.

We frequently misjudge people by not taking sufficient account of the situational influences on their behavior. That is, we assume people are always acting in character, so to speak. Yet, if the truth were known, people are often constricted by their immediate circumstances. For example, I recall a young man who constantly yawned and looked sleepy in class. I got the impression he was bored with the course. Later, when I discovered he worked in a manual labor job from midnight to 7 A.M., I realized he had good reason for his sleepy appearance in class. To avoid misjudging people, we must take account of the powerful and changing influences of their situation. This is also why it is wise to observe someone in a variety of different situations across time in order to know what that person is really like.

Shyness

"Everyone but me was having such a good time laughing and talking," said Diane. "My boyfriend was moving around the room greeting friends. And there I was trying to think of something to say to this woman I was talking to. She must have felt sorry for me. I couldn't wait until the party was over."

This sounds familiar, doesn't it? Shyness—the tendency to avoid contact or familiarity with others—afflicts people of all ages, but especially the young. According to a study of shyness by Philip Zimbardo (1977) and his colleagues, about 40 percent of American college students label themselves as "currently shy." Another 40 percent say they used to be shy, but have outgrown it. In addition, about 15 percent of the students are "situationally shy." That is, they feel shy only in certain situations, such as on blind dates, giving speeches, and talking with people in positions of authority. Contrary to the myth of the shy female, men and women reported shyness with equal frequency.

Shyness means different things for different people and covers a wide range of feelings and behaviors. At one end of the spectrum are those who are not especially apprehensive about meeting people when necessary. But most of the time they prefer being alone, being in nature, or working with ideas or things rather than people. In the middle range are those who are easily embarrassed, lack self-confidence and social skills. Such individuals hesitate to ask for a date or a favor from others. At the other extreme are individuals whose shyness has become a neurotic self-imprisonment. These people judge themselves with impossible rules that result in avoiding unfamiliar people and situations, thus minimizing the possibility of rejection.

Almost all of us tend to be shy in some situations, such as meeting strangers, dealing with people of the opposite sex, and being in large groups. But people who are habitually shy are different: they see shyness as something within themselves, that is, as a personal trait. Yet they dislike being shy. Shyness also creates many problems for them, including feeling lonely, overly self-conscious, and unassertive, as well as having difficulty making friends. Shy people are also often misunderstood by others. They are apt to be regarded as aloof, condescending, emotionally "cold" and disinterested. (See Table 8–1.)

Table 8–1. THE EXPERIENCE OF SHYNESS.

Thoughts and feelings	Percent of shy people
Self-consciousness	85
Concern for impression management	67
Concern for social evaluation	63
Negative self-evaluation	59
Thoughts about unpleasantness of the situation	56
Physiological reactions	
Increased pulse	54
Blushing	53
Perspiration	49
Butterflies in stomach	48
Heart pounding	48
Overt behavior	
Silence	80
Lack of eye contact	51
Avoiding others	44
Not taking action	42
Speaking in low voice	40

Adapted from *The Silent Prison of Shyness*, Phil Zimbardo, Paul Pilkonis, and Robert Norwood (Glenview, IL: Scott, Foresman College Division, 1974), p. 12.

If you or someone you know suffers from shyness, consider the following suggestions. First and foremost, strive to reduce the inner monitoring of your thoughts, feelings, and actions, especially the concern for how people see you. Instead, focus on your participation in the activities around you and with the people around you. Second, identify those aspects of situations that elicit shyness, such as meeting new people, as well as the social skills that may be lacking. Third, develop your social skills, such as how to initiate and carry on a conversation and how to assert yourself. Fourth, keep in mind that shyness subsides when you step out of your usual identity, as in role-playing, or when you become totally absorbed in something, or when you are helping others. Fifth, if shyness has become too disabling, seek counseling or therapy. One young woman said, "I was so shy I couldn't even tell the guy I was going with how I felt about him." After counseling she was considerably less shy. Finally, remember that shyness is widespread. When a stranger at a party doesn't look at you or speak to you, why not introduce yourself? If you feel up to it, for an entire day make it a point to say "Hi" or "Hello" to everyone you meet. See what response you get. You may be pleasantly surprised.

WHAT ATTRACTS US?

Think back to how you met your friends. Can you recall what attracted you to each other? Frequently we're attracted to people with whom we have a lot in common. We may be interested in the same career goals or taking the same course. In some instances, we're attracted to people who are different from us: perhaps they complement us in some way. Of course, a person's physical attractiveness also makes a difference, especially in the attraction between men and women. Then too, a lot depends on the "chemistry" or subjective factors when people meet. We seem to get along with some people better than others almost from the start.

Interaction and Liking

Chances are that at some time your friends lived nearby, attended the same school, or worked at the same place. Nearness is especially important in the early stages of attraction. First, the more you come into contact with people the more opportunities you have for getting to know them better. There's also a strong association between interaction and liking. That is, the more you get to know someone, the more you like that person. And it works the other way, too: the more you like someone, the more you associate with him or her. We also tend to emphasize the positive qualities and minimize the negative qualities of people we associate with every day. Otherwise, if you feel you're stuck with an unpleasant coworker or roommate, you may feel a lot of resentment. Then too, social norms imply cooperative relationships with others, so that we make a special effort to get along with people we live or work with. Otherwise, life might be miserable.

If it's true that the more you associate with someone, the more you like that person, then the longer couples are married the happier they should be—right? Since this is obviously not the case for many couples, other factors, such as compatibility, are involved. As a result, when there are serious differences or basic incompatibilities between two individuals, close contact may lead to overt conflict, resentment, and alienation. In such cases, "familiarity breeds contempt." It is well known among those who work with people that in assault and murder cases, the leading suspects are likely to be lovers, spouses, or ex-spouses.

Physical Attractiveness

We're warned "don't judge a book by its cover." But when it comes to physical attractiveness, we do anyway, don't we? There's a wealth of evidence suggesting that we find people, especially those of the opposite sex, more attractive and likeable when they resemble the cultural standards of beauty. Traditionally—and unfairly—it has been considered more important for women to be physically attractive than men, as seen in a sexist ad by a dating service inviting applications from *attractive* women and *successful* men. Yet, many women will admit that physical attractiveness is also important in a man as well. This was brought out in a study in which college students kept careful records of every social interaction of 10 minutes or more during several 10-day periods throughout the college year. The results showed that the relationship between physical attractiveness and the amount of social interaction was more significant for men than for women. The most likely explanation is that attractive men are more assertive in meeting women, have had more successful experiences with them, and thus are more apt to approach women than less attractive men. Because of cultural conditioning, many women may be less likely to initiate opposite-sex relationships. Furthermore, men may fear rejection from beautiful women and may look for partners among women with moderate attractiveness (Reis, et al., 1982).

The adage that "beauty is in the eye of the beholder" suggests that physical attractiveness is partly subjective. Thus, you may not find my partner as attractive as I do, and vice versa. Then too, the norms of attractiveness differ somewhat between the sexes, such that a woman considered attractive by men may not be so regarded by other women. Nevertheless, there are certain notions in each culture that make for attractiveness. In Western society, women often prefer men who are tall, have broad shoulders, thin waists and legs, and small, tight buttocks. Men prefer women who are shorter than themselves, somewhat slim, with medium-sized breasts, legs, and buttocks (Baron and Byrne, 1984). In regard to the face, women often show a preference for men with strong facial features such as a jutting chin and beard; men are more apt to be attracted to women with large eyes and rounded features, such as a small nose and chin (Cunningham, 1981).

As you look around, it is obvious that few people of either sex possess such an ideal face or figure. Most of us have some attractive features as well as others we'd like to change. At the same time, each of us manages to modify the cultural expectations regarding physical attractiveness to fit ourselves and our partners. For example, the better we like someone, the more we modify our subjective evaluation of that person's physical attractiveness. Thus, you may find someone attractive regardless of others' opinions. Because beauty is partly, at least, in the eye of the beholder, there are many people in the world who would probably consider each one of us highly attractive, which is a good thing to keep in mind.

Each of us might fantasize about having a highly attractive opposite sex partner. But when it comes to choosing a date or romantic partner, we usually settle for someone like ourselves, at least in regard to physical attractiveness. This tendency has been labeled the matching hypothesis. For example, sixty-seven couples who were introduced by a dating service in Los Angeles were later judged in terms of their attractiveness and romantic attachment. Not surprisingly, there was a positive association between the similarity of physical attractiveness and increasingly deeper romantic involvement (Folkes, 1982). The same principle has been observed among married couples, with the similarity of attractiveness being greater than would be expected by chance (Price and Vandenberg, 1979). If you're going steady with someone or are married, to what degree does the matching hypothesis apply to your relationship? Can you think of couples who are exceptions to this rule? All things considered, how important do you think physical attractiveness is in love and marriage?

Likes or Opposites?

"Birds of a feather flock together," said Aristotle, suggesting that we're attracted to people like ourselves. Indeed, there has been a great deal of empiri-

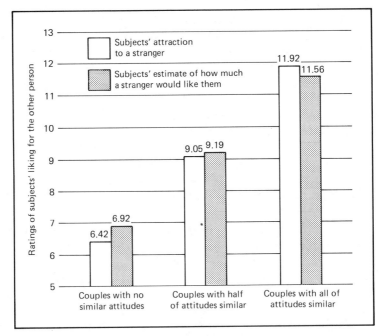

Figure 8–1. ATTITUDE SIMILARITY AND ATTRACTION.   The above ratings were a sum of two 7-point scales indicating subjects' liking for and desire to work with the other person.

From M.H. Gonzales, J.M. Davis, G.L. Loney, C.K. Lukens, and C.M. Junghans, "Interactional approach to interpersonal attraction," *Journal of Personality and Social Psychology*, 1983, 44, 1192-1197. Copyright © 1983 by the American Psychological Association. Reprinted by permission of the publisher and author.

cal support for this notion, especially in regard to attitudes, values, and social characteristics such as educational level. One result is Byrne's *law of attraction*, which states that we're attracted to people directly according to the proportion of similar attitudes shared (Clore and Byrne, 1974). For example, Linda and Tom share attitudes toward school, dating, and politics. But they disagree on matters such as beer drinking, sex, and religion. The proportion of similar attitudes here is 50 percent, though the number of items is three. Yet, they would like each other less than another couple sharing similar attitudes in just two areas but disagreeing on only one. In the latter case, the couple agrees in 66 percent of attitudes, though the number of items is only two. That is, it is the *proportion* of shared attitudes rather than the absolute number of them, that makes for attraction. For instance, one study of attitude similarity and attraction compared couples with no attitudes in common, similarity in half of their attitudes, and similarity in all of their attitudes. As expected, the results showed that the attraction between partners increased directly according to the proportion of their similar attitudes (Gonzales, et al., 1983). (See Figure 8–1.)

There is less agreement about the importance of similarity in attraction when it comes to needs and personal traits. According to one view, people with similar needs and personalities are attracted to each other; the other view is that people who are complementary (opposite but compatible) in their needs and traits are attracted. Actually, the theory of complementarity needs tends to

We tend to be attracted to individuals who are distinctive in some way. (Charles Gatewood)

apply mostly in regard to specific traits rather than to the meshing of two personalities as a whole. That is, a talkative person may become attracted to someone who is quiet; a dominant individual might seek out a more dependent partner. Also, complementarity probably isn't important in the early stages of attraction, though it may become more important in a long-term relationship like marriage. Nevertheless, even among married couples, the weight of evidence seems to favor similarity. For example, a study of 108 married couples showed that couples with similar needs experienced greater marital happiness and adjustment than those with dissimilar needs (Antill, 1983).

BECOMING FRIENDS

The more we get to know someone, especially when we're mutually attracted, the more likely our relationship will ripen into a friendship—the affectionate attachment between two or more people. We usually think of a friend as someone we've known a long time, which is often true. Yet, friendship has more to do with the quality of the relationship than the frequency of association. Friendships provide a warmth and closeness that is often missing in daily transactions. As society becomes more complex and mobile, and thus more impersonal, we cherish close friendships all the more.

We select our friends from a wide diversity of people, according to a *Psychology Today* survey on the subject. The results of this survey are helpful in that it includes a large proportion of young adults, from the late teens through the 40s, as well as singles and married people. About half (47 percent) of these people have close friends from a different ethnic or religious background. Almost as many (38 percent) report having close friends of a different racial group. Many individuals also report having close friends of the opposite sex, though a slight majority (55 percent) say most of their friends are of the same sex. Almost everyone thinks it's possible to be friends with your parents, children, coworkers, bosses, and neighbors (Parlee, et al., 1979).

When Friends Get Together

Not surprisingly, one of the most common activities among friends is having an intimate talk. This is the most or second-most frequently mentioned activity by both men and women in the *Psychology Today* survey. (See Table 8–2.) You may call up a friend to tell her about an incident that happened to you at work. Or your friend may want to talk about the trouble he's having with his girlfriend or wife. In both instances, sharing your feelings and getting someone else's reaction on the subject may be extremely helpful. Another frequently mentioned activity, especially for men, is doing a favor for a friend. Perhaps you'll ask your friend to write a letter of reference for you. Or your friend may want you to witness a legal document for her. Asking or doing a favor for some-

Table 8–2. WHAT FRIENDS DO TOGETHER. Respondents in the *Psychology Today* Survey on Friendship were asked, "Have you done the following with friends in the past month?" The first column shows the percentage of men and women who said they had done an activity; the second shows the ranking of that activity for each sex.

Women	Men		Women	Men
90	78	Had an intimate talk	1	2
84	80	Had a friend ask you for a favor	2	1
84	77	Gone to dinner in a restaurant	3	3
80	75	Asked your friend to do a favor for you	4	4
75	70	Had a meal at home or at your friend's	5	5
67	64	Gone to a movie, play or concert	6	6
62	64	Gone drinking together	7	7
62	49	Went shopping	8	10
45	55	Participated in sports	9	8
41	53	Watched a sporting event	10	9
38	41	Quarreled	11	11
36	32	Attended a meeting of an organization you both belong to	12	14
34	40	Smoked pot together	13	12
30	32	Had sexual intercourse	14	13
24	19	Done something with your children	15	16
22	30	Conducted a business transaction	16	15
16	15	Taken a vacation together	17	17

Source: Mary Brown Parlee and the editors of *Psychology Today*, "The Friendship Bond," *Psychology Today*, October 1979, p. 53. Reprinted with permission from *Psychology Today* Magazine. Copyright © 1979 American Psychological Association.

one else presupposes a great deal of trust as well as give and take in a relationship, both important qualities of friendship.

One of the greatest favors friends can do for each other is to lend a listening ear. Sometimes a casual friend becomes a close friend because that person listens sympathetically to some personal problem of yours. Faced with such crises, many people will turn to a friend before talking about it with their families. A friend may serve as a sounding board and provide needed support without the conflict of kinship loyalties. Do you have friends you could turn to in a personal crisis? If so, who are they? At the same time, people who ask their friends to share serious problems that are more properly discussed with a professional may be asking too much of their friends. In these instances, it's often best to refer your friend to the appropriate help, while remaining supportive.

Mutual Self-disclosure

As the relationship between two people changes from strangers to acquaintances to close friends, individuals disclose a greater breadth and depth of information about themselves (Altman, 1975). For example, Connie and Marybeth shared an apartment during summer school. At the beginning of the semester, they talked about familiar topics such as their courses, teachers, and food preferences, including one intimate topic, namely, their feelings about their boyfriends. By the end of the summer they felt comfortable talking about a greater variety of subjects, such as their career goals, clothes preferences, leisure activities, and more intimate matters such as health concerns, parents, religious beliefs, and sexual experiences. As Connie and Marybeth became good friends, they developed greater trust in each other and shared matters that might threaten a weaker relationship. On one occasion, Connie told how she and another 17-year-old had lied about their ages, gone to a singles bar, and then left with two men. When the men offered them drugs, they panicked and escaped through a bedroom window, all of which Connie had never told her parents.

Increasing levels of self-disclosure do not always lead to greater intimacy between two people. Ordinarily, the more you disclose about yourself the more your friend will do likewise. Otherwise, your friend would hold a power advantage over you, knowing intimate details about you not ordinarily shared with others. However, if your friend does not feel sufficiently comfortable or trustful in the relationship, he or she would not reciprocate in such intimate self-disclosure. Eventually, you'd back off and restrict your communication to more superficial matters. In other instances, someone may share information that presents a conflict in the relationship, such that both partners may retreat to more superficial levels of sharing. For example, a young man in his late 30s told his wife about a brief sexual affair he'd had while out of town on business a few months earlier. He reassured his wife that he felt no affection for this other woman and promised never to see her again. The young man also said he felt better for having shared this affair with her and hoped it would bring them closer together. He was wrong. His wife became extremely resentful and suspicious. Ever since then, she has doubted that he loves her and is worried about what he's doing while he's out of town. Both partners have become more guarded, with a reversal of intimacy occurring.

In some cases, because of shared intimacy and self-disclosure, former close friends and lovers may agree to remain just friends. In other cases, especially with ex-spouses, both partners may want nothing more to do with each other.

Individuals also differ in their willingness to share personal information for several reasons. Those who enjoy high self-esteem not only feel more comfortable sharing personal information about themselves but feel greater security that comes with close relationships. Others with low esteem are more apt to withhold personal information and thereby fail to learn about themselves through closeness with others. Then too, men and women often differ in their willingness to share personal matters. Pairs of women characteristically engage in more intimate disclosure than do pairs of men (Cohn and Strassberg, 1983). Even though many men have become more open and willing to share intimate information about themselves in recent years, men who disclose a lot about themselves tend to be evaluated negatively. In one study, men and women pretended to reveal very intimate details about themselves to strangers. They talked about a parent's suicide, their sex preferences, and their feelings of competitiveness and desires for success. Women who disclosed a lot about themselves in regard to the family suicide and sex preferences were liked much more than women who disclosed less about themselves. In general, though, men who disclosed a lot about themselves to strangers were evaluated negatively. However, neither sex was evaluated positively when talking about competitiveness and success, especially the women. Apparently, it may appear unfeminine to want to compete and succeed (Kleinke and Kahn, 1980).

All things considered, the association between liking and mutual self-disclosure depends a lot on the particular individuals, how compatible they are, and how comfortable they feel sharing intimate matters. Also, with the influence of diminishing sex-role stereotypes, we can expect men to engage in more self-disclosure than has been the case in the past, especially with their friends and lovers.

Intimacy and Growth

Ideally, as two friends or lovers become closer to each other, their relationship deepens in a way that fosters growth in each of them. But this is not always the case, is it? Increasing disclosure may also bring about a greater awareness of differences and conflicts, as evident in the love/hate relationships among lovers. Then too, insecure individuals who are threatened by closeness may become jealous and manipulative toward their partners. Also, one partner may be more emotionally involved than the other in the relationship, with such one-way relationships much more likely to dissolve than those in which both partners are mutually involved.

A related issue has to do with intimacy and sex. Can you be a close friend with someone of the opposite sex without being romantically or sexually involved with this person? Some people remain skeptical about this. But now that men and women are working side by side just about everywhere, more individuals of both sexes are choosing friends of the opposite sex. At the same time, most people feel that opposite-sex friendships are different, in that they may easily turn into erotic relationships. Almost half the respondents in the *Psychology Today* survey had a friendship turn into a sexual relationship. Although this strengthens some friendships, it may jeopardize others. This is especially true when one or both friends are married to someone else. Do you think married people can have friends of the opposite sex? Would you agree that a lot depends on how happily married the couples are? Then too, a lot depends on whether both friends respect the marriage bonds of one or both partners (Parlee, et al., 1979).

One of the most common barriers to healthy intimacy is an excessive sense of dependency on the part of one or both partners. When this is the case, friendship or love relationships may easily turn into "addictive relationships." Like those addicted to alcohol or other drugs, dependent people need increasingly larger doses of affection and reassurance to feel secure in their relationships. Preoccupied with their own relationship, the partners become jealous of outside involvements that would interfere with their own security. They cut themselves off from other friends. John, 32, is going with Valerie, a 28-year-old single parent. They share many interests and have grown closer over the past 6 months. Yet Valerie is concerned about her dependency on John. "At times, I feel like my entire life revolves around John, what he wants and how he feels about me," says Valerie. "I don't feel that's good." Then too, she has grown increasingly uneasy about John's possessiveness. "If I have lunch with my best girlfriend, John starts asking 'What did you two talk about? I don't understand why you want to see her so much.' When John sees me talking with another man at a party, he comes running over to join us, as if he doesn't trust me." Valerie's friends have also noticed John's possessiveness and have warned her about it. Now Valerie is worried about the future of their relationship.

By contrast, healthy intimacy not only makes for a more satisfying relationship but also fosters greater autonomy and growth in each person as well. Feeling accepted and trusted, each partner feels freer to be himself or herself and to keep up other friendships. Outside interests and involvement provide variety to their own friendship or marriage. Also, each person welcomes change in the other as a way of adding vitality and richness to their relationship. Realistically, though, many close relationships are neither addictive nor healthily intimate. Most of our friendships and love relationships fall somewhere in between these two extremes. What about your close friendships or love relationships? Take a few minutes to reflect on your own close relationships and answer the following questions:

How does this relationship affect each of us?

Is each of us free to change and grow?

If lovers, are we also friends?

Does each of us give as well as receive love?

Can we experience closeness without giving up our individuality?

Answers to such questions may help each of us to assess how healthy our close relationships are.

Staying Friends or Breaking Up

"There's no friend like an old friend," goes the time-honored saying. With old friends we can relax and be ourselves without fear of rejection. We're familiar with each other's mannerisms and make allowances for each other's weaknesses. Apparently, most people are fortunate enough to have old friends. According to the *Psychology Today* survey on the subject, more than three-fourths of the respondents reported having friends of 6 years duration or longer. About a fifth of them report having friendships longer than 20 years. Generally, people feel that their friendships have become more important to them as they grow older, though this sentiment is less evident among those with higher income and educational levels (Parlee, et al., 1979).

Staying friends depends more on the special quality of the relationship than the frequency of contact between two people. Most of us have some friends we don't see very often, But we still consider them friends. We may keep in touch by calling up occasionally or exchanging cards or letters. Class reunions and vacations also afford additional opportunities for renewing old ties. At the same time, physical separation often exacts a toll on friendship. When respondents in the *Psychology Today* survey were asked why friendships cool off, the most frequently given reason was that one person had moved away (Parlee, et al., 1979).

Apart from moving away, the most common reason for ending a friendship is feeling betrayed by a friend. Perhaps this shouldn't be surprising, given the importance of trust and the ability to keep confidence in friendship. In another study, about one-third of the people said that their basic expectations in friendship had been violated by a best or close friend. In some instances, there were minor infringements, such as using a personal item without asking permission. But other cases involved more serious offenses, such as "repeating things I said in confidence" or "trying to seduce my wife." In some instances, people still claimed someone as a friend, but with such qualifications as "You have to watch what you tell her, she gossips a lot" or "You just can't trust him" (Davis, 1985).

Friendships may also cool off or break up because the individuals discover they have very different views on matters that are important to them. Not surprisingly, this was the third most frequently cited reason for ending a friendship. Other reasons, in descending order, were: one of us got married, my friend became involved with or married someone I didn't like, my friend borrowed money from me, we took a vacation together, one of us had a child, one of us became more successful at work, one of us got divorced, one of us became much richer, and I borrowed money from my friend. In some cases, increasing intimacy between friends, such as may be occasioned by taking a vacation together, may make them even more aware of their differences. More often than not, though, friends' lives begin moving in different directions, such as getting married or divorced, and they have less in common. But friendship is such a deeply satisfying experience that each of us will continue making new friends throughout life, while cherishing the special closeness that comes with a long-lasting friendship.

Summary

Meeting People

1. In the initial stages of relationships, we form impressions of other people through the process of person perception.

2. We tend to form extensive impressions of others on the basis of limited information, usually judging by such factors as a person's physical appearance, especially his or her attractiveness, speech, and nonverbal behavior.

3. The most common reason we misjudge people is the lack of sufficient information about them. Instead, we usually rely on things like false cues and stereotypes and fail to take into account the situational influences on people's behavior.

4. Shy people, who avert our eye gaze and hesitate to speak up, are often misunderstood as aloof, conceited, and emotionally cold.

What Attracts Us?

5. We're attracted to people for a variety of reasons, usually including such factors as greater familiarity, physical attraction, and similar backgrounds and interests.

6. The more we get to know someone, the more we like that person, unless we discover serious differences or basic incompatibilities between us.

7. We tend to evaluate physically attractive people more favorably than others, even on matters that have little or nothing to do with physical appearance.

8. Although we're generally attracted to people with similar attitudes and interests as ourselves, when it comes to the level of needs and personal traits, we often relate to others on a blend of similarity and complementarity.

Becoming Friends

9. As society becomes more complex, mobile, and impersonal, we value close friendships all the more. At the same time, we're choosing our friends from a wider diversity of people than in the past, including more opposite sex friends.

10. Close friends frequently get together for a good talk and companionship, in addition to sharing a variety of other activities.

11. We're apt to disclose a lot about ourselves with good friends, strengthening the bond of friendship between us in the process.

12. Healthy friendships tend to foster autonomy and growth on the part of each person and involve a minimum of dependency and possessiveness.

13. Staying friends with someone depends more on the special quality of the relationship than the frequency of contact. The most common reasons we break off a friendship is because we feel we've been betrayed or we have grown apart from another person.

Self-test

1. We tend to form extensive impressions of people on the basis of:

    a. their education
    c. their family background
    b. very little information
    d. body language

2. We frequently misjudge people by not taking sufficient account of how their behavior is affected by:

    a. unconscious motives
    c. situational influences
    b. pride
    d. money

3. Which characteristic describes people who are especially apt to be misjudged as aloof and conceited?

    a. intelligent
    c. aggressive
    b. shy
    d. artistic

4. The more you get to know someone, the more you tend to:

    a. criticize that person
    c. like that person
    b. dislike that person
    d. envy that person

5. According to the matching hypothesis, we tend to choose a romantic partner who is similar to ourselves in regard to:

    a. attitudes
    c. family background
    b. personal traits
    d. physical attractiveness

6. According to Byrne's law of attraction, we're attracted to people with whom we share:

    a. similar attitudes
    c. similar IQs
    b. complementary needs
    d. complementary traits

7. One of the most common activities among friends is:

    a. going shopping
    c. having an intimate talk
    b. having sex
    d. taking a vacation

8. There is a strong positive association between mutual self-disclosure and:

    a. liking
    c. intimacy
    b. friendship
    d. all of the above

9. A common barrier to healthy intimacy is the presence in one or both partners of:

    a. undue dependency
    c. a fear of homosexuality
    b. a critical attitude
    d. excessive empathy

10. One of the most frequent reasons friendships break up is that at least one person feels:

    a. exploited
    c. betrayed
    b. overinvolved
    d. inadequate

Exercises

1. *First impressions.* Look around in your classes and select someone you haven't met. Jot down your impressions of this person. Then make it a point to introduce yourself and become better acquainted with this person. To what extent was your initial impression accurate or inaccurate?

2. *Do you ever suffer from shyness?* If so, in which situations? How has shyness affected your life? What steps have you taken to overcome your shyness?

3. *Write a personal ad about yourself.* Suppose you were writing a personal ad for the classified ad section of a magazine devoted to introducing singles. How would you describe yourself? How would you describe the type of person you're looking for? Write a short paragraph for this purpose.

4. *Self-disclosure.* Write a paragraph or two including your thoughts on the following matters: How comfortable do you feel sharing personal information with friends? With whom do you share the most? Which topics? If married, do you share more with your spouse or friends? Would you agree that the rewards of mutual self-disclosure outweigh the risks?

5. *Who can you turn to?* If you were experiencing a personal crisis, who would you turn to for help—your family or friends? Which person would you seek out first? Explain the reasons for your answers.

6. *Intimacy and growth.* Think of a close friendship or love relationship. Then describe your relationship in a page or so, including your thoughts on the following points: Do you both maintain other friendships? If lovers, are you also friends? Can each of you experience closeness without giving up your individuality? To what extent does this relationship encourage each of you to grow as a person?

Questions for Self-reflection

1. How much do you judge by first impressions?
2. Do you make a good first impression on others?
3. Are you ever bothered by shyness?
4. Do you usually find that the more you know someone, the better you like the person?
5. How important are good looks in being attracted to someone of the opposite sex?
6. Do some of your friends have interests and personalities quite different from yours?
7. Who is your best friend?
8. Which people do you feel most comfortable sharing secrets with?
9. Do you have a close friend of the opposite sex?
10. Have you ever been betrayed by a close friend?

Recommended Readings

Burns, David D. M.D. *Intimate Connections.* New York: New American Library, 1985 (paperback). Suggestions for making friends and finding love partners.

Kleinke, C. L. *First Impressions.* Englewood Cliffs, NJ: Prentice-Hall, 1975 (paperback). A discussion of the various factors that influence our initial impressions of other people.

Rubin, Theodore Isaac. *One To One.* New York: Viking, 1983 (paperback). A psychiatrist interprets the nature of one to one relationships.

Rubinstein, C., and P. Shaver. *What It Means To Be Lonely.* New York: Delacorte Press, 1982. An in-depth understanding of loneliness based on the authors' research studies.

Sager, C. J., and B. Hunt. *Intimate Partners.* New York: McGraw-Hill, 1979. A discussion of the hidden patterns in love relationships.

Zimbardo, P. G. *Shyness.* Reading, Mass: Addison-Wesley, 1977 (paperback). An examination of shyness in relation to the cultural forces that produce it, with suggestions for overcoming shyness.

9 Sexuality

If you discovered that your partner or spouse was romantically involved with another person, would you suspect the motive would be love or sex? Gregory White (1981) posed such a question to 150 couples, including those who were dating casually, going steady, living together, or married. Although individual answers varied considerably, several patterns emerged. Women were likely to believe that their partners were seeking greater sexual variety, thus reinforcing their image of men as "sexual animals." On the other hand, men felt that if their partners strayed outside the relationship it would be because of their search for greater commitment, reflecting their image of women as "marriage-oriented." However, for both sexes, the more threatened a partner was, the more he or she tended to think the other partner's outside involvement would be a quest for sex. Thus, White surmises, suspicions of a partner's sexual involvement with someone else may reflect underlying fears about one's own sexual attractiveness.

MALE AND FEMALE

Although we've come a long way from the time when sex was considered "dirty," the popular notions just cited suggest that our understanding of sex continues to be hampered by sexual stereotypes—widespread generalities about the sexual characteristics and behavior of males and females. Such generalities exaggerate the real differences between men and women, thereby setting the stage for misunderstanding and frustration between the sexes. The extent to which such stereotypes are passed along from one generation to another can be seen in a study by Beverly Romberger (1985). In an effort to find out what women think about men, Romberger conducted in-depth interviews with women whose backgrounds cut across the lines of age, economics, lifestyle, and religion. One of the themes that emerged from these interviews was the sharing of "commonplaces"—beliefs or truisms that are passed along from one generation to another through cultural lore—usually acquired at an early age. Here are some of the 250 commonplaces about men:

> Men are after only one thing—sex.
>
> Men don't respect easy women.
>
> It's up to the woman to say "no."
>
> A woman should make herself attractive to men but shouldn't give in to their advances.

Some of the truisms about women included:

> Getting pregnant is the worst thing that can happen to an unmarried woman.
>
> The right time to have sex is after marriage.
>
> A woman must keep the house clean.
>
> It's a woman's job to keep her man's shirts ironed.

Whether or not women actually believe these truisms, admitted Romberger, is open to debate. But these potent messages persist into adulthood, often overruling, or at least contesting with, the intellect. This is why we begin the chapter by dispelling several of the familiar stereotypes held by men and women.

Beyond Stereotypes

There's a long-standing but mistaken belief that men have a stronger sex drive than women. Although this stereotype is beginning to diminish as younger generations are socialized differently, many men and women still subscribe to it. Even "normal" women, it is assumed, don't enjoy sex as much as men do. Sex is something women do mostly to please the man they love. By contrast, men are regarded as "sexual animals" ever in search of sexual variety and inclined to "play around" with other women even after marriage. Yet there is no convincing evidence that the female sex drive is any less intense or "animalistic" than the male's. The main difference is that women, especially in the past, have been taught greater restraint in expressing their sexuality. As women affirm their sexuality and enjoy satisfying relationships with men, as more and more women are doing, they enjoy sex as much as men. In some instances a woman's sexual responsiveness may surpass that of a man, though this varies more widely among women than men, and within a particular woman at a particular time (Masters, Johnson, and Kolodny, 1985).

There's also the mistaken notion that when it comes to sex, men are the "sexperts" and women are naive. And men are not the only ones who subscribe to this idea. In one study, about half of the women felt that a "real man" should be skillful in bed (Tavris, 1977). Of course, many men enjoy the role of teacher. But others feel it's a burden. "Why is it always my responsibility to know what my partner wants in lovemaking?" asks one man. "I get tired of running the show." Actually, many women today are better aware of their sexual needs than any of their partners are. Furthermore, women frequently complain that their male partners are ignorant or unskilled in lovemaking (Hite, 1976). By contrast, men are usually pleased to discover women who initiate sex, play an active role in lovemaking, and take responsibility for their own pleasure. More and more, it seems women are inclined to regard men as sexual equals.

Then there is the stereotype that women are natural "controllers" in sexual matters. That is, having been taught that men are lustful creatures with "sex on the brain," a woman feels she must assume the role of controller. Instead of enjoying the cuddling and kissing with a man, she may turn her attention to how to keep his hand off her breasts or genitals. After years of putting the brakes on sexual intimacy, it's not surprising that many women have difficulty experiencing pleasure in lovemaking once they give up the controlling role, as in a satisfying love relationship or marriage. By the same token, a man may be conditioned to regard a woman as a challenge, to see "how far" he can go with her. Men, regarding the touching and cuddling women value so much as only a means to an end, may rush into intercourse. Consequently, men may also have a hard time being receptive to genuine sexual sharing, or may be threatened by a woman who takes the initiative in sex (Crooks and Baur, 1983).

Still another stereotype is that there is something wrong with people who engage in homosexual behavior—sexual behavior with those of one's own sex. Yet, homosexual men and women do not exhibit any higher incidence of psychopathology than do heterosexuals. Nor is there one homosexual personality type. Instead, there is a wide diversity of homosexual lifestyles, ranging from individuals who prefer close, stable relationships with others to those who have few partners and engage in little sexual activity. Few homosexuals conform to society's stereotypes of them (Bell, Weinberg, and Hammersmith, 1981). Furthermore, Masters and Johnson found no differences in the physiological responses during sexual activity and orgasm between homosexual and heterosexual couples (Masters, Johnson, and Kolodny, 1985). As a result, homosexuality is no longer regarded as a psychological disorder, except in those cases in which it has become a problem for the individuals themselves (DSM-III, 1980). Homosexuality is increasingly being viewed as another variant of human sexual behavior, one that is now preferred by a significant minority of Americans.

Sexual Communication

Talking *about* sex is hard enough. Sharing our sexual feelings and needs is even more difficult. One reason is that we've grown up associating a sense of discomfort, if not shame, with the sexual aspects of our bodies. Then too, our parents and teachers haven't taught us how to talk about sex in a matter-of-fact way. So, by the time we're eager to communicate sexual needs we don't know how to go about it. In one study, 200 college students were asked to indicate the word or phrase they used to describe the sex organs and sexual intercourse. The results showed that men used a greater variety of terms and varied them more with different listeners. With most people, men were inclined to use slang terms like "pussy" or "dick." They also used aggressive terms such as "screwing" for sexual intercourse. Women were more apt to stick to clinical terms for the genitals, such as "vagina" and "penis." Women usually preferred the term "making love" for sexual intercourse, while men used this phrase mostly when speaking with a lover or spouse (Sanders and Robinson, 1979). This suggests that in talking about sexual matters, it's important for each couple to determine which words and phrases are agreeable and comfortable for their relationship.

Probably the most important part of sexual communication is the attitude partners have toward each other, such as trust and mutual empathy—the sense that each cares for the other and knows this is reciprocated. A lot depends on the spirit and tone of voice in which you say something, and on your partner's willingness to discuss it in good faith. A good way to initiate sexual communication is to share your own feelings and preferences in regard to sex. You might say something like, "I usually enjoy doing something together, such as taking a stroll on the beach, before going to bed." Such personal sharing tends to evoke a similar disclosure from your partner. You may also have an opportunity to do this when comparing notes with your partner. When planning an evening out, it's natural to discuss each other's preferences, such as, "Would you like to go dancing or attend a movie?" When you feel comfortable enough in the relationship, you might also like to share notes about your romantic and sexual preferences. Such a candid approach may avoid the slow, and often awkward, trial-and-error process that results in a great deal of misunderstanding. Yet, it's important not to become calculating or clinical in discussing sex. Couples may also find it helpful to share their feelings after a time of physical intimacy or lovemaking—what was most satisfying, and what might be improved.

The sense that each person cares for the other is an important part of sexual communication.
(Teri Leigh Stratford)

You may also use questions to discover your partner's needs and preferences. You might ask a yes-or-no question, such as "Did you enjoy that?" Or you could use an open-ended question, such as "Which aspects of our lovemaking would you most like to change?" Some individuals prefer either/or questions, such as "Would you like to talk about it now or at another time?" Either/or questions encourage more participation from your partner than a simple yes-or-no answer.

Giving and receiving criticism in sex is a touchy but important matter. When you feel the urge to criticize, ask yourself, "What's the reason for my saying this?" If there's no good reason, it's better not to say it. Also, wait for the appropriate time and place to offer such criticism. When you feel you must criticize, express your remarks in a nonjudgmental way. Whenever possible, demonstrate what you mean. If a woman felt her partner was too rough in stimulating her, she might place his hand on hers and show him how she'd prefer him to stimulate her clitoris. When receiving criticism try not to overreact. Remember that criticism is often a way your partner shows he or she cares for you. Look beyond the words to what your partner is trying to tell you. Ask what the criticism means, then try to take it to heart (Weisinger and Lobsenz, 1981).

Finally, remember that much of our communication is nonverbal, especially in sex. How close your partner sits next to you or the way your partner touches and caresses you reveals a lot about his or her attitude at the moment. Then too, your partner's facial expressions and sounds communicate a lot. Many individuals find rapid breathing, moans, groans, and orgasmic cries very arousing. The absence of such sounds can be very frustrating.

Initiating and Refusing Sex

Nowhere is sexual communication put to the test more than in initiating and refusing sex. Some couples don't communicate very well in this area and expect their partners to be mind readers. Others have developed nonverbal cues or elaborate rituals to signal their interest in sex. One woman says, "When John gets out the champagne and suggests we watch a movie on TV, I know what he's thinking."

Men have traditionally taken the initiative in sexual intercourse. But nowadays men and women are moving away from such restricted notions of what "men must do" or what "women must not do." You might expect that individuals of both sexes are learning to share the roles of initiator and refuser equally, which is true to some extent. But the old traditions are still alive, as seen in Blumstein and Schwartz's study of *American Couples* (1983). Among married couples, men take the initiative in sex a little over half the time, with men and women sharing the initiator role about a third of the time. Among cohabiting couples, or those living together, the partners share the initiative or the man takes the initiative equally often, about 40 percent of the times respectively. Cohabiting women are somewhat more likely than married women to take the initiative in sex, but still only do so about 15 percent of the time. Among gay and lesbian couples, the partners alternate or share the initiative equally, about one-third of the time for each of these options respectively. (See Figures 9–1 and 9–2.)

Interestingly, the more emotionally expressive the partner, regardless of sex, the more he or she initiates lovemaking. This pattern holds true among married couples, cohabiting couples, and gay and lesbian couples alike. Men and women who express their feelings readily tend to feel comfortable making the first move because they are sensitive about how to approach their partner. The more they succeed, the more they inherit the role. Also, the more expressive partner is less likely to refuse sex. On the other hand, the more powerful partner of the two, usually the person who is less emotionally involved in the relationship or less in love, is more likely to refuse sex. By refusing sex, a partner can become a force to be reckoned with.

The more couples can initiate and refuse sex on an equal basis, the more satisfied they are with their sex life. Not surprisingly, they also engage in sex more frequently than other couples. Among married and cohabiting couples

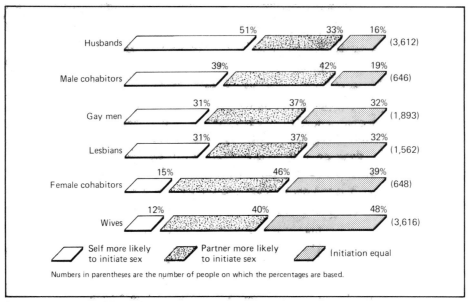

Figure 9–1. INITIATING SEX.

From *American Couples* by Philip Blumstein, Ph.D., and Pepper Schwartz, Ph.D. Copyright © 1983 by Philip Blumstein and Pepper W. Schwartz. By permission of William Morrow & Company, 1983, p. 207.

alike, 80 percent of the couples who share the initiator and refuser roles equally are satisfied with the quality of their sex life, compared to only two-thirds of the couples in which sexual initiation is not equal.

HUMAN SEXUAL RESPONSE

Much of sexual behavior, especially intercourse, takes place in private, so that it's difficult to know what occurs. Even the participants themselves are so emotionally involved that their recall is often inaccurate. For years people simply filled in the gaps of their sexual knowledge with jokes and stories, obscuring their understanding of sex with half-truths and myths. Fortunately, this situation is changing, thanks largely to the pioneering work of Masters and Johnson and the growing field of sex therapy.

The Sexual Response Cycle

Through an extensive series of interviews and controlled observations of volunteers masturbating and engaging in sexual intercourse, Masters and Johnson (1966, 1985) have identified the basic sexual response patterns of men and women. (See Figures 9–3 and 9–4.) These patterns consist of certain common

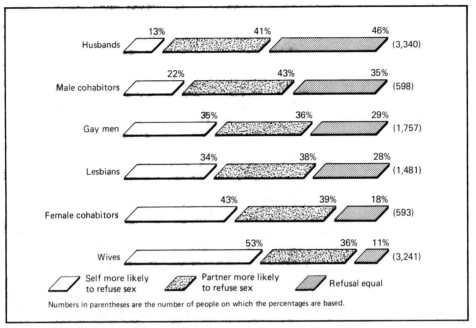

Figure 9–2.   REFUSING SEX.

From *American Couples* by Philip Blumstein, Ph.D., and Pepper Schwartz, Ph.D. Copyright © 1983 by Philip Blumstein and Pepper W. Schwartz. By permission of William Morrow & Company, 1983, p. 221.

physiological changes that occur in a predictable sequence and are collectively labeled the sexual response cycle. What follows is a modified version of the cycle, incorporating some of the recent changes suggested by other authorities in the field. We'll describe five phases of the sexual response cycle: (1) transition, (2) excitement, (3) plateau, (4) orgasm, and (5) resolution.

Transition. In the sexual response cycle, *transition* is the gradual shift from a nonsexual to a sexual state of being, and it includes the awakening of sexual desire and a readiness for sexual arousal (Knoepfler, 1981). We're all familiar with the importance of "getting ready" for a special evening out. The same is true with sex. Although individuals vary widely in regard to what puts them in the mood for sex, some things commonly facilitate the transition to sex. Anything that induces relaxation, with a shift from a goal-centered to a more process-centered awareness almost always helps. Some people enjoy a relaxed meal, including a small to moderate amount of alcohol. Others may prefer dancing, listening to music, or watching a romantic or erotic movie. Physical touching, massage, or relaxing in moving hot water, such as in hot tubs and Jacuzzis, are favorite ways to get into the mood for sex. It is quite possible that many problems with lack of sexual desire stem from one partner's *unreadiness* for sex. Men in particular tend to be more impatient and less in tune or interested in the need for transition than women. Many women prefer a more gradual transition, accompanied by emotional sharing and tender caressing.

Excitement. Sexual arousal, or *excitement*, involves a combination of mental and sensory stimulation. Each partner's anticipation of sex, often accompanied by sexual fantasies, is an important part of getting in the mood for sex. Sexual desire is also heightened through the stimulation of the senses. Although individual preferences vary widely, sights and sounds, the sense of smell and even taste, all combine to heighten the mood. Touching is especially important. Mutual caressing of various parts of the body, especially the erogenous zones, almost always intensifies sexual arousal, even when sexual desire is initially low in one partner. As one woman says, "Sometimes in the beginning I'm not much in the mood for sex, but I rarely end up feeling indifferent."

Sexual arousal activates two types of basic changes. First, there is an increased muscle tension (myotonia) throughout each partner's body, which builds until the eventual release in the involuntary contractions of orgasm. There is also an increased heart rate, blood pressure, and engorgement (vasocongestion) of blood vessels throughout the sexual parts of our anatomy. The man's penis may become erect and subside several times during this time. The woman's breasts enlarge, with her nipples becoming erect. Her clitoris and vaginal opening swell in size. The inner two-thirds of the vagina also lengthens and becomes lubricated.

Plateau. The *plateau* phase is usually quite brief, lasting anywhere from a few seconds to several minutes. It's difficult to define the onset of this phase because there is no clear outward sign, such as erection of the man's penis or lubrication of the woman's vagina. Actually, the usual signs of sexual arousal become more pronounced as the individuals approach orgasm, which is why some authorities

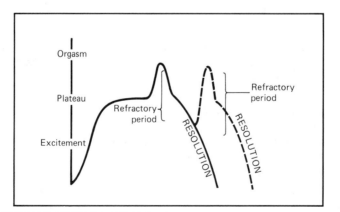

Figure 9–3. THE MALE SEXUAL RESPONSE CYCLE. Masters and Johnson identified one typical male response pattern, though men have reported considerable variation in their response patterns.

From William H. Masters and Virginia E. Johnson, *Human Sexual Response* (Boston: Little, Brown, 1966). © 1966 by William H. Masters and Virginia E. Johnson.

are now referring to this as the *charge* phase (Crooks and Baur, 1983). The heart beats faster and breathing grows more rapid. Increasing muscle tension and blood pressure leads to engorgement of the sex organs, promoting the partners' readiness for orgasm. Men rarely lose their erection at this phase. Women also experience a marked increase in the swelling of the outer third of the vagina, or the "orgasmic platform," making stimulation by the male even more pleasurable. At this point, the partner who is moving faster toward orgasm, often the man, may need to slow down or vary the stimulation from time to time, so that both partners may reach orgasm at the same time, or nearly so.

Orgasm. As the climax of sexual excitement approaches, the partners may sense that *orgasm* is inevitable. This is especially true for men, who usually achieve orgasm once they reach the plateau or charge phase of arousal. However, women may reach the heightened sexual tension of the plateau phase without necessarily achieving orgasm, as authorities have observed: "This is often the case during penile-vaginal intercourse, when the man reaches orgasm first or when effective manual or oral stimulation is replaced with penetration as the female approaches orgasm" (Crooks and Baur, 1983, p. 178).

In both sexes, orgasm is experienced as a highly pleasurable release from tension, accompanied by involuntary muscle spasms throughout the body and uncontrollable cries and moans. Muscles in and around the man's penis contract rhythmically causing the forceable ejaculation of semen. Similarly, the outer third of the woman's vagina contracts rhythmically along with the pulsation of her uterus. For both sexes, the first few contractions are the most intense and pleasurable, followed by weaker and slower contractions.

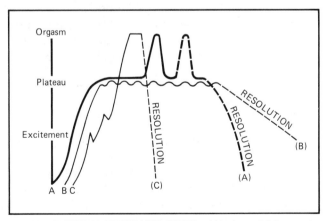

Figure 9–4. THE FEMALE SEXUAL RESPONSE CYCLE. Masters and Johnson identified three basic patterns in the female's sexual response. Pattern A most resembles the typical male pattern, except for the lack of a refractory period between orgasms. Variations include an extended plateau phase with no orgasm (B), or a rapid rise to orgasm (C) with no definitive plateau and a very brief resolution.

From William H. Masters and Virginia E. Johnson, *Human Sexual Response* (Boston: Little, Brown, 1966). © 1966 by William H. Masters and Virginia E. Johnson.

Individuals of both sexes vary considerably in their subjective reports of orgasm. Yet the underlying physiological processes are basically the same. When individuals of both sexes have submitted anonymous descriptions of orgasm, experts are unable to reliably distinguish between the accounts from men and those from women (Wiest, 1977). Similarly, the physiological process of orgasm in females seems to be the same, regardless of the method of stimulation. Women do report subjective differences, however, in their experience of orgasm by clitoral stimulation as opposed to vaginal intercourse. Orgasms from direct clitoral stimulation, whether manual or oral, tend to be sharper and more locally intense. Orgasms from vaginal intercourse are less intense, with slightly fewer vaginal contractions, though they are more diffused throughout the woman's body (Masters, Johnson, and Kolodny, 1985; Hite, 1976). As a result, women vary in their preference for clitoral or vaginal stimulation .

Resolution. When no further stimulation occurs, orgasm is immediately followed by the *resolution* phase. The body returns to the normal, nonexcited phase. Heart rate, blood pressure, and breathing quickly subside. Muscle tension usually dissipates within 5 minutes after orgasm. Men lose about 50 percent of their erection within a minute or so after orgasm, with the remaining loss of erection occurring in the next several minutes. Men also enter into a *refractory* period—a time when no added stimulation will result in orgasm. The length of time varies widely, from a few minutes to several days, depending on such factors as the man's age, health, and frequency of previous sexual activity as well as the sexual desire for his partner. Women experience no equivalent refractory period. Most women are physically capable of another orgasm, though they may not desire it. Ordinarily, the woman's clitoris descends to its usual overhanging position within a few seconds, though the engorgement of the shaft and glans dissipates more slowly. Nipple erection also subsides. Women who have not reached orgasm after high levels of arousal usually experience a slow resolution, with discomfort throughout the genital and pelvic area. However, when both partners have reached orgasm, they generally find this is a pleasant and relaxed time.

Individual and Sex Differences

We've stressed the similarity in men and women's sexual response in accordance with the more recent knowledge of the sexual response cycle. This helps to dispel the old notion that men and women are worlds apart in their experience of sex, encouraging better communication between them. Yet there are some important differences between men and women's experience of sex (in addition to the refractory period in males noted above).

A major difference is the greater orgasmic variation among women compared to men, both in the physiology of orgasm and in the individual's subjective awareness of sexual climax. Masters and Johnson (Masters, Johnson, and Kolodny, 1985) have identified three basic patterns of the sexual response cycle in women, though only one for men. (See Figure 9–4.) Pattern A most resembles the male pattern and differs mainly in the woman's capacity for additional orgasm. Pattern B shows a prolonged, fluctuating plateau phase, with small surges toward orgasm, followed by a gradual resolution. This is sometimes referred to as "skimming," due to the lack of a single intense climax, and is most often reported by young or sexually inexperienced women. Pattern C shows a rapid rise in sexual excitement leading to a single, intense orgasm and quick resolution. Masters and Johnson suggest that after many experiences of intercourse, some women gradually change their sexual response patterns. The developmental sequence begins with the minor orgasm pattern (B), changes to the intense-orgasm pattern (C), and finally to multiple orgasmic responses in A.

Although men exhibit fewer variations, it would be a mistake to assume all men experience the sexual response cycle in the same way. Some men have reported extended periods of intense sexual stimulation before reaching orgasm. Others have experienced several mild sexual climaxes finally leading to an expulsion of semen. Still others have prolonged pelvic contractions after ejaculation (Zilbergeld, 1978).

Marked difference between the sexes has to do with the ability to experience multiple orgasms—two or more sexual climaxes within a short period of time. Although it is not at all uncommon for women to have several orgasms in quick succession, multiple orgasms are the exception rather than the rule for men. But despite the greater potential for multiple orgasms, only about one in six women report having such climaxes regularly (Crooks and Baur, 1983). Why so few? One reason may be that men tend to stop stimulating their partners after having their orgasm, so women are less likely to continue sexual activity beyond their initial climax. Then too, the reports of multiple orgasms are usually based on the rates typical of vaginal intercourse as against clitoral stimulation. Some authorities suggest that if women who are capable of having regular orgasms are properly stimulated within a short period after their first climax, in most instances they will be capable of having several additional orgasms before they are fully satisfied (Masters, Johnson, and Kolodny, 1985).

Mutiple orgasms are much less common among men, though they do occur. They are more likely to be reported by very young men, with their frequency declining with age. Yet a few men are capable of experiencing a series of orgasms in a relatively short period of time. These men usually experience a series of preejaculatory orgasms culminating in a final climax with ejaculation. The final orgasm accompanied by the expulsion of semen triggers a refractory period. These reports suggest that orgasm and ejaculation are not always associated with each other, so that men who learn how to experience orgasm without ejaculation may be able to experience a series of closely timed orgasms more like women (Robbins and Jensen, 1978).

There's a popular notion that in a series of orgasms, each successive climax is more intense than the last. But is this always so? A lot depends on the person's gender and makeup. Women who experience multiple orgasms in Masters and Johnson's lab did report that their subsequent orgasms were more intense and pleasurable than the first. By contrast, most men who had multiple orgasms reported the opposite, namely that their first orgasm was more pleasurable. The usual explanation is that the greater volume of semen, the more superior the orgasm, with the initial ejaculation producing the most semen. Yet some men report the opposite experience, and derive greater pleasure from subsequent orgasms. One middle-aged man said, "I discovered that I could have more than one orgasm in one session, and while it may take me a long time to come again, the getting there is a very nice part. My partner likes it, too!" (Crooks and Baur, 1983, p. 188). Such accounts suggest that the pleasure of orgasms also involves other factors, such as the man's greater staying power, heightened awareness, and greater appreciation of his partner's response in later orgasms.

At the same time, multiple orgasm is best seen as a potential area to be explored by some, rather than an ultimate goal for all. Women's greater capacity for multiple orgasms should not be construed to mean that they "must" have more than one climax to be satisfied. Many women prefer to have one orgasm or perhaps none at all. Similarly, the infrequency with which men report multiple orgasms does not mean that they cannot have them. Much depends on the particular person, with individual differences often exceeding those between the sexes. Finally, the more relaxed the partners are about sex, the more opportunities they will have to experience the full range of their sexual potential.

Love and Sex

So far we've been focusing on sex as a physical act. But what about the attitude and relationship of the partners involved? Must they be in love to enjoy sex? Not necessarily. Healthy, guilt-free people *can* function well sexually and derive pleasure from sex without being love. In one survey of college students, 70 percent of the women and 79 percent of the men felt that while love enriches sex, it is not necessary for its enjoyment. Yet, the same survey discloses a double standard among men and women. That is, about 30 percent of the women indicated that sex was either not enjoyable or totally inappropriate without love, whereas only 12 percent of the men felt this way (Crooks and Baur, 1983). Couples living together express a more liberal attitude. The majority of both sexes endorse sex without love, with only 12 and 13 percent of men and women respectively disapproving of sex without love. On the other hand, married couples hold a more conservative attitude. Over 40 percent of the women and 27 percent of the men disapprove of sex without love (Blumstein and Schwartz, 1983).

Actually, the relationship between sex and love depends largely on the values of the people involved. This was brought out clearly in a study of 231 couples who had been dating steadily for about 8 months (Peplau, Rubin, and Hill, 1977). The couples were surveyed in depth about a number of issues pertaining to love and sex, including their attitudes toward sex, emotional intimacy, frequency of sex, and whether they had initiated sexual intercourse early or late in their relationship. On the basis of the results, the researchers divided the couples into three groups: the sexually traditional, the moderate, and the liberal couples respectively. Those labeled sexually traditional, a minority of couples sampled, believed that abstaining from sex until marriage indicated their love and respect for each other. The sexually moderate couples felt that sex is an expression of love that only comes with time. Accordingly, they didn't begin having intercourse until about 6 months after they had been dating. The couples labeled sexually liberal viewed sex as an activity that is enjoyable in itself and which may also help the partners get to know each other better. Not surprisingly, the latter couples generally began having sexual intercourse soon after they met.

When the couples were divided again on the basis of whether they had begun sex early or late in their relationship, the link between sex and love was much stronger among the later-sex couples. Couples who began having sex later in their relationship were more often in love, felt more intimate ties, and were more inclined to marry their partners than those who had started having sex earlier in the relationship. They also engaged in sex less frequently, averaging two to three times a week compared to the four or five times a week for the early-sex couples. Yet, a followup study conducted 2 years after the original survey showed that there was no significant relationship between the couple's sexual activity and their overall satisfaction with their relationship or its permanence. Couples who either abstained from sex or engaged in it early and often stayed together or broke up with equal frequency.

A time of emotional sharing and caressing helps to put a couple in the mood for sex. (Teri Leigh Stratford)

At the same time, love tends to enrich sex, especially in a long-term relationship like marriage. The affection and commitment a couple enjoys in their relationship may enhance their overall pleasure, compensating somewhat for the loss of sensual excitement that usually occurs after years of marriage. By contrast, couples who go to bed mechanically, especially when one or both partners have little or no affection for each other, soon discover that sex itself is no longer satisfying. George Leonard, in his book *The End of Sex* (1983), points out that the popular emphasis on sex for pleasure has led to manipulative relationships that eventually undermine sex; hence, the theme of his book—sex is dead, long live love. But it is *erotic* love that Leonard proclaims. Erotic love includes a healthy acceptance of sex and sensuality. Erotic love not only strengthens the love between a man and a woman, it also makes for better sex. It is no coincidence that couples refer to intercourse by the phrase "making love"; sex and love belonging together.

SEXUAL PROBLEMS

The emphasis on sexual fulfillment in recent years has had many beneficial effects. There is more objective information about sex, increased sexual communication between partners, and less anxiety and guilt over harmless sexual practices like masturbation. At the same time, such changes have been accompanied by new anxieties. Many sexually normal men worry about their sexual performance. Women who are not orgasmic may suffer the same loss of self-esteem as the man who has a weak erection. Then too, increasing sexual activity outside of marriage has accentuated the perennial problems of birth control, unwanted pregnancies, and sexually transmitted diseases.

Sexual Dysfunctions

Even sexually experienced couples discover that each time they make love sex is different. Sometimes sex is highly pleasurable for both partners; at other times it is less satisfying for one or both of them. Such occasional problems are usually not serious; often they are caused simply by excessive alcohol, fatigue, or stress. However, when sexual problems persist or become distressful to the individuals involved, they may be classified as sexual dysfunctions. Unfortunately, because the inability to perform sexually is associated with a loss of self-esteem, individuals may resist seeking help. Fortunately, this situation is changing with the greater openness about sex and the general availability of sex therapists.

Sexual dysfunctions may be grouped according to the phase of sexual response cycle in which they occur. They include difficulties of desire, arousal, and orgasm.

Inhibited sexual desire (ISD) is a common sexual difficulty among both sexes. About one out of every five men, single and married, suffers from this problem, with an even higher incidence among women (Leo, 1984). Primary ISD is rare and occurs among those who have never masturbated or expressed any curiosity about sex. As adults they have little or no interest in sex or in the sexual aspects of a relationship. More commonly, people develop secondary ISD, either at a particular point in their lives or in a specific situation. That is, a woman may experience ISD with her spouse but not in masturbation or with a lover. Actually, because sexual desire varies so much between people and within the same individual at different times, it is difficult to define what constitutes lack of sexual desire. In some instances it may be a realistic response, such as with a partner who practices poor hygiene or is verbally abusive. Generally, the term ISD is reserved for cases in which the lack of sexual desire becomes a source of distress to either the individual or his or her partner.

In many cases, the lack of sexual desire reflects the individual's preoccupation with a life problem like divorce, a death in the family, or a problem at work. Emotional factors are often involved. Boredom is a frequent cause of inhibited sexual desire. So is anger, especially buried anger. Other factors are anxiety, guilt, low self-esteem, depression, and the fear of intimacy. Prolonged frustration from the lack of arousal or orgasm may result in low sexual desire. And a person who feels pressured into sex or feels guilty about saying no may become less and less interested in sex. Some people may be so fearful of sexual pleasure or closeness that they unconsciously prevent themselves from feeling sexual desire by developing a "turn-off" mechanism. By becoming angry, fearful, or distracted, they draw on the natural inhibiting mechanisms that suppress sexual desire. The lack of desire appears to emerge automatically. They do not realize that they have control over the focus of their thoughts and thus contribute to their own problems (Kaplan, 1979).

Another type of sexual dysfunction is *inhibited sexual arousal*, which occurs most often as *erectile inhibition* (impotency) and *inhibited vaginal lubrication*. Men who suffer from this problem usually have secondary erectile inhibition—that is, they've previously experienced erections but are consistently unable to have an erection of sufficient firmness to penetrate the woman's vagina. Most men experience occasional difficulties with having an erection, usually because of fatigue or stress. It's only when this difficulty continues to occur or becomes distressful to the man or his partner that it should come to the attention of a professional. Many factors may contribute to erectile failure.

Physiological factors of erectile inhibition include severe diabetes and the effect of certain drugs, especially alcohol, narcotics, amphetamines, and some prescribed medications. Worry and criticism from a partner may also lead to an erectile failure. In most instances, erectile inhibition presents only a passing problem. But sometimes these experiences may generate such concern and anxiety that they develop into a pattern. The man's anxiety assumes the form of a "spectator's role." That is, instead of relaxing and letting his erection occur spontaneously, he watches and judges his own performance. By doing so, the man's critical attitude and tenseness contribute to the erectile failure. Treatment consists of helping the man learn how to relax and let things happen. It's especially important not to overreact to the temporary loss of erection. After all, men usually have and lose several erections during the excitement phase, without even noticing it.

Inhibited vaginal lubrication in the woman is similar to the man's lack of erection because in both cases sufficient vasocongestion doesn't occur. Normally, during sexual stimulation the massive congestion of blood vessels in the vaginal walls secrete droplets of fluid, which eventually form a shiny film on the walls of the vagina. Lack of lubrication doesn't always mean something is wrong. Frequently, the woman is not sufficiently stimulated. And feelings of apathy, boredom, anger, or fear may inhibit her arousal. Also, during prolonged intercourse with lengthy plateau periods the woman may have a decrease in vaginal lubrication. In such instances, increased stimulation of the woman's clitoris or other parts of her body may help to increase vaginal lubrication. Older women who have passed the menopause age sometimes supplement their vaginal lubrication by adding small amounts of vaginal jelly purchased from the local pharmacy.

The most common *difficulty of the orgasm phase* in the sexual response cycle is *premature or retarded ejaculation* on the man's part and *delay or absence of orgasm* for the woman. Premature ejaculation consists of reaching orgasm so quickly it significantly lessens the man's enjoyment of sex and/or undermines his partner's satisfaction. It is a common problem for men. In one survey of college students, one-fourth of the men reported premature ejaculation was an ongoing difficulty for them, with another half saying it was sometimes a problem (Crooks and Baur, 1983). The most common reason is that men have become accustomed to reaching orgasm quickly, either to allay their anxiety, demonstrate their sexual prowess, or to avoid discovery. Too little vaginal lubrication may also increase the friction of the penis during intercourse, thereby leading to rapid ejaculation. Fortunately, this condition is readily treatable through measures such as the stop-start or squeeze techniques. The man, usually with the aid of his partner, practices recognizing the sensations of impending orgasm and momentarily stopping stimulation, until he gradually learns to delay ejaculation.

The most common problems for women are slowness or inability to reach orgasm. Since orgasm is a reflex, an involuntary reaction, and differs considerably from one individual to another, it may help to see this problem in the context of womens' overall sexual response, as described by an authority:

> Clinically, female orgasm seems to be distributed more or less along a bell-shaped curve. On one extreme are the women who have never climaxed at all. Next are women who require intense clitoral stimulation when they are alone and not "disturbed" by a partner. Women who need direct clitoral stimulation but are able to climax with their partners fall in the middle range. Also near the middle are women who can climax on coitus but only

after lengthy and vigorous stimulation. Near the upper range are women who require only brief penetration to reach their climax and, at the very extreme, are the women who can achieve an orgasm via fantasy and/or breast stimulation alone. (Kaplan, 1975, pp. 72–73)

Women who have never reached orgasm often lack knowledge of their own sexual response cycle, learned often through masturbation. These women may be helped to reach orgasm by minimizing their inhibitions and by maximizing their sexual stimulation through masturbation. A more common complaint is slowness or failure to reach orgasm through intercourse with a partner. This problem is not surprising, considering orgasm is usually triggered through sensory stimulation of the clitoral area, and this is accomplished only indirectly in intercourse. Consequently only about one-third to one-half of women reach orgasm solely through intercourse (Kaplan, 1975). Those who prefer vaginal orgasm and are unable to attain it often need more lengthy thrusting on the man's part. But there are many more women who need direct clitoral stimulation, either by manual or oral stimulation from the man or self-stimulation, in addition to the penile-vagina thrusting during intercourse to reach climax. Women frequently complain that men don't know how to give clitoral stimulation. Men tend to be impatient, rubbing the clitoris directly or too long, thereby irritating the clitoris. Women usually prefer a more indirect, playful approach, which may include caressing one side of the clitoral shaft or use of an indirect, circular motion of the whole clitoral area. Occasionally, women have difficulty reaching orgasm even with adequate clitoral stimulation. In some instances, women may be plagued by feelings of anxiety, anger, or guilt. Or they may be ambivalent about their relationship with their partner. Some women may fear losing control of their feelings or behavior with a particular partner. We should also keep in mind that even healthy, sexually experienced women do not always reach orgasm, whether because of fatigue or temporary, situational factors. Nor is this necessarily a problem. Although Hite (1976) found that no more than one-fourth of her respondents reached orgasm through intercourse alone, 87 percent of them said they enjoyed intercourse because of the feelings of closeness and security associated with it.

Birth Control

The availability and use of reliable birth control methods has become increasingly important in recent years for several reasons. Obviously, unmarried couples want to avoid an unwanted pregnancy. Yet even among married couples, there's a growing tendency to have planned and wanted children. Many couples wait several years or more after marriage to strengthen their relationship and acquire financial stability before having their first child. And women who want to combine a career with parenthood can accomplish this better through the use of dependable birth control methods.

American women are not particularly happy with the contraceptive choices available to them. According to a national survey, about 60 percent of them feel that no one method of birth control is completely satisfactory, whether due to inconvenience or side effects. And this level of dissatisfaction varies little with the woman's age, marital status, or income. Most women have tried several contraceptive methods in the search for one that suits them best, but feel that every method requires trade-offs between safety and effectiveness. What women want are birth control methods that do not require them to make such trade-offs (Yankelovich, Skelly, and White, 1982).

Table 9–1. COMPARATIVE EFFECTIVENESS OF BIRTH CONTROL METHODS. Adapted from Robert A. Hatcher, M.D. et al., *Contraceptive Technology 1984–1985,* 12th rev. ed. (New York: Irvington Publishers, 1984), p. 3.

Method	Theoretical Failure Rate	Actual Failure Rate	Advantages	Disadvantages
Tubal ligation	0.04	0.04	Extremely reliable; permanent	Initial expense; Not considered reversible
Vasectomy	0.15	0.15	Extremely reliable; permanent	Initial expense; Not considered reversible
Combined birth control pills	0.5	2.0	Very effective	Cost; daily use; side effects
Progestin-only pill	1.0	2.5	Fewer potential side effects than combined pill	
IUD	1.5	5.0	Effective; little attention after insertion	Increased risk of infection; heavier menstrual period
Condom	2.0	10.0	Effective; protects against STD	Interrupts sexual activity; reduces sensation
Diaphragm (with spermicide)	2.0	19.0	Effective; inexpensive	Interrupts sexual activity
Sponge (with spermicide)	—*	10–20	Easy to use; minor side effects	Unreliable when not carefully used
Cervical cap	2.0	13.0	Inexpensive; few side effects	Difficult to obtain; lack of research on use
Foams, creams, jellies, and vaginal suppositories	3–5	18.0	Inexpensive; few side effects	Unreliable when improperly used
Withdrawal	16.0	23.0	No cost	Interrupts sexual activity; unreliable
Fertility awareness techniques (includes mucus, rhythm, and basal body temperature methods)	2–20	24.0	Inexpensive; no side effects; acceptable to Roman Catholic Church	Less reliable for women with irregular cycles; requires periods of abstinence
Douche	—	40.0	Inexpensive	Very unreliable
Chance (no birth control method)				

*Inadequate data to know the lowest observed failure rate of this new method of birth control.

The effectiveness of the various contraceptives, along with their advantages and disadvantages, is shown in Table 9–1. Generally, the condom and the pill are most popular among people in their teens and 20s. Those over 30 favor methods that combine high effectiveness with maximum safety, such as vasectomy for men and tubal ligation for women (Forrest and Henshaw, 1983). Yet, it is important for couples to choose the method of birth control that suits them best. The primary concern is that the method be effective without jeopardizing either partner's health. But there are other considerations too, such as the convenience and expense. Women need to ask themselves: "Will I have trouble remembering to use this method? Are there any objections because of my religious beliefs? Will this method interrupt lovemaking?"

Then too, there is the matter of men sharing the responsibility for birth control. Shared responsibility for birth control can enhance a relationship. When the man takes an active interest in contraception, the woman is less likely to feel resentment over assuming all the responsibility for birth control. Men may share responsibility for birth control in several ways. An important step is discussing the matter of birth control before first engaging in intercourse. This initial step is rarely taken, however, mostly because of the fear of spoiling the spontaneity of sex. In long-term relationships, men can share the expense of any medical exams or the cost of contraceptives. In addition, the man might help by inserting the diaphragm into his partner's vagina before intercourse, or by using a backup method such as a condom, especially with a vaginal form or suppository.

Sexually Transmitted Diseases

A variety of diseases may be contracted through sexual interaction. These are called sexually transmitted diseases (STD), a broader and less value-laden term than venereal disease. Although most of these diseases can be treated successfully, many of them are on the increase, largely because of increased sexual activity and a tendency to have more than one sexual partner, especially during one's youth. The incidence of STD is highest among those in the 20- to 24-year-old group, with the next highest incidence among those in the 15- to 19-year-old group (NIAID, 1981).

Gonorrhea continues to be one of the most common sexually transmitted diseases. It increased dramatically through the 1960s and 1970s, mostly because of the rising use of the pill. The use of a condom may help prevent gonorrhea during intercourse, but it doesn't guarantee immunity. Early symptoms in men include a bad-smelling cloudy discharge from the penis and a burning sensation upon urination. Many women fail to seek treatment because they have so few early symptoms that they don't realize they are infected. Untreated gonorrhea is the single most common cause of sterility among men. Women with untreated gonorrhea may experience inflammation of the fallopian tubes, infertility, birth malformations, or menstrual disorders. Fortunately, gonorrhea is easily treated with pencillin in most cases.

The incidence of sexually transmitted diseases is highest in the 20-to-24-year-old group. (Charles Gatewood)

Syphilis, though less common than gonorrhea, is a far more serious disease. It is caused by a spiral-shaped bacteria that is transmitted through sexual contact. The early signs of syphilis are a painless sore at the place of sexual contact, usually the man's penis and the inner walls of the woman's vagina or cervix. Although the sore usually disappears within a month or two, a skin rash and sores may appear, along with sores on other parts of the body in a later stage. These symptoms eventually disappear, but if the disease is left untreated it may progress to an advanced stage causing brain damage, heart failure, blindness, or paralysis. Fortunately syphilis is readily detected through a blood test, and there is a highly effective treatment similar to that for gonorrhea.

Genital herpes, one of several herpes viral infections, has increased dramatically in recent years and affects millions of people. It appears to be transmitted primarily through sexual contact. Symptoms of genital herpes usually appear within several days after sexual contact with an infected partner. The symptoms consist of one or more small, red, painful bumps (papules) in the genital area, such as the man's penis and the woman's labia and inner vaginal walls. These bumps change into blisters, which eventually rupture into painful open sores. The person continues to be contagious throughout this time. In addition to the periodic discomfort, genital herpes can have serious complications. Pregnant women may require a Caesarean section if active herpes is present in the birth canal at the time of delivery. Furthermore, women infected with genital herpes are eight times more likely to contact cervical cancer than others (*Harvard Medical School Health Letter*, 1981). So far there is no real cure for genital herpes, but medical researchers are pursuing an effective treatment on many fronts. Current treatment consists of reducing discomfort and speeding healing during an outbreak of herpes.

Chlamydia infections, which cause inflammation of the urethral tube, now rival gonorrhea as the most sexually transmitted disease. It is now estimated to occur at three times the incidence of gonorrhea in men (Hatcher, et al., 1984). Men who contact the infection have symptoms similar to gonorrhea, such as a discharge from the penis and a mild burning sensation during urination. Women with chlamydia infections show little or no symptoms and are often unaware of the disease until they are informed by an infected partner. Yet a woman may have the infection for a long time, during which she may pass it on to her sexual partners. If left untreated in women, the disease may result in cervical inflammation or pelvic inflammatory disease and, in cases of pregnancy, may cause eye damage to infants at birth. In men, it may spread to the prostate. It is important that an infected person get a laboratory diagnosis before receiving treatment because the symptoms are often confused with those of gonorrhea, though the disease is usually treated with a different drug, tetracycline, rather than penicillin.

AIDS (Acquired Immune Deficiency Syndrome) is a new disease in humans that has achieved national prominence in recent years because of the growing threat it poses. AIDS is caused by a virus, commonly named HTLV-III (for human T-lymphotropic virus, type 3), which destroys the T-helper cells in the body's immune system. Thus, many germs that ordinarily would be harmless to a person with a normal immune system can produce devastating, ultimately lethal, diseases in the persons with AIDS (*Harvard Medical School Health Letter*, 1985).

Not everyone with the AIDS virus develops the deadly AIDS syndrome. There were 12,000 cases of AIDS reported in the United States by the summer of 1985, but not all individuals who manifest the AIDS-related complex (ARC), also develop the full-blown AIDS syndrome. In addition, a much larger number of people, estimated at one million or more, are carriers of the virus but have little or no symptoms. How many of these people eventually develop AIDS remains to be seen (Wallis, 1985).

Although AIDS has become established primarily as a sexually transmitted disease, it is communicated through blood or blood products containing the virus. By all indications, the AIDS virus does not spread easily, such as in a handshake or sneeze. It does not readily penetrate intact body surfaces and does not last long outside the body. Instead, the AIDS virus seems to be acquired by direct exposure of one's bloodstream to the virus, which is carried by body fluids—notably blood and semen. Among homosexually active men, who make up the largest fraction of AIDS patients in the United States, the main source of transmission has been anal intercourse. But the virus can also be transmitted through vaginal intercourse, from men to women or, less commonly, vice versa. The risk of intravenous drug users, who are likely to share needles, comes through direct exposure of the blood stream to someone else's infected blood. The risk of AIDS to people receiving blood transfusions, especially hemophiliacs, has diminished considerably by virtue of more careful screening of donors. There is not, and never has been, a risk to blood donors of contacting AIDS. Since saliva can contain the AIDS virus, though rarely so, it is conceivable that intense kissing could disrupt the lining of the mouth, and thus serve as a means of contagion. But, there appears to be very little risk of getting AIDS from kissing. A final matter concerns the incubation period—the time from the infection to the appearance of symptoms—which tends to be years rather than months, sometimes taking up to 5 years.

To date, no screening tests can clearly identify people in the early stages of AIDS. Instead, such tests identify people with antibodies to the AIDS virus, meaning they have been infected. But the results do not distinguish between those who carry the virus but are not affected by it and those who will develop the AIDS-related complex or the AIDS syndrome itself. Although there is no cure for AIDS yet, there are several forms of treatment. These include the use of powerful drugs (1) to help compensate for the lost immune abilities; (2) to bolster the patient's own immune system; and ultimately, (3) to eliminate the virus that is causing AIDS. Although there are several projects underway to fight AIDS at its source, it is too soon to know what long-term benefits these promising drugs will have.

Meanwhile, here are some practical guidelines for preventing AIDS. First, people who are sexually active outside monogamous relationships of several years' standing, or who have a single partner who may be sexually active, should take measures to protect themselves from the transfer of body fluids. This means using a condom during intercourse and avoiding oral exposure to semen. Although it is not known whether spermicidal creams destroy the AIDS virus, when used in conjunction with a condom they may add a measure of protection. Controlling the spread of AIDS among intravenous drug users might be aided by lifting the ban against the sale of injection equipment. For instance, in the United States, where needles are purchased by prescription, up to 26 percent of AIDS patients have been intravenous drug users; in Canada, where needles are sold over the counter, the figure is only 0.5 percent. Now that blood donors are being screened more carefully, the risk of recipients of blood has been reduced considerably. At the same time, the banking of one's own blood before elective surgery is recommended, to prevent not only AIDS but other complications that may result from the transfusion of blood from one person to another (HMSHL, 1985).

Ultimately, the surest way to prevent the infection will be the development of a vaccine. Although research efforts are underway, there are no guarantees and it may very well take a long time. Meanwhile, AIDS will be a major influence in many lives for the rest of this decade, if not for the rest of this century. Among other things, it may well alter the attitude toward casual sex among heterosexuals as well as homosexuals.

Summary

Male and Female

1. The understanding of sex has been distorted by sexual stereotypes—widespread generalizations about the characteristics and appropriate behavior for males and females.

2. Fewer people than in the past subscribe to the mistaken notions that men have stronger sex drives and are more skilled in sex than are women.

3. Sexual communication involves the mutual sharing of sexual needs and feelings in a relationship, and it depends on a variety of factors, such as each partner's attitudes and nonverbal behavior as well as words.

4. An important part of sexual communication is learning how to initiate and, on occasion, to refuse sex. Couples who share the initiator and refuser role equally have a more satisfactory sex life than other couples.

Human Sexual Response

5. The sexual response cycle of men and women includes the transition, excitement, plateau, orgasm, and resolution phases. Considerable variation among individuals as well as between men and women is evident during the sexual response cycle.

6. A major difference between the sexes is the greater variation among women in the physiology and subjective awareness of orgasm, especially in the woman's ability to have several orgasms in quick succession.

7. Although a significant number of men and women believe it's possible to enjoy sex without love, most of them agree that love enhances sex.

Sexual Problems

8. Common sexual dysfunctions include the lack of sexual desire: erectile inhibition and premature ejaculation in men; inhibited vaginal lubrication and slowness or inability to reach orgasm in women.

9. Birth control methods vary considerably in their reliability, with the final choice often involving a trade-off between the safety and effectiveness of a given method.

10. Sexually transmitted diseases such as gonorrhea, syphilis, genital herpes, chlamydia infections, and AIDS present a health hazard, though many of these diseases, with the notable exception of AIDS, can be effectively treated.

Self-test

1. Which of the following is a stereotype?
   a. men have stronger sex drives than women
   b. women are natural "controllers" in sexual matters
   c. men are more knowledgeable about sex than women
   d. all of the above.

2. The most important part of sexual communications is the partners':
   a. attitudes toward each other
   b. factual knowledge about sex
   c. use of correct clinical terms
   d. skills of persuasion

3. Married and unmarried couples alike tend to be more satisfied with their sex lives when the initiative for sexual intercourse is:
   a. taken mostly by the man
   b. shared equally by both partners
   c. taken mostly by the woman
   d. determined randomly by throwing dice

4. Sexual arousal is heightened through a combination of mental and sensory stimulation in which of the following phases of the sexual response cycle?
   a. orgasm
   b. resolution
   c. excitement
   d. transition

5. There is greater variation in both the physiology and the individual's subjective awareness of sexual climax among:
   a. married couples compared to unmarried couples
   b. men compared to women
   c. homosexuals compared to heterosexuals
   d. women compared to men

6. Peplau, Rubin, and Hill's study of dating couples found that couples who engaged in sex, compared to those who didn't, were:
   a. more satisfied with their relationship
   b. likely to break up sooner
   c. no more or no less satisfied with their relationship
   d. more prone to feelings of regret

7. Inhibited sexual desire is caused mostly by:
   a. psychological factors
   b. neurological factors
   c. genetic factors
   d. hormonal factors

8. People over 30 years of age tend to favor birth control methods that combine high effectiveness with maximum safety, such as:
   a. the condom for men
   b. the pill for women
   c. sterilization for both sexes
   d. vaginal jellies

9. The incidence of sexually transmitted diseases is highest among those in which of the following age groups:
   a. 15–19
   b. 20–24
   c. 25–30
   d. over 30

10. The symptoms of which sexually transmitted disease below appear within several days after contact with a infected partner and consist of small red, painful bumps that turn into blisters and painful sores?

a. syphilis

b. AIDS

c. gonorrhea

d. genital herpes

Exercises

1. *Sexual concerns.* Think over some of the concerns, problems, or worries you have about sex. Now write one or two of them on a 3 by 5 card. Have someone collect the cards and give them to the instructor. Give the instructor an opportunity to look over the cards before class. Then have the instructor read each card aloud and make a brief comment on each question or problem, before asking members of the class for additional comments.

2. *Sexual communication.* If you're married or sexually active with someone, write a page or so on the sexual communication in your relationship. How well do you communicate sexually? If possible, get your partner's views on this. Also, include the effectiveness of nonverbal communication as well as words. Does one person take the initiative for intercourse more often than the other? Or do both partners share this equally? How do you think the sexual communication can be improved?

3. *Shared responsibility for birth control.* How do you feel about men sharing the responsibility for birth control? What are some of the pros and cons of this? Does this present any special problems for the woman, especially in a short-term relationship?

4. *How important is love for sex?* Do you feel two people can enjoy sex without being in love? Or do you feel people must be in love to have good sex? Write a short paragraph explaining your views about sex and love.

5. *Sharing sexual fantasies.* If you're married or sexually active in a secure relationship, share some of your sexual fantasies with your partner. Such sharing is usually more helpful when it is mutual. It may be wise to begin with mild fantasies that can help desensitize fears and embarrassment, and enable you to judge the impact of such sharing on your partner as well as yourself. It's also best to avoid sharing fantasies that would shock your partner or threaten the relationship.

Questions for Self-reflection

1. When was the last time you read a book about sex by a recognized authority in the field?

2. How well do you and your partner communicate about sex?

3. Do you and your partner share the initiative for making love? Or does one of you usually initiate sex?

4. Must physical hugging and touching always lead to sexual intercourse?

5. Are you aware of what is sexually arousing for your partner?

6. Do you and your partner agree about the relationship between sex and love?

7. Are you aware that an occasional sexual dysfunction may be due to emotional stress?

8. How safe is your method of birth control?

9. Can you recognize the symptoms of genital herpes and gonorrhea?

10. Are you familiar with the practical guidelines for avoiding AIDS?

Recommended Readings

Comfort, Alex. *Joy of Sex.* New York: Simon & Schuster, 1985 (paperback). An anthology of lovemaking, illustrated with tasteful art.

Masters, W. H., V. E. Johnson, and R. C. Kolodny. *Human Sexuality,* 2nd ed. Boston: Little, Brown, 1985. An informed explanation of the sexual response cycle, with helpful illustrations.

McCarthy, B. W., and E. J. McCarthy. *Sex and Satisfaction After 30.* Englewood Cliffs, N.J.: Prentice-Hall, 1981 (paperback). Suggestions for enhancing sexual fulfillment during the middle years.

Penny, Alexandra. *How To Make Love To Each Other.* New York: Berkeley Publishing Company, 1984 (paperback). Suggestions for improving lovemaking.

Slaff, James I., M.D. *The AIDS Epidemic.* New York: Warner Books, 1985 (paperback). An informative book which includes practical steps you can take to avoid getting AIDS.

Westheimer, Dr. Ruth. *Dr. Ruth's Guide To Good Sex.* New York: Warner Books, 1983 (paperback). A practical manual for handling sexual problems and enhancing one's sex life.

10 Love and Marriage

If you are going steady, living with someone, or married, can you recall how you and your partner met? Did you meet in familiar ways, such as through mutual friends, at school, or at work? Or did you meet each other accidentally? Apparently, the answer to such questions depends a lot on whether the situation is real life or the movies. Jay Bogar (1984) has observed that in the movies romance usually begins with the "cute meet." Although there is no exact formula for the cute meet, some features are generally present. The people involved tend not to be in control of what happens. They experience embarrassment, discomfort, or fear. And they usually begin by disliking each other intensely. Sometimes the lovers-to-be find themselves in the same cramped quarters. Almost always, they meet in an accidental way. In *Irreconcilable Differences*, Ryan O'Neal is hitchhiking on a rainy night and persuades Shelley Long to give him a ride. In *Romancing the Stone*, Kathleen Turner, a love-starved novelist traveling in a foreign country, takes the wrong bus, which later runs into Michael Douglas's jeep, thus setting the stage for their unlikely meeting.

The cute meet has become a standard feature of Hollywood films. Interestingly, while most of us would object if characters wore clothing out of keeping with the movie's era, we continue to accept the most unlikely romantic encounters without a complaint. Perhaps the cute meet appeals to the romantic streak in us. Deep down, each of us likes to feel that someday, somehow, that special person will appear in our lives.

LOVE

When we meet that special person, our lives may change dramatically as a result of "falling in love." Occasionally, people fall in love abruptly and precariously. More often, love blossoms in time, whether over days or weeks. In either case, the love-struck person's actions are ruled more by the heart than the head. As such, love is notoriously unpredictable, and frequently disappears as quickly as it came. In contrast, couples who have built an enduring, satisfying relationship tend to describe their love in a different way. They would be the first to admit that mature love is something you "grow into," often through many ups and downs. Such love involves learning how to get along with another person day in and day out, and how to accept that person despite personal differences and occasional feelings of anger. Love also calls for a certain degree of personal maturity, with each person learning what it means to give love as well as to receive it—something many couples never learn.

We'll begin the chapter by taking a look at the psychological understanding of love. Then we'll explore the importance of the relationship aspects of love and marriage, including the deeper meaning of love in long-term relationships. In succesive sections, we'll discuss various aspects of marital adjustment, as well as divorce and remarriage.

Romantic Love

Romantic love—a strong emotional attachment to someone of the other sex—has long been celebrated by poets, songwriters, and lovers all around the world. Such love can be seen in the partners' preoccupation with each other, including a great deal of physical touching, hugging, and gazing into each other's eyes. Most of us have little difficulty recognizing when we're in love because of the folklore about romantic love expressed in songs, stories, and movies. Love is something we feel, a kind of warm glow within. Yet it isn't fully under our control, and we often fall in love against our better judgment. Also, we tend to idealize the person we love. He or she can do no wrong. Love is also "blind," leading us to overlook a person's faults that may be perfectly obvious to everyone else. Romantic love is also possessive. We want this person to ourselves. Jealousy is regarded as a sign of our love. Furthermore, under the spell of romantic love, lovers do sentimental, foolish things, such as putting a marriage proposal on a highway billboard. When we're in love, there's an acute longing to have our love returned, making our moods dependent on such reciprocation. Finally, romantic love includes a great deal of ambivalence and suffering, expressed in such clichés as "It's too good to last" and "True love never runs smooth."

Psychologists explain the intensity and irrationality of romantic love in various ways. Some point out that romantic love taps deep, unconscious aspects of our experience, especially those associated with early parental relationships. Others emphasize that romantic love flourishes in the soil of unfulfilled needs

Couples in love engage in a great deal of touching and gazing into each other's eyes. (Teri Leigh Stratford)

and self-dissatisfaction. People who are dependent, insecure, and lonely are especially likely candidates for romantic love. Psychologists have demonstrated this by devising scales to measure both love and dependency. The results showed that the more dependent people were, the more "in love" they were with their partners. Those most in love were also the most dependent. People who "didn't know" whether they were in love or not were less dependent on their partners (Berscheid and Walster, 1978).

Romantic love also heightens the potential for both positive and negative aspects of close relationships. This was brought out in a series of studies comparing romantic relationships with friendships. Keith Davis (1985) and his colleagues found that while love and friendship are alike in many ways, there are some crucial differences that make love relationships both more rewarding and more volatile. They identified several key components that make love relationships unique, namely the "passion" cluster and "caring" cluster of characteristics. Accordingly, individuals in love were more preoccupied with their partners, had an exclusive relationship with their partners, and desired physical intimacy with them. They also cared enough to give their utmost when their partners were in need, even more so than among friends. At the same time, because of the greater exclusiveness and emotional involvement between them, lovers experienced greater ambivalence, conflict, distress, and mutual criticism in their relationships than did friends. In sum, love relationships are both more satisfying and more frustrating than good friendships are.

Staying Together or Breaking Up

When love quickly fades, it may have been infatuation—a highly emotional, often physical, short-lived love. In other cases, true love runs its course, and dies. Fortunately, love often leads to a long-term relationship. But in each instance, whether couples stay together or break up depends on more than romantic love.

In one study, Hill, Rubin, and Peplau (1976) followed over 200 dating couples for a 2-year period. During that time, over half of the couples stayed together; the other half broke up. The people who stayed together tended to be more similar to each other in regard to age, intelligence, career plans, and physical attractiveness than those who broke up. Apparently, similarities between people not only attract them to each other, but also foster lasting relationships between them. In contrast, serious differences or disagreements encourage people to eventually go their own ways.

Relationships were also more likely to end if one partner was more emotionally involved in the relationship than the other—a common finding. Among couples who initially reported that one partner was more emotionally involved in the relationships, 54 percent eventually broke up during the 2-year period. But among couples in which both partners were equally involved, only 23 percent broke up. Emotional commitment between partners must be somewhat mutual if a relationship is to develop into a satisfying and lasting relationship.

There's also some evidence that the longer couples date before marrying, the better their chances for a happy marriage. In one study, married women of all ages were divided into four groups—those who had dated less than 5 months, 6 to 11 months, 1 to 2 years, and more than 2 years. The results showed that each group in succession was happier in their marriage than the preceding one. Apparently, with longer periods of acquaintance individuals are better able to screen out incompatible partners (Grover, et al., 1985).

Why People Marry

Despite all the pessimism about marriage, Americans continue to hold marriage in high regard. Even the high rate of divorce indirectly reflects people's high expectations of marriage. About 94 percent of people in the United States eventually marry—most of them in their 20s. The median age of *first* marriage has risen somewhat, and is now about 25 years of age for men and 23 years of age for women. But the growing number of divorces and remarriages raises the average age of *all* marriages still further (U.S. Bureau of the Census, 1985).

The great majority of Americans eventually marry—most of them in their twenties. (Ken Karp)

People marry out of mixed motives, many of them not even clear to themselves. Yet when people are asked why they married, their answers are suggestive. In one survey of 75,000 women, the major reason given for getting married and staying married was love (Tavris and Jayaratne, 1976). Furthermore, women who married primarily for love were happier with their marriages than those who had married mostly for other reasons, such as to have a family or to achieve financial security. Close behind love as the reasons for marrying and staying married were companionship and fulfillment. Companionship takes on many qualities of an intimate friendship, with happily married wives regarding their husbands as their best friends. The importance of fulfillment suggests that marriage is also expected to fulfill a variety of psychological needs such as intimacy, security, and growth, reflecting the importance of personal fulfillment in our society.

When people in lasting relationships, especially the happily married, speak of "love," it's most likely to be "companionate love"—the affection people feel for someone with whom their life is deeply intertwined (Berscheid and Walster,

1978). Although such love has its romantic side, it pertains mostly to the compatibility and closeness between two persons. Companionate love involves the mutual sharing of feelings of trust and respect for each other, with a willingness to give and take on both sides. Fantasy and idealization gradually give way to reality. The partners come to accept each other as they really are. As one husband put it, "My wife accepts me as I am, instead of trying to make me into someone else." Mature, companionate love is also based on self-acceptance instead of self-dissatisfaction. Having accepted themselves, both partners are more able to reach out and accept each other more fully in a way that makes them more lovable. Finally, mature love grows stronger with time. There is less of the love-hate conflict so characteristic of romantic, passionate love. Not that all is harmony and peace for happily married couples. Far from it. Such couples also have their disagreements and problems. But their trust and respect for each other encourages them to manage their problems in a positive way. In the long run, even the shared struggles as well as the joys strengthen their love for each other.

THE MARRIAGE RELATIONSHIP

A landmark study of Americans' mental health found that more couples are happier with their marriages today than in the past. About three-fourths of married couples report they are happier than average with their marriages, compared to just two-thirds of married couples in the 1950s. At the same time, more couples report having problems in marriages, 61 percent today compared to just 46 percent in the 1950s. Such contradictory findings can be explained through a third, common factor, namely the growing importance of the personal relationship in marriage (Veroff, Douvan, and Kulka, 1981).

The Importance of the Relationship

When the same couples were asked what was the best thing in their marriage, the most frequently given answers revolved around the marriage relationship itself, such as how much the partners enjoyed being with each other. When asked what was the worst thing about their marriage, couples cited relationship factors, such as difficulties in communicating with each other, as often as they mentioned situational factors, such as unhappiness at work. In other words, when the individuals are happy with each other, they tend to be happy in their marriage. But when they are not getting along well in their relationship, their married life as a whole suffers, despite other considerations such as a nice family or good income (Veroff, Douvan, and Kulka, 1981).

Individuals and couples alike tend to have different priorities in regard to the relative importance of close relationships and work. This was brought out in a study by Philip Blumstein and Pepper Schwartz (1983), which included cohabiting couples as well as married couples. They found that in about half the married couples, one partner is relationship-centered while the other is more work-centered. (See Figure 10–1.) In many instances the husband devoted most of his energies to the job and the wife to the needs of their relationship. Yet this was not always the case. There was also a tendency for the partner most inclined to be understanding and compassionate, regardless of sex, to put the relationship first. In a few instances, the roles were reversed, with women putting the work role first. In one-fourth of the married couples, and slightly more of the cohabiting couples, both partners were relationship-centered. In both instances, relationship-centered couples were the happiest of all. Couples in which one partner was relationship-centered were somewhat less happy in their marriage. At the other extreme, couples in which both partners were work-centered were the least happy and committed to their marriage. With work demanding so much of a person's energies today, and with more dual-career couples, the relationship may easily become a secondary aspect of the individual's and couple's life. Although many work-centered couples may not really want to see their relationship go under, if no one is putting the relationship first, they may risk losing what makes their life together special.

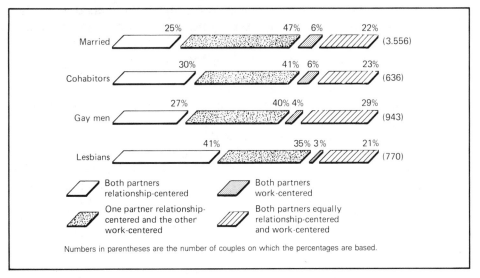

Figure 10–1. RELATIONSHIP-CENTERED COUPLES, WORK-CENTERED COUPLES, AND MIXED COUPLES.

From *American Couples* by Philip Blumstein, Ph.D., and Pepper Schwartz, Ph.D. Copyright © 1983 by Philip Blumstein and Pepper W. Schwartz. By permission of William Morrow & Company, 1983, p. 171.

Communication and Conflict

Hundreds of experienced marriage counselors were asked to indicate the main causes of marital difficulties among the couples they worked with. The findings were then combined to show the frequency with which the different problem areas occurred. One or more of the usual things blamed for marriage failure—conflicts over children, money, sex, infidelity, relatives, and leisure—occurred in 35 percent of all the couples. Other difficulties such as disagreements about housekeeping chores and physical abuse occurred less frequently, in 16 percent of the couples. However, at the top of the list, far above the rest, was a problem cited by a whopping 86 percent of all couples—difficulty in communication. Again and again, husbands and wives complained, "We just can't talk to each other" (Mace and Mace, 1977).

Why can't couples communicate? Married people talk with each other all the time. They say things like "What are we having for dinner?" and "I'll be home later than usual tonight." This type of communication is easy enough. The failure in communication tends to occur at a deeper level of sharing feelings, expectations, intentions, and personal needs. It's in these areas that partners have trouble getting through to each other. In most instances both partners long for intimacy and tenderness. But the price is being open and vulnerable. Accordingly, each tends to hold back, settling into a kind of guarded communication. When feelings are expressed, they're likely to be the "safer" negative feelings like anger. Individuals are more reluctant or embarrassed to express their positive feelings of love and tenderness.

These difficulties in communication are further compounded as couples try to mesh their lives more closely. As they become more involved with each other, some areas of disagreement are inevitable. As they struggle to resolve their disagreements, the sparks begin to fly. Feelings of irritation, frustration, exasperation, and hostility accumulate. The harder they try to resolve their disagreements, the more anger is generated. Each partner wants closeness; yet each feels cheated. Their love is blocked by anger. So instead of loving each other, they find themselves hating each other.

How couples manage conflict makes the crucial difference in marriage. When one partner is clearly dominant in the relationship, that person often resorts to the "hammer" approach. The person may get angry and demand that his or her partner give in. The person may even threaten to leave if the partner doesn't agree. Stability is achieved through one partner being dominant and the other submissive. The more controlling a partner is in the relationship, the more inclined he or she is to use "hard tactics" of anger, threat, and domination (Kipnis and Schmidt, 1985).

Another type of solution more commonly seen among partners committed to companionship is emotional alienation. The sharing of power makes for a democratic, two-vote system. Yet this approach is difficult to operate successfully when the partners disagree over a matter they both feel strongly about. Conflicts are not resolved because neither is willing to give ground. The clash of conflicting wills generates increasing tension and resentment. Such a state becomes so intolerable that the partners withdraw emotionally from their relationship. Conflicts are not resolved, but an uneasy peace is achieved at a price— an "emotional" divorce. Unfortunately, this is probably the most familiar type of marriage, with the partners drifting apart, experiencing fewer conflicts, to be sure, but also less satisfaction in an "empty" marriage.

A third approach to conflict management, usually advocated by marriage and family counselors, is based on rational, problem-solving and negotiation skills. The assumption here is that conflict is not all bad. Indeed, conflict is an inevitable part of vital close relationships; it may help individuals learn more about themselves and each other and may deepen their relationship. Such an approach involves five overlapping stages:

1. *Acknowledge the conflict.* As easy as this sounds, this is often the most difficult part. Conflict is so anxiety-arousing in close relationships that couples tend to avoid or deny it, which results in nagging, boredom, and indifference. Instead, it's better to acknowledge the conflict openly. This helps to clear the air and set the stage for a constructive solution.

2. *Identify the problem.* The biggest difficulty here is our tendency to be judgmental and blame the person instead of focusing on the problem behavior. We say, "You're selfish" instead of "When you go ahead without asking my preference, I feel left out." Both partners need to use nonjudgmental "I" messages and reflective listening skills to say how they see the problem, how they feel about it, and what each is saying and doing—and *not* doing—that contributes to the problem.

3. *Explore alternatives.* Both partners should explore a variety of alternatives and try to look at the advantages and disadvantages of each. Focusing on a mutually acceptable solution taps the "we" motivation of both parties and helps them to move from an adversarial to a more cooperative relationship.

4. *Reach an agreement.* Your chances of reaching agreement are better in regard to changes in overt behavior than underlying perceptions and personalities. The most important thing here is mutual consent. Does the solution incorporate the best interests of both parties? It often helps to make a written note of such an agreement to avoid future misunderstanding.

5. *Implement the plan of action.* The sooner you act on the agreed-upon solution, the better. Both partners should be clear as to what is to be done, when, where, and by whom. Also, after a reasonable period of time, it's often advisable to reassess the situation and make further changes as mutually agreed upon.

Not surprisingly, couples who rely mainly on such rational tactics and compromise tend to be the most satisfied with their marriage relationships (Kipnis and Schmidt, 1985).

Commitment

A crucial factor in each couple's relationship is commitment—the pledge or promise to make it work. But it's important to point out that partners may make many different types of commitment, ranging from the sharing of emotional ties to marriage as a legal contract. We've already seen that when a couple's love or emotional involvement is mutual, this makes for a stronger and more lasting relationship. Otherwise, when emotional involvement is one-sided, or one partner's commitment is tentative, the relationship becomes less stable and usually less satisfying. For example, Lisa and Mark had been going together for 3 years, without a hint of marriage. When Lisa broached the subject, Mark resisted, saying, "I'm not ready to make that type of commitment." Yet, when Lisa grew restless and began dating other men, Mark became angry and accused her of being disloyal. Lisa replied, "If you aren't prepared to talk about marriage after all this time, I feel free to date other men." Heated arguments and numerous late-night phone calls ensued for the next several weeks. They also sought the help of a counselor who helped them clarify their relationship. Several months later they became engaged. Mark and Lisa discovered that they needed a firm mutual commitment at that point in their relationship in order for it to thrive.

Unmarried couples who live together represent another level of commitment—that of sharing physical intimacy, everyday lives, and often their financial resources. The number of cohabiting couples has more than tripled since 1970, resulting in about 2 million unmarried households by the mid-1980s. Most of these couples are under 40 years of age, with many partners never having been married. (See Table 10–1.)

Typically, people drift into this type of arrangement, often keeping a place of their own. Such couples enjoy greater intimacy compared to other dating couples their age. Yet their rates of breaking up or getting married are about the same as other couples. Once married, these couples are also about as happy, no more but no less so, than other couples (Risman, et al, 1981).

At the same time, the commitment in such an arrangement may not be as mutual as it appears. In one survey, when men were asked if they planned to marry the woman they were going with, there was no difference between the responses of cohabiting and noncohabiting men. Yet cohabiting women were slightly more inclined to believe that their live-in partner would eventually marry them than noncohabiting women (Macklin, 1974). The discrepancy between each partner's commitment among cohabiting couples became widely publicized during the 1979 "palimony" trial between singer Michelle Triola and actor Lee Marvin. Michelle Triola sued Lee Marvin for a share of his financial assets during their 6 years of living together, even though she had since moved out. During the trial, when Lee Marvin was asked whether he had loved Michelle Triola, he hedged a bit and admitted that while he had loved Michelle it was not the sort of love that involved a long-term loyalty. In other words, Lee may have once loved Michelle without feeling or making any lasting commit-

Table 10–1. UNMARRIED COUPLES BY SELECTED CHARACTERISTICS, 1970 to 1984, AND BY MARITAL STATUS OF PARTNERS, 1983. An unmarried couple is here defined as two unrelated adults of the opposite sex sharing the same household.

Presence of Children and Age of Householder	1970	1980	1983	1984	Marital Status of Male	Total	Marital Status of Female			
							Never married	Divorced	Widowed	Married, husband absent
Unmarried couples . . .	523*	1,589	1,891	1,988	Total, 1983 . .	1,891	965	625	163	137
No children under 15 yr	327	1,159	1,366	1,373	Never married . .	1,010	695	209	67	41
Some children under 15 yr . .	196	431	525	614	Divorced	638	195	340	47	55
					Widowed	78	10	25	39	4
					Married, wife absent	164	64	53	10	39
Under 25 yr. old	55	411	455	432						
25–44 yr. old . .	103	837	1,082	1,208						
45–64 yr. old . .	186	221	233	234						
65 yr. old and over	178	119	121	114						

*Numbers of couples are in thousands

From: U.S. Bureau of the Census, *Statistical Abstract of the United States 1984*, 105th ed. (Washington, D.C.: U.S. Government Printing Office, 1984), p. 40.

ment to her. But Michelle may not have perceived this distinction and felt that he was both in love with her and committed to her (Kelley, 1983).

Marriage is often regarded as the highest level of commitment a couple can make. But even this is subject to different interpretations. In their book *American Couples*, Philip Blumstein and Pepper Schwartz (1983) point out that many couples who marry legally hold to the concept of "voluntary marriage." The implicit assumption is that their marriage will last as long as their love does. When the couple is no longer "in love," it's understood they will get divorced. Does this mean that the traditional marriage vows of "till death us do part" have become irrelevant? Not necessarily. Jeanette Lauer and Robert Lauer (1985) surveyed several hundred couples who had been happily married for 15 years or more to see what made their marriages last. The most frequently given reason for an enduring and happy marriage was genuinely liking one's spouse—or a rewarding personal relationship—as described earlier in this chapter. The second key to a lasting marriage was the belief in marriage as a long-term commitment. Many respondents felt too many people in the present generation take the marriage vows too lightly and are unwilling to work through difficult times. Some felt divorce was not an option. Others viewed the marriage commitment more as a determination to stay together and work things through despite unhappy times. No doubt, couples differ as to how much unhappiness they are willing to put up with in their relationship or how long they will work at it. But their commitment to marriage as a long-term relationship may motivate them to work all the harder at it, thereby increasing their chances of success.

MARITAL ADJUSTMENT

One of the major differences between couples today and those of the past is the lack of clearly defined roles for husbands and wives. The changing nature of male and female roles creates problems for all types of couples as they settle down to live together. Even the most mundane tasks may become a problem. Who cooks? Who takes out the trash? Who writes the checks? Yet, such tasks are only a part of a much larger issue, namely how men and women relate to each other. Getting along in marriage involves the larger questions of authority, fairness, and the respective fulfillment of needs. In this section, we'll take a look at several important areas of marital adjustment, including the sharing of marriage responsibilities—such as the provider and housekeeping roles—as well as handling money, marital sex, and the changes in the couple's relationship over time.

Sharing Marital Responsibilities

Marriage partners are sharing marital responsibilities to a greater degree today than in the past. As a result, the respective role expectations between husbands and wives are becoming more flexible and functional. More wives are sharing the provider role by working outside the home. Husbands are expected to provide greater emotional support in the marriage, including help with child-rearing. Decision making has become more democratic, especially among dual-career couples. There's a tendency for the person with the greatest competency, interest, or time to perform a given task. For example, Tom travels a good bit in his job and his wife Carol assumes greater responsibilities for things such as writing the checks. She also doesn't hesitate to mow the lawn or take the car in for repairs, though she often talks this over with her husband. Tom makes it a point to call home several times a week to keep in touch with Carol and the kids and to assist with things such as making sure the kids are doing their homework. Like many couples today, Tom and Carol are less concerned about who does which task than what works for them as a couple and how it affects their relationship.

A major area of marital adjustment for many couples has to do with the wife's working outside the home. Most married women would like the option of working outside the home and feel it would help their marriage. Although many husbands agree with this idea, a substantial minority do not. In one survey, three-fourths of the wives either strongly favored the wife working outside the home or felt neutral about it; only 25 percent of the women opposed the idea. However, only two-thirds of the husbands favored their wives working or felt neutral about it, with 34 percent of them objecting to the idea. There was greater agreement on this issue among cohabiting couples, though, once again, women felt more strongly than men did about this. Interestingly, when women work outside the home, couples tend to share power more equally and are more satisfied with their marriages than couples without working wives (Blumstein and Schwartz, 1983).

One difficulty that comes with the increased sharing of marital responsibilities is the issue of fairness. More specifically, there is a tendency for each partner to want greater rewards at no additional costs. For example, a husband may favor his wife working to help pay the bills, but still expect her to continue doing all the things she did around the house before taking a job. In turn, a working wife may want to keep most of her earnings while expecting her husband to help out more around the house. Take the matter of housework among married couples. Although working wives do less housework than full-time homemakers do, they still do most of the household chores. Even though husbands of working wives help out around the house more than husbands of full-time homemakers do, their contribution is not impressive (Blumstein and Schwartz, 1983). (See Figure 10–2.)

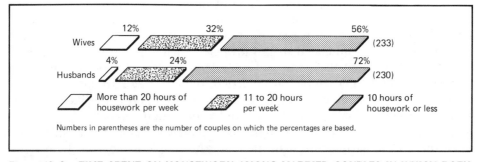

Figure 10–2. TIME SPENT ON HOUSEWORK AMONG MARRIED COUPLES IN WHICH BOTH ARE EMPLOYED FULL-TIME AND BOTH FEEL STRONGLY THAT HOUSEWORK SHOULD BE SHARED EQUALLY.

From *American Couples* by Philip Blumstein, Ph.D., and Pepper Schwartz, Ph.D. Copyright © 1983 Philip Blumstein and Pepper W. Schwartz. By permission of William Morrow & Company, 1983, p. 145.

Managing Money

Money has become an increasingly important factor in marriage in recent years, probably because of things like inflation and a tight job market. Yet conflicts over money usually reflect struggles over larger issues, such as power, equality, trust, and interdependence in the relationship. The conflict over money usually revolves around three issues: the couple's income, their management of money, and whether to pool their financial resources or not.

In their study of American couples, Blumstein and Schwartz (1983) found that the amount of money a person earns establishes relative power in the relationship. Because husbands generally earn more, they tend to exert more power in the relationship, especially in money matters. The greater the difference between the husband and wife's income, the more likely the husband will exert greater authority in the marriage. Yet the couple's attitude toward the male provider role also makes a difference. When one or both partners believes the provider role should be shared, husbands are less likely to hold greater authority in the relationship regardless of his income. As you would expect, whether or not a wife has a separate income also plays an important role. In one survey, 80 percent of the wives worked outside the home. Most of them felt that their income gave them greater self-esteem and power in the relationship. But when the wife earned more than her husband, the couple often argued about money (Rubenstein, 1981). Although the couple's income is not generally the central problem with money, it is important. The more disappointed couples are with their overall income, the less satisfied they are with their relationship (Blumstein and Schwartz, 1983).

Couples argue more about how to manage their money than about how much they have, according to the findings of Blumstein and Schwartz. And this seems to hold true at all income levels, among married and unmarried couples alike. Married couples are especially apt to fight over money matters. Since married couples have accumulated shared property, such as a house and cars, they must make many joint decisions, and such decisions have a high potential for conflict. But the longer couples are married, the less they fight about money. Perhaps they've had enough experience to reach a mutually agreeable policy or have established a high level of trust and cooperation, or both. Cohabiting couples are slightly less inclined to fight about money than married couples. Yet when the woman earns more than the man, the couple is more likely to fight over money, much the same as married couples do. At the same time, when the partners feel they have achieved equality in their relationship, whether married or not, they have fewer conflicts over money.

Couples must also decide whether to pool their financial resources or not. From one point of view, it's natural for each partner to want to retain some financial independence. On the other hand, we've been brought up to believe that love involves subordinating our self-interest for the greater good of the relationship. Yet there are drawbacks to pooling of financial resources. Nevertheless, most married couples come down in favor of pooling their resources. More than three-fourths of the couples married 10 years or more favor pooling, though women are somewhat less enthusiastic about it than their husbands. Here again, the partners' attitudes toward their marriage also affect their policies on money. More than eight out of 10 husbands and wives who believe marriage is a lifetime relationship favor pooling, whereas only five out of ten spouses subscribing to the idea of "voluntary marriage" like the idea. Cohabiting couples generally feel less favorably toward pooling their money and property. Actually, those who keep their money separate have fewer fights over money. But they also have weaker ties, making it easier for them to dissolve their relationship. The longer unmarried couples live together, the more likely they are to pool their resources (Blumstein and Schwartz, 1983).

Couples with young children value
their time together as a family.
(Ken Karp)

Sex in Marriage

Most everyone recognizes that a good sex life is an important part of a
couple's marriage. Yet sex is rarely an isolated act. The partners' sexual satisfaction usually mirrors their life together outside the bedroom, especially how they
feel about each other. When things are going well in their marriage, sex
becomes a satisfying physical bond that strengthens their relationship. But when
there are disagreements about money or rearing the children, this often spills
over into their sex life. The resulting dissatisfaction with sex then begins to con-
taminate the rest of their marriage as well.

The longer couples, married and unmarried alike, live together, the less
frequently they have intercourse. Reasons usually cited include the lack of time
or physical energy. Perhaps a more important factor is the decline of sexual
ardor because the partners have become "accustomed to each other." The
decrease in physical vigor associated with aging is also a related factor, especially
among couples in middle and late adulthood. Less frequent intercourse leads to
diminished satisfaction in sex, but not greatly so. In one survey, 67 percent of
the couples married 10 years or more described their sex life as "good" or "very
good," compared to 82 percent of newly married couples. A lot depends on the

particular couple, with sexually satisfying marriages tending to remain that way, while sexually lukewarm marriages turn even cooler (Levin, 1975). Then too, couples assign different priorities to sex. For some, sex is a major bond, with one or both partners complaining when sex occurs too infrequently. For others, sex is less central to the marriage. Jeanette and Robert Lauer (1985), in their study of what makes marriages last, found some couples who remained happily married despite a less than ideal sex life, though men were more apt to complain about this than women.

Couples who have been married for a long time usually pay more attention to the quality of sex than its frequency, though these are not mutually exclusive. What counts most is how much they enjoy making love and whether it is mutually satisfying. For instance, the more frequently intercourse leads to orgasm for women, the more they report being satisfied with their sex lives (Levin, 1975). Couples frequently complain about the effect children have had on their sex lives. But it is the quality rather than the frequency of sex that is usually found wanting. Giving an example of how children get in the way, one man said, "We have to wait until the kids are asleep to make love. By then we're both tired and we have to keep 'quiet.' Sex isn't as much fun anymore." Actually, there is a strong positive relationship between the quality and frequency of sex, such that couples who enjoy their sex life the most also tend to have sex more frequently (Blumstein and Schwartz, 1983). But again, it's almost impossible to distinguish cause and effect. Is it because the partners are happy in their marriage that they enjoy sex? Or does a satisfying sex life serve to strengthen a couple's love? It's hard to tell. One point is clear: for most couples, though not necessarily all, a good sex life and a happy marriage go together.

Most couples hold to the ideal of sexual monogamy, whether they adhere to it or not. But when asked if they've ever had sex outside marriage, it's a different story. Unfortunately, it's difficult to get a realistic picture of marital infidelity because the statistics vary so widely between different surveys, especially those done in the mass media. However, in a careful study of American couples, Blumstein and Schwartz (1983) found that one in four husbands and one in five wives admitted having had extramarital sex. Wives were more likely than husbands to have had an affair rather than just casual sex. In most instances, husbands and wives were well aware when their partners were having extramarital sex, whether they openly confronted their partners about this or not.

Traditionally, the double standard in sex has permitted husbands to engage in extramarital sex more than wives, but this too is changing. Today more women are engaging in extramarital sex. Marital infidelity is especially common among women who have engaged in sex before marriage and who work outside the home. Working wives are twice as likely as full-time homemakers to have sex outside of marriage. Although women who participate in extramarital sex tend to be dissatisfied with their marriage, including their sex life, the difference is not striking. Furthermore, a small minority of wives who engage in extramarital sex report enjoying their marriage, including their sex life, suggesting that some of the motivation for extramarital sex may be experimental or recreational rather than from dissatisfaction or for retaliation (Levin, 1975).

Changes in Marriage Over Time

Let's suppose four couples with similar backgrounds get married. Then after a few years of marital bliss, couple A goes steadily downhill in their marriage. Couple B experiences an up and down pattern in their relationship through the years. Couple C, after 2 or 3 years of happiness, experiences a decline in their marital satisfaction, but once the kids leave home, marriage becomes more rewarding again. Couple D reports their marriage has become happier with each passing year.

Which of these four patterns is the most common? It would be gratifying to say it is the increasing happiness of couple D. But practically no studies find this to be a *common* pattern, despite particular couples here and there who report such an experience. More often, marriages tend to devitalize over time, with the steady decline in marital satisfaction in couple A characteristic of those who are unhappily married, and the fluctuating pattern of marital happiness in couple C characteristic of the average marriage. The latter pattern resembles a U curve, with marital satisfaction declining, then leveling off, and later increasing in the "empty nest" years of marriage. Andrew Greeley (1981) and his col-

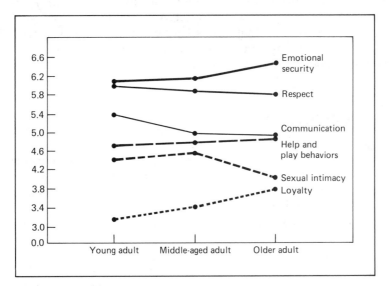

Figure 10–3. CHANGES IN TIME COMPONENTS OF SATISFYING LOVE RELATIONSHIPS ACROSS THE LIFE SPAN.

From M.N. Reedy, J.E. Birren, and K.W. Schaie, "Age and sex differences in satisfying love relationships across the adult life span," *Human Development*, 24, 1981, pp. 52-66. Reprinted by permission of S. Karger AG, Basel, Switzerland.

leagues found that the fluctuations in marital satisfaction usually depended on such things as the duration of the marriage and the age of the children. Generally, there was a high degree of marital happiness in the first 2 years, followed by a sharp decline between the second and eighth year, with a strong rebound about the ninth or tenth year of marriage. The ebb and flow of marital satisfaction continued, with low points about the end of the second decade of marriage and just before the twenty-fifth anniversary. Perhaps this has something to do with the presence of teenagers in the home and the burden of paying for a college education. In any event, once the kids left home, many couples reported an increase in marital happiness. In fact, those who were still together at their fiftieth anniversary reported levels of marital happiness rivaling their first 2 years of marriage.

Couples, like couple D, who are happily married all along also experience growth in their relationships. In order to discover how satisfying love relationships change over the years, Reedy, Birren, and Schaie (1981) studied 102 happily married couples in early, middle, and late adulthood respectively. The changes in the various components of satisfying love relationships can be seen in Figure 10–3. As you can see, sexual intimacy and communication were relatively more important among young adult couples, whereas feelings of emotional security, mutually satisfying behaviors, and loyalty were increasingly important among older couples. For some reason, women rated emotional security as more important in love than men did. And, surprisingly, men, more than women, rated loyalty as more characteristic of their love relationship. There were no sex differences for communication and sexual intimacy. The fact that emotional security and respect were ranked consistently high by couples at all ages suggests that a satisfying marriage depends a great deal on the trust and commitment in the relationship, with sexual intimacy playing an important but subordinate role in marriage.

DIVORCE AND REMARRIAGE

Unfortunately, as we all know, many marriages now end in divorce. The divorce rate among Americans has more than doubled in the past 25 years, with one out of every two marriages now ending in divorce (U.S. Bureau of the Census, 1984). Each year over 1 million couples get divorced, most of them within the first 10 years of their marriage. Why the dramatic rise in the divorce rate? Many different reasons have been put forth, ranging from the lack of preparation for marriage to the fading of religious values. A major factor has been the gradual shift away from the traditional notion that marriage is forever to the idea that the primary goal of marriage is happiness and fulfillment. This shift in values has also been accompanied by changes in the laws that make it easier for couples to get divorced.

The Divorce Experience

The decision to divorce usually comes after a long period of mutual alienation, often accompanied by a separation, in which both partners suffer from hurt, damaged self-esteem, and loneliness. In many instances, the couple may have sought help from professionals such as marriage counselors and family therapists. Yet no matter how good or bad the marriage has been, the process of getting divorced is almost always painful. Divorce is also a complex experience because so many things are happening at once. Bohannan (1975) has identified six overlapping experiences that are common to the experience of divorce, although they may occur in different order and with varying intensities from one couple to another.

The *emotional* divorce usually comes first. The partners tend to withdraw emotionally from each other, or coexist with a great deal of mutual antagonism. The cold-war atmosphere of this emotional divorce often does more damage to the children than the legal divorce that follows.

The *legal* divorce is necessary if the individuals ever wish to remarry. In some states couples may divorce only if there are sufficient grounds for divorce, such as mental or physical cruelty, infidelity, or the abuse of alcohol or drugs. Because such laws punish the "guilty" partner and reward the "innocent" party, most states also provide for a "no fault" divorce on such grounds as irreconcilable differences. Either way, the legal aspects of divorce are not only expensive but emotionally draining as well.

The *economic* divorce deals with the settlement of property and money. Although alimony ("giving food") has traditionally been granted to wives, it may now be given to the partner of either sex with the lesser income, or it may not be given at all. As long as they are physically and financially able, however, fathers are generally responsible for child support payments until their children become of legal age.

The *coparental* divorce has to do with the custody of the children and visitation rights. The courts tend to follow the principle of "the best interests of the child." Traditionally this has meant that custody was generally given to the wife. But today there is a tendency to award joint custody and in some cases custody to fathers. The partner who is not granted physical and legal custody of the children is usually granted certain visitation rights.

The *community* divorce comes in the form of disapproval and rejection by friends and acquaintances. The increasing number of divorces as well as the support groups available for divorced people help to alleviate much of the loneliness that inevitably accompanies divorce.

The *psychic* divorce is almost always the last and most difficult part of divorce. It consists of separating one's self from the influence of a former partner and becoming an autonomous social being again. This may be quite frightening at first. Yet this is also potentially the most constructive aspect of divorce in which the individual may experience considerable personal growth. Nevertheless, it takes most people 2 or 3 years to fully recover from the distress of a divorce.

Single-parent Families

Divorce has a psychological impact on the children as well as on the divorcing couple. If the current divorce rate continues, it is projected that anywhere from one-third to one-half of all children under 18 will have experienced the divorce of their parents by the mid-1990s (Glick, 1984). *How* children are affected by their parents' divorce varies considerably, depending on such factors as the age, sex, and personality of the child, custody arrangements, the custodial parent-child relationship, and use of various support systems.

In an attempt to determine how children are affected by divorce, Wallerstein and Kelly (1980) interviewed parents and children of sixty families, then did a followup interview 18 months later, and again after 5 years. They found children of all ages experienced anger, loneliness, and sadness. Younger children had the most difficulty understanding divorce and tended to blame themselves, feeling they were being punished for being bad. Although adolescents were less likely to blame themselves, they did feel especially vulnerable to being forced to take sides with one parent. Adolescents were also likely to hide their hurt feelings, thus prolonging their adjustment to divorce. The first year after the divorce was especially stressful for the children and parents alike. By the end of the first year and a half, however, most of the children and adolescents had adjusted reasonably well to their new home situation. However, a disturbing number of them remained intensely dissatisfied even after 5 years.

An increasing number of children live in single-parent families. About one in five families is headed by one parent, with double that number among black families. More than three-fourths of single-parent families are headed by women. (See Figure 10–4.) Single-parent mothers generally face economic hardship. They must usually take a job outside the home while balancing the conflicting claims of work, childrearing, and domestic chores, not to mention personal loneliness. In some instances, a "coercive cycle" may develop between single mothers and their sons. The mother, feeling overwhelmed with her responsibilities as a single parent, becomes strict with her son. At the same time, boys, because of their tendency to engage in aggressive behavior, are apt to rebel and manifest discipline problems at home, academic and social problems at school, and delinquency. Girls who grow up without a father have fewer problems in school and delinquency. But they may have greater difficulties relating to boys than girls in intact marriages. Depending on the personal makeup of the girl and her age at the time of the divorce, girls may either become shy and insecure around men or they may compensate by becoming flirtatious and aggressive with the opposite sex. They usually begin dating at an earlier age and become more sexually active than other girls. They also experience more conflicts with their mothers and hold more negative attitudes toward their fathers (Hetherington, Cox, and Cox, 1979).

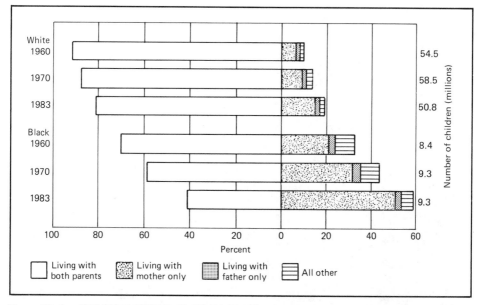

Figure 10–4. CHILDREN UNDER 18 BY RACE LIVING WITH BOTH PARENTS OR A SINGLE PARENT: 1960, 1970, and 1983.

Adapted from U.S. Bureau of the Census, *Social Indicators* (Washington, D.C.: Government Printing Office, 1980), p. 25. Information for 1983 from U.S. Bureau of the Census, *Statistical Abstract of the United States 1984*, 105th ed. (Washington, D.C.: Government Printing Office, 1984), p. 46.

The growing tendency of the courts to consider the genuine needs of the child in relation to both parents in awarding custody rights has resulted in more joint custody arrangements and more single-parent families headed by men. During the 1970s, the number of single-parent families headed by fathers doubled. About one out of ten single-parent families is now headed by a father (U.S. Bureau of the Census, 1984). Boys may benefit from such an arrangement in the sense that the father may be more accepting and even encouraging of the traditional masculine behaviors such as rough-and-tumble play and participation in sports. However, girls may feel their fathers are less sensitive to their own needs than mothers are. Fathers with custody rights are more likely than mothers to use supportive services such as babysitters, relatives, and daycare centers. At the same time, father-custody children have more frequent contact with the noncustodial parent than their counterparts in mother-custody homes. While boys in father-custody families show more independence than girls do in this situation, girls tend to show more independence in mother-custody families (Santrock, Warshak, and Eliot, 1982).

The effects of divorce are not all bad. In some instances, children of divorce may experience less anguish and maladjustment than those growing up in homes with intact but conflict-ridden marriages (Bane, 1979). Also, because of their situation, children of divorced parents may become more responsible

Single-parent families headed by fathers, once a rarity, are becoming more common. (Ken Karp)

and self-reliant at an earlier age. At the same time, it is true that children of divorce are more likely to get divorced themselves, probably because they have learned that divorce is a viable solution to marital conflict (Pope and Mueller, 1979). Otherwise, surveys do not indicate any clear difference in personal adjustment between those who grow up in broken homes and those who come from intact marriages (Kulka and Weingarten, 1981).

Remarriage

Despite the painful experience of divorce, most divorced people remarry. One-fourth of them remarry within 1 year of their divorce. Half of them will have remarried within 3 years after the divorce, and three-fourths within 9 years (Glick, 1977). Men remarry at an average age of 35 years, women at an average age of 32 years. In most instances, a divorced person marries another divorced person, probably because they share similar experiences. Then too, participation in support groups such as Parents Without Partners increases the likelihood of divorced people meeting and marrying someone like themselves.

Slightly fewer women than men remarry, an average of three out of four women compared to four out of five men, probably for several reasons. First, and foremost, with advancing age, the ratio of available men to women decreases—giving new meaning to the familiar saying "a good man is hard to find." As a result, a woman's chances for remarriage decrease with age as follows: a woman in her 20s has a 76 percent chance, a woman in her 30s has a 56 percent chance, a woman in her 40s a 32 percent chance, and a woman in her 50s less than a 12 percent chance for remarriage. The fact that most men marry younger women adds to the problem, though this tendency is changing to some extent. Whether a woman has children also affects her chances of remarriage, though less so than the age factor. For example, a woman who has three children but is still in her 20s has a 72 percent chance of remarriage. If she has no children but is in her 30s, her chance of remarrying is only 60 percent (Blumstein and Schwartz, 1983).

Interested people often ask, "How successful are second marriages?" And to be frank, it's difficult to answer because the record is mixed. Statistically, second marriages are even more likely to end in divorce. We should hastily add that there are a small number of "repeaters" who marry and divorce several times, thus inflating the overall figures. At the same time, many second marriages are quite successful, both in terms of marital happiness and longevity. When the divorce repeaters are removed from consideration, the outlook for second marriages may be even better than previously thought. At least six out of ten second marriages last until death, which is higher than first marriages. Also, the remarriage of divorced people over 35 years of age further enhances their chances for a successful remarriage (Hunt and Hunt, 1977). Partners in a second marriage often benefit from their mistakes in an earlier marriage. They know full well the value of give and take in a close relationship like marriage. Age and maturity also help. Most of all, remarried people usually realize the value of commitment and often work harder at their second marriage.

An increasing number of remarriages now involve children. Remarried couple households account for about one out of every six households, and include 10 million children under 18 years of age. Half of these children have stepparents, mostly stepfathers because of the tendency of children to live with their mothers. The remaining children are born after the remarriage of the partners. The majority of remarried couples have children from the previous marriages of just one spouse. A much smaller number of families have children from the previous marriages of both spouses. And only a very small number of remarried couples have children of their own in addition to children from the previous marriages of both partners (Cherlin and McCarthy, 1985).

Remarriages involving children pose special demands on both the adults as well as the children. In addition to learning how to live with a new person, one or both partners must also become accustomed to a ready-made family. When the children are young, the stepparent has more opportunity to develop rapport and trust with the children. But when there are adolescents involved, it's more difficult for everyone involved. If a father too quickly assumes the authority of a parent, especially in matters of discipline, the stepchildren may resent it. Both parents must make allowance for their stepchildrens' initial suspiciousness and resistance. Part of the problem is that the role of stepparent is not well defined. This is often compounded by the child's continued interaction with the remaining biological parent. Yet when both parents develop a good working relationship, talking things out, and cooperating on such issues, blended families may do at least as well as intact families, if not better in many cases. Furthermore, as nontraditional families become a more substantial proportion of all families, both generations may assume their respective roles more easily.

Summary

Love

1. We began with a discussion of romantic love—the strong emotional, sexual attachment to someone of the opposite sex—and how such love heightens both the positive and negative potential of close relationships, making them more satisfying and more frustrating then friendships.

2. Yet no matter how much in love two people are, they are more likely to stay together if they share similar attitudes and interests as well as a mutual emotional involvement.

3. Although couples marry primarily for love and companionship, those who remain happily married do so because of "companionate love"—the affection people feel for someone with whom their life is deeply intertwined.

The Marriage Relationship

4. The marriage relationship plays a central role in marriage today, with couples in which both partners are relationship-centered being the happiest of all.

5. Couples continue to report that communication is their main problem in marriage, either because of difficulties resolving their differences or the emotional alienation that often results. Good communication consists more in how couples resolve conflict than its absence.

6. Commitment also plays an important role in marriage, with many couples citing their belief in marriage as a permanent contract as the main reason they have achieved a happy and lasting marriage.

Marital Adjustment

7. A major change in marriage is the lack of fixed roles for husbands and wives, with a greater sharing of marital responsibilities among partners than in the past.

8. Couples are more apt to fight over how to spend their money than how much they have. Partners who feel they have equality in their relationship also have fewer conflicts over money.

9. A good sex life is also an important part of marriage, though sex usually goes hand in hand with a satisfying marriage.

10. Although the average marriage tends to devitalize over time, partners who remain open to each other and continue growing in their relationship report increasing happiness in their marriage.

Divorce and Remarriage

11. The divorce rate has more than doubled in the past 25 years, with one out of every two marriages now ending in divorce.

12. Getting a divorce involves six overlapping experiences, including the emotional, legal, economic, coparental, community, and psychic divorce.

13. How children are affected by divorce depends on a variety of factors, such as the age and sex of the child and the custody arrangements. Many children are now growing up in single-parent families.

14. Most divorced people eventually remarry, with many of them achieving happy marriages. Remarriages involving children from a previous marriage pose special demands on the adults as well as the children.

Self-test

1. Dating couples are more likely to break up when the individuals are:
- **a.** from similar backgrounds
- **b.** mutually involved
- **c.** not mutually involved
- **d.** extremely intelligent

2. The main reason couples give for getting married is:
- **a.** financial security
- **b.** sexual fulfillment
- **c.** having a family
- **d.** love

3. The happiest married couples are those in which:
- **a.** both partners are relationship-centered
- **b.** one partner is relationship-centered
- **c.** both partners are work-centered
- **d.** both partners are equally relationship-work-centered

4. Married couples tend to have their biggest problem with:
- **a.** sex
- **b.** communication
- **c.** finances
- **d.** in-laws

5. Most married women would like to have the option of:

   a. taking separate vacations   **c.** not preparing meals
   b. working outside the home   **d.** all of the above

6. When it comes to money, couples tend to argue mostly about:

   a. their income   **c.** money management
   b. pooling their resources   **d.** who earns the most

7. Over time, the average American marriage tends to:

   a. become devitalized   **c.** become happier
   b. remain unchanged   **d.** remain conflict-habituated

8. According to Bohannan, the last and most difficult part of the divorce experience is the:

   a. legal divorce   **c.** coparental divorce
   b. psychic divorce   **d.** community divorce

9. About one in five families is headed by:

   a. fathers   **c.** mothers
   b. foster parents   **d.** one parent

10. Most divorced people tend to:

    a. remarry another divorced person   **c.** never marry again
    b. remarry within 1 year of their divorce   **d.** remarry someone who has never been married

Exercises

1. *Qualities desired in a mate.* Make a list of some personal qualities you would like in a marriage partner. You might list a dozen such qualities, and then go back and check the three most important ones. Write a short paragraph telling why you think these three qualities are the most important.

   You might do the same for personal qualities you would not like in a marriage partner. Again, list a dozen such qualities, and then check the three most important ones. Why do you think these qualities are undesirable?

2. *Qualities you offer to a prospective mate.* Make a list of the major personal strengths and weaknesses you would bring to a marriage relationship. What are the three most desirable qualities you have to offer? What are some of your less desirable qualities that might affect the marriage?

   If you are going steady with someone or if you are married, you might ask your partner to add to your list. Try to list more desirable qualities than undesirable ones.

3. *Cohabitation.* If you are currently living with someone of the opposite sex or have had such an experience, write a page or so telling what you learned from this experience. To what extent is your experience similar to that of cohabitating couples described in this chapter? Did cohabitation include serious plans for marriage? What are some of the values of cohabitation? The hazards? Would you recommend this experience to others?

4. *The marriage relationship.* If you're going steady, living with someone, or married, describe the type of relationship you have with your partner. If lovers, are you also friends? Do you and your partner return each other's love? Or is one of you more emotionally involved in the relationship than the other? To what extent are both of you relationship-oriented?

5. *Marital adjustment.* If you're living with someone or married, what has been your major adjustment in learning to live together? Has this been learning how to communicate and handle conflict? Or has it had more to do with specific problems involving money and sex? Select one or two of the most difficult adjustments you've had in marriage, or your current relationship, and write a page or so about it.

6. *The divorce experience.* If you have gone through a separation or divorce, write up your experience in a page or so. To what extent did you experience the six overlapping phases of divorce described in this chapter? How has the divorce experience influenced your desire to remarry?

    If you came from a home with divorced parents, you might write up your experience telling how you have been affected by your parents' divorce. How has your experience influenced your outlook on marriage? On divorce?

Questions for Self-reflection

1. How can you tell whether your partner loves you?
2. If you are going steady or are married, what attracted you to your partner?
3. Why do you think companionship is so important in today's marriages?
4. Are you and your partner equally involved emotionally in your relationship?
5. Do you and your partner "fight fair" so you can disagree without undermining the relationship?
6. If you are living together or married, do you and your partner share the housework?
7. If married, do you pool your money?
8. To what extent do you feel that sexual satisfaction and marital happiness go together?
9. If you or your parents have gone through a divorce, what was the hardest part for you?
10. If you are a single-parent, what is the biggest challenge you face?

Recommended Readings

Blumstein, Philip, and Pepper Schwartz. *American Couples.* New York: William Morrow and Company, 1983. Discusses the importance of money, work, and sex in close relationships, based on an in-depth survey of married and unmarried couples.

Branden, Nathaniel. *The Psychology of Romantic Love.* New York: Bantam, 1981 (paperback). A positive interpretation of romantic love, including the conditions in which it grows and dies.

Klagbrun, Francine. *Married People.* New York: Bantam, 1985. Basic guidelines for strengthening one's marriage in an age of divorce.

O'Conner, Dagmar. *How To Make Love To the Same Person for the Rest of Your Life.* New York: Doubleday, 1985. Practical suggestions for keeping sex enjoyable within long-term relationships.

Stuart, Richard B., and Barbara Jacobson. *Second Marriage.* New York: W. W. Norton and Company, 1985. An upbeat approach to making remarriage a successful experience.

Weiss, R.S. *Marital Separation.* New York: Basic Books, 1975 (paperback). Helpful information about the nature of relationships between partners before, during, and after separation and divorce.

11 Work and Leisure

Richard Bolles, a Harvard-educated clergyman, suddenly found himself without a job. He had been fired by Grace Cathedral in San Francisco as part of a cost-cutting measure in the economic doldrums of the late 1960s. Bolles used his $800 severance pay for the services of an executive search agency, which dutifully mailed out 900 resumes with little results. An employment agency and a perusal of the want ads were equally fruitless. Eventually, through the help of a friend, Bolles found a job.

By this time, Bolles had become curious. Why are some people so much more successful than others in changing jobs or careers? It was an intriguing problem. Coming from a family of journalists (his father, grandfather, and brother all had been journalists), he decided to investigate. For the next two years he traveled around the United States, covering 65,000 miles, talking endlessly to career experts, counselors, job hunters, and employment agencies. When he had finished, he proceeded to distill the principles that successful job hunters and successful employment agencies had in common. Expecting only a modest response, he published his book himself, using the photocopying machine in his office. Sales increased slowly but steadily. Then during the tight job market of the 1970s, the book became a best seller. Eventually, it became the best-selling book on job hunting and career changing in the history of the nation (Bolles, 1985). Since then, Richard Bolles has become a recognized authority in the field, and acquired some wealth in the process.

CHOOSING A CAREER

Richard Bolles' experience illustrates some of the perils and promises of finding your niche in the American workplace. On the minus side, you can see that no matter how talented and well-educated you are, you can still end up without a job. A major reason is the lack of a system of matching people with careers and jobs. Bolles himself has said that job hunting in the United States is still Neanderthal or primitive. As a result, in addition to millions of unemployed people, it has been estimated that more than three-fourths of the people in our country are *underemployed*—working in a job beneath their abilities and/or education.

On the plus side, Bolles' success story shows what you can do when you take the initiative and make the most of your opportunities. Notice that in reassessing his career Bolles took stock of what he had to offer: his own talents as a writer and his experiences of unemployment. Then too, observe how Bolles found his best opportunities in meeting a genuine need: helping people to find work in an increasingly competitive job market. Finally, one of the keys to Bolles' success, both in his professional life and in his book, has been his emphasis on the individual's positive, take-charge attitude, as opposed to the conventional image of job applicant as panhandler cowering before employers. All of these points are relevant for our own lives as we, too, face the challenges of choosing a compatible career and finding a job that uses our talents, as we'll see in the rest of this chapter.

Self-assessment

In choosing a career goal, it's best to begin by taking stock of yourself. Such self-assessment should include a consideration of your interests, abilities, personality, and personal values. What are your interests? Which school subjects do you like the most? The least? Which hobbies do you enjoy? Think about your recreational and sports activities. In each case, try to determine what it is that most interests you, whether it's the activity itself or the people you're doing it with. Generally, the intrinsic enjoyment of the activity is your best guide to the choice of a career.

What are you good at? People often balk at this question. They say, "I haven't done anything but go to school" or "I've been busy raising three kids." The implication of such remarks is that they don't have any marketable skills. But when they are confronted with a checklist of things they can do, the picture brightens. For example, a woman who has run a garage sale, organized trips for children, and had charge of the family budget has had considerable experience with management skills, a very important ability for a variety of jobs. Another way to find out what you're good at is to reflect upon your achievements, including those in school. Select several achievements in each of the 5-year periods of your life. What do these achievements have in common?

Your personality also offers valuable clues for choosing a compatible career. Each of us is a unique combination of traits, needs, and motives that make some work environments more compatible than others. For example, a meticulous homemaker may be good working with computers, a field that requires the ability to manage details with precision. A young man who has never cared much for school may like working with his hands, such as rebuilding car engines. Many times our experience in part-time and summer jobs helps us to see which type of work environments we like the most. For example, after spending a summer working with a tree service, one young woman realized how much she enjoyed working outside.

Your personal values are also an important consideration. We often take our values for granted, becoming aware of them mostly when faced with an important decision. An example would be choosing between a job we enjoy but that doesn't pay well and one that we don't especially like that offers good pay. You might make up a list of some of your personal values, such as personal fulfillment, family, helping others, security, and the like. How do your values compare to those in the fields you're interested in?

Identifying Compatible Careers

Once you have a better understanding of your interests and abilities, you're ready to match yourself with a compatible career. With more than 20,000 different careers to choose from, this can be a formidable task. Fortunately, there are many helpful resources, such as the *Occupational Outlook Handbook* (OOH), published by the United States Department of Labor Statistics. This handbook contains more than twenty basic career groups, each with dozens of related careers. For example, health-related careers would include physicians, physician's assistants, registered nurses, practical nurses, medical technologists, and the like. For each career, the handbook provides information on the type of work involved, places of employment, entrance requirements, working conditions, and employment outlook. The OOH also has an introductory section with helpful information on such topics as how to find a job and employment opportunities. The OOH, revised every 2 years, is available in most libraries and counseling centers and can also be purchased from any of the regional centers of the Bureau of Labor Statistics.

In indentifying compatible careers, it's often advisable to talk over your plans with an interested teacher, school counselor, or someone in your field of interest. Professionals in school counseling centers and career guidance centers spend a good part of their time assisting people with their career planning. They also have access to a wide assortment of inventories for this purpose. These inventories may furnish valuable leads as to which career is most compatible for someone with your interests, especially when discussed with a counselor.

John Holland's *Self-directed Search* (SDS) may be completed by yourself or taken under the supervision of a counselor. When taking the SDS you indicate choices in regard to your career daydreams, activities, abilities, career prefer-ences, and self-estimates. The results are then tabulated to indicate which three personality-occupational types you most resemble and in which order. See the descriptions of Holland's six personality-occupational types in the box. Using a separate occupational-finder booklet, you match your preferred personality-occupational types with representative compatible careers. If you have access to a computer, there's also the *System of Interractive Guidance and Information* (SIGI), published by the Educational Testing Service, Princeton, N.J. You sit at a termi-nal and enter into a dialogue with the computer, examining your values, explor-ing career options, and making tentative career choices that can be tested realistically and revised. In this way you may learn more about the strategies involved in the choice of a compatible career.

Holland's Six Personality-Occupational Types

The following are descriptions of Holland's six personality-occupational types. These descriptions are, most emphatically, only generalizations. None will fit any one person exactly. In fact, most people's interests combine all six themes or types to some degree. Even if you rate high on a given theme, you will find that some of the statements used to characterize this theme do not apply to you.

The archetypal models of Holland's six types can be described as follows:

REALISTIC: Persons of this type are robust, rugged, practical, physically strong, and often athletic; have good motor coordination and skills but lack verbal and interpersonal skills, and are therefore somewhat uncomfortable in social settings: usually perceive themselves as mechanically inclined; are direct, stable, natural, and persistent; prefer con-crete to abstract problems; see themselves as aggressive; have conventional political and economic goals; and rarely perform creatively in the arts or sciences, but do like to build things with tools. Realistic types prefer such occupations as mechanic, engineer, electri-cian, fish and wildlife specialist, crane operator, and tool designer.

INVESTIGATIVE: This category includes those with a strong scientific orientation; they are usually task-oriented, introspective, and asocial; prefer to think through rather than act out problems; have a great need to understand the physical world; enjoy ambigu-ous tasks; prefer to work independently; have unconventional values and attitudes; usually perceive themselves as lacking in leadership or persuasive abilities, but are confident of their scholarly and intellectual abilities; describe themselves as analytical, curious, inde-pendent, and reserved; and especially dislike repetitive activities. Vocational preferences include astronomer, biologist, chemist, technical writer, zoologist, and psychologist.

ARTISTIC: Persons of the artistic type prefer free unstructured situations with maxi-mum opportunity for self-expression; resemble investigative types in being introspective and asocial but differ in having less ego strength, greater need for individual expression, and greater tendency to impulsive behavior; they are creative, especially in artistic and musical media; avoid problems that are highly structured or require gross physical skills; prefer dealing with problems through self-expression in artistic media; perform well on standard measures of creativity, and value aesthetic qualities; see themselves as expres-

The *Strong-Campbell Interest Inventory* (SCII), usually administered by a professional counselor, is also widely used for career guidance. In the SCII you indicate your preferences (like, dislike, or indifferent) for various careers, school subjects, activities, amusements, and types of people as well as something about your own personal characteristics. Computer-scored printouts present the results organized around Holland's six occupational-personality types. The results from the SCII include information in several areas, including general career themes, basic career interests, and specific careers you're most compatible with. Discussion of the results with a counselor usually provides valuable leads as to the best compatible careers for you.

How helpful are these inventories? A lot depends on how they are used. If you take them in hopes that they'll tell you which career you *should* choose—a

---

sive, original, intuitive, creative, nonconforming, introspective, and independent. Vocational preferences include artist, author, composer, writer, musician, stage director, and symphony conductor.

SOCIAL: Persons of this type are sociable, responsible, humanistic, and often religious; like to work in groups, and enjoy being central in the group; have good verbal and interpersonal skills; avoid intellectual problem-solving, physical exertion, and highly ordered activities; prefer to solve problems through feelings and interpersonal manipulation of others; enjoy activities that involve informing, training, developing, curing, or enlightening others; perceive themselves as understanding, responsible, idealistic, and helpful. Vocational preferences include social worker, missionary, high school teacher, marriage counselor, and speech therapist.

ENTERPRISING: Persons of this type have verbal skills suited to selling, dominating, and leading; are strong leaders; have a strong drive to attain organizational goals or economic aims; tend to avoid work situations requiring long periods of intellectual effort; differ from conventional types in having a greater preference for ambiguous social tasks and an even greater concern for power, status, and leadership; see themselves as aggressive, popular, self-confident, cheerful, and sociable; generally have a high energy level; and show an aversion to scientific activities. Vocational preferences include business executive, political campaign manager, real estate sales, stock and bond sales, television producer, and retail merchandising.

CONVENTIONAL: Conventional people prefer well-ordered environments and like systematic verbal and numerical activities; are usually conforming and prefer subordinate roles; are effective at well-structured tasks, but avoid ambiguous situations and problems involving interpersonal relationships or physical skills; describe themselves as conscientious, efficient, obedient, calm, orderly, and practical; identify with power; and value material possessions and status. Vocational preferences include bank examiner, bookkeeper, clerical worker, financial analyst, quality control expert, statistician, and traffic manager.

College graduates enjoy the highest lifetime earnings and the lowest unemployment. (Laimute E. Druskis)

common misunderstanding—you'll probably be disappointed. Nor will the results predict how successful or happy you'll be in a given career, since these depend on such things as your abilities and personal motivation. Instead, these inventories are best used as an *aid* in making an informed career choice. For instance, the results of the SCII have proven quite useful in predicting which people will remain in a given field. Those who choose a career very similar to their career profiles tend to remain in their careers, whereas those who enter a career highly dissimilar to their profile eventually tend to drop out of it. When you consider all the time and money invested in preparing for a career, this information can be extremely helpful to you.

Arriving at a Decision

If you're like most people, you'll end up with not just one but a number of potentially compatible careers. Ultimately, you must make a decision as to which is the best career for you. The process of decision making is so important that we've devoted the better part of a chapter to it—Chapter 12, Personal Freedom and Decision Making. You might pay close attention to the steps in decision making—especially the balance sheet procedure. The latter consists of listing all the pluses and minuses involved in a given course of action, such as the choice of a career goal. Such an approach helps you to make a comprehensive appraisal of what is involved. It also promotes contingency planning, that is, figuring out what to do if one or more of the unfavorable consequences in the minus column were to materialize.

In the process of deciding on a career, there are certain pitfalls to guard against. One is the accidental choice, which consists of choosing a career mostly because of one's first job. People who do this may discover later, to their regret, that they would have been happier or more successful in another line of work. Another pitfall is the choice of a career or job because of its external trappings, like money, prestige, or power. In the long run, it's better to choose a work activity that is enjoyable in itself, as long as the financial rewards are adequate. A major mistake is waiting for things to happen. Instead, you must take the initiative and engage in an active process of finding a compatible career as we've already discussed.

Still another pitfall has to do with the timing of your decision, with the risk of making a premature decision or undue delay. This was brought out in a well-known longitudinal study by Daniel Levinson (1978) and his colleagues, in which they followed young men through middle age. A major finding was that the choice of a career was more difficult and complex than ordinarily portrayed. Men who made strong career commitments in their 20s, before they were fully informed about it, often regretted their choices later. On the other hand, those who delayed making a career commitment until their 30s usually deprived themselves of the necessary experience to make a wise choice. Levinson concludes, "One of the great paradoxes of human development is that we are required to make crucial choices before we have the knowledge, judgment, and self-understanding to choose wisely. Yet, if we put off these choices until we feel truly ready, the delay may produce other and greater costs" (Levinson, 1978, p. 102). All of this suggests that we need to choose a career goal, but keep open to modifying that choice in light of our subsequent experience and growth.

Preparing for Your Career

As soon as you've chosen a career goal, you'll need to know how to prepare for it. As you might expect, there are a variety of ways to prepare for a career. Some careers are entered through an apprenticeship, vocational-technical school, or on-the-job training program. Others require a 2-year or 4-year college degree. In addition, careers such as accounting and nursing also require a state license or some type of certification. Professions such as medicine and law also require an advanced degree, supervised training, and a state license. Since most of you are already enrolled in some sort of post-high-school education, you may have begun the appropriate preparation for your career. Others of you, especially those in a liberal arts program of study, may not yet have selected a career goal. Nor must everyone in college have a career goal. But, in either case, an integral part of career planning is finding out the appropriate educational requirements.

Until recently, the advantages of a college education have been taken for granted. College is supposed to make you a better informed person and provide access to the higher status, better paying careers. Admittedly, college graduates continue to have the highest average lifetime earnings. According to one projection, a 25-year-old male who has a 4-year college degree can expect lifetime earnings of about 2.2 million dollars, as compared with 1.7 million dollars for someone who has a 2-year college degree, and 1.4 million for a high school graduate (U.S. Bureau of the Census, 1984). A female of the same age and education would normally have lower lifetime earnings, though continuing efforts to eliminate inequities in the workplace may modify these projections in the coming years. Although the proportion of college-educated workers has increased, a college degree does not guarantee you a job, as we'll explain later in the chapter. (See Figure 11–1.)

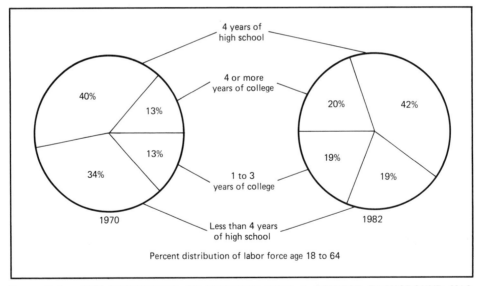

Figure 11–1.   THE PROPORTION OF WORKERS WITH A COLLEGE BACKGROUND HAS INCREASED SUBSTANTIALLY.

Source: U.S. Bureau of Labor, Bureau of Labor Statistics, *Occupational Outlook Handbook*, 1984-85 (Washington, D.C.: U.S. Government Printing Office, 1984), p. 16.

As a result, there has been a marked shift toward career-oriented programs in such fields as business, nursing, and computer science. This is especially evident in the 2-year community colleges, which now enroll almost half of all the students in the first 2 years of college. Then too, there is greater aware-ness of the need to keep flexible in one's career options. One way to do this is to carry a dual major, like business and computers or nursing and education. Another way is the willingness to change one's career goal or, if necessary, to drop out of college to get more work experience in order to clarify one's career goal. Finally, there's the need to modify one's career goals in the light of avail-able opportunities. In one survey including a large proportion of college gradu-ates, 40 percent of the respondents reported that they had gotten into their careers by chance without too much deliberation. Another 16 percent said they had settled for their present career because they couldn't get a job in their pre-ferred field. Only 23 percent of the respondents were working in the career of their first choice (Renwick and Lawler, 1978). All this underlines the impor-tance of flexibility and the willingness to modify your career goal in light of experience and the available opportunities.

GETTING ALONG ON THE JOB

Most of us have gained work experience through a variety of part-time and summer jobs, and, in some cases, full-time jobs. Although these jobs may not have been especially interesting or related to our career goals, they do provide practical knowledge. Experience in the workplace helps us to learn how to budget our time, take pride in a job well done, and most important of all, learn how to get along with other people (Cole, 1980). Getting and holding a satisfy-ing full-time job is usually more involved.

Job Satisfaction

Although recent graduates tend to get jobs with modest incomes and responsibilities, they're apt to have high morale for the first few months or more on the job. In addition to being pleased to have a job, there's the novelty of the work activity itself as well as the stimulation of getting to know new peo-ple. However, after the first year or two, morale drops considerably. After 3 to 5 years, job satisfaction is at its lowest point. For those who stay with the same employer 5 years or more, job satisfaction increases. Seasoned workers tend to adjust to the realities of the job and reevaluate their career aspirations as well (Halloran, 1983).

Despite all the griping you hear on the job, most people are satisfied with their jobs. Depending on the survey, anywhere from two-thirds to more than three-fourths of American workers are either "somewhat" or "very" satisfied with their jobs (*New York Times*, Dec. 17, 1981). College-educated workers, espe-cially those in the professions and executive positions, are usually more satisfied with their jobs than those with less education. Older workers are also more satis-fied with their jobs, partly because of their greater job security. Surprisingly, women are generally as satisfied with their jobs as men are. Yet, women are apt to be more dissatisfied with certain aspects of their jobs, such as having less freedom on the job, less participation in decision making, fewer chances for promotion, and lower pay (Renwick and Lawler, 1978). The most dissatisfied workers tend to be black, under 25 years of age, and in the lower-level jobs, such as laborers and machinery operators (Landy, 1984).

Satisfaction on the job depends on a combination of things, especially the work activity itself and the conditions in which it's done. People generally prefer work that is interesting, enjoyable, and useful to others. When workers are doing something that is intrinsically enjoyable, they tend to feel competent and satisfied with their jobs (Deci and Ryan, 1980). Yet, job satisfaction also depends heavily on the working conditions on the job. Workers generally prefer having friendly, cooperative coworkers, considerate supervisors, good pay, and chances for promotion. Workers are also happier with work that allows them to make decisions on their own without checking everything out with their supervisors. Pay is also important, but it's not usually at the top of the list. When people feel their work is uninteresting or they're being paid unfairly, money is a powerful

---

Working with a Difficult Boss

When Michael Lombardo and Morgan McCall asked highly successful executives about their experiences with difficult bosses, they discovered that two-thirds of the executives had worked with such people. The names given to the commonly encountered types suggest their respective characteristics: Attilas (as in Hun), egotists, dodgers, incompetents, detail drones, Rodneys (as in Dangerfield), slobs, and snakes-in-the-grass. Although there was no one best way to cope with such bosses, suggested strategies included:

1. *Be patient and cope with adversity.* Intolerable bosses may help us learn how to handle conflict without destroying the relationship. They may also remind us that we work for the company rather than the boss.

2. *Look for common ground.* Don't blame everything on your boss. If you must disagree on one matter, be supportive on others.

3. *Modify your behavior.* Emphasize cooperation whenever possible. Minimize complaints.

4. *Make it a learning experience.* Successful executives learned what *not* to do by observing their boss's bad habits.

It is unwise to remain in an intolerable situation indefinitely, especially if your principles are being compromised or your health affected. But it's best to regard a difficult boss as a problem situation that may be improved, if not resolved, before taking the more drastic step of quitting your job.

Source: M. M. Lombardo and M. W. McCall, Jr., "The Intolerable Boss," *Psychology Today,* January 1984, pp. 44–48. Reprinted with permission from *Psychology Today* Magazine. Copyright © January 1984 American Psychological Association.

incentive. But when people find their jobs interesting or rewarding in other ways, money becomes less of an incentive (Jenks, 1983). At the same time, for the majority of people in the middle and working classes who are caught between materialistic aspirations and economic pressures, pay continues to be an important part of job satisfaction.

Perhaps you've heard that workers don't care about their jobs the way they used to. But is this true? Apparently so, judging by Gallup polls, which asked: "Do you enjoy your work so much that you have a hard time putting it aside?" When a cross-section of American workers were asked this question in the 1950s, 52 percent of them said yes. But when the same question was asked in the 1980s, only 34 percent answered yes (Glenn and Weaver, 1982). At the same time, Daniel Yankelovich (1982) points out that the work ethic is still very much alive, it's simply *under*employed. Surveys have shown that four out of five American workers feel "an inner need to do the best job I can regardless of pay." The majority of workers also believe they exercise a great deal of control over the quality of work they do on the job. Yet, fewer than one out of five workers say they are exercising that control to do the best job they can. Why? Perhaps workers feel unmotivated. For example, in studies when workers are asked who benefits from their labors, most of them assume that the chief beneficiaries are others—consumers, managers, and stockholders. In other words, most workers are not only willing to work harder but want to do so, *if* they are given the proper encouragement and incentives by management.

Women in the Workplace

Women have become a more significant part of the labor force in recent years, with over half of them employed outside the home at any given time. Actually, the participation rate of women in the workplace varies somewhat, depending on factors such as their age and marital status. For instance, almost two-thirds of married women in the 25–44 age group work outside the home, with an even higher rate among women the same age who are single, divorced, or widowed (U.S. Bureau of the Census, 1985).

In many cases, women work to support themselves and help with the family support. But even if they had the means to maintain their current standard of living without working, three out of four young women workers say they would continue to work (La Farge, 1983). Jobs provide women with a sense of competence and a chance to apply talents not used in motherhood and housework alone.

Now that it is illegal to discriminate against women in hiring, women are breaking down job barriers in many fields. Women now work as carpenters and astronauts as well as doctors and lawyers. In 1970 women earned only 5 percent of the law degrees and 10 percent of the medical degrees. By 1980, women earned 20 percent of the degrees in each of these fields (Spain and Bianchi, 1983). Yet there are many obstacles to equality of the sexes in the workplace. The most notable inequity is the earnings gap between the sexes. Women on the average earn only 60 cents for each dollar a man earns (U.S. Bureau of the Census, 1985). One reason is that many women have less education and work experience than men. Only recently has the same proportion of women as men enrolled in college. Another reason is that the majority of women continue to enter the low-paying service fields. More than three-quarters of the women are crowded into just twenty of the Labor Department's 427 job categories. Women are overrepresented in such jobs as secretary, waitress, house servant, nurse, and elementary school teacher. But they are underrepresented in such jobs as auto mechanic, police officer, miner, and construction worker. Only a small proportion of women belong to unions and apprenticeship programs in the trades (Lewin, 1984).

Table 11–1. MALE- AND FEMALE-DOMINATED CAREERS.

Selected male-dominated careers (percent men)	
Plumbers	99.2
Auto mechanics	99.0
Dentists	96.7
Police	93.3
Carpenters	93.0
Selected female-dominated careers (percent women)	
Secretaries	99.2
House servants	95.9
Registered nurses	95.6
Bookkeepers	92.0
Telephone operators	91.9

Source: U.S. Bureau of the Census, *Statistical Abstract of the United States, 1984,* 104th ed. (Washington, D.C.: U.S. Government Printing Office, 1984).

More than half of the married and divorced women in the workplace have children at home. But the effect a working mother has on her family depends on so many factors it is hard to generalize. Blumstein and Schwartz (1983) found that the more satisfied women are with their jobs, the happier they are with their marriages and families. Conversely, when things are not going well at work, women are more likely to bring their problems home. At the same time, women with husbands who are supportive of their working and who help with the kids may get over such times with less detrimental influence on their families than other women. Even though the conventional wisdom about the need for having the mother at home during the child's preschool years has not been confirmed, many men and women are still convinced of its truth. As a result, when the wife works, couples argue more about how the children should be reared. Affluent women try to reduce their worries by hiring housekeepers or finding promising preschool programs. But mothers with more limited means have greater difficulty finding childcare facilities they consider an adequate substitute for the mother. All in all, a lot depends on the quality of the mother's relationship with her children, how she spends her time with them, how much cooperation with the childrearing responsibilities she receives from her husband as well as the availability of daycare services.

Is There a Future In It?

Advancement in one's job or career is often associated with more money and prestige. But promotion also means wider responsibilities on the job and, hopefully, being more useful to others. The increase in pay that goes with promotion is usually needed just to keep up with inflation. Accordingly, what society calls "promotion" is necessary just to stay even. Lack of promotion means going backward (Bolles, 1985).

The lack of advancement, along with low pay, continues to be a major source of worker dissatisfaction. This is especially true among women workers and those from minority groups. Workers who are not promoted often complain of favoritism. In one survey, including a large proportion of college educated workers, almost half the respondents felt that getting ahead on the job depended more on "who you know" than what you know. Since this response was given more frequently by dissatisfied workers, some of the cynicism might be sour grapes (Renwick and Lawler, 1978). Yet it's an attitude often expressed in private company that cannot help but affect worker morale.

All of this suggests the importance of knowing how promotions are made in the organization you work for. Many companies make their policies on promotion clear in the employment interview or at the time of hiring. If not, you should inquire about this. You should know to what extent promotions are based on such factors as education, work experience, job performance, and seniority. For example, Lisa was hired by a real estate broker to bolster sagging sales. She did so in record time. She initiated an innovative advertising campaign and never hesitated to take clients around to see houses or property during the evening hours or weekends. As a result, she sold more real estate every year than anyone else in her company. But no promotion was forthcoming. Someone from the outside was brought in to become the new manager. When Lisa asked why, she was told that coworkers and clients alike had complained of her aggressive, high-handed style. Lisa had expected to be promoted on the basis of her results, but her superiors had judged her by a more inclusive standard. Such misunderstanding could have been avoided if either Lisa or her boss had clarified the policy on promotion at the outset.

Opportunities for promotion may be more difficult to come by than in the past. Major changes are occurring in the labor market because of technological change and the loss of jobs to foreign markets. As a result, the continuous spectrum of jobs is being replaced by a two-tier system in which the vast majority of jobs will be low-paying service jobs at one end and a very few technological, managerial, highly paid jobs at the other end. Gone will be the middle-range jobs, with their upward mobility and career ladder opportunities. The growth

More than half of American women now work outside the home. (Laimute E. Druskis)

of high-level, professional opportunities will be lower than in the previous two decades, making it more difficult for many college graduates to get the type of job with a promising future (Nielsen, 1983).

CAREER OUTLOOK

How promising your job is often depends on the outlook for your field. Do you know the outlook for your chosen career? Are the job openings in your field expected to remain stable? Or is there a rapid growth of jobs projected? Although it's difficult to answer these questions, the Bureau of Labor Statistics periodically makes informed projections of jobs in the various careers. Since employment projections, by their nature, are somewhat imprecise, you should not use them as the sole basis of a career decision. But such projections can help you assess future opportunities in the careers that interest you.

Projected Growth

Tomorrow's economy, like today's, will require workers in many different fields. The number and types of workers needed will depend on the interaction of economic, demographic, social, and technological influences. By analyzing changes in the economy and the factors involved, the Bureau of Labor Statistics develops projections of future demands for many careers. To make these projections authorities must make some assumptions about the growth of the labor force, productivity, inflation, and unemployment. Accordingly, they make three types of projections, based on a low, moderate, and high growth pattern respectively. The projections in Table 11–2 are based on moderate growth.

Job prospects depend not only on job openings but also on the number of workers looking for these types of jobs. Generally, the labor force is expected to grow through the mid-1990s but at a slower rate than in the recent past. Much of the growth in the labor force will be the continued, though slower, rise in the number and proportion of women seeking jobs. Women will account for nearly two-thirds of the labor force growth between now and 1995. The number of young people in the 16–24 age bracket is expected to decline, resulting in less competition for entry level jobs. This could be particularly important for the Armed Forces—the single biggest employer for men in this age group. At the same time, the number of people in the 25–54 age group is expected to increase considerably, from two-thirds to nearly three-fourths of the labor force. Since these people have more work experience, this may result in higher productivity in the workplace, but it may also serve to keep the job market competitive for people this age. The number of people 55 years of age and older is expected to decline somewhat, reflecting the trend toward early retirement (U.S. Bureau of Labor, 1985).

Although employers always want to hire the best qualified person available, this does not mean they always choose those with the most education. Only about one-fourth of all jobs require a college degree. But you should be aware of the continuing rise in educational attainment of the work force. The median educational level of the work force is now over 12 years. Among workers in the 25–34 age group, nearly half have completed at least 1 year of college. Those who have graduated from college continue to have the lowest rates of unemployment, while those with less than 4 years of high school have the highest unemployment rate. Yet a college degree no longer guarantees success in the job market. The proportion of college graduates employed in the professions, managerial, and technological areas has declined because these careers have not been expanding rapidly enough to absorb the available college graduates. As a result, one out of five college graduates has not been able to find a job that requires a college degree (OOH, 1984). However, not all careers requiring a college degree will be overcrowded. Good opportunities will exist for a number of careers, such as engineers and systems analysts.

TABLE 11–2. OCCUPATIONS WITH THE LARGEST PROJECTED JOB GROWTH, 1984–1995.
The numerical projections are in thousands.

Occupation	Employment		Change in employment 1984-95	
	1984	1995	Number	Percent
Cashiers	1,902	2,469	556	29.8
Registered nurses	1,377	1,829	452	32.8
Janitors and cleaners, including maid and housekeeping cleaners	2,940	3,383	443	15.1
Truck drivers	2,484	2,911	428	17.2
Waiters and waitresses	1,625	2,049	424	26.1
Wholesale trade salesworkers	1,248	1,617	369	29.6
Nursing aides, orderlies, and attendants	1,204	1,552	348	28.9
Salespersons, retail	2,732	3,075	343	12.6
Accountants and auditors	882	1,189	307	34.8
Teachers, kindergarten and elementary	1,381	1,662	281	20.3
Secretaries	2,797	3,064	268	9.6
Computer programmers	341	586	245	71.7
General office clerks	2,398	2,629	231	9.6
Food preparation workers, excluding fast food . .	987	1,205	219	22.1
Food preparation and service workers, fast food	1,201	1,417	215	17.9
Computer systems analysts, electronic data processing	308	520	212	68.7
Electrical and electronics engineers	390	597	206	52.8
Electrical and electronics technicians and technologists	404	607	202	50.0
Guards	733	921	188	25.6
Automotive and motorcycle mechanics	922	1,107	185	20.1
Lawyers	490	665	174	35.5
Cosmetologists and related workers	524	674	150	28.7
Cooks, restaurants	463	601	138	29.7
Maintenance repairers, general utility	878	1,015	137	15.6
Bookkeeping, accounting, and auditing clerks . .	1,973	2,091	118	6.0
Bartenders	400	512	112	27.9
Computer operators, excluding peripheral equipment	241	353	111	46.1
Physicians and surgeons	476	585	109	23.0
Licensed practical nurses	602	708	106	17.6
Carpenters	944	1,046	101	10.7
Switchboard operators	347	447	100	28.7
Food service and lodging managers	657	746	89	13.6
Electricians	545	633	88	16.2
Teacher aides and educational assistants	479	566	88	18.3
Blue-collar worker supervisors	1,470	1,555	85	5.8
Receptionists and information clerks	458	542	83	18.2
Mechanical engineers	237	317	81	34.0

Source: *Monthly Labor Review*, U.S. Department of Labor, Bureau of Labor Statistics, November 1985. Washington, D.C.: U.S. Government Printing Office, 1985, p. 51.

Changing Jobs or Careers

Looking over the job projections and alternative career patterns may start you thinking about your own career goal. Perhaps many of you already have a firm career goal and are busily preparing for it. Others may have doubts or reservations about your career goals. Either way, remember that it's perfectly natural to modify your career goal with experience and a greater knowledge of career opportunities. Students are often reluctant to change their career goals, for many reasons. Sometimes they would rather keep to their original goal than risk disappointing their parents, spouses, or peers. They forget they are choosing for themselves. Switching career goals may also be regarded as an admission of failure. But to continue in a direction you have doubts or misgivings about will only make matters worse. Then too, individuals may overestimate the price of changing career goals. After gathering all the facts, the penalties may not be as great as expected. The longer you delay changing career goals or careers, the more difficult it is. Nevertheless, about one in nine workers changes his or her career each year (OOH, 1984). More often than not, the positive gains outweigh the costs involved.

People are also changing jobs more frequently than in the past. The time a worker keeps a job has steadily declined to an average of $3\frac{1}{2}$ years. The typical American worker has ten or more different jobs (or employers) in his or her lifetime, compared to half that number during the 1950s. An individual tends to hold several brief jobs in the first few years after graduation, then settles into a position that lasts several years. Workers in their 30s who stay with the same employer for 5 years or more are likely to remain in that job for a long time. As people get older, they make fewer job changes, with little difference between men and women. By the age of 40, workers will make about two more job changes; at 50, only one more. Few people change jobs in their 60s, and most of them are probably moving into second careers because of retirement. At the same time, there are exceptions to this pattern. A small number of workers exhibit extremely stable job patterns throughout their careers. Others change jobs every few years until they reach retirement (Crittenden, 1980).

LEISURE

All work and no play would make life pretty dull. So it probably comes as no surprise that most people spend as much time in leisure activities as they do at work, anywhere from 30 to 40 hours a week. People in the 18–25 age bracket and those over 50 years of age spend twice as much time in leisure as they do in work (Social Indicators III, 1980). Although economic pressures have curtailed leisure time somewhat in the past few years, the long-term trend is toward increased leisure.

Unwinding in the sun. (Laimute E. Druskis)

What Is Leisure?

Leisure ordinarily refers to "free time" apart from work. Yet, there are many things wo do outside work that are anything but leisure. Examples would be cleaning up after meals, lawn work, studying, and visits to the dentist. Such activities are usually labeled as *maintenance* activities. In contrast, leisure has to do with the *way* we use our free time, our motivation for doing it, the meaning it has for us, and how it affects our lives. The purpose of leisure, Aristotle believed, is the cultivation of the self and the pursuit of the higher things of life.

Leisure may be defined as any activity we've freely chosen to do, excluding work and maintenance activities. Playing a musical instrument primarily for the enjoyment of it or bicycling for pleasure would be examples of unconditional leisure. Many forms of leisure—such as vacations—involve planning and, to a certain degree, prescribed activities. On the other hand, when you're so tired you feel like "doing nothing," you're probably recuperating from work, which is more of a maintenance activity. People who have a satisfying leisure life, such as those who play tennis, often find they must acquire certain skills and play often enough to keep up their game. At the same time, individuals who are highly competitive or perfectionistic may become so concerned about their performance that they end up taking the pleasure out of their leisure actvitities. Leisure also implies the absence of monetary reward. That is, we do something primarily for the enjoyment we get out of it. As a result, professional athletes should not consider their chosen sport a leisure activity no matter how much they enjoy it.

Table 11–3 HOUSEHOLD PARTICIPATION IN LEISURE ACTIVITIES. Based on a national sample survey of 1500 households as of mid-July 1983 conducted by the Gallup Organization.

TYPE OF ACTIVITY	Number (mil.)	Percent[1]	TYPE OF ACTIVITY	Number (mil.)	Percent[1]	TYPE OF ACTIVITY	Number (mil.)	Percent[1]
Watching television	68	81	Camping	17	20	Golf	10	12
Listening to music	54	64	Vacation trips in			Swimming in own		
Sewing/needlepoint	27	32	U.S.	29	34	pool	7	8
Going to the movies	36	42	Bicycling	19	22	Horseback riding	8	9
Vegetable gardening	35	42	Tennis	10	12	Racquetball	6	7
Pleasure trips in			Workshop/home			Skiing (downhill)	5	6
cars	37	44	repair	25	29	Boating (power)	8	10
General exercise/			Jogging	16	19	Vacation trips		
Physical fitness	26	31	Bowling	17	20	outside U.S.	5	6
Watching professional			Hunting	14	16	Snowmobiling	3	4
sports (TV)	33	39	Photography	17	20	Cross-country skiing	3	4
Fishing	26	31	Hiking	12	14	Archery	3	4

[1]Percent of all households.

Source: U.S. Bureau of the Census, *Statistical Abstract of the United States, 1984*, 104th ed. (Washington, D.C.; U.S. Government Printing Office, 1984). p. 238.

Work and Leisure

Many people regard their work and leisure activities as separate—and perhaps unrelated—parts of their lives. One person may be unhappy in her job, but enjoy her hobbies and recreational life. Another person may have a very satisfying career, with little or no time for play. In each instance a person's involvement and satisfaction in work and leisure is related to personal characteristics, needs, and values. Accordingly, several work and leisure patterns have been identified, together with the personal characteristics of those who resemble each pattern (Kabanoff and O'Brien, 1980).

1. *Passive involvement.* This pattern pertains to low levels of involvement and satisfaction in both work and leisure. It is characteristic of people who are marginal, resigned, or alienated in society, especially men with little education and income. Fred, a high school dropout, had difficulty holding jobs. Eventually, he got a steady job inspecting water meters, though he dislikes the work. Fred, divorced with few friends, uses his leisure time watching television and visiting the neighborhood bar.

2. *Live for leisure.* As the title implies, this pattern is seen among people with a compensatory view of leisure. They engage in recreational activities mostly to "blow off steam" accumulated in a frustrating job. It is especially prevalent among older women in dead-end menial jobs. Marge has a secure but boring job in the county courthouse. But she enjoys a rewarding life outside work. She is active in her church and community affairs and enjoys keeping up with all her nieces and nephews.

3. *Work-centered.* This is a pattern of high involvement and satisfaction in work, with little time for leisure. Since men have traditionally been regarded as the major breadwinners, it is probably no surprise that they are the single largest group exhibiting this pattern. Charlie, a self-confessed workaholic, takes pride in having worked his way up to sales manager of a construction equipment company. But he spends most of his time at work. Charlie's leisure life, such as it is, consists mostly of an occasional evening out with his wife plus an annual fishing trip with his sales personnel.

4. *Self-fulfillment.* People who fit this patten are enthusiastically engaged in their careers and leisure activities. They tend to be college-educated, well paid, and they enjoy their work very much. Leisure activities serve mostly to fulfill self-actualizing needs not met in their careers. Linda has built up a successful career in real estate sales. She genuinely enjoys her work. Yet she also takes time to experiment with gourmet cooking, go sailing, and take family camping trips.

Not everyone fits neatly into the above patterns. But most of us resemble one pattern more than the other. Which pattern most reflects your involvement and satisfaction in work and play? In what ways would you like to change your pattern?

Using Leisure Positively

By the time people have driven home after a hard day's work and eaten dinner, they're often too tired to do anything else. When asked their favorite way to spend an evening, the majority say watching television. Adults now watch television an average of 3–4 hours a day, most of it in the evening. Although people watch television primarily for entertainment, and to a lesser extent for the news, watching TV is also a time to relax and unwind, or to recuperate, which is mostly a maintenance activity. The ease with which someone may push a button and be entertained hours on end remains a great temptation. At the same time, individuals who have curtailed their television habits are usually amazed at how many other interesting things there are to do in life.

In contrast, the positive use of leisure requires a certain degree of choice and planning. Ideally, you should select activities that are compatible with your interests and lifestyle, rather than simply doing whatever is convenient at the time or what your friends want to do. To enjoy an activity to the fullest, you

A major reason for taking a vacation is having an opportunity to relax with the entire family. (Great Adventure)

usually have to acquire the necessary skills. You must also budget your time and money to keep it up. For example, people who take pride in their golf game tend to play regularly and probably derive greater satisfaction than those who play only occasionally.

A favorite form of leisure is taking a vacation. According to one survey, about half the population takes some type of vacation each year, typically a 1- or 2-week vacation. Most people feel little or no guilt taking time off for a vacation. But when asked the main reasons for taking a vacation, their responses reflect a variety of motives. The most common motive is to relax. Other motives are intellectual stimulation, family togetherness, adventure, self-discovery, and escape. After the vacation, most people are glad to be back home and look forward to returning to work. Only a few feel depressed at facing the familiar routine. Most people feel that work is more important than leisure. They seek not so much a leisure-filled life as a better balance of work and leisure. Now that more women are working outside the home, leisure has become even more important for families. Furthermore, the shorter working week and flexible schedules enable people to take more long weekends, which promises to make vacations a regular event rather than a once-a-year affair (Rubenstein, 1980).

Leisure becomes increasingly important from midlife on because of all the changes in people's lives. By this time in their lives, people are reassessing their needs and values and what they want out of life. Also, people this age tend to have more job security, available money, free time, and paid vacations than younger adults. For many, this may be the first time they've been able to follow their own inclinations without having to worry about the productiveness of their efforts. Now they can take up interests and express abilities not previously used in career and family responsibilities. In short, leisure becomes a means of personal growth. Constructive leisure activities are also an important way to prepare for retirement. People who have developed rewarding leisure activities as well as a network of social and family relationships are all the more able to make the crucial shift from full-time work to full-time leisure.

Summary

Choosing a Career

1. It's best to begin the choice of a career goal by taking stock of your own interests, abilities, and personality.

2. Once this is done, you're ready to explore the careers options available to you, realizing, if needed, there are a variety of inventories that may help to identify the most compatible careers for someone like yourself.

3. You should also be aware of certain pitfalls in decision making, such as arriving at a career goal prematurely or unduly delaying the choice of a career.

4. It's best to keep your career goal flexible and be willing to modify it in light of subsequent experience, especially while you're in college.

Getting Along on the Job

5. Satisfaction at work depends on a variety of working conditions, such as supervision, coworkers, chances for advancement, and pay, as well as your enjoyment of the work activity itself.

6. Although women are breaking down job barriers in many parts of the workplace, the majority of them are still overrepresented in the low-paying service jobs.

7. Lack of advancement on the job, along with low pay, continues to be a major source of job dissatisfaction.

Career Outlook

8. Employment opportunities are expected to increase in most careers through the mid-1990s, along with a considerable rise in the number of people in the 25–54 age group.

9. College graduates have the lowest rate of unemployment, though one out of five graduates has not been able to find a job that requires a college degree.

10. Since the average person holds ten or more jobs in his or her lifetime, each of us must become skilled in job-hunting as well as our primary job competencies.

Leisure

11. Leisure has to do with how we use our free time apart from work or maintenance activities.

12. There are several ways in which people's involvement in work and leisure are related, with each pattern related to their personal characteristics.

13. The positive use of leisure becomes increasingly important from midlife on as we reassess what we want out of life.

Self-test

1. Inventories such as Holland's Self-directed Search may be helpful in predicting which career you:

a. will be happy in
b. should choose
c. are compatible with
d. will succed in

2. In the process of choosing a career, a major pitfall is:

a. being too impatient
b. waiting for things to happen
c. emphasizing money
d. changing your mind too often

3. The most dissatisfied workers tend to be those who are:

a. black
b. under 25
c. in lower-level jobs
d. all of the above

4. The biggest inequity between men and women in the workplace is the gap between their:

a. education
b. job qualifications
c. earnings
d. job productivity

5. A major source of worker dissatisfaction is lack of:

a. supervision
b. advancement
c. fringe benefits
d. education

6. Between now and 1995, the biggest numerical increase in workers will occur among those in what age group?

a. 18 to 20
b. 21 to 24
c. 25 to 54
d. 55 and over

7. During his or her career, the American worker holds an average of how many different jobs?

a. 5
b. 8
c. 10
d. 15

8. Something we've freely chosen to do outside of work is:

a. leisure
b. moonlighting
c. nonleisure
d. maintenance activity

9. Which pattern of work and leisure refers to low levels of involvement and satisfaction in both work and leisure?

   a. live for leisure

   b. work-centered

   c. self-fulfillment

   d. passive involvement

10. The most common reason for taking a vacation is:

    a. relaxation

    b. to escape

    c. self-discovery

    d. family togetherness

Exercises

1. *Exploring your career interests.* Make an extensive list of all the activities you've enjoyed doing. Include school courses, extracurricular activities, full- and part-time jobs, hobbies, and sports. Then select a dozen of the most satisfying activities and rank them from the most enjoyable down. Ask yourself what made each activity satisfying. Was it the activity itself? Or was it mostly the people you did it with or the recognition or money involved? Activities that are intrinsically enjoyable are usually the best indications of the types of careers you'll enjoy.

2. *Identifying compatible careers.* Read over Holland's six personality-occupational types and select the three types that best characterize you, ranking them 1, 2, 3. Then look at the sample careers listed under each of your selections. Have you considered any of these careers?

   Better still, do a self-directed career inventory like *Holland's Self-directed Search*, or one which requires professional supervision like the *Strong-Campbell Interest Inventory*. These inventories are usually available in your college counseling center or career guidance center.

3. *Becoming better informed about your career goal.* How much do you know about your chosen career? You might find it helpful to look up some basic information about it in a resource like the *Occupational Outlook Handbook*. Look up your chosen career or one you're interested in. Then write down information on the following: (1) description of the work; (2) typical places of employment; (3) educational and entry requirements; and (4) employment outlook. This exercise should give you a more realistic view of your career goal and how to prepare for it.

4. *Write up your experience finding jobs.* If you've held part- or full-time jobs, how have you found out about them? Did a friend tell you about the job? Or did you use the wants ads or see a notice posted? How much luck was involved? Would you agree that when it comes to finding a job you need to use as many different resources as you can?

5. *Your experience as a woman in the workplace.* Describe your experience as a woman worker in part-time and full-time jobs, paying special attention to the working conditions on the job, such as pay, supervision, and promotion. If you're married and have children, has your family been supportive? If you're a single parent, what special problems has this presented for you?

6. *Your work and leisure pattern.* Reread the four patterns of work and leisure described in the chapter. Which one most resembles your level of involvement and satisfaction at work and leisure? How do you account for this? In what ways would you like to change your pattern at work or play?

Questions for Self-reflection

1. Do you have a specific career goal?
2. If not, are you actively engaged in choosing a career—or are you "waiting for things to happen"?
3. Do you believe that hard work eventually pays off?
4. What are the three most important things you look for in a job?
5. If you won a half million dollars in the state lottery, would you continue to work?
6. What is the projected outlook for your career?
7. If you were to change careers, what would your alternate career choice be?
8. Have you ever been unemployed?
9. What is the most important thing you've learned from your part-time jobs?
10. What is your favorite leisure activity?

Recommended Readings

Bolles, Richard N. *What Color Is Your Parachute?* Berkeley, CA: Ten Speed Press, 1986 (paperback). A practical manual for those changing jobs or careers, updated annually.

Irish, Richard K. *Go Hire Yourself an Employer.* New York: Doubleday, 1978 (paperback). A creative approach to the age-old problem of job hunting.

Jackson, Tom J. *How To Get the Job You Want in Twenty-Eight Days.* New York: E. P. Dutton, 1982 (paperback). Practical suggestions for finding the job you want.

Mitchell, Joyce Slayton. *I Can Be Anything,* 3rd ed. New York: College Entrance Examination Board, 1982. This book is especially helpful for exploring the career options for women.

Nadler, Burton J. *Liberal Arts Power! How To Sell It on Your Resume.* Princeton, NJ: Peterson Guides, 1985. Guidelines for making your college education an asset in job hunting.

Occupational Outlook Handbook. 1986-1987 Edition. Washington, D.C.: Bureau of Labor. U.S. Government Printing Office, 1986 (paperback). Basic information about a wide range of careers, together with trends and projected growth of jobs, revised every 2 years.

Rohrlich, J. B. *Work and Love.* New York: Crown Publishing Company, 1982 (paperback). Deals with the vital balance between successful at work and in close relationships.

12 Freedom and Decision Making

Stan, a 26-year-old married student, came up to me after class to talk about an important choice he was facing. It seems he had lost his job in a steel plant during the past year. Then after months of unsuccessful job hunting and agonizing over his future, Stan had decided to enroll in college to become an engineer. Recently, and unexpectedly, Stan's former employer called and offered him a chance to return to work. "It's a tempting offer," Stan said. "But I'm not sure I want to go back." Stan pointed out that by taking his old job back he would be able to support his wife and two small children more adequately. "But then I'd always worry about when the next layoff is coming," he said. I agreed, pointing out this was an important consideration. At the same time, Stan was under great stress attending school full-time while supporting his family. He was having a difficult time paying the bills, and he was constantly tired. Nor was there any assurance he would get a good job as an engineer once he got his degree. "Well," he said, as he turned to leave, "I'll let you know as soon as I make up my mind."

PERSONAL FREEDOM AND CONTROL

Stan, like most of us, finds that taking charge of his life means making important decisions. It's not simply a matter of whether to accept his old job back or to remain in school, as hard a choice as this is. It goes deeper than that. Such decisions also involve important value choices in regard to what he wants out of life, what's he's willing to settle for, and how hard he's willing to work to get what he wants. It's no surprise this has been a trying time in Stan's life, with many sleepless nights and numerous heart-to-heart talks with his wife, who supports his decision to attend college. You may be interested to know that eventually Stan refused the offer of his old job. Later, he admitted that this experience had actually helped to reassure him that he is doing what he really wants to do.

All this reminds us that exercising personal freedom and control over our lives is intimately bound up with making decisions. We'll begin by taking a look at our inner sense of freedom, or *perceived freedom*, and how this affects our decision making. Then we'll devote the rest of the chapter to the practical process by which we make decisions, and how we may improve our decision-making skills. Finally, we'll explain how you can use decision making to promote personal growth.

Perceived Freedom

William James once said about freedom that "the perception of the thing and the thing itself are the same," suggesting that our awareness is an important factor in freedom. For example, if you believe that you have no choice but to remain in an extremely frustrating job or marriage, you're likely to feel desperate and trapped despite the options available to you. On the other hand, if you're actually in a highly restrictive job or marriage, but *perceive* you have some options, such a belief itself enhances your freedom in this situation.

Accordingly, modern researchers are discovering that the freedom we attribute to ourselves, however real or illusory, is itself a powerful force with real consequences in our lives. Perhaps you've noticed how much more you enjoy doing something when you've have had a choice in the matter. This was brought out in an experiment with volunteers who agreed to wear electronic pagers as they went about their activities during an ordinary week. At random intervals throughout each day, the beeper sounded and the respondents were asked to indicate what they were doing, how they felt, and to what extent they would prefer to be doing something else. Half the time, people were doing something they wanted to do. One-quarter of the time they were doing things they felt they had to do. At other times, they checked both options or said they had nothing else to do.

Generally, people felt least free when doing things expected of them, such as working and doing household chores. They felt the greatest sense of free-

The more freely we choose an activity,
the more we tend to enjoy it.
(John Pitkin)

dom when engaging in leisure activities, socializing with friends, watching television, reading, and playing sports and games. On the whole, men felt freer than
women in all but three activities: public leisure, socializing, and eating out in a
restaurant. At the same time, each sex perceived the same activities differently.
For example, women felt less free than men when doing household chores—
most likely because such duties are often expected of women. On the other
hand, men felt much freer than women when cooking, probably because for
most men cooking is a voluntary and occasional activity. The results also showed
that the freer people felt in a given activity, the more they enjoyed it. Conversely, when they were doing something compulsory, their attention was
divided between performing the task and wishing they were doing something
else. The study also showed that to a considerable extent the inner experience
of freedom is independent of external conditions. That is, when people felt an

activity was freely chosen, regardless of the circumstances, they became more involved with the task and enjoyed it more (Csikszentmihalyi & Graef, 1979). (See Figure 12–1.)

Threats to Freedom and Control

Have you ever felt someone was exerting undue influence over you, and, in reaction, you resisted all the more? If so, you're already familiar with the experience of *reactance*—the negative reaction to the threatened loss of our personal freedom and control. Whenever we feel our sense of freedom or personal control is being threatened or restricted, we strive all the harder to assert ourselves, often to the point of doing the opposite of what is expected. Everyday examples would be adolescents rebelling against authoritarian parents or consumers resisting hard-sell sales pitches.

The strength of reactance behavior depends on a variety of factors. In the first place, whenever the restrictions on our freedom are perceived as fair and legitimate, reactance may not occur. For example, when parents restrict television viewing because a child has misbehaved, the punishment may be felt as justified by the child as well. Furthermore, when there are available alternatives similar to those being restricted, reactance behavior may not occur, or, if it does, only to a mild degree. On the other hand, the more important the restricted freedom is to us, the more we expect to exercise control in regard to a matter; and the harsher the threats to our freedom and control are, the more intense our reactance will be.

Suppose you walked into a restroom and saw a sign on the wall that said "Do NOT Write on the Walls!" What would you do? How do you think other students who use the restroom would react? Whatever your response, you may be interested in a related study of restroom graffiti. One of four signs was placed on toilet walls as follows: (1) high threat/high authority—Do NOT Write on the Walls, signed by the chief of college security; (2) low threat/high authority—Please Do Not Write on the Walls, signed by the chief of college security (3) high threat/low authority—Do NOT Write on the Walls, signed by the grounds committeeperson; and (4) low threat/low authority—Please Do Not Write on the Walls, signed by the grounds committeeperson. Results showed that the most graffiti was written on the walls with the high threat/high authority signs. The least amount of graffiti occurred on the walls with the low threat/low authority signs (Pennebaker and Sanders, 1976).

As long as we expect to exercise control in a situation, we'll fight all the harder to assert ourselves when faced with the possible loss of control. But when the restriction is severe or prolonged, our resistance may eventually wear down until we give up. Martin Seligman (1975) has described this state as one of *learned helplessness*—the condition in which we've learned that our efforts have little to do with the outcome of a situation. Learned helplessness may help to

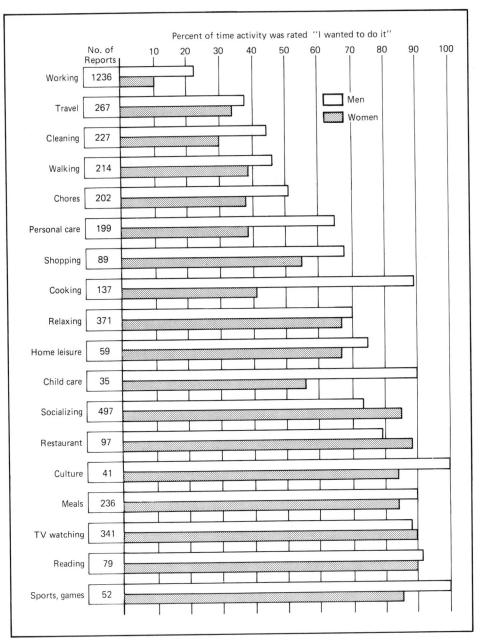

Figure 12–1. REPORT FROM THE FREEDOM RATERS. The number of reports shows the total number of times people were engaged in each activity when queried by the researchers.

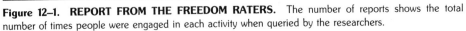

From Mihaly Csikszentmihalyi and Ronald Graef, "Feeling free," *Psychology Today*, December 1979, p. 90. Reprinted with permission from *Psychology Today* Magazine. Copyright © December 1979 American Psychological Association.

Don't Read This Item!

There is a handwritten sign in a parking lot on Sansom Street in Philadelphia that begins, "PLEASE DO NOT READ THIS STATEMENT."

The message then continues to warn customers to wait for attendants to pick up their cars, not only for the customers' protection but to avoid chipping car paint when opening the car door. So why are people told not to read the statement? Could it be? Precisely, my dear Watson—reverse psychology!

Parking lot manager Bob Gosson says more people read the sign when they are told not to. "You know," Gosson says, "I've had people put on their eyeglasses to read it cause it says don't do it."

From *The Philadelphia Inquirer*, April 21, 1981, p. 2-B.

explain a wide range of human behavior, including depression and unexplained deaths. Seligman has suggested that learned helplessness may play an important role in many types of depression, especially those occasioned by external failure and loss. The most prominent symptom of both conditions is a sense of passivity, seen in decreased activity and a general loss of interest in just about everything. While most of us experience disappointment and loss, those most vulnerable to bouts of depression tend to overreact to such experiences because of their attitude of learned helplessness. Case histories of such people have shown that they see themselves as "born losers." Even their dreams are characterized more by frustration, powerlessness, and a loss of self-esteem than by a desire for suffering or punishment sometimes ascribed to depressed people. Learned helplessness may also help to explain why women are twice as susceptible to depression as men. Traditionally, women have been brought up to be overly dependent on others—their parents, boyfriends, husbands, bosses. As a result, they may eventually come to feel ineffectual and prone to depression. Yet, Jessie Bernard (1977) suggests that as women discover that their problem is more oppression than depression, the incidence of depression among women may well decrease.

If the sense of helplessness becomes severe, it may lead to death. Indeed, learned helplessness has been offered as an explanation for a variety of enigmatic deaths, including voodoo deaths among African or Caribbean people; premature, unexplained deaths; and higher death rates among inmates in concentration camps and other institutions. Seligman (1975) gives a dramatic example of how the sense of helplessness may contribute to premature death, as seen in a study of unexpected deaths in a home for the aged. Fifty-five women over 65 years of age (their average age was 82) applied for admission to a home for the aged in the Midwest. Each woman was asked several questions such as: "How much choice did you have in moving to this home?" "How many other

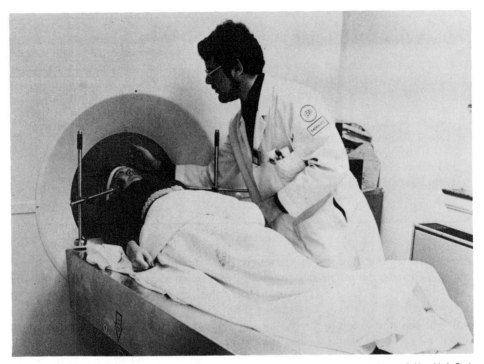

Being immobilized in a small space makes us apprehensive. (Courtesy of St. Vincent's Hospital, New York City)

possibilities were open to you?" and "How much pressure did your relatives apply?" Seventeen of the women stated they had no alternative but to move into the home. After only 4 weeks in residence, eight of these seventeen women died. A total of sixteen of them died after only 10 weeks in residence. Yet, only one person of the thirty-eight who voluntarily entered the home died in the same period of time. All the deaths were called unexpected by the staff, indicating that the psychological influences such as a sense of hopelessness and helplessness were definitely involved.

Perceived Freedom and Decisions

Given the importance of personal freedom and control, and the potentially disastrous effects of losing control, it's not surprising to find that there's a close connection between perceived freedom and decision making. Researchers are finding that the ease or difficulty of making decisions is vitally affected by our perceived freedom and vice versa. We'll point out how our perceived freedom is affected by the number and types of alternatives we face. We'll also see how our perceived freedom affects our willingness to assume responsibility for our decisions.

Common sense tells us that the more alternatives we have to choose from, the freer we feel—which is true up to a point. However, having too many alternatives makes decision making difficult and costly. This is especially true in a competitive, rapidly changing economy when companies, in an effort to increase their sales, proliferate the number of models and styles of their products, but with little or no real difference between the options. There comes a point when choice becomes overchoice, thereby diminishing rather than increasing our freedom. When it takes a lot of time and trouble to evaluate the options, people feel less free than with a smaller number of options. By contrast, when people feel they can evaluate the alternatives quickly and easily, they feel freer, with more options (Harvey & Jellison, 1974).

We also feel freer making decisions that involve positive rather than negative outcomes (Harvey, Harris, & Barnes, 1975). For example, it may be easier to choose between taking one 2-week vacation or two 1-week vacations than whether to withhold extra income for taxes from each paycheck or at the end of the year. Our felt freedom also depends on the value differences between alternatives. When there is little or no difference, you may decide just as easily by flipping a coin. But when the differences are great, a wise decision may be more obvious. For example, when given a chance to choose among opportunities for investing our money, we may feel more freedom of choice when there are significant differences in the net gains among the various choices.

The degree to which we're willing to assume responsibility for our decisions also depends on how much choice we exercise in a situation. Many studies have shown a strong positive relationship between an individual's perceived freedom and his or her felt responsibility for decision (Harvey, Harris, & Barnes, 1975). For example, a student who enrolls in college after some deliberation may feel more responsible for her performance than one who simply attends college because it's expected of her. We might even generalize and say that the greater the person's feelings of freedom, the greater the accompanying responsibility. But this generalization holds true only up to a certain point. In some instances, a great sense of freedom becomes very stressful, exposing people to increased anxiety, conflict, criticism, and self-recrimination, as well as the temptation to escape their responsibilities.

As much as we prize the freedom to direct our own lives, we may sometimes find ourselves "freezing up" in the face of an important decision. Walter Kaufmann (1975) has coined the word "decidophobia" for the fear of making decisions. Not that people necessarily fear making all decisions. Indeed, those most plagued by this fear may immerse themselves in making small decisions about trivial things as a way of avoiding the more important decisions. Kaufmann suggests that most of us, at one time or another, have used the following strategies to avoid making serious, fateful decisions in our lives. A common strategy is drifting. Instead of choosing how to live, people simply drift along, either by living according to the status quo or by dropping out, as do those whose lives are guided by no ties, code, tradition, or major purpose. Another

---

More Freedom of Choice Today

Judging by a survey of 1500 people carried out by Yankelovich, Skelly, and White, the majority of Americans feel they have more freedom of choice in how to live their lives than their parents did. Most feel that their parents' lives were hemmed in by all kinds of social, educational, and economic constraints that they themselves have escaped.

The survey showed that 73 percent of Americans feel they have more freedom of choice than their parents did, 17 percent feel they have the same level of choice as their parents, and 8 percent believe they have fewer choices. Only 2 percent were not sure.

Most people felt confident they would be able to carry out their choices and live the way they truly wanted. Typical statements were: "I have more options than my parents did." "I can do what I want to do with my life; my parents couldn't."

People who perceive their parents this way do not necessarily feel they are better people than their parents. But they do believe they have more options in the important areas of education, work, sex, marriage, family, travel, friends, possessions, where to live, and how to live. Would you agree?

From: Daniel Yankelovich, *New Rules* (New York: Random House, 1981).

---

strategy is based on shared decision making, as in committees and marriage. Instead of really making a decision, people just talk until something happens. They presume a consensus, often never questioning it. But if things turn out badly, no one feels responsible. Each merely went along. A frequently used strategy is based on an appeal to some type of authority, such as an expert, a movement, a religion, or an institution. Although individuals may experience a tension between their loyalty and their personal conscience, they find innumerable ways to justify either alternative.

Truly autonomous persons rely on none of these strategies. Instead, they accept responsibility for their lives and carefully scrutinize the alternatives available to them. But they also keep their eyes open and have the courage to admit when they are wrong and need to change. The Russian novelist Alexander Solzhenitsyn is an example of the truly autonomous person who resisted all the temptations of the "decidiphobic," making one fateful decision after another, often against overwhelming odds. The ability to make autonomous decisions, an important mark of adulthood, doesn't just consist of making decisions on our own, as important as they may be. It also means making decisions without undue fear of disapproval from others, such as our parents, peers, and those in positions of authority. Above all, it means taking responsibility for our decisions, without blaming others or fate for what happens to us, as we'll discuss in the final section of the chapter.

DECISION MAKING

From the moment we awake until we go to sleep at night, we must make decisions. Fortunately, many of our day-to-day decisions, such as when to get up and what to eat for breakfast, are made with little effort, mostly because of our basic commitments and habits. It is mainly when we encounter a new problem or face an important choice, such as whether or not to accept a promising job offer, that we become acutely aware of the need to make a decision. Even then we may become so overwhelmed analyzing the alternatives, or so caught up in the mental anguish of considering the consequences of our choice, that we procrastinate making a decision. Worse still, we may make a hasty decision to "get it over with," thereby increasing the risk of a poor decision. In both instances, we lose sight of the overall procedure needed to arrive at a decision we can live with. Here in this section we'll take a look at some of the familiar ways people make important decisions in their lives. Then we'll discuss the necessary steps in making sound decisions, along with some suggestions for improving decision-making skills.

Decision-making Strategies

In one study, individuals were asked how they went about making important decisions. An analysis of the results showed that the following types of decision-making strategies were most commonly used:

Impulsive
Taking the first alternative with little thought or examination. (Don't look before you leap.)

Fatalistic
Leaving it up to the environment or fate. (It's all in the cards.)

Compliant
Letting someone else decide. (Anything you say.)

Delaying
Postponing thought and action. (We'll cross that bridge later.)

Agonizing
Becoming overwhelmed analyzing alternatives. (I don't know what to do.)

Planning
Using a rational procedure with a balance between reason and emotion. (Weighing the facts.)

Intuitive
Basing a decision on inner harmony. (It feels right.)

Paralysis
Accepting responsibility but unable to approach a decision. (I can't face up to it.)

The distribution of individuals who followed each strategy was: planning, 25 percent; impulsive, 18 percent; compliant, 17 percent; delaying, 11 percent; fatalistic, 10 percent; agonizing, 6 percent; intuitive, 6 percent; and paralytic, 6 percent (Dinklage, 1966). Which of these strategies do you use most often? Which is most characteristic of you?

Since all important decisions involve some risk or uncertainty, decision-making strategies can also be classified according to the element of risk

Some people dislike shopping
because of all the decisions involved.
(Laimute E. Druskis)

involved. At least four types of risk-taking strategies have been identified: the
wish, escape, safe, and combination strategies. The *wish strategy* involves choosing the alternative that could lead to the most desirable result regardless of risk.
An example would be someone who applies for a position as an astronaut even
though the chances of being selected are very small. The *escape strategy* involves
choosing the alternative that is most likely to avoid the worst possible results. An
example would be the pitcher who, realizing the game is tied and nobody is on
base, intentionally walks a batter who leads the league in home runs. The *safe
strategy* consists in choosing the alternative that is most likely to bring success. An
example would be a part-time student who decides to earn money by taking a
job with set hours and salary rather than selling on a commission. The *combination strategy* involves choosing the alternative that combines high probability and
high desirability. An example would be a patient who elects to undergo surgery
that has a high success rate with highly desirable health benefits (Gelatt,
Varenhorst, & Carey, 1972).

It is important to use the strategy that is most compatible for the individual
and situation. Because of their training, experience, or interests, some people
like to "take a chance" while others prefer to "play it safe." Then too, emotions
and personality traits may alter people's estimate of risk. Confident people may
underestimate the risk involved, while fearful people may overestimate it.
Moreover, a person has to balance the risk against the desired outcome or
achievement. That is, people who are fearful of rejection may risk too little,
while highly ambitious people may risk too much. On the other hand, those
high in achievement motive usually take more moderate risks, thereby increas-

Which Job Would You Choose?

First, make your selection. Then read the rest of the exercise.

A	B	C
A job that pays a low income, but which you are sure of keeping.	A job that pays a good income, but which you have a 50-50 chance of losing.	A job that pays an extremely good income if you do well, but one in which you lose everything if you don't do well.

When 46,000 high school seniors in Minnesota were asked this question, 50 percent of them chose B, with another 25 percent each choosing A or C. But there were important differences within the three groups. Generally boys chose a greater risk than girls; college-bound youth a greater risk than those who went directly to work; and city kids a greater risk than country kids. In fact, boys from the city who went to college chose risk C 44 percent of the time, while girls from the country who went to work after high school chose risk C only 10 percent of the time.

Try to analyze your answer in order to learn more about yourself.

Source: H. B. Gelatt, B. Varenhorst, and R. Carey, *Deciding* (New York: College Entrance Examination Board, 1972), p. 40. Copyright © 1972 by the College Entrance Examination Board, New York. Adapted with permission.

ing their actual chances of success. It is good to keep in mind that the purpose of making a decision is to bring about desired results and avoid undesirable ones. In this sense, what constitutes a "good" or "bad" decision varies with the individual and situation. Yet in order to bring about preferred results consistently, you need to be aware of the essentials of decision making.

Steps in Decision Making

Books on this subject usually tell us how decisions *ought* to be made. Instead, Irving Janis and Leon Mann (1977) have formulated the following five steps in decision making based on how people have actually made and carried out difficult decisions, ranging from weight loss to national emergencies.

Appraising the Challenge. This involves recognizing a challenge for what it is, guarding against both faulty assumptions or oversimplifying a complex problem. Key question: "What are the risks of doing nothing, or not changing?"

Surveying the Alternatives. What is most needed here is an attitude of openness and flexibility, with a concern to gather information about all possible alternatives, obvious or not. Key question: "Have I considered all the alternatives?"

Weighing Alternatives. All the options are evaluated as to their practicality and consequences, especially the possible gains and costs. Key question: "Which is the best alternative?"

Making a Commitment. The cumulative tension of considering alternatives can be resolved only by making a commitment. Yet there is a danger of acting impulsively to "get it over with." Key question: "When do I implement the best alternative and allow others to know my decision?"

Following Through. Since every decision involves some risk, it is important not to overreact to criticism and disappointment, either by changing your mind prematurely or by justifying your choice and shutting out valuable criticism. Key questions: "Are the risks serious if I don't change? Are they more serious if I do change?"

Successful decision making involves what Janis and Mann call "vigorous information processing." Yet there are situations in which decision makers habitually fail to gather sufficient information, especially the following:

1. When there appears to be little risk in your present course of action, you are unlikely to look for alternatives.

2. When there is a high risk to what you're doing and the prospects of a low-risk alternative, you're likely to choose the latter.

3. If all the alternatives look risky and there appears to be little opportunity of your coming up with a better one, you're likely to put off a decision, often denying a problem exists.

4. When you feel there is an option that may disappear if you wait to investigate other alternatives, you may panic and choose prematurely.

Gathering information takes time and energy, disrupting our routines and building tension and conflict, all of which are unpleasant. Consequently, we're more willing to look for new information when we expect the benefits of a decision to outweigh the costs involved. Unfortunately, in making important decisions such as that of a career, we tend to underestimate the benefits of information gathering, and often pay a high price for it. There's nothing so agonizing as discovering an ideal choice *after* you're already committed yourself to a less desirable course of action—right?

Group Decision Making

Many matters are decided through a process of shared decision making. Often this is done informally, as when several friends agree on a movie they want to see or a couple buys a house. At other times, the process of decision making becomes more formalized, as in the deliberations of a jury or a town meeting. In both cases, the question arises: Are group decisions superior to those made by individuals? Actually, it can work either way, depending largely on the group.

The saying "A camel is a horse that was put together by a committee" suggests group decisions are mostly compromises. In accordance with this notion, Irving Janis (1982) has found that groups tend to engage in *groupthink*. That is, in the desperate drive for consensus and conformity, people tend to suppress critical thinking. For the most part, this is nondeliberate and unconscious. Members also share the illusion of invulnerability, leading them to take riskier courses of action and fail to heed warnings of danger, which can be disastrous in national policy and military actions.

At the same time, group decisions *can* be superior to those made by individuals, especially when they use conflict creatively. In a comparison of ad hoc groups and trained groups, Jay Hall (1971) found that the latter groups arrived at superior decisions because of better conflict management. In the typical group, conflict is seen as disruptive, with the usual conflict-reducing techniques leading to compromise solutions. But in trained groups, it's just the opposite. Conflict is viewed as a way of generating a wider range of alternatives and thus a more creative solution. Some guidelines for achieving creative consensus are:

1. Present your views, but listen to those of others.

2. Don't feel that someone has to win and someone has to lose.

3. Strive for the best possible solution.

4. Avoid conflict-reducing techniques such as the majority vote.

5. Realize that differences of opinion are natural and may lead to better solutions.

Aids in Making Decisions

While the process of gathering information, weighing alternatives, and making a commitment is complex enough, it is further complicated by many personal factors, such as our values, attitudes, tolerance for anxiety and conflict, and the like. Consequently, we may improve our decision-making skills by keeping in mind the following principles.

Use Sounder Judgment. Judgment, the raw material of decision making, involves drawing inferences from data. Many decisions are doomed from the start because of poor judgment, often because of the human tendency to simplify complex matters into familiar ideas, especially stereotypes. Richard Nisbett and Lee Ross (1980) suggest replacing simplistic, intuitive strategies with the more empirical orientation that guides scientists, asking ourselves such questions as: What are the facts? How representative are they? What do the alternatives look like? How much is due to situational and chance factors? Sounder judgments may lead to better decisions.

Draw up a Balance Sheet. This consists of listing the various advantages and disadvantages of a given course of action. The sample balance sheet in Table 12–1 represents the situation of Cheryl, a 25-year-old secretary who contemplates returning to school to become a computer programmer. Students like Cheryl as well as adults of all ages have found that the balance sheet procedure helps them to make a comprehensive appraisal of a situation requiring a decision, and promotes contingency planning, that is, figuring out what to do if something in the minus column materializes. People who use the balance sheet procedure are more likely to stick to their decisions and express fewer regrets about the options not taken (Janis and Wheeler, 1978).

Table 12–1. CHERYL'S BALANCE SHEET.

Projected Consequences	Positive Anticipations	Negative Anticipations
Tangible gains and losses for me	1. Good job opportunities 2. Better income 3. Challenging career	1. Hard courses 2. Financial difficulties 3. Short-term loss of job security
Tangible gains and losses for others	1. Parents proud of me 2. Substantial help with family income 3. Positive role model for daughter	1. Less time for boyfriend 2. Conflicts between career and family goals
Self-approval or disapproval	1. Confidence in mastering challenge 2. Pride in being computer programmer	1. Lingering doubts about working with computers
Social approval or disapproval	1. Admiration for a woman working with computers	1. Future husband may disapprove of wife working with computers

Clarify Your Values and Objectives. Many conflicts arise from confusion over values rather than over the conflicting alternatives. Since values are neither "good" nor "bad" in themselves, this requires a personal examination. Once you have clarified your values, they can be translated into tangible objectives that guide your decisions. For example, students are sometimes torn between the need to study, work, socialize, or play, often vacillating in their decisions. Yet those who have made a clear choice about what they hope to gain from college will be more likely to resolve their daily decisions effectively.

Accept Reasonable Results. Nothing is so devastating to decision making as the wish for an "ideal" solution. People with perfectionistic tendencies are especially susceptible to this. Yet constant striving for perfection guarantees failure. It is usually wiser to accept the most reasonable results under the circumstances. Among the methods of combatting perfectionism suggested by David Burns (1980) are recognizing the advantages and disadvantages of perfectionism and comparing how perfectly you did something with how much you enjoyed it. For example, you may feel that you didn't play tennis very well, but you enjoyed it nevertheless because of the exercise and compansionship.

Make the Best of Faulty Decisions. Because of limitations in human judgment, circumstances, and unforeseen events, when it comes to decisions, "You can't win 'em all." But people are apt to waste time berating themselves or trying to justify their poor decisions. Roger Gould (1978) says it may be wiser to realize that more often than not we made the best possible decision at the time, to attempt to learn from our mistakes, and whenever possible, to modify our decision to achieve a more desirable result. For example, a woman who dropped out of college, married, and had two children regretted giving up her plans to be a writer. Once her children were in school, and encouraged by her husband, she began spending her mornings writing, eventually publishing several novels and winning national recognition.

DECISIONS AND PERSONAL GROWTH

I once asked a colleague who works with alcoholics at what point in the treatment program clients began making significant progress. "It's hard to say," he

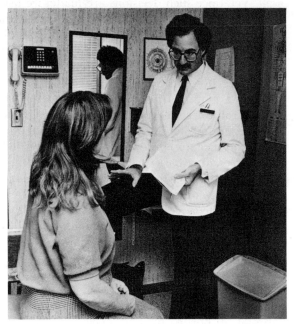

Gathering information
is essential for making an
informed choice. (Laimute E. Druskis)

said, "because so much depends on when a person makes up his or her mind to change. In fact, we won't even admit people into our program until they have made some sort of commitment to change." A similar realization led Harold Greenwald (1973, 1984) to adopt a new approach in treating clients, namely *direct decision therapy*, Greenwald found the main thing that happens in therapy, regardless of the techniques used, is that the person is helped to make a decision to change and then is supported in carrying out that decision. Decision therapy is aimed at helping clients see their problems as the result of previous decisions, to examine the consequences and alternatives of such decisions, and then to choose a more satisfying alternative. Dr. Greenwald readily admits that this approach has been helpful in his own personal life, including an earlier decision to become a psychologist. He has also found that many people who have never participated in therapy have benefited from applying the principles of decision therapy to their personal lives, especially in terms of personal growth.

Finding the Basic Decisions in Your Life

According to Greenwald, a good beginning point is to find the basic decisions underlying our everyday behavior, especially problem behavior. Although we may be conscious of our behavior being a reaction to people and situations, on closer examination we may find that we have *chosen* to act a certain way. Greenwald speaks of the "decision behind the decision," referring to basic life choices involving our needs and motivation, which we're only dimly aware of if at all. Yet, once such decisions are made, we usually organize our lives around them and our perceptions as well, so that we understand everything that happens to us a certain way. Some practical examples illustrate the point.

Have you ever wondered why people procrastinate or fail to put forth their best efforts on important matters? Often such behavior is the outgrowth of a basic life choice to protect themselves from failure or hurt, though they may not be aware of it. For example, the boy who habitually waits until Friday afternoon to call for a date that evening or the girl who waits until August to apply for college admission have something in common. In both instances, they have a face-saving excuse if they fail—"I was too late." Somewhere in the dim past, each has made a basic decision to play it safe, because of a fear of failure or getting hurt. Only when they change that decision will they put forth their best efforts and enjoy a greater chance of success.

Much negative behavior, such as rebelliousness and defiance, is also the result of a basic life decision though again not in the person's awareness. For example, a young man left home in his mid-teens because of constant fights with his overly strict father. Nevertheless, even after leaving home, he was still known to be "touchy" and "hard to get along with," even by his friends. He was always doing the opposite of what people expected of him, often with disappointing results. This young man had made a choice in opposition to coercive parental authority; he had decided "No!" Until this rebellion, he was an appendage of his parents. But after rebelling, he felt more in charge of his life. Nor should that surprise us, since the defiance of the young child or adolescent is often the initial step toward autonomy. However, as long as this young man remains stuck in this initial but negative stage of independence, his life will be controlled more by what he is against than what he is for.

Using Decision Making for Personal Growth

Greenwald has outlined the following suggestions for applying the principles of decision therapy to yourself:

1. *State your problem as clearly and completely as you can.* Your problem need not be acute or a crisis, just something you would like to deal with. You may even find it helpful to write things down.

2. *See each problem not as something that just happened to you, but as the consequence of a decision you have made.* Such a problem could be something you decided to do, something you decided to be, or some way you decided to regard other people.

3. *Look for the basic decision behind the decision.* Did you decide to have the problem in order to avoid something? If so, what were you avoiding?

4. *List the advantages and payoffs of the decision.* These may be actual positive gains or may include the avoidance of anxiety. In either case, they are still payoffs.

5. *What was the context in which you made the original decision?* Were you very young? What was the situation then? Was your decision a sound one, given the circumstances?

6. *Ask yourself if the context is different now that you're older.* Maybe the payoffs are not so important or have become more trouble than they are worth.

7. *List the alternatives to each decision you've made.* Examine them in terms of the advantages and disadvantages of each.

8. *Now choose one of the alternatives and decide to put it into practice.* Sharing your decision with friends or colleagues may help you carry it out.

9. *If you have trouble putting the decision into practice, go back to the first suggestion to see if you're still operating under an old decision.* Remember that what you actually do is the best clue to the decision you've made, not what you'd like or wish to do.

10. *Remember that it's not enough to make your decision only once.* You must reaffirm your decision repeatedly. For example, if you decide to lose weight, each time you sit down to eat you must reaffirm your decision.

11. *If you fail occasionally in carrying out your decision, that doesn't mean that you have to give up altogether.* Since most of us are not infallible, we must be able to accept an occasional failure, pick ourselves up, and continue with our decision.

Adapted from Harold Greenwald, *Direct Decision Therapy* (San Diego, CA.: Edits, 1973).

Making New Decisions

In Greenwald's view, it is only when a *wish* to change leads to a *decision* to change that we really change and grow. For example, many smokers dislike their smoking habit. They say things such as "I'd *like* to stop smoking" and "I *hope* to give it up soon" and "I *plan* to cut down on my smoking." But until they make a basic decision to stop smoking and learn how to implement that decision, nothing happens.

So far we have assumed that people will automatically decide to change for the best. But this is not always the case. In some instances, people may become so overwhelmed with the anxiety and risks of change, that they will decide to remain the way they are, however unsatisfying or painful that may be. Nor can someone be forced into growth, especially by therapists who are militant about people living up to their human potential. As Greenwald (1973) aptly says, "Why the hell does anybody have to live up to his potential unless he wants to?" (p. 295). However well-intentioned such therapists may be, they can make the same mistakes that parents and spouses are prone to make—namely, trying to tell someone else what they ought to decide. Rather, the therapist's task is to help the client first discover what he or she wants to do and then make a personal decision to do it. As most of us have discovered, once you know what you want to do and really decide to do it, you're well on your way.

Some Practical Applications

One of the most common examples of decision making is "decision by default." Putting things off, whether temporarily or indefinitely, is itself a decision. An example that comes to mind is a young man who was having considerable difficulty completing his doctoral dissertaion, partly because of emotional blocks in writing and partly because of conflicts with his advisor. Things became so frustrating that this young man simply turned his efforts elsewhere. He took an administrative post at the university ("while I finish my degree") and spent more time painting ("to take my mind off my problems"). Several years later when I asked him how his degree program was progressing, I wasn't surprised to hear that he had finally "decided" to give it up. Actually, he had made that decision earlier. The failure to make a positive decision is itself a decision with fateful consequences.

Overcoming negative, self-defeating behavior usually involves making a positive decision at a basic level of motivation. An example concerns a 28-year-old librarian who was bothered by depression and a poor relationship with her supervisor. She reported that she was constantly complaining at work and was especially critical of her boss, often without an apparent reason. During therapy this woman discovered that earlier in her life she had learned to suppress her anger for fear of parental disapproval. She had become a passive, good little girl, but resented those on whom she remained dependent. Gradually, she learned to take more initiative, to show her anger more directly, but as an expression of her feelings rather than as judgmental remarks that might put others on the defensive. As this woman became more assertive, she felt less depressed and enjoyed a more satisfying relationship with those in authority. She also returned to school for a master's degree and later assumed a supervisory position at another library.

Sometimes it is wise to make a decision that counters or reverses an earlier commitment that has led to undersirable consequences. An example is a 45-year-old lawyer who married the daughter of a senior partner in his firm. He admits having married out of "mixed motives." That is, while he had been genuinely attracted to his wife, he had also hoped that his "connections" would enhance his career. Yet he soon discovered that conflicts with his father-in-law complicated his life both at work and at home. Consultation with a specialist about his asthma attacks, which seemed worse during joint vacations at his wife's family summer place, suggested these were brought on by emotional conflicts over his in-laws. Gradually, this man realized that it had not been a good idea to marry the "boss's daughter," and eventually he decided to start his own firm. Although he went through a few lean years, he soon had a flourishing law practice and was much happier in his marriage as well. Failure to make such a courageous decision often results in feeling trapped in one's career, drinking problems, or extra-marital affairs.

Sometimes dramatic improvements involve group decision making. In one instance, the quality of work had gotten so bad that a company was considering simply closing an automobile assembly plant. As a final gesture, the manager suggested they inform the workers of the situation and ask for their suggestions. They discovered that the workers themselves were well aware of their poor work, although they justified it because of their poor working conditions. Yet they wanted to improve the situation just as much as the company officials did. A group decision was reached to save the plant, involving concessions from both management and labor. During a 6-month probationary period, a new policy was adopted involving workers' suggestions to improve assembly-line production, to improve treatment of workers, and to make the work more meaningful. Each team of workers followed a car through the assembly line and became responsible for the acceptance of the final product. The improvement in productivity and quality of work was so dramatic that the plant not only survived but became a model for the rest of the plants in the parent company.

Summary

Personal Freedom and Control

1. We began the chapter by noting that perceived freedom, or the freedom we attribute to ourselves, however real or illusory, is itself a powerful force with real consequences in our lives.

2. However, when we feel our personal freedom or control is being threatened or diminished, we strive all the harder to assert it.

3. The ease or difficulty with which we make decisions is also affected by our perceived freedom in several ways, such that we are usually freer in choosing between a reasonable number of alternatives than an excessive number of them.

Decision Making

4. Although there are a variety of decision-making strategies, it's best to use the strategy that is most compatible for the individual and situation at hand.

5. The actual process by which people arrive at important decisions covers at least five basic stages, including appraising the challenge, surveying the alternatives, weighing them, making a commitment, and a reasonable adherence to one's course of action.

6. We also discussed several aids in decision making, such as the use of better judgment, the balance sheet procedure, clarifying objectives, and accepting reasonable results.

Decisions and Personal Growth

7. According to Greenwald's direct decision therapy, it helps to see each of our problems not as something that just happened to us, but as the consequence of a decision we've made.

8. It's only when a wish to change leads to a decision to change that we really change and grow.

9. We must also reaffirm our decisions repeatedly, accepting an occasional failure and picking ourselves up and continuing with our commitment to change.

Self-test

1. The freedom we attribute to ourselves, however real or illusory, is:

   a. reactance   **c.** perceived freedom
   b. false freedom   **d.** unconscious freedom

2. The condition in which we've learned that our efforts have little to do with the outcome of a situation is known as:

   a. perceived freedom   **c.** psychic reactance
   b. learned helplessness   **d.** pseudo-freedom

3. We tend to feel freer making decisions that involve:

   a. mostly positive outcomes   **c.** positive and negative outcomes
   b. the maximum number of alternatives   **d.** value conflicts

4. A decision-making strategy that usually involves postponing thought and action is:

   a. impulsive   **c.** fatalistic
   b. compliant   **d.** delaying

5. In making important decisions, the initial step is usually:

a. making a commitment

b. surveying the alternatives

c. appraising the challenge

d. weighing the alternatives

6. Successful decision making generally involves:

a. making decisions quickly

b. vigorous information processing

c. agonizing over decisions

d. all of the above

7. One of the suggestions for improving decision-making skills is to:

a. use sounder judgment

b. strive for perfection

c. put your values aside

d. make decisions quickly

8. Use of the balance sheet procedure in making decisions helps:

a. to make a comprehensive appraisal

b. people to stick to their decisions

c. to promote contingency planning

d. all of the above

9. According to Greenwald's direct decision therapy, we should state our problems:

a. as something that just happened to us

b. in terms of a value conflict

c. as the consequences of decisions we've made

d. in terms of the unconscious conflicts involved

10. Once you've made a decision to change your behavior in some way, such as to lose weight, you:

a. should never accept even an occasional failure

b. must reaffirm this decision repeatedly

c. automatically begin to change your behavior

d. always talk it over with other people

Exercises

1. *Freedom and enjoyment.* This exercise is based on the research findings that showed that the freer people felt in a given activity, the more they enjoyed it. To see how this applies to your experience, select several activities you've enjoyed very much and an equal number you have disliked. Then compare these activities according to your perceived freedom in each of them. Do you find there is a close relationship between how free you feel and how much you enjoy an activity? What are some of the other factors that affect your enjoyment of an activity?

2. *Reactance behavior.* Recall several situations in which your sense of personal freedom or control was threatened or greatly diminished. Examples would be when you're the object of a hard-sell approach, when an application of yours has been denied, or when you are treated in a high-handed manner by someone in a position of authority. Did you find yourself exhibiting "reactance behavior?"—that is, asserting yourself all the harder in the face of such restriction?

3. *Decision-making strategies.* Look over the various decision-making strategies discussed in the subsection by the same title as above. Included here are the impulsive, fatalistic, compliant, delaying, agonizing, planning, intuitive, and paralysis strategies. Which of these strategies do you use most often? Do you find that one of them is especially characteristic of you? To what extent do you vary your decision-making strategy with the particular situation?

4. *Risk taking.* Reread the material on decision-making strategies based on the degree of risk involved—the wish, escape, safe, and combination strategies respectively. Do you tend to use one of these strategies more than the others? If so, which one? To what degree do you take risks when making decisions? Do you find that this depends somewhat on the particular situation?

5. *Steps in decision making.* Review the material on Janis and Mann's five steps in decision making, including (1) appraising the challenge, (2) surveying the alternatives, (3) weighing the alternatives, (4) making a commitment, and (5) following through despite criticism. Then select an important decision you've made, and analyze it in terms of this procedure. Did you find yourself spending much more time in some of these steps than others? If so, which steps?

6. *Decision making and personal growth.* Select some aspect of your life, such as a habit or problem behavior, that you would like to change. Then analyze it in terms of Greenwald's principles of direct decision therapy. Is the problem behavior partly a consequence of a decision you've made, whether you were aware of it or not? Are you convinced that you must make a deliberate decision to change this behavior?

Questions for Self-reflection

1. Do you feel that generally you have more freedom of choice than your parents did?
2. When you think you have "no choice" in a situation, what do you do?
3. How do you go about making important decisions?
4. Are you aware that decisions are only as good as the judgments on which they are based?
5. How often do you "decide" things by *not* deciding?
6. Are you willing to take calculated risks?
7. What was the best decision you ever made? What was the worst one?
8. How much truth is there in the saying that "life is what happens to us while we're making other plans"?
9. Under what conditions are group decisions likely to be better than those of individuals?
10. How much control do you feel you have over your life?

Recommended Readings

Cammaert, L. P., and C. C. Larsen. *A Woman's Choice.* Champaign, IL: Research Press, 1980 (paperback). A practical handbook to aid women in making the best possible choices about their lives.

Greenwald, Harold, and Elizabeth Rich. *The Happy Person.* New York: Avon Books, 1984 (paperback). How to use the principles of direct decision therapy to make the most of your life.

Keyes, Ralph. *Chancing It.* Boston: Little, Brown 1985. Examines the role of risk-taking in everyday life.

May, Rollo. *Psychology and The Human Dilemma.* New York: W. W. Norton, 1980. A noted existentialist explains the meaning of human freedom in relation to the promises and perils of human existence.

Rubin, Theodore Isaac. *Overcoming Indecisiveness.* New York: Harper & Row, 1985. A psychoanalyst explains the eight states of effective decision-making.

Wheeler, D. D., and I. L. Janis. *A Practical Guide for Making Decisions.* New York: The Free Press, 1980. A practical guide for decision making based on the authors' own studies.

13 Psychological Disorders

Cathy, 32, has taken exactly the same route to and from work for several years. One day recently she tried walking down a different street. Midway down the unfamiliar block, Cathy broke out in a cold sweat. She felt dizzy and had heart palpitations. "I began to panic," she said. Cathy is suffering from an *anxiety disorder.*

Don, an engineer in his mid-40s, has been doing poorly at work. He has lost interest in his home life and feels tired all the time. Also, he has trouble getting to sleep at night and has begun drinking heavily every evening. He can't seem to enjoy anything these days. Don suffers from *depression.*

Nancy, 28, an accountant, lives at home and has few friends. She complains that people are talking about her and calling her names behind her back. In recent months, she has begun hearing imaginary voices telling her that she must get rid of her mother. After a violent argument with her mother, Nancy is taken to a local clinic where she is diagnosed as having a schizophrenic disorder.

UNDERSTANDING PSYCHOLOGICAL DISORDERS

The family and friends of these people might refer to their eccentric behavior in more familiar, judgmental terms than those we've used. Cathy's friends might view her as "neurotic." Don's family might call him an "alcoholic," without recognizing the underlying depression. And Nancy's coworkers might say she's having a "nervous breakdown." Psychologists and other mental health workers generally avoid such terms because they are too vague to be of help. Instead, professionals are concerned about more relevant matters, such as the emotional discomfort suffered by these people and the degree of impairment in their everyday functioning—in short, which disorder they have—and thus how best to help them so that they may resume their usual activities.

The study of psychological disorders is often associated with abnormal behavior, because many disorders involve thoughts, feelings, or actions that are not considered normal. Yet, neither abnormal behavior nor psychological disorders are easy to define. For instance, a brilliant scientist's thoughts may be unusual but not necessarily abnormal in the usual sense of this term. On the other hand, some forms of depression are too common to be labeled abnormal, but are nevertheless classified as a psychological disorder. Then too, other behaviors may be considered socially deviant, such as bathing nude at a public beach, without being a psychological disorder. Consequently, we'll begin by taking a look at some of the common standards used in defining psychological disorders, the incidence of such disorders, and how they are classified.

Defining Disorder

Many people are surprised to discover that there is no precise and universally agreed upon definition of a psychological disorder. Even the experts disagree among themselves in regard to this matter. However, there are some standards commonly used for defining disorders, and we will take a look at these in this section.

A major factor is the individual's level of *personal discomfort* or *distress*. An individual who experiences a painful symptom such as a chronic fear of heights or a marked change in mood as in severe depression may be diagnosed as having a psychological disorder, whereas an individual who behaves eccentrically but is otherwise happy would not be so diagnosed. Many professionals have already adopted the idea of level of personal distress in regard to their view of homosexuality. That is, homosexual behavior itself is no longer considered a disorder. It is only when individuals are seriously unhappy about their homosexual orientation that such behavior is considered a psychological disorder (DSM-III, 1980). As useful as this standard is, it isn't sufficiently comprehensive by itself. What about the rapists who feel no remorse for the suffering inflicted on their victims? Or what about the eccentric loner who claims to be receiving messages from outer space, but is content with his own life and doing no harm to others?

Such considerations suggest another important factor in defining psychological disorders, namely, *maladaptive behavior*. Individuals may suffer significant impairment in one or more areas of functioning, such as the inability to work or get along with family and friends. This is a practical approach because it focuses on behavior that is relative to life circumstances. But it fails to distinguish between those situations in which one should and should not adapt. For instance, would we diagnose as maladaptive the people who couldn't accept Hitler's regime and fled the country? Or would we say that people who fail to accept the conventional practices of racial and sexual discrimination are sick?

Still another way of defining psychological disorder involves the violation of *social norms*. People in every society live by certain rules of what is acceptable and unacceptable behavior. For instance, in regard to eating behavior, it may be acceptable to eat at a rock concert but not at a symphony concert. Yet, acceptable eating behavior varies around the world. In most societies, people commonly eat in public but urinate in private, though it is just the reverse in other societies. Consequently, what is considered abnormal varies somewhat from one culture to another and within the same society in different eras.

As you can see, there is no single satisfactory standard for defining psychological disorder. In practice, mental health professionals and others rely on a combination of these standards to judge whether a given behavior is a disorder. The presence of painful symptoms or personal distress, significant impairment in one or more areas of functioning (including impairment due to organic causes), and the social acceptability of the individual's behavior are all taken into account, though in varying degrees.

Incidence of Disorders

During any 6-month period, one in five adults will suffer from some type of psychological disorder, ranging from disabling anxiety to a severe illness such as schizophrenia. Yet, only one-fifth of those afflicted will seek help from a psychiatrist or a psychologist. Most of the others will consult someone other than a mental health specialist, such as their family physician or clergy. These are some of the findings of an extensive survey conducted by the National Institute of Mental Health (Robins, et al., 1984), among 20,000 Americans in five communities around the nation. Each subject was interviewed up to 2 hours and asked to respond to a list of 200 questions about specific symptoms, such as loss of interest in sex or feelings of panic about leaving the house. The symptoms correspond to 15 specific psychological disorders described in the Diagnostic and Statistical Manual of Mental Disorders described in the next subsection. The data were analyzed by the computer and then used to project statistics of the population as a whole.

Anxiety disorders, including phobias, panic attacks, and obsessive-compulsive behaviors, are the most widespread disorders, affecting 13 million Americans or 8.3 percent of the adult population. About 10 million people, or 6.4 percent of the population, are abusers of alcohol or drugs, with most of these cases related to alcohol. Almost as many, or 9.4 million people (about 6 percent of the population), suffer from some type of affective disorder, including both chronic depression and manic depression. Another 1.5 million people, or 1 percent of the population, suffer from schizophrenia, with an equal number of people exhibiting some sort of severe cognitive impairment or disordered thinking. About 1.4 million people suffer from antisocial personality, a set of traits that includes a lack of remorse for wrongdoing and often a pattern of criminal and violent behavior.

When all disorders are taken into account, men and women are equally likely to suffer from psychological disorders. However, the patterns of disorders differs somewhat among the sexes. Women suffer more from phobias and depression, while men are more apt to abuse alcohol or drugs and exhibit long-term antisocial behavior. At the same time, women are twice as likely as men to seek help, which may have given the impression in the past that women were more troubled than men. In both sexes, the incidence of disorders drops by about half after 45 years of age. This is especially true for alcohol and drug abuse as well as antisocial behavior. Among the other findings was that about one out of every three persons interviewed had experienced at least one psychological problem in their lifetime, with college graduates reporting fewer such ailments than noncollege graduates.

Classifying Disorders

One of the most authoritative guides for classifying the various psychological disorders is the *Diagnostic and Statistical Manual of Mental Disorders*, third edition, published by the American Psychiatric Association, usually referred to as the DSM-III. The authors of this manual acknowledge there is no satisfactory definition that specifies precise boundaries of psychological disorders. Nor are there sharp boundaries between the various disorders, or between psychological disorders and no disorder. Within these limitations, the manual classifies, defines, and describes over 200 psychological disorders, using precise, practical criteria as the basis of classification.

Throughout the DSM-III, the emphasis is on classifying *behavior* patterns, rather than people. Thus, the manual refers to people who exhibit the symptoms of schizophrenia, rather than "schizophrenics." Also, the terminology refers to "mental health professionals" and "clinicians" instead of psychiatrists, thereby acknowledging the broader range of human service workers who deal with psychological disorders. Finally, the emphasis is on *describing* rather than interpreting psychological disorders, especially when the causal factors are unknown. We'll describe several of the more common or serious disorders, such as the anxiety disorders, affective disorders, and schizophrenia, and highlight some of the other disorders in the boxed items. A list of the major categories of disorders in the DSM-III is shown in Table 13–1.

Table 13–1   SELECTED CATEGORIES OF PSYCHOLOGICAL DISORDER IN THE DSM-III.

Organic mental disorders	Psychological or behavioral abnormalities associated with a temporary or permanent brain dysfunction.	Senile dementia*
Disorders arising in childhood or adolescence	Disorders that are first evident in these stages of development.	Hyperactivity Infantile autism Mental retardation
Substance use disorders	Undesirable behavioral changes associated with the use of drugs that affect the central nervous system.	Alcohol abuse or dependence* Amphetamine abuse or dependence
Schizophrenic disorders	Serious alterations of thought and behavior that represent a split from reality.	Disorganized, paranoid, catatonic, and undifferentiated types of schizophrenia*
Affective disorders	Disturbances of mood that pervade one's entire life.	Depression* Bipolar disorder*
Anxiety disorders	Disorders in which the main symptom is anxiety or attempts to escape from anxiety.	Panic attacks* Phobias* Obsessive-compulsive disorder*
Somatoform disorders	Disorders involving physical symptoms with no known physical cause, often associated with stress.	Psychogenic pain disorder
Dissociative disorders	Sudden loss or alteration in the integrative functions of consciousness.	Amnesia (not caused by organic mental disorder) Multiple personality*
Psychosexual disorders	Disorders of sexual functioning or identity caused by psychological factors.	Sexual dysfunctions, e.g., erectile dysfunctions, inhibited orgasm*
Factitious disorders	Physical or psychological symptoms voluntarily produced by the individual, often involving deliberate deceit.	Factitious disorder with psychological symptoms
Disorders of impulse control	Difficulties controlling one's emotions or behavior.	Pathological gambling
Adjustment disorder	Impaired functioning due to identifiable life stresses, such as family or economic crises.	Adjustment disorder with depressed mood Adjustment disorder with academic inhibition
Personality disorders	Long-standing patterns of thought and behavior that are maladaptive.	Antisocial personality*

*Asterisks denote disorders that are discussed in this chapter or another chapter of the book.

Source: *Diagnostic and Statistical Manual of Mental Disorders*, 3rd ed. (Washington, D.C.: The American Psychiatric Association, 1980).

ANXIETY DISORDERS

As you may recall from earlier chapters, anxiety may be helpful in mobilizing us to meet some threat, such as studying for an important exam. However, in an *anxiety disorder*, the anxiety is out of proportion to the situation or occurs in the absence of any specific danger. Anxiety can be experienced in several different ways in these disorders. In a generalized anxiety disorder, the anxiety itself becomes the predominant disturbance. Either the person is anxious all the time or suffers from periodic anxiety attacks. On the other hand, in a phobic disorder the anxiety is evoked by some dreaded object or situation. In the obsessive-compulsive disorder, anxiety occurs if the person does *not* engage in some thought or behavior, which otherwise is senseless and often embarrassing.

Panic Attacks

The main characteristic of the generalized anxiety disorder is a persistent sense of "free-floating" anxiety. People who are chronically anxious can't say what they are afraid of. All they know is that they feel on edge all the time. They generally worry a lot and anticipate that something bad will happen to them. They often feel the symptoms associated with anxiety, such as cold sweat, the pounding heart, and the dry mouth. Anxiety may disrupt their everyday functioning, such that may find it hard to concentrate and make decisions. People with this disorder may also develop headaches, muscular tension, indigestion, a strained face, and fidgeting. Frequently they become apprehensive about their anxiety, fearing their condition will give them ulcers, a heart attack, or make them go crazy.

Chronically anxious people may also suffer from panic attacks. In some instances, the attack occurs in response to a specific phobic situation, such as driving in city traffic or getting up to speak publicly. However, when such an attack occurs in the absence of a feared situation, this condition is called a *panic disorder*. In a panic attack, anxiety increases to an almost intolerable level. The person breaks out in a cold sweat, feels dizzy, and may have difficulty breathing. Almost always there is the feeling of inescapable doom, as if one won't make it or will die. Panic attacks may last only a few minutes or continue for hours. Afterwards, the person feels exhausted. Since panic attacks are unpredictable, they often create additional anxiety, with the person avoiding certain situations in which he or she fears losing control or being helpless.

For example, Cynthia suffered from periodic panic attacks at college. She couldn't concentrate on her studies, had difficulty sleeping, and complained of stomach pains. The college counselor observed that these attacks occurred toward the end of the semester, usually before a long holiday. Cynthia said she loved her parents and looked forward to going home. Yet, as the end of semester approached, she became more susceptible to panic attacks. In her discussions with the counselor, Cynthia discovered that her anxiety was precipitated by problems at home. She felt caught in a conflict between her parents, who were separated. Because she was unable to cope with the pressure to take sides with her mother or her father, the prospects of going home for the holidays evoked intense anxiety.

Someone experiencing acute anxiety.
(Laimute E. Druskis)

Phobias

Phobic disorders are characterized by a persistent and irrational fear of a specific object or activity, accompanied by a compelling desire to avoid it. Most of us experience an irrational avoidance of selected objects, like spiders or snakes, but this usually has no major impact on our lives. By contrast, when the avoidance behavior or fear becomes a significant source of distress to the individual and interferes with his or her everyday behavior, the diagnosis of a phobic disorder is warranted (DSM-III, 1980). There are several major types of phobic disorders: simple and social phobias, which generally involve a circumscribed stimulus, and agoraphobia, which involves an intense fear of unfamiliar situations.

Simple phobias are the most common type in the general population, though not necessarily among those seeking treatment. Objects commonly feared include animals, particularly dogs, snakes, insects, and mice. Other simple phobias are acrophobia, fear of heights, and claustrophobia, the fear of closed places. Most simple phobias originate in childhood and disappear without treatment. However, the more intense fears that persist into adulthood generally don't disappear without treatment.

Social phobias involve a chronic, irrational fear of and a compelling desire to avoid situations in which the individual may be scrutinized by others. If confronted with the necessity of entering such a situation, the individual experiences marked anxiety and attempts to avoid it. Examples would be an intense fear of speaking or performing in public, eating in public, using public lavatories, and writing in the presence of others. Although this type of disorder itself is rarely incapacitating, it does result in considerable inconvenience such as avoiding a trip that involves the use of a public lavatory. Also, in an effort to relive their anxiety, individuals with this disorder often abuse alcohol, barbiturates, and other antianxiety medications.

Multiple Personality

Multiple personality is one of the dissociative disorders, in which the individual alternates between two or more distinct personalities. Or there may be a dominant personality with a variety of subordinate ones.

Clinical studies have shown that most cases of multiple personality have certain features in common. First, there are marked differences in the memories and mannerisms of each personality. Also, each personality tends to emerge in response to a particular situation. Then too, each personality takes on a particular role or emotional experience for the others. That is, one personality may take on a controlling role; another one may play a more rebellious role. In many cases, the dominant personality is unaware of the activities of the other personalities, which may account for the "lost time" reported by people suffering from multiple personality (Putnam, 1982).

Although multiple personality is a relatively rare disorder, there has been a marked increase in the number of such patients reported in the past few years. Most are women. And the majority of them have been victims of physical or sexual abuse in childhood. It appears that when faced with overwhelming stress, such children escape emotionally by imagining separate personalities to deal with the suffering (Coons, 1980).

During treatment, therapists help the person integrate the different personalities, sometimes through the use of hypnosis. But it is usually a long and difficult process. In the widely publicized case of Sybil, for example, it took 11 years to integrate her sixteen personalities into a stable, coherent personality (Schreiber, 1975).

Agoraphobia, classically known as "fear of open spaces," is typically the most severe phobic reaction and the one for which people most often seek treatment. Agoraphobia is a cluster of different fears, all of which evoke intense anxiety about panicking in unfamiliar places. Situations commonly avoided include being in crowds, such as a crowded store, in elevators or tunnels, or on public transportation or bridges. This type of phobia tends to occur in the late teens or early 20s, though it can occur later in life, and is often precipitated by separation anxiety in childhood or a sudden loss of significant objects or persons. During the outbreak of this phobia, the individual is often housebound. Or if the person goes out, great care is taken to avoid certain situations such as being in an elevator.

Obsessive-compulsive Disorder

The essential features of this disorder are recurrent obsessions or compulsions, or, as is usually the case, both. An *obsession* is a thought or image that keeps recurring to the mind, despite the individual's attempts to ignore or resist it. Similarly, a *compulsion* is an act that the individual feels compelled to repeat again and again, usually in a ritualistic fashion or according to certain rules. The act is performed with a sense of compulsion, coupled with a desire to resist such action, at least initially. The individual usually recognizes the behavior is senseless and does not derive pleasure from carrying it out, though doing so provides a release of tension.

Most of us experience mild obsessions from time to time. We might keep humming a tune we heard recently. Or our thoughts might keep going back to an article about a tragic accident we read in the daily newspaper. But these minor obsessions are temporary and do not interfere with our everyday activities. In contrast, pathological obsessions reoccur day after day. They also tend to involve thoughts of lust and violence, partly because of their association with the individual's anxiety and guilt, which makes them even more demoralizing to the person. Examples would include the fear of being contaminated by germs, the fear that one will kill one's child or spouse, or the temptation to have sex with a forbidden partner.

Pathological compulsions tend to fall into two categories (Rachman and Hodgson, 1980). The first group includes checking rituals, such as making certain the windows are closed, the doors are locked, or the stove is turned off. For instance, a person may switch off the car engine to reenter the house several times and make certain the stove is turned off. The second group are cleaning

Antisocial Personality Disorder

Unlike the anxiety disorders, the personality disorders are characterized by long-standing habits of thought and behavior that cause less distress to the individuals themselves than to the people involved with them. Individuals with the antisocial personality disorder, which is usually evident by midadolescence, have a history of chronic antisocial behavior, with little or no regard for the rights of others. For example, one person wooed and married 105 women, some of them more than once, but all without the benefit of a divorce. Another individual spent his entire life as an impostor, passing himself off at various times as a minister, teacher, zoologist, prison warden, psychologist, college dean, Trappist monk, and surgeon (Van Atta, 1982).

How can individuals get away with such outrageous acts? One reason may lie in their superficial charm, poise, and good intelligence. Then too, they tend to be insincere, callous, and manipulative such that they can lie with a straight face. Lacking a sense of responsibility, they can engage in impulsive and reckless behavior, giving the appearance of being "free." Yet, they can also be dangerous, and can kill with little or no guilt. They are incapable of establishing close, lasting relationships with others. Nor are they able to learn from their experience.

Individuals with this disorder tend to come from a home characterized by the absence of love, harsh punishment, with one or more parents exhibiting this disorder (DSM-III, 1980). Particular patterns of brain wave activity have also been found in these people, suggesting they have a lower arousal level than most people (Mednick, et al, 1982). Also, some observers contend that Western society may encourage antisocial tendencies by glamorizing fame and success, such that antisocial individuals' superficial charm and lack of concern for others may help them to get ahead (Smith, 1978).

rituals, which include cleaning floors, keeping the bathroom immaculate at all times, and changing clothes several times a day to insure they are spotless. Whatever their routine, individuals afflicted with this disorder become very anxious if they are unable to engage in it. Accordingly, this disorder can be disabling, usurping much of the person's time and energy. For example, one woman compulsively washed her hands over 500 times each day in spite of the painful sores incurred by such behavior. She had a strong fear of being contaminated by germs, and felt she could temporarily alleviate her fear only by washing her hands (Davison and Neale, 1982).

DEPRESSION AND SUICIDE

Most of us go through periods of time when nothing seems to go right. The car breaks down, we're overdrawn at the bank, and problems arise in our close relationships. We may say we're "depressed." But we're usually not suffering from a psychological disorder. Our mood is one of mild dejection that generally passes within a matter of days. In contrast, when the disturbance of one's mood is more severe and persistent, it may be classified as a clinical depression, one of the affective disorders. Without counting the normal times when people feel down, depression is one of the most common disorders in our society. It is sometimes referred to as "the common cold of mental illness." But whereas the common cold never killed anyone, clinical depression often does. As many as half of the suicides in the United States are committed by people suffering from depression (Greenberg, 1982).

The Range of Depression

Depression may assume a variety of forms, some of which are more severe and chronic than others. In many instances, people experience the symptoms of depression only to a mild or moderate degree, such that they may continue their everyday activities. They may suffer from any number of the common symptoms of depression, including decreased energy, loss of interest in everyday activities such as eating, feelings of inadequacy, periods of crying, and a pessimistic attitude. It is estimated that three-quarters of all college students suffer some symptoms of depression during college; one-quarter of them at any one time. In almost half of these students, the depression is serious enough to require professional help. Depression may be triggered by the stress of student life, academic pressures, and the felt need to make a career decision. Yet, depression is often brought on by "cognitive distortions," such as exaggerating the importance of getting good grades or the loss of a love relationship. When students confront their actual problems instead of dwelling on their distorted self-perceptions, they tend to have more success in breaking out of their depression (Beck and Young, 1978).

People who suffer from major depression experience many of the same symptoms mentioned earlier, except in a more severe and chronic way. In some cases, a major depression includes psychotic features such as delusions and hallucinations. This condition almost always interferes with one's everyday functioning. In many instances, periods of hospitalization may be necessary. Contrary to popular belief, a major depression may occur at any age. The age of onset is fairly evenly distributed throughout adult life. It is estimated that 8 to 11 percent of men and 18 to 23 percent of women will experience a major depression at some point in their lives. More than half of those who experience one episode of major depression will eventually have another one (DSM-III, 1980).

Why is depression more common in women than in men? One explanation is that women are closer to their emotions and can admit illnesses more readily than men can. Also, women are twice as likely to seek help for depression, which further distorts the figures. However, it is now thought that the prevalence of

Depressed people suffer from feelings of inadequacy and a pessimistic outlook. (Laimute E. Druskis)

depressions among men may be closer to that of women, except that depression among men is often masked by alcoholism and drug addiction. Support for this view comes from a study among the Amish people of Pennsylvania. The results showed that while depression was the most common form of mental disturbance, there was no difference in the prevalence among men and women, largely because the Amish have no alcoholism (Egeland and Hostetter, 1983).

Bipolar Disorder

In some instances, people may experience an alternation of elated and depressive moods. Popularly known as manic-depression, this condition is now termed *bipolar disorder*. Usually, this disorder first appears in the form of a manic episode, in which the individual exhibits such symptoms as an expansive mood, increased social activity, talkativeness, sleeplessness, and reckless behavior. For example, one man took a leave of absence from his job, purchased an expensive car and a large number of cuckoo clocks. He rarely slept, and he spent every evening in bars drinking heavily while "wheeling and dealing." By the time he was admitted to the hospital, he was several thousand dollars in debt

---

Famous Manic-depressives

King Saul of Israel—*I Samuel* records his plight. Uncontrollable outbursts of irritability and suspiciousness alternated with a depressed state. While manic he tried to kill David and later his own son, Jonathan. On another occasion he stripped off all his clothes and lay down naked all that day and night. When in a depressed state he committed suicide.

Ernest Hemingway—The novelist experienced manic phases of activity—fishing, hunting, writing, fighting, loving—that alternated with depressions. When manic he believed he was immortal, which may partially explain his frequent accidents and automobile collisions. Committed suicide in 1961.

George III of England—The "mad monarch" asked rapid fire questions while waiting for answers, bolted his food, rode his horse to death, and had episodes of sleep depriving energy.

Theodore Roosevelt—Irrepressible, all action and energy, he could work for days with little sleep; he was constantly occupied with talking, telephoning, and writing. During his governorship and presidency, he wrote 150,000 letters and wrote an estimated 18 million words in his lifetime.

Winston Churchill—Brilliant, impulsive, and domineering, Britain's Prime Minister had high periods when he talked nonstop and said whatever came to mind, alternating with bouts of deep depression that he called his "Black Dog."

Robert Schumann—The peak years of his musical output occurred during his manic phase; while depressed he created nothing. He tried to drown himself in the Rhine, and spent the last 2 years of his life in a mental hospital.

From: J. Ingram Walker, M.D., *Everybody's Guide to Emotional Well-being* (San Francisco: Harbor Publishing, 1982). © 1982 by J. Ingram Walker, p. 41.

and had driven his family to exhaustion with his excessive activity and overtalkativeness (Spitzer, et al., 1983).

The subsequent episodes may occur in any one of different patterns. The initial manic episode may be followed by periods of normal activity, followed by a depressed episode, and then another normal period. Or one mood may be followed immediately by its opposite, with normal intervals occurring between the manic-depressive pairs. In rare forms, the mood may alternate between manic and depressive episodes, with no intervals of normal functioning. In another rare form, the mixed type, the individual may experience syptoms of both moods simultaneously, such as being expansive and yet weeping and threatening suicide.

In addition to the manic episodes, there are other characteristics that distinguish bipolar disorder from major depression (Hirschfeld and Cross, 1982). First, bipolar disorder is much less common than major depression, affecting between 0.4 and 1.2 percent of the population. Second, bipolar disorder is equally prevalent among men and women. Third, unlike major depression which occurs more frequently among the lower socioeconomic classes, bipolar disorder is more prevalent among the upper classes. Fourth, while married people are less susceptible to major depression, they enjoy no such advantage in regard to bipolar disorder. Fifth, although major depression can occur at any time in life, bipolar disorder usually appears before the age of 30. Sixth, bipolar episodes tend to be briefer and more frequent than in major depression. Finally, bipolar disorder is more likely to run in families than major depression.

Suicide

It's difficult to know exactly how many people take their own lives. One reason is that many people who commit suicide prefer to make their deaths look accidental, thereby enabling their survivors to collect insurance or be spared the stigma associated with suicide. Then too, should they fail, suicide is still listed as a felony in several states. Also, if the truth were known, a significant number of single-car accidents are actually suicides. Despite incomplete statistics, a conservative estimate is that more than 26,000 Americans commit suicide each year (U.S. Bureau of the Census, 1984). Furthermore, as many as two to eight times this many people attempt suicide each year (Shneidman, 1980).

The rate of suicide for youth in the 15- to 24-year-old group has increased sharply in the last 30 years. Suicide now ranks as the second highest cause of death among males and the third highest cause of death among females in this age group. However, suicide rates generally increase with age before decreasing for everyone except white men. (See Figure 13–1.) Men are five times more likely than women to commit suicide. One reason is that men tend to use more swift and violent means, such as a gun. By contrast, women are more likely to take pills, which often permits intervention. As a result, many of these unsuccessful suicide attempts are regarded as a cry for help (U.S. Bureau of the Census, 1984).

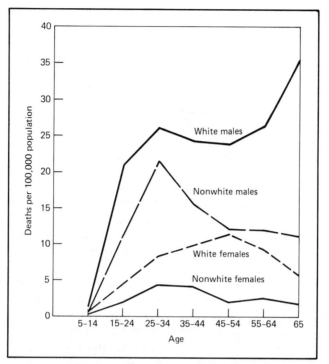

Figure 13–1. SUICIDE MORTALITY RATES BY AGE, SEX, AND RACE.

Adapted from U.S. Bureau of the Census, *Statistical Abstract of the United States*, 1985
(Washington, D.C.: U.S. Government Printing Office, 1984), p. 79.

Why do people commit suicide? Surprisingly, suicide is more prevalent in affluent
societies, so much so that it has been described as a disease of civilization. At the
level of individual behavior, many possible motives have been suggested. These
include: escaping from pain or stress, attempts to rid one's self from unacceptable feelings, turning aggression inward, punishing others by making them feel
guilty, and acting impulsively on one's momentary feelings of desperation. For
some, suicide may be seen as the best means for withdrawing from seemingly
unsolvable problems in living. The tragedy is that such problems are often tran-
sitory, whereas the solution of suicide is permanent.

Suicide is also related to psychological disorder, especially depression. A
study of people hospitalized after attempting suicide found that four out of five
of them were suffering from depression. Curiously, severely depressed people
are more likely to take their lives as things are looking up for them. When they
are most depressed, they may not have sufficient energy to take their own lives.
Usually, it's when they start to feel better and get their energy back that they
commit suicide. At the same time, autopsies of suicide victims have found
abnormally low levels of serotonin—a neurotransmitter which has been linked

to depression—suggesting that biochemical deficiencies may play a role in suicide (Greenberg, 1982).

People who commit suicide often feel overwhelmed by a combination of problems. In one study of teen-age suicide, 505 suicide attempters seen in the emergency room of a large hospital were compared with the same number of individuals matched for age and sex who had been treated in the emergency room but not for suicide. Among the attempters, girls outnumbered boys three to one. Compared to the controls, the attempters had more psychological problems, greater history of alcohol and drug abuse, and more prior psychological treatment. Furthermore, their families had more psychological problems, more history of suicide, and more parental absence through death or divorce (Garfinkel, et al, 1982).

The prevention of suicide has received greater attention in recent years. One approach is to make it more difficult to commit suicide by having tighter control over the prescription of sedatives, more gun control legislation, and protective measures (such as putting a wire fence around the observation platform of the Empire State Building in New York City). Another approach is to increase the community awareness and resources for dealing with suicide. Many communities now have suicide hotlines available 24 hours a day. Volunteers usually have specific goals, such as determining the seriousness of the suicide threat, establishing contact, conveying empathy and understanding of the caller's problems, informing the person of the available resources, and getting some sort of agreement that the caller will seek help.

Warning Signs

Here are some warning signals of suicide:

- Expression of suicidal thoughts or a preoccupation with death

- Prior suicidal attempt

- Giving away prized possessions

- Depression over a broken love relationship

- Despair over a chronic illness or one's situation at school or work

- Change in eating habits

- Change in sleeping habits

- Marked personality changes

- Abuse of alcohol or drugs

- Sense of hopelessness

Contrary to the myth that people who threaten to kill themselves seldom carry through with it, most people who commit suicide express some suicidal intent, directly or indirectly, within several months of their deaths. It helps to recognize these warning signs as noted in the accompanying boxed item. Perhaps you've heard that questioning depressed people about their suicidal ideas will give such thoughts greater force. But this isn't true. Providing these people with an opportunity to talk about their suicidal thoughts often helps them to overcome such wishes and know where to turn for help. If you notice the warning signals of suicide in a family member or friend, do your best to see that the person gets professional help.

SCHIZOPHRENIA

Most of us can understand what it's like to be panic-stricken or depressed. But the bizarre behavior of the schizophrenic individual is strange to us. For instance, you may recall the young woman mentioned at the beginning of the chapter, who hears imaginary voices and believes everyone is talking about her. She seems to be living in a different mental world than the rest of us. Such individuals are difficult to understand and are even harder to treat. Yet, at least one out of every 100 people will suffer from a schizophrenic episode sometime during his or her life. Schizophrenia is so disabling that as many as 40 percent of the mental hospital beds in the United States are occupied by people with this disorder (U.S. Department of Health and Human Services, 1981).

Because schizophrenia is a label given to a group of related disorders, it's impossible to describe the "typical" patient. The essential features of these disorders include the presence of psychotic behavior such as hearing voices during the active phase of the disorder, characteristic symptoms involving multiple psychological processes such as blunted emotions, a marked deterioration from the previous level of functioning, onset before 45 years of age, and a duration of at least 6 months (DSM-III, 1980).

Symptoms

1. *Disorders of thought.* One of the most striking features about individuals suffering from schizophrenia is their peculiar use of language—both in the form and content of thought and speech. There is a loosening of associations of thought and rambling, disjointed speech. Words that have no association beyond the fact that they sound alike, such as clang and fang, may be juxtaposed with each other. The major disturbance of the content of thought involves delusions—beliefs that have no basis in reality. For example, an individual may feel he is being spied upon or plotted against by his family.

2. *Distorted perception.* Individuals suffering from schizophrenia seem to perceive the world differently from other people. They have difficulty focusing on certain aspects of their environment while screening out other data. Instead, their inner world is flooded with an undifferentiated mass of sensory data, resulting in odd associations, inner confusion, and bizarre speech. In addition, many of them experience hallucinations—sensory perceptions that occur in the absence of any appropriate external stimulus. The most common hallucination is hearing voices, which characteristically order the person to commit some forbidden act or accuse him or her of having done some terrible misdeed.

3. *Blunted or inappropriate emotions.* Schizophrenia is characterized by a blunted affect, or in more severe cases, a lack of emotions. Schizophrenic individuals may stare at you with a blank expression or speak in a flat, monotone voice. Or they may display inappropriate emotions, such as giggling when telling you about some painful experience.

4. *Social withdrawal.* People who eventually have a schizophrenic episode tend to be loners, often preferring animals, nature, or inanimate objects to

---

Subtypes of Schizophrenia

On the basis of their symptoms, individuals are usually diagnosed as having one of the several subtypes of schizophrenia as follows:

Paranoid schizophrenia. Individuals experience delusions and hallucinations related to the themes of persecution or grandeur. They may claim immense powers or adopt a delusional identity with some famous figure like Napoleon or Christ. The onset of paranoid schizophrenia tends to occur later in life than the other subtypes, and it is the diagnosis most commonly given on first admission (Sarason and Sarason, 1984).

Catatonic schizophrenia. The distinguishing feature of this subtype is a marked disturbance in psychomotor behavior. Patients may become mute and remain in a bizarre posture for long periods of time. Or, they may alternate between such immobility and periods of frenzied activity, including violent behavior. Either way, these individuals usually require hospitalization. Once common several decades ago, this subtype is now rare in Europe and the United States (DSM-III, 1980).

Disorganized schizophrenia. Traditionally known as "hebephrenic" because of the characteristic childish behavior, individuals with this diagnosis display a marked incoherence of speech and disturbed affect. They tend to make funny faces, giggle constantly, and generally act silly, along with their delusions and hallucinations. The onset of disorganized schizophrenia is usually early and insidious, with a poor prognosis.

Undifferentiated type. This is a miscellaneous category that is used for individuals whose symptoms do not fit into any of the above types or overlap with the symptoms of the other types. Since many patients have aspects of more than one subtype of schizophrenia, this is a diagnosis commonly given (Bootzin and Acocella, 1984).

human company. Perhaps they are preoccupied with their inner world. Or, having learned that they are often misunderstood, they may prefer to keep to themselves. But there is also a marked avoidance of people. They avoid eye contact, and tend to stand or sit at a greater distance from people than others do. They are also emotionally distant, making it difficult to establish satisfying close relationships with them.

Causes

Despite extensive research and treatment, the causes of schizophrenia are not fully understood. For a long while, the prevailing view was that this disorder was brought on by environmental stress, especially deviant family patterns. Some authorities emphasized the role of overprotective but rejecting mothers and weak, ineffectual fathers. Others pointed to faulty family communications. In one study, deviant communication by parents proved to be an accurate predictor of whether their adolescents would be diagnosed as schizophrenic 5 years later (Doane, et al., 1981).

Famous Schizophrenics

Virginia Woolf—Novelist who had intermittent psychotic episodes throughout her life. During periods of illness she would talk with imaginary birds in Greek. She believed that the leaves of trees were controlling her thoughts and feelings. She heard sounds in the universe that signalled the birth of a new religion. When not floridly psychotic she was reclusive and depressed. Some authorities think she had manic-depressive illness; others opt for schizophrenia.

Vaslav Nijinsky—Russian ballet dancer who was a patient of Eugene Bleuler, the psychiatrist who coined the term schizophrenia. Nijinsky wrote in his *Diary:* "I am God. . . I love God, and therefore I smile upon myself."

Friedrich Nietzsche—The great nineteenth-century German philosopher said that in crying out against the madness of God, he had gone mad himself.

Zelda Fitzgerald—Wife of the writer, F. Scott Fitzgerald, Zelda was ill most of her adult life despite receiving the best psychiatric care available. She died in a 1948 Highland Hospital fire.

Vincent Van Gogh—Hot tempered painter who was not recognized as a great artist until long after his death. Sensitive and withdrawn, he believed that people were trying to poison him; on one occasion he attacked his friend Gauguin with a razor; later he cut off his own ear and presented it to a prostitute; he died of a self-inflicted gunshot wound.

From: J. Ingram Walker, M.D., *Everybody's Guide to Emotional Well-being* (San Francisco: Harbor Publishing, 1982). © 1982 by J. Ingram Walker, p. 63.

In recent years, there has been increasing evidence that schizophrenia may be due to genetic, neurological, and biochemical factors. Family studies have shown that the more closely one is related to a schizophrenic individual, the greater the likelihood of developing this disorder (Gottesman, 1978). Furthermore, brain studies have found that chronic schizophrenics have enlarged brain ventricles, which are associated with cognitive impairment, poor response to drug treatment, poor premorbid adjustment, and more negative than positive symptoms (Andreasen, et al., 1982). There are biochemical abnormalities as well, with schizophrenic individuals having an excessive activity of those parts of the brain that use dopamine as the neurotransmitter. The major evidence comes from research on the antipsychotic drugs that work by blocking the brain's receptor sites for dopamine (Meltzer, 1979).

A third approach is that schizophrenia is caused by an interaction of the individual's inherited predisposition to the illness and environmental stress. Yet it is not clear which stresses are most likely to precipitate this disorder. Many of the crises of schizophrenic individuals are not especially stressful for other people. It appears that the problems that most people would greet with annoyance arouse more anxiety in schizophrenic individuals, especially chronic schizophrenics (Bootzin and Acocella, 1984).

Course

For the diagnosis of schizophrenia to be made, there must be continuous signs of the illness for at least 6 months. This includes an active phase of psychotic symptoms, and often, though not always, a prodromal (forerunner) and residual phase as well.

The Prodromal Phase. The onset of schizophrenia usually occurs in adolescence or early adulthood. It may occur abruptly, with marked changes in the person's behavior appearing in a matter of days or weeks. Or there may be a gradual, insidious deterioration in functioning over many years.

During this phase, individuals tend to be socially isolated. They may show blunted or shallow emotions and have difficulty communicating with others. They may neglect personal hygiene, school work, or their jobs. By this time, such individuals may have begun to exhibit the bizarre behavior and psychotic symptoms signaling the onset of the active phase.

The Active Phase. The onset of the active phase is often precipitated by intense psychological stress, such as the loss of a job, rejection in love, or the death of a parent. During this period the psychotic symptoms become prominent. Schizophrenic individuals begin to hallucinate, hold delusions, and exhibit the incoherent and illogical thought and bizarre behavior characteristic of this disorder. However, no one patient manifests all these symptoms; each individual exhibits a somewhat different pattern.

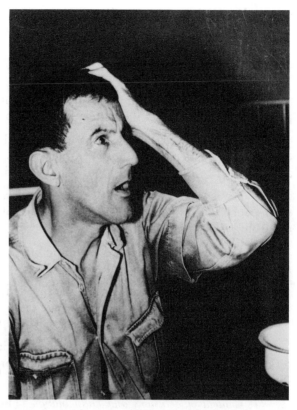

People suffering from schizophrenia usually require intensive treatment. (WHO Photo)

The Residual Phase. Individuals may recover in a matter of weeks or months. Some of the psychotic symptoms, such as hallucinations or delusions, may persist, though no longer accompanied by intense emotion. Such individuals may continue to exhibit eccentric behavior and odd thoughts, such as thinking they are able to control events through magical thinking. As a result, most of them are not ready to fully resume everyday responsibilities, whether holding a job or running a household.

Outlook

There is considerable difference of opinion about the outlook for individuals who have suffered a schizophrenic episode. Furthermore, comparative outcomes of schizophrenic individuals based on long-term studies vary considerably, partly because of the criteria used in the selection of patients, what constitutes recovery, and the social era in which individuals are treated. Nevertheless, an extensive followup study of 1000 people who suffered a schizophrenic episode by Manfred Bleuler (1978) showed that 25 percent of them resumed normal functioning, 50 to 65 percent of them alternated between the residual phase and a reoccurence of the active phase, and 10 percent of them remained schizophrenic the rest of their lives.

How well an individual recovers from a schizophrenic episode depends on many things, especially the following factors:

1. *Premorbid adjustment.* The more adequately the individual functions prior to the active phase, the better the outcome (DSM-III, 1980).

2. *Affective behavior.* Conscious anxiety and the presence of other emotions, including depression, are favorable signs. A state of hopelessness not accompanied by depression is a poor sign (Arieti, 1981).

3. *Precipitating event.* If the episode occurred after specific precipitating events, such as a broken engagement or the loss of a job, the possibility of recovery is favorable (DSM-III, 1980).

4. *Sudden onset.* The more acute the onset, the more favorable the prognosis (DSM-III, 1980).

5. *Age of onset.* The later in life the first schizophrenic episode occurs, the better. Men are more at risk before the age of 25; women are more at risk after 25 (Lewine, 1981).

6. *Type of schizophrenia.* Paranoid and catatonic schizophrenics have a better chance of recovery; undifferentiated schizophrenics have the poorest chance (Sarason and Sarason, 1984).

7. *Content of delusions and hallucination.* The more the delusions involve feelings of guilt and responsibility, the better the prognosis. Conversely, the more delusions and hallucinations blame others and exonerate the individual, the more severe the psychosis (Arieti, 1981).

8. *Response to the illness and treatment.* The more insight patients have as to what made them ill and the more cooperative they are with their therapists and staff, the better their chances for recovery. The more resigned they are to being sick, the poorer the outlook (Arieti, 1981).

9. *Supportive family.* When families of schizophrenics are taught why the patient acts strangely and how to talk out and solve their problems, the patient's chances for a good recovery improve dramatically (Falloon, et al., 1982).

The larger the number of these positive indicators that apply to a given individual, the better the person's chances for a good recovery. Yet, as Joseph Zubin (1983) suggests, even though schizophrenia is not necessarily a permanent disorder, individuals with a predisposition for this disorder will remain vulnerable to it. That is, when stressful life events combine with the person's vulnerability to this disorder, schizophrenic behavior may reoccur. However, if such individuals have access to a structured and supportive environment and develop better coping skills so that the unavoidable life stresses will not affect them so adversely, they may well live normal and fruitful lives.

Summary

Understanding Psychological Disorders

1. We began the chapter by noting that abnormal behavior and psychological disorders tend to be defined by a combination of standards, such as personal discomfort, maladaptive behavior, and the violation of social norms.

2. During any 6-month period, one in five adults will suffer from some type of psychological disorder, ranging from the mildly disabling anxiety disorders to severe ones like schizophrenia.

3. In DSM-III, an authoritative guide for the various psychological disorders, the emphasis is on describing the characteristic behavior patterns rather than interpreting the possible causes of the psychological disorders.

Anxiety Disorders

4. The main characteristic of the generalized anxiety disorder is a persistent sense of diffuse anxiety, with some chronically anxious people also suffering from acute panic attacks.

5. Phobic disorders are characterized by a chronic, irrational fear of a specific object or activity, together with a compelling desire to avoid the same.

6. The essential features of the obsessive-compulsive disorder are recurrent obsessions or compulsions, or usually both.

Depression and Suicide

7. The affective disorders cover different types of mood disturbances, including states of extreme elation and depression.

8. Depression may range from a state of mild despondency to a major depressive disorder, which is so disabling it requires hospitalization.

9. Bipolar disorder, another affective disorder, known to some as manic-depression, involves an alteration between moods of extreme elation and depression.

10. Almost half the suicides in the United States involve people suffering from depression, with the incidence of suicide among white males rising with age.

Schizophrenia

11. The most severely disabling psychological disorder is schizophrenia, which will affect about 1 percent of Americans sometime during their lives.

12. The symptoms of schizophrenia include disordered thinking, perceptual distortions such as hearing imaginary voices, blunted or inappropriate emotions, and social withdrawal.

13. Although the causes of schizophrenia are not fully understood, it is thought that the disorder results from an interaction of genetic predisposition and environmental stress.

14. The typical course of schizophrenia includes an active phase of psychotic symptoms, and often, though not always, a prodromal and residual phase.

15. There is considerable difference of opinion about the outlook for individuals who have suffered a schizophrenic episode. But certain factors, such as a sudden onset at midlife, indicate a more favorable recovery.

Self-test

1. A psychological disorder is usually defined by a combination of standards such as:

a. maladaptive behavior
b. the violation of social norms
c. personal discomfort
d. all of the above

2. The most widespread psychological disorders in the United States are the:

a. schizophrenic disorders
b. anxiety disorders
c. affective disorders
d. phobic disorders

3. People with phobias are most likely to seek treatment when they have:

a. a simple phobia
b. agoraphobia
c. a social phobia
d. claustrophobia

4. In what type of disorder is an individual bothered by a chronic state of free-floating anxiety?

a. phobic
b. obsessive-compulsive
c. generalized anxiety
d. depressive

5. The onset of a major depression:

a. is evenly distributed throughout adult life
b. usually occurs during adolescence
c. rarely requires hospitalization
d. is most likely to happen in middle age

6. Almost half of the suicides in the United States are committed by people suffering from:

a. phobias
b. anxiety disorders
c. depression
d. panic attacks

7. In what age group does the highest incidence of suicide occur?

a. 15 to 24
b. 25 to 34
c. 35 to 44
d. over 65

8. Persons who hear imaginary voices, feel everyone is talking about them, and are socially isolated are probably suffering from:

a. a bipolar disorder
b. schizophrenia
c. a phobic disorder
d. depression

9. The characteristic symptoms of schizophrenia become prominent during the:

    a. active phase   **c.** prodromal phase
    b. residual phase   **d.** precurser phase

10. Which one of the following factors generally indicates a favorable recovery for someone who has experienced a schizophrenic episode?

    a. early age of onset   **c.** sudden onset
    b. absence of a precipitating event **d.** lack of conscious anxiety

Exercises

1. *Have you ever experienced a panic attack?* Even if you've only experienced intense anxiety, write a page or so describing what it was like. Be sure to include what occasioned the anxiety and how it affected you. Also, how well do you cope with similar situations today?

2. *Are you bothered by an intense fear or phobia?* If you were to list your worst fears, which ones would you include? Do you share some of the more common fears, such as the fear of dogs, snakes, or closed places? Or are you bothered by other fears? What are you doing to overcome your fears?

3. *Managing the "blues."* Most of us have times when we feel down. The important thing is knowing how to handle ourselves so that we can snap out of such low moments. Write a page or so describing how you cope with feelings of discouragement and depression. How effective is your approach?

4. *Have you known someone who committed suicide?* To what extent did this person exhibit the characteristics discussed in the chapter? Also, in retrospect, did the person display any of the warning signs of suicide? At this point, do you think you're better able to recognize individuals with a high risk for suicide?

5. *Psychological disorders in the family.* Do you have relatives who have suffered from a psychological disorder? If so, which ones? Are any of these disorders those which tend to run in families, for example, alcoholism, schizophrenia, and major depression? What steps, if any, are you taking to avoid such problems?

6. *Distinguishing schizophrenia and multiple personality disorder.* People tend to confuse these two disorders. Do you know the difference between them? To test yourself, you might write a paragraph or so explaining how these two disorders are different from each other. Ask your instructor to check your answer to make certain you really understand the differences.

Questions for Self-reflection

1. What are the advantages and disadvantages of tolerating greater deviance in today's society?

2. When you become very anxious about something, how does this affect your behavior?

3. How do you cope with occasional feelings of despondency?

4. Why do you think women are more apt to seek help for their depression than men?

5. Would you agree that depression among males is often masked by drinking or drug problems?

6. Why do you think the suicide rate is rising among youth?

7. How would you account for the high suicide rate among white men and low suicide rate among black women?

8. What are some of the *chronic* self-destructive behaviors people engage in?

9. Do you know the difference between schizophrenia and multiple personality?

10. Are you aware that some individuals who have experienced acute schizophrenic episodes resume normal lives?

Recommended Readings

Arieti, Silvano. *Understanding and Helping the Schizophrenic.* New York: Touchstone Books, 1981 (paperback). Guidelines for understanding and helping schizophrenic individuals by a noted authority in the field.

Hazleton, Lesley. *The Right To Feel Bad.* New York: Ballantine Books, 1984 (paperback). Practical suggestions for coping with depression.

Keyes, Daniel. *The Minds of Billy Milligan.* New York: Random House, 1981. A true story of Billy Milligan, the first case of a multiple personality being acquitted of a major crime under this plea.

Mack, J. E., and H. Hickler. *Vivienne: The Life and Suicide of an Adolescent Girl.* Boston: Little, Brown, 1981. The true story of a sensitive and lonely girl and her suicide.

Melville, J. *Phobias and Obsessions.* New York: Penguin Books, 1977. An explanation of the meaning and function of the various phobias and obsessions in human behavior.

Vonnegut, Mark. *The Eden Express.* New York: Praeger, 1975. A personal account of the author's experience with schizophrenia and his eventual recovery.

Walker, J. Ingram, M.D. *Everybody's Guide To Emotional Well-being.* San Francisco: Harbor Publishing Co., 1982 (paperback). A lucid and interesting explanation of common emotional problems and how to cope with them. (Available from Dr. Ingram at 705 Landa Street, New Braunfels, Texas 78130.)

# 14 Therapy

Few of us escape having problems at home or at work at one time or another. Most of the time we manage such difficulties on our own. We may feel better after a heart-to-heart talk with a friend. Then too, some problem situations tend to work themselves out with time. But when our difficulties persist, especially to the point of interfering with our everyday lives, it's time to get professional help. You may recall from the last chapter that only one-fifth of the adults with a serious psychological problem or disorder seek help from a mental health professional such as a psychiatrist or psychologist. What about the other four-fifths of the people who need help? Most of them will be seen by family physicians, the clergy, and other types of counselors. Yet, 22 percent of the people who need help, or about 8 million people, will receive no treatment at all. Think about it—8 million people with serious problems, including schizophrenia, rely on their neighbors, bartenders, beauticians or whoever to get by (Walker, 1982).

GETTING HELP

Why do so few people in need seek help? In some instances, people don't know how to go about getting help. Or they may feel that therapy is too costly. Some individuals are so disturbed they don't even realize they need help. But in many instances, social attitudes are the crucial factor. Some individuals, especially those with little education, are reluctant to seek help because of the stigma associated with it. In the popular mind, therapy is for people who are "crazy." Then too, in a society that puts a high value on self-sufficiency, people may feel that getting help is an admission of weakness. This is probably a major reason why men are less likely than women to seek professional help for psychological problems. It's more acceptable for women to express their emotions and admit weakness. Men are expected to cope on their own, and, as a result, often hide their problems with alcohol. Fortunately, Americans of both sexes are more willing to admit their need for personal help and to seek it than in the past. In part, this reflects a greater desire for personal well-being, as well as an increased orientation toward psychology to explain experience (Veroff, Douvan, & Kulka, 1981).

One of the hardest parts of therapy is selecting a *therapist*—a person trained to help people with psychological problems or disorders. Generally, it's not a good idea to rely solely on the yellow pages of the phone book. It's better to talk with someone who is well informed in this matter. This could be a trusted professional in a related field, such as the family physician, a respected teacher, or one's clergy. You might also talk with someone who has gone through therapy. Then too, most towns have a publicly-funded community mental health center that offers a wide range of psychological services, including referral to the appropriate therapists in the community.

In selecting a therapist, psychiatrist J. Ingram Walker (1982) suggests that we consider two key questions: (1) Is the therapist professionally trained and certified? and (2) Do I feel comfortable with this person? Ordinarily, people must be properly qualified in order to list themselves as a psychiatrist or psychologist in the telephone book. Also, when professionals are licensed by the state, they are supposed to display their certificates in a prominent place in the office. But we also want to know whether we'll feel comfortable talking to the therapist. Is he or she warm and empathetic without being smothering? Once you've selected a therapist, in the initial session it's appropriate to ask this person about his or her approach to therapy. It's also wise to discuss such matters as the length of therapy, the fees, whether such treatment is covered by your health insurance. If you do not feel comfortable with the therapist after a session or two, you might want to change therapists. But you should also be aware that in therapy, as in all close relationships, there will be rocky as well as gratifying times. Therapy can become so uncomfortable that you may feel like quitting. However, if you put yourself into it and keep going, you'll usually find it's a rewarding experience in the long run.

Who Are the Therapists?

Unlike law or medicine where there is a single path to professional practice, there are many routes to becoming a psychotherapist. Since few states regulate the practice of psychotherapy as such, the question of who may legitimately conduct psychotherapy is governed by state law or professional boards within the respective professions.

Psychiatrists are medical doctors who specialize in the treatment of mental illness. They usually spend 3 to 4 years training in a clinical setting following their medical degree and can treat the psychological disorders requiring drugs and hospitalization.

Psychoanalysts are generally psychiatrists who have received several years of additional training in personality theory and the therapeutic methods of one of the founding analysts, such as Freud, Jung, Adler, or Sullivan.

Psychologists are individuals who receive clinical training in the methods of psychological assessment and treatment as part of a program in clinical, counseling, or school psychology. They may have a Ph.D., Ed.D., or Psy.D. degree.

Psychiatric social workers receive supervised clinical training as part of their master's degree program in the field of social work, and some earn a doctorate as well. They tend to be community-oriented and usually work as part of a clinical team, though sometimes in private practice.

Counselors are people who receive training in personality theory and counseling skills, usually at the master's degree level. Their counseling emphasis tends to reflect their respective professional affiliations, depending on whether they are doing marriage counseling, career counseling, pastoral counseling (clergy), or some other type of counseling.

Paraprofessionals (*para* meaning "akin to") are people with 4- or 2-year degrees (or sometimes no degrees at all) who work in the mental health field. Sometimes as many as half the staff members of a community mental health center work at the paraprofessional level, assisting in the helping process in a variety of ways.

INSIGHT THERAPIES

Another difficulty in choosing a therapist is sorting through the various approaches to therapy. There are now more than 250 different schools of therapy, including the various insight therapies as well as many types of behavioral and group therapies. Despite their differences, most therapies share certain common goals. All of them afford clients relief from their symptoms, such as intolerable anxiety or depression. Many of them afford the client better understanding of his or her thoughts, feelings, motives, and relationships. They also help clients to modify their problem behaviors, such as excessive fear. In addition, many therapies help clients to improve their relationships with others at home and work. Different schools of therapy emphasize some of these goals more than others; some may put more emphasis on adjustment, while others may emphasize growth.

We'll begin with the *insight* therapies—those which bring change through increasing the person's self-understanding.

Psychoanalysis

According to Sigmund Freud (1965), the founder of psychoanalysis, psychological disturbances are due to anxiety that we feel about hidden conflicts between the different parts of our unconscious personality. If not expressed directly, these unconscious impulses and conflicts seek indirect release in all kinds of symptoms. The therapist's purpose is to help the individual gain insight or conscious awareness of these unconscious desires or conflicts, thereby gaining emotional release and eventual mastery of them.

The psychoanalyst may use a variety of techniques to accomplish this end. One of the earliest of these was *free association*. The client is asked to lie down on a couch, relax, and talk about anything that comes to awareness. Sometimes the client is encouraged to talk about his or her dreams. Though these recollections might appear irrelevant, the well-trained analyst may see relationships and meanings that eventually shed light on the client's problems.

When an individual hesitates or is reluctant to talk about some painful experience, this is seen as a sign of the client's resistance. The therapist may simply wait or may use another approach to the area of resistance, so that eventually this can be overcome. By analyzing an individual's resistances, the therapist helps the client to see how he or she handles anxiety-provoking material. The overall process of free association, dream association, and the interpretation and overcoming of the resistance is called "working through."

Freud also discovered that his clients would often treat him the same way they had treated the significant figures earlier in their life, especially their parents. This is called *transference*. At the appropriate time, the therapist interprets these feelings and actions to the client, thereby helping the client to achieve additional self-insight.

Traditionally, psychoanalysis involved hour-long sessions three to five times a week, often lasting several years. But at the level of current fees, this would make psychoanalysis prohibitively expensive for all but the privileged few who could afford the necessary $15,000 to $20,000 a year. As a result, there have been many changes in this approach. Now psychoanalytic therapy may involve only one or two sessions a week, and often lasts only twenty or thirty sessions. The therapist sits facing the client and takes a more active role in therapy than the impenetrable "mirror" role advocated by Freud. Psychoanalytic therapists are also likely to be more eclectic than in the past, using techniques from other approaches when appropriate. At the same time, the emphasis of this approach remains on the individual's gaining insight and self-mastery of the unconscious forces affecting one's behavior.

The Person-centered Approach

One of the major alternatives to psychoanalysis is Carl Rogers' humanistic approach to therapy. In recent years, Rogers (1980) has changed the name of his approach from client-centered therapy to the person-centered approach, as a way of indicating that the same principles apply to a variety of fields of human interaction as well as psychotherapy.

Rogers developed his view of therapy out of his own experience as a therapist. Early in his career he was counseling a mother about her son, who was having problems. No matter what strategy he tried, he got nowhere. Finally, he admitted his failure. As the mother walked toward the door, she turned and asked Rogers if he ever saw adult clients. When he replied, "Yes," the woman returned to her seat and began pouring out her own problems. She spoke of her own sense of confusion and failure and her despair about her marriage, all of which was more pertinent to her son's problems than the sterile case history approach they had followed before. After many more interviews, the woman felt better about her marriage, and her son's problem behavior dropped away as well. Rogers felt the improvement had come because he had followed her lead, because he had listened and understood rather than imposed his diagnostic understanding on her. This was the first of many experiences that gradually led Rogers to the view that therapeutic progress comes mostly from respecting and responding to the client's own frame of reference.

Therapists using this approach believe that all of us have within ourselves vast resources for self-understanding and altering our behavior, and that these resources can be tapped if the proper climate for change can be provided. According to Rogers (1980), three conditions must be present in order for a therapeutic climate to be growth-producing. All of them pertain to the client-therapist relationship. First, the therapist must be genuine, or "congruent" in the relationship, rather than maintaining a detached professional facade. That is, there is a congruence, or close matching, between what the therapist experiences at the gut level and what is expressed to the client. The second essential is an attitude of acceptance and caring. When the therapist is experiencing acceptance and caring toward the client at the moment, therapeutic change is more likely to occur in the client. But such caring is nonpossessive. The therapist accepts the client unconditionally, such that the client is free to feel what is going on within himself or herself at the moment—whether confusion, resentment, fear, or love. The third aspect of the therapeutic relationship is empathetic understanding. This means that the therapist accurately senses the feelings and personal meanings the client is experiencing and communicates this understanding to the client. Rogers holds that as clients are understood and accepted, they accept themselves more fully and listen more accurately to the flow of their inner experience. They also become increasingly self-directed and feel greater freedom to become the true, whole person they would like to be. During the early stages of therapy, one young woman said that whenever she looked within herself she felt nothing but emptiness: "There was just a cavern."

Later, speaking about the change in her life, the same woman said:

> It's real: I am in a very dynamic process of becoming. I'm not on top of the world yet (maybe, as Joe suggests, I'm somewhere around five on the process scale), but now I know I will be. The cavern is filling with experiencing, and feeling— and I'm in there—ME—A PERSON." (Rogers, 1980, p. 218)

Therapy and Discontent

It is often assumed that following therapy individuals will feel more content with themselves. But not necessarily. Using Maslow's hierarchy of needs, Marcine Johnson (1980) hypothesized that the level of discontent might rise as one result of psychotherapy. That is, as the basic needs are satisfied, the person might still be discontented because higher-level, growth needs are not fulfilled. In Johnson's study, thirty women sorted items in a Q-sort technique, a way of ranking one's self-concept, before and after therapy. The results showed that these women exhibited more high-level discontent at the conclusion of therapy. As Carl Rogers points out, "A client may have changed significantly and still be as dissatisfied as at the beginning of therapy, but the nature of that dissatisfaction needs to be evaluated. 'I'm not realizing all my potential' is quite different from 'I can't stand my job' " (Rogers, 1985, p. 14).

A Variety of Approaches

New forms of insight therapy continue to appear on the scene and take their place along side the more established ones described above. Many of these newer approaches are attempts to add or emphasize aspects of therapy thought to be missing in existing therapies. For instance, in contrast to the so-called value neutral approach to therapy, two other therapies—*existential therapy* as practiced by Rollo May and *logotherapy*, developed by Viktor Frankl—stress the importance of each individual clarifying those values that give personal meaning and purpose to one's life. This requires that individuals have the courage to make choices, break away from restrictive lifestyles, and take responsibility for their lives. Similarly, Greenwald's *direct decision* therapy, described in the chapter on freedom, emphasizes the importance of individuals taking responsibility for their lives, especially in terms of the decisions they have made or need to make. *Gestalt* therapy, founded by Fritz Perls, also puts great value on the individual's responsibility in therapy, but makes more use of the here-and-now nonverbal behavior in the therapy session as a way of helping clients to unify their feelings and actions. *Actualization therapy*, developed by Everett Shostrom, combines elements of the person-centered approach, gestalt therapy, and rational-emotive therapy, as a way of maximizing the individual's growth or self-actualization.

There are, as always, many therapists who continue to practice the type of therapy in which they have been trained, modifying their orientation somewhat with experience. But an increasing number of therapists would characterize themselves as eclectic in the sense of having been exposed to more than one theoretical orientation in their training and continuing to add new techniques to their repertoire of therapeutic strategies. They seem more intent on being able to use the most appropriate treatment strategy for a given client's problems than remaining within a particular school of therapy. As a result, in practice, many therapists incorporate aspects of more than one insight therapy as well as different behavioral techniques (Smith, 1982).

A supportive relationship is an important part of most psychotherapies. (Ken Karp)

BEHAVIOR THERAPIES

Instead of searching for the underlying causes of the client's difficulties, as in the insight therapies, behavior therapists focus directly on the problem behaviors involved. Their aim is to help individuals replace their maladaptive behaviors with more appropriate and satisfying ones. Typically, this involves: discovering the factors that trigger and reinforce the problem behavior, to specify a target behavior to replace it, and then, by manipulating these factors, to bring about the desired target behavior. In the process, behavior therapists help clients to develop the necessary skills to cope more effectively with their life situations. In the next few pages, we'll take a look at several of the more widely used behavioral treatment strategies, including desensitization, social skills training, and cognitive restructuring.

Desensitization

Many of our fears are acquired through the process of conditioned responses, that is, on the basis of the principles of classical conditioning described by John Watson. Desensitization, developed by Joseph Wolpe, is the attempt to reverse this process by learning a new response that is incompatible with the fear. By linking the feared object or situation to something pleasant, like relaxation, the client becomes "desensitized" to the feared situation.

Desensitization is especially effective with fears and phobias. Wolpe (1973) tells of a 24-year-old art student who came for treatment because of her fear of taking examinations, which had resulted in repeated failures. Wolpe began by making up a hierarchy of imagined situations that made her anxious, culminating with the day of the examination. Then he taught her how to relax her body muscles and gradually associate such a relaxed state with each of the feared situations. After seventeen sessions, the art student felt free from anxiety at the highest level of the hierarchy. Four months later she took and successfully passed her examinations without any disruptive anxiety.

In addition to confronting the client with imagined scenes of the situation, as in systematic desensitization, therapists may also use variations of this technique. In behavior rehearsal, for example, the client role-plays the feared situation. In the real-life method, the individual gradually approaches the feared situation directly.

Social Skills Training

One of the major therapeutic innovations developed by social learning therapists is training in social skills. Many problems arise for people simply because they are inept or socially inhibited in dealing with everyday situations. Most of us can think of certain situations in which we do not handle ourselves very well because of felt inadequacies, such as speaking up in class. But this is especially true for people with serious psychological disorders, such as those suffering from schizophrenia. Social skills are sets of responses that enable such individuals to become more effective in dealing with others in a variety of social situations. Social skills involve knowing what to say and do in a given situation (content), what to do to elicit a desired response (consequences), how to do it (style), and when a given response is appropriate (timing). Many social learning therapists recommend using behavior rehearsal, including the use of modeling the desired behavior, role playing, instructions, behavioral contracts, and repeated practice of what to say and do with specific feedback. This approach

Overcoming Your Fears

Although desensitization is ordinarily done under professional supervision, it can also be used on a do-it-yourself basis with one's milder fears.

There are four steps in desensitizing yourself.

First, on separate 3 × 5 cards write down each situation you associate with a given fear or apprehension. Include at least ten but no more than twenty-five items in your stack of cards.

Next, arrange these cards in a hierarchy from the least to the most threatening situation, preferably with small steps of anxiety arousal between each situation. For example, suppose you are afraid of riding in a crowded elevator. You might construct a hierarchy including imagined situations such as the following:

1. You're entering a building that has an elevator.

2. You're walking down the hall toward the elevator.

3. You're standing alone in front of the elevator.

The next step is to train yourself in relaxation techniques. Sit in a comfortable chair or lie on a couch or bed. Then, beginning with your forehead and scalp, practice relaxing and letting your muscles go limp. Then progress to your jaw muscles, then your neck, and so on. You may vary this technique by alternately tensing and relaxing each set of muscles. Or, you can combine this with deep breathing, as described in the chapter on stress. Whichever method you use, spend two or three sessions practicing your relaxation techniques until you can become reasonably relaxed.

Now you're ready for the fourth step. Take the top card from the pile and look at it. Then close your eyes and visualize the situation as vividly as you can in your imagination. As soon as you experience *any* anxiety, stop imagining the scene and go back to your relaxation techniques. When you are completely relaxed, then look at the card again. Repeat this until you can look at the card without feeling anxious. Then progress to the next card. You can heighten the realism of the imagined scenes by using such aids as pictures, recordings, slides, and videotapes.

It is important not to rush. Don't be upset if you can only visualize a few scenes in the hierarchy in each session. Each person has his or her own rate of progress. It's also a good idea to begin each new session with the last hierarchy scene that didn't arouse anxiety in the previous session.

has been used to establish or strengthen a variety of social skills, including assertiveness training, dating behavior, and job interviewing skills (Zimbardo, 1985).

Cognitive Restructuring

Although many behavioral techniques involve cognitive processes, there is one school of behavior therapy in which cognitive processes are the main focus, namely, cognitive behaviorism. Albert Ellis' *rational-emotive therapy* (1979), Aaron Beck's *cognitive therapy* (1979), and Donald Meichenbaum's *self-instructional training* (1977) all fall under the general heading of cognitive restructuring. Although these therapies differ in emphasis and tone, they share a common approach. The central assumption is that emotional problems result from the individual's distorted thoughts and reactions to external events rather than the events themselves. In each case, the goal is to change the client's problem behavior by changing the irrational thoughts that produced the behavior.

Lisa has just discovered that she made a low grade on her first test in psychology. She feels discouraged and engages in self-defeating thinking: "How stupid can I be! I'll never make a good grade on the course. I might as well drop it." A cognitive therapist might point out that Lisa is "awfulizing," that is, overreacting to her poor performance. The therapist would point out the irrationality of Lisa's thinking and model a more realistic evaluation of her situation, for example: "This was the first test, not the final exam." Then the therapist would help Lisa take positive steps to improve her situation, such as talking to the teacher to discover why she did poorly on the test, how she can improve her performance on the next test, and what are her chances for eventually making a good grade on the course. The therapist might instruct Lisa in monitoring and correcting her thoughts and how to begin preparing more effectively for the next test now.

In practice, behavior therapists tend to use a combination of behavioral techniques, depending on the individual and the types of problems involved. As a result, Arnold Lazarus (1981) has developed "multimodal therapy," a comprehensive and flexible approach to behavior therapy. Lazarus holds that since human problems are multidimensional in nature, it is essential to attend to these different dimensions for lasting changes to occur. Accordingly, multimodal therapy begins with a comprehensive and systematic assessment of the BASIC-ID, an acronym for behavior, affect, sensation, imagery, cognition, interpersonal relationships, and drugs. Assessment and treatment includes the deficits and excesses that arise within each of these dimensions. For example, a client's lack of assertiveness would represent a deficit that needs to be supplemented; compulsive eating would be an excess that needs to be reduced or eliminated. The therapist then employs a variety of cognitive-behavioral techniques to reeducate the client.

GROUP APPROACHES TO THERAPY

Group approaches to therapy have mushroomed in number and variety in the past several decades, to such an extent that they now constitute one of the most promising approaches to therapy.

Groups offer several advantages over individual therapies. The most obvious one is that groups offer opportunities for individuals to interact with others with similar problems, thus releasing the powers of empathy, mutual support,

Some Irrational Ideas Commonly Held

Albert Ellis has identified a dozen irrational ideas or assumptions that are widespread in our society and when believed tend to lead to self-defeating behavior. These are:

1. The idea that you must—yes, *must*—have sincere love and approval almost all the time from all the people you find significant.

2. The idea that you must prove yourself thoroughly competent, adequate, and achieving, or that you must at least have real competence or talent at something important.

3. The idea that people who harm you or commit misdeeds rate as generally bad, wicked, or villainous individuals and that you should severely blame, damn, and punish them for their sins.

4. The idea that life proves awful, terrible, horrible, or catastrophic when things do not go the way you would like them to go.

5. The idea that emotional misery comes from external pressures and that you have little ability to control your feelings or rid yourself of depression and hostility.

6. The idea that if something seems dangerous or fearsome, you must become terribly occupied with and upset about it.

7. The idea that you will find it easier to avoid facing many of life's difficulties and self-responsibilities than to undertake more rewarding forms of self-discipline.

8. The idea that your past remains all-important and that because something once strongly influenced your life, it has to keep determining your feelings and behavior today.

9. The idea that people and things should turn out better than they do and that you have to view it as awful and horrible if you do not quickly find good solutions to life's hassles.

10. The idea that you can achieve happiness by inertia and inaction or by passively and uncommittedly "enjoying yourself."

11. The idea that you must have a high degree of order or certainty to feel comfortable, or that you need some supernatural power on which to rely.

12. The idea that you can give yourself a global rating as a human being, and that your general worth and self-acceptance depend upon the goodness of your performances and the degree that people approve of you.

Source: Albert Ellis and Robert A. Harper, *A New Guide to Rational Living* (Englewood Cliffs, NJ: Prentice-Hall, and Hollywood: Wilshire Books, 1975), pp. 83–85. Reprinted by permission of the publishers and the author.

and control among their members. Then too, groups present a microcosm of the larger society, thus facilitating the transfer of learning from therapy to outside life. Groups are also more cost efficient, saving time and money. Instead of seeing one client for an hour, a therapist may see eight or ten. As a result, each client pays less for the therapist's time. And, more importantly, more people can receive help, an important consideration in a society where mental health resources are in short supply.

Virtually every theory or technique employed in individual therapy has been or can be applied to groups as well, so that we find psychoanalytic groups, behavioral groups, and gestalt groups, along with countless others. Some of these approaches include preexisting groups like couples or families. Others consist of strangers who share a common problem or concern. Some groups focus on therapy; others are designed primarily for learning and growth. In the following pages, we'll describe several of the more common group approaches, namely family therapy, mutual help groups, and community services.

Sometimes people may be helped more effectively in group therapy. (Ken Karp)

Marital and Family Therapy

Married and unmarried couples alike usually come to therapy because of some particular problem, such as infidelity on the part of one partner, poor communication, or trouble with in-laws. A common problem encountered is when one partner, usually the more dominant person in the relationship, has threatened to leave, while the other partner wants to stay in the relationship. Although couples coming for help often blame their partners for their problems, professionals in this field tend to focus more on their interaction or the marriage relationship itself. The therapist may begin with the specific problems presented by a couple, but attention is also given to how such problems are related to their marital interaction. If one partner has committed infidelity, instead of joining in the blame for that partner, the therapist may ask what brought it about. Perhaps one partner sought to fill a void in an empty marriage or indulged in a hostile attempt to get back at the other partner. Either way, the therapist helps each partner become more aware of their give-and-take relationship, how they compete with and hurt each other, and so forth. The therapist also helps them clarify the decision as to whether they want to separate or work at their marriage. If it becomes evident that the partners are willing to work at their marriage, the therapist helps them express better communication and supportive concern for each other.

Family therapy, as the name implies, involves the larger family unit, including children. Family therapists differ in regard to their procedures as well as theoretical orientations. Some therapists prefer to see the entire family from beginning to end. Others may see the identified client or parents for a couple of sessions and then the identified client with his or her parents and siblings in the remaining sessions. There are also a variety of theoretical orientations, including the *communications, behavioral,* and *systems* approaches.

Contextual family therapy, initially developed by Nagy, is an intergenerational approach that emphasizes each person's search for fair treatment. As a client, your attitudes and behavior are understood not only in relation to your immediate family, but also within the context of your family over more than one generation. Special attention is given to certain patterns of owing and receiving and indebtedness and entitlement that have developed and the resulting struggle toward a balance of fairness through successive generations within a given family. The central concept is each individual's search for fairness, or justice, both given and received, within one's family tradition (Nagy and Krasner, 1986).

For example, if in my family of origin I feel unfairly treated by my parents or siblings, I may be left with a sense of "being owed" or entitled to what I believe I didn't receive. I may then try to collect this debt or felt injustice from my mate or my children. I may take from them in such a way that they, in turn, feel unfairly treated by me. The resulting struggle tends to be passed on from one generation to another. The same is true for fair treatment. If I feel fairly treated by my parents, I may approach my mate and children with a feeling of indebtedness, or need to "over-give" to them in order to correct the balance of relational justice between the generations.

The goal of therapy is to help individuals earn freedom from their felt wrongs or indebtedness through a rebalancing of felt justice. This goal is achieved through the therapeutic dialogue between various family members who have most influenced the identified client. Each family member expresses his or her views and, in turn, is willing to listen to others' viewpoints. Dialogue entails recognition of others' views and the right to hold such views, rather than simple agreement with them. The therapist encourages clients to be authentic and to identify their wants. Feelings are translated into concrete wants—for example, not "How do you feel about your wife," but "What do you want from your wife." In addition, clients are encouraged to examine what they are willing to give—for example, not "How do you feel toward your wife," but "What do you want to give your wife?" Clients are encouraged to make their just claims directly to the appropriate person. Often parents, children, spouses, and ex-spouses are called into therapy sessions so that the therapist can facilitate the clients making their claim. For example, if your problem is your father, then you deal with him face-to-face. Clients are taught to build trust by learning new modes of communication. They are discouraged from obtuse, indirect, and manipulative statements and encouraged to give clear, direct "I" statements. Often it is the therapist's responsibility to affirm the client's right to express his or her entitlement. Finally, it is the responsibility of the therapist to help the client identify resources—mother, father, siblings, and friends—who can emotionally give to the client, and thereby enable the client to establish mutually gratifying relationships with other people.

Mutual-help Groups

In the past several decades, there has been a marked increase in self-help or mutual-help groups among peers. These are groups of people who share a common problem or concern and meet regularly to discuss their problems without the guidance of professionals, in this case, mental health professionals. There are now an estimated half-million such groups, which deal with almost every conceivable human problem (McCormack, 1981).

Although these groups frequently have multiple functions, such as fostering self-care and lobbying for reform, they all have the same underlying purpose—to provide emotional support and practical help in dealing with a problem common to all members. A major assumption is that no one understands you or may help you better than someone who has the same problem. Knowing that someone else truly understands one's feelings because of having "been there" may bring a sense of relief to someone who has suffered in isolation. New members may approach their first meeting with apprehension, wondering what the group can do for them or what it will ask in return. Yet, experienced members, well aware of these mixed emotions, encourage new members to feel relaxed and feel welcome. In an atmosphere that is friendly and compassionate, new members soon realize that their participation is voluntary with no strings attached—no commitments, no enforced disclosures, and no group constraints. There is usually an unwritten code of confidentiality within the group. Even when there is a series of steps to recovery, as in the various "Anonymous" groups, members can proceed at their own pace. A veteran member may describe the organization, distribute literature, and help the new member to feel at home. Some groups, especially those that deal with addictive behavior or emotional disorders, may use a "buddy" system so that a new member can count on a familiar person for encouragement and support. All in all, mutual-help groups provide an atmosphere of acceptance and support that encourages their members to share their sorrows and frustrations, and from there they can begin to communicate more openly, view their problems more objectively, and find more effective coping strategies (McCormack, 1981).

Information on Mutual-help Groups

If you fail to find the mutual-help group of interest in your phone book, write or phone:

National Self-Help Clearing House
33 West 42nd Street,
New York, NY 10036
Tel: (212) 840-1259

Also, the National Institute of Mental Health has prepared a fact sheet on mutual-help groups that is available at no charge from:

Consumer Information Service
Department 609K
Pueblo, CO 81009

Community Services

Since the late 1950s, the introduction of antipsychotic drugs, along with convincing evidence that custody care in large mental hospitals is bad for patients, has led to the release of large numbers of ex-patients into the community. Since most of these patients required some type of treatment, as do others in the community who wish to avoid hospitalization, mental health professionals began developing more community-based services. The passage of the Community Mental Health Centers Act in 1963 aimed to create one mental health center for every 50,000 people in the United States. Everyone in the *catchment area*, an area of geographical coverage, would be able to receive the needed psychological services without having to leave the community. Although the actual services provided by these centers have fallen far short of the initial vision, they have been a major factor in the nationwide shift to community-based mental health care.

Not surprisingly, the outpatient services are the most heavily used services of these mental health centers. As a result, since 1955, outpatient services have increased twelve-fold, to about 4.5 million clinical episodes (Kiesler, 1982). The goal of such outpatient services is to provide help for individuals without disrupting their normal routine. Most mental health centers also offer short-term therapy for individuals with a variety of problems in the community. The more comprehensive centers provide alternatives to hospital care, such as emergency services, day hospitals, halfway houses, and hotlines. Over 1000 day hospitals have been established throughout the United States. These hospitals provide individuals with the needed therapeutic services on a nine to five basis and then allow them to return to their families in the evening. Another agency that has proliferated in recent years is the halfway house—a residence in which newly released patients or exaddicts can readjust to community life under supervision. The best halfway houses are small residences and are usually staffed by paraprofessionals who help the residents learn to live together and acquire the appropriate skills to return to community life. Also, a variety of hotlines are now available in many communities. Almost 200 suicide-prevention and 600 youth and/or drug abuse hotlines have been established throughout the United States (Trowell, 1979).

The majority of people with emotional problems seek help in a community mental health center. (Ken Karp)

Community-based services often fall short of what is needed, mostly because of insufficient funding and the resultant inadequacies in facilities, staffing, and carefully thought out programs that address the needs of the community. Because of these inadequacies, the return of patients to the community has slowed significantly. Even when patients return to the community, they lack the necessary supervision and support to stay there. Many of them become "street people" before returning to the hospital. As a result, in many places, the number of admissions to mental hospitals has *increased* rather than decreased, leading to a "revolving door" policy. Yet the average length of stay in hospitals has decreased—to less than 2 weeks in general hospitals, which account for most psychiatric admissions, and less than 6 months in large state mental hospitals, which normally keep the more severely disturbed patients.

HOW WELL DOES THERAPY WORK?

For many years, hardly anyone bothered to ask such a question. Therapists and clients alike held a kind of blind faith that therapy does work. Then after reviewing various studies on the subject in 1952, Hans Eysenck shocked the world of therapy by concluding that as many clients with neurotic complaints improved with the passage of time as did from psychotherapy. Eysenck's claims were hotly contested and challenged by other studies. Since then, extensive studies have confirmed that therapy tends to have modest positive effects. In a comprehensive review of 475 studies, one investigation has shown that the average client receiving therapy is generally better off than 75 percent of those who do not receive therapy. And the improvement rate is even higher in regard to the alleviation of anxiety and fear. Equally important, the researchers found that the different types of therapy—psychodynamic, humanistic, and behavioral therapies—do not differ significantly in their rates of effectiveness (Smith, Glass, and Miller, 1980).

Much of the current research is focused on more specific, measurable factors that make therapy effective. For instance, one investigation (Howard, et al, 1986), including 2,431 clients in 15 studies, found a positive relationship between the length of treatment and client improvement. About one-third of the clients improved within the first three sessions, regardless of the ultimate duration of treatment. Similarly, half of them had improved by eight sessions. And approximately three-fourths of the clients had improved by 26 sessions. At the same time, the rate of improvement varied considerably among different types of clients. Depressed clients generally showed improvement after the first few sessions. But clients with anxiety disorders usually took a somewhat higher number of sessions before showing improvement, and the more severely disturbed psychotic clients required the highest number of sessions of all. While such findings do not prove that time-limited therapy is as effective as time-unlimited therapy, 26 sessions could be used as a point in the treatment process at which cases that have not shown any measurable improvement would be subjected to a clinical review.

Another concern is the relative effectiveness of drugs and psychotherapy. Some people object to the extensive use of drugs in therapy because they simply alleviate symptoms rather than resolve the psychological difficulties involved. Although this criticism has some justification, it applies to some types of psychological disorders more than others, and more especially, in various degrees to different individuals with the same disorder. One comparative study, conducted at Camarillo State Hospital in California, included 228 schizophrenic patients

Drug Therapy

Drugs are commonly used in the treatment of psychological disorders, with or without other types of therapy. The three main classes of psychoactive drugs used are: antianxiety drugs, antidepressant drugs, and antipsychotic drugs.

Antianxiety drugs, or minor tranquilizers, are the most commonly prescribed psychoactive drugs in the United States. In most cases, family physicians prescribe these drugs for people going through a difficult time. But they are also used in the treatment of anxiety disorders, stress-related disorders, and for withdrawal from alcohol and other drugs.

Antidepressants are used to elevate mood in depressed patients. These drugs help to relieve many of the typical symptoms of depression, such as sleeplessness or excessive sleepiness, chronic fatigue, loss of appetite, loss of sex drive, sadness, and feelings of worthlessness. One of the limitations of these drugs is that they usually take several weeks to become effective.

Antipsychotic drugs, as the name suggests, are used to treat the symptoms of the severe disorders like schizophrenia. These drugs tend to reduce symptoms such as hallucinations, delusions, and bizarre behavior. But they do not cure the apathy, social withdrawal, or interpersonal difficulties found in people with schizophrenia. They also have several side effects, with a small proportion of patients developing *tardive dyskinesia*—characterized by jerking movements around the neck and face and involuntary protrusions of the tongue. Despite the criticisms surrounding the use of such drugs, most professionals who work with schizophrenic patients believe the value of these drugs outweighs their potential abuse.

who were first admissions at the hospital. All of them were considered to be average in regard to their prospects for recovery. Each patient was assigned to one of five treatment groups: (1) milieu therapy, (2) electroconvulsive therapy, (3) drug therapy, (4) individual psychotherapy, and (5) individual psychotherapy plus drugs. The results indicated that the two best treatments for the average schizophrenic patient were the drugs-alone and the psychotherapy-plus-drugs approaches (May, Tuma, and Dixon, 1981). Although psychotherapy appears to be considerably more effective with many types of depression than with schizophrenia, at least one study involving depressed patients has shown that drug therapy combined with psychotherapy was more effective than either of these treatments alone (Rounsaville, Klerman, and Weissman, 1981). Despite such findings, drugs often remain the major form of treatment for schizophrenia and depression in many institutions, primarily because they are the least expensive form of treatment.

As we've shown throughout this chapter, there is a wide range of therapies for people with all sorts of difficulties, including individuals temporarily overwhelmed by the problems of living as well as those with serious psychological disorders. A major problem is making the help available to those who need it, and getting them to use it. All too often, the people most likely to seek therapy are those who need it least, that is, the affluent, educated individuals with mild disturbances. In contrast, the people who need therapy the most are least likely to seek it out, that is, those with the most serious psychological disorders, who are also less receptive to therapy and less able to pay for it. Closing this gap is a continuing goal of community-based mental health services.

Summary

Getting Help

1. Only about one-fifth of the people suffering from a psychological disorder seek therapy from a mental health professional, mostly because of the stigma associated with getting help.

2. It's best to get recommendations for a therapist from a trusted professional and then in the initial session discuss such matters as the fees and type of treatment offered.

3. One of the difficulties in selecting a therapist is the bewildering variety of schools of therapy, including insight, behavioral, and group therapies.

Insight Therapies

4. The goal of insight therapy is to bring about change through increasing the individual's self-understanding.

5. Modern psychoanalysis uses many of Freud's ideas and techniques for achieving insight and self-mastery of the unconscious forces of life, but in a shorter period of time.

6. Rogers' person-centered approach holds that individuals have within themselves vast resources for self-understanding and growth, which may be actualized when they are provided with a caring and empathetic environment conducive to change.

7. There are a variety of other insight therapies, many of them attempts to add or emphasize aspects of therapy thought to be missing in existing therapies, such as the importance of decision making in direct decision therapy.

Behavior Therapy

8. Behavior therapists focus directly on the client's problem behaviors, with the aim of replacing maladaptive behaviors with more appropriate and satisfying ones.

9. In desensitization, the client learns to substitute a new response, such as relaxation, for an old, maladaptive response, such as anxiety or fear.

10. Social skills training includes a variety of behavioral techniques that help clients learn more adequate ways of handling social situations.

11. The aim of cognitive restructuring is to modify clients' problem behaviors by changing the irrational thoughts that produce this behavior.

Group Approaches to Therapy

12. Group approaches to therapy have mushroomed in the past several decades, such that they now constitute one of the most promising approaches to therapy.

13. Marital and family therapy generally approach the individual's problem as a function of the marriage relationship or family structure and encourage all members of the group to work for mutually satisfying relationships.

14. Mutual help groups among peers, such as Alcoholics Anonymous, provide emotional support and practical help in dealing with a problem common to all members.

15. The shift of mental health care from the state hospitals to community-based services has been made possible by the establishment of community mental health centers, which provide individual therapy, emergency services, and outpatient services for newly discharged mental hospital patients.

How Well Does Therapy Work?

16. Studies show that psychotherapy generally works better than no therapy at all, with the different schools of insight and behavior therapy being approximately equal in effectiveness.

17. The comparative effectiveness of drugs versus psychotherapy varies somewhat among different disorders and individuals, with the combination of drugs and psychotherapy generally bringing the greatest improvement.

Self-test

1. Approximately what percent of the adults with a psychological disorder will seek help from a mental health professional?

a. 20   **c.** 50
b. 30   **d.** 75

2. The process of helping clients gain insight into their unconscious conflicts through such techniques as dream interpretation is called:

a. cognitive therapy   **c.** psychoanalysis
b. behavior therapy   **d.** gestalt therapy

3. According to Carl Rogers, the client-therapist relationship tends to be conducive to personality change when the therapist:

a. is congruent in the relationship   **c.** exhibits empathetic understanding
b. has an attitude of acceptance   **d.** all of the above

4. Desensitization is especially effective with:

a. schizophrenia   **c.** depression
b. phobias   **d.** bipolar disorder

5. To modify the client's behavior through changing the irrational thoughts that produce the behavior is the goal of:

a. gestalt therapy

b. desensitization

c. family therapy

d. cognitive therapy

6. An intergenerational approach to family therapy that emphasizes each person's search for fair treatment is called:

a. behavioral therapy

b. contextual therapy

c. gestalt therapy

d. existential therapy

7. There is an assumption that no one understands and can help you better than someone who has the same problem in:

a. mutual-help groups

b. psychoanalysis

c. gestalt therapy

d. social skills training

8. The most heavily used services of community mental health centers are the:

a. emergency services

b. day hospitals

c. outpatient services

d. halfway houses

9. A comprehensive review of the effectiveness of therapy has shown that psychoanalysis generally is:

a. superior to humanistic therapy

b. as effective as other therapies

c. inferior to behavior therapy

d. little better than no therapy

10. Comparative studies have shown that by 26 sessions of therapy, improvement is seen in what proportion of clients?

a. one-third

b. one-half

c. three-fourths

d. all clients

Exercises

1. *How do you feel about getting help?* Write a paragraph or so describing your attitude toward getting help for a psychological problem. To what extent do you feel that getting psychological help is a sign of personal weakness? How severe would the problem have to be before you sought help? Be honest.

2. *Who would you turn to for help?* Suppose you needed psychological help immediately, who would you turn to? Write down the name, address, and telephone number of the person or agency. If you're unable to do this from memory, you might ask around for appropriate referrals. Regardless of who you select, also write down the name, address, and phone number of the nearest mental health center or similar agency for your local community.

3. *Distinguishing between psychiatrists and psychologists.* People often confuse these two professionals. Reread the boxed item on "Who are the therapists?" Then write a paragraph or so describing the differences between these two types of professionals. What services are usually reserved for psychiatrists? What types of problems or psychological disorders are most appropriate for psychiatrists and for psychologists? You might ask your instructor to comment on this.

4. *First-person account of therapy.* If you've participated in counseling or therapy, write a page or so describing your experience. In what ways was it beneficial? Do you have any misgivings about it? On the basis of your experience, what suggestions would you make to people considering therapy?

5. *Desensitization.* Reread the boxed item on do-it-yourself desensitization. Then apply the material to one of your mild to moderate fears, such as test anxiety or the fear of riding a crowded elevator. If you're unsure of how to proceed, check with your instructor or an experienced counselor.

6. *Social skills training.* Workshops are given on a variety of social skills, such as assertiveness training, communication skills, job interviewing skills, and overcoming shyness. If you were to take part in such a workshop, which social skill would you be most interested in improving and why?

7. *Mutual-help groups.* Perhaps you've participated in a group like Parents Without Partners or Toughlove. If so, write a page or so describing your experience. If not, which type of mutual-help group would you be most interested in joining and why? You might write the National Self-help Clearing House to get a list of such groups.

Questions for Self-reflection

1. Do you believe that friends can be good medicine?
2. If you were looking for a therapist, either for yourself or someone else, whose recommendation would you seek?
3. What are some personal qualities you would look for in a therapist?
4. Have you ever considered using desensitization to reduce your own anxieties or fears?
5. Can you recall times when you aggravated a problem by irrational expectations or thoughts?
6. Do you think some of your limitations or problems might be related to your family patterns, either present or past?
7. Have you ever belonged to a mutual help group?
8. Would you agree that people have to want to change in order to benefit fully from therapy?
9. Do you realize that asking for help when you need it is itself a mark of maturity?
10. Are you aware that many people experience personal growth as well as the relief of symptoms in psychotherapy?

Recommended Readings

Burns, **David.** *Feeling Good.* New York: William Morrow and Company, 1980. A psychiatrist explains how to conquer your depression by changing your thoughts and perceptions.

Ellis, Albert, and R. A. Harper. *A New Guide To Rational Living.* Englewood Cliffs, NJ: Prentice-Hall, 1975 (paperback). An application of cognitive-behavioral principles to everyday problems.

Kovel, J. A. *A Complete Guide To Therapy.* New York: Pantheon Books, 1977 (paperback). A therapist's view of what motivates people for therapy, along with descriptions and evaluations of the various therapies.

Lazarus, Arnold A. *The Practice of Multimodal Therapy.* New York: McGraw-Hill, 1981. An overview of the behavioral strategies used in therapy.

Mahoney, Michael J. *Self-change.* New York: W. W. Norton, 1981. A high-level self-improvement book containing practical strategies for solving personal problems.

Shephard, Martin. *The Do-it-yourself Psychotherapy Book.* New York: Permanent Press, 1980 (paperback). A psychiatrist explains how to use many of the principles of psychotherapy to improve yourself.

15 Adult Life Stages

The funny thing about aging is the way it sneaks up on you. One morning you wake up and you're 30 or 45, and you wonder how you got there. You may not feel any different. But your birthdays betray your age. It seems that, at least unconsciously, each of us remains the same age throughout our lives. Or it may be, as Sydney Harris (1985) suggests, that each of us has an "optimum age" at which we'd like to remain. Some people have a mental image of themselves as still in their 20s. Others don't seem comfortable with themselves until they are older. However, there are some people who never find their optimum age. As teenagers, they can't wait to grow up. But in middle age, they want all the privileges of adults but not the responsibilities. And in old age, they regret what they feel they missed in their youth. Speaking personally, I continue to think of myself as someone in his 30s, though I'm reminded otherwise each time I look in the mirror. It usually comes as a surprise when my body rebels. I don't feel older, except in those rash moments when I overexert myself, such as riding my bike up a steep hill. Nevertheless, virtually all of us have been hit with the admonishment, "Act your age." But what if your chronological age isn't the age you feel? And it rarely is.

EARLY ADULTHOOD

Regardless of how we feel about ourselves, we do grow older. Up through adolescence, much of our development is associated with changes that tend to occur at a given age, such as puberty and high school graduation. In contrast, adult development depends more on events and influences that may occur at any age, such as an unwanted divorce or the decision to change careers. As a result, high school classmates who meet again, say at a high school reunion, usually discover that they are much more different from each other at 40 years of age than they were at 18. At the same time, certain changes such as leaving home and the midlife transition commonly occur in everyone's life so that it has become customary to describe adult development in terms of three broad stages, early, middle, and late adulthood respectively.

In a longitudinal study of adult development, Daniel Levinson (1978) and his colleagues discovered what parents and young people themselves have long suspected, namely, that the transition to adulthood is more complex and strung out than ordinarily understood. In their view, early adulthood begins with an "early adult transition," roughly from the late teens until the early 20s, and lasts well into a person's late 30s. The major developmental tasks of this period are leaving home, choosing and preparing for a career, establishing close relationships like friendship and marriage, and, if desired, starting a family of one's own.

Leaving Home

Essentially, this stage has to do with coming to see ourselves as autonomous adults separate from our families of origin. Since the separation from our families is never complete, as Levinson (1978) points out, it may be more accurate to understand "leaving home" in terms of the transformation of emotional ties between young persons and their families that takes place during this period. The external aspects include moving out of the family home, becoming less dependent financially on our parents, and entering new roles and responsibilities. The internal aspects include increasing differentiation of oneself from parents and more autonomous decision making. It is this psychosocial transition, however, that is most essential for entering adulthood. That is, some youths may run away from an unhappy home at an early age, but take a long time before growing up emotionally. Others, mostly because of a lengthy education, may remain home well into their 20s, choosing to achieve self-sufficiency in other ways. In both cases, it is the "symbolic" leaving home that is so crucial to attaining emotional autonomy.

In his book *Leaving Home*, Jay Haley (1980) points out that maladjustments at this stage often reflect problems in separating both from home and from the dynamics of the family itself. Separation troubles can take many forms, including drug addiction, delinquent behavior, emotional disturbances, failure at school or work, paralyzing apathy, or suicide. In many instances young people have difficulty leaving home because of their parents' unwillingness to "let go." Such parents may complain of a young person's problems at school or with drugs, while deriving an unconscious satisfaction from knowing they are still needed as parents. Young people themselves also experience conflicts over leaving home. On the one hand, they may feel impatient and resentful toward their parents for their attempts to control them, but they may also feel anxious about their ability to make it on their own.

Going away to college often tips the balance of forces toward independence, and in the process improves the relationship between young people and their parents. This can be seen in a study by Kenneth and Anna Sullivan (1980) that included 242 male students from twelve high schools in Pennsylvania, New Jersey, New York, and Massachusetts. They compared two groups of students: those who attended residential colleges and those who remained at home and commuted to school. Questionnaires completed by students and their parents at the high school and college stage included questions about the affection and communication between parents and students as well as the latter's independence. The level of the young man's independence was measured first by whether his family encouraged him to make his own decisions or criticized him and tried to dictate such things as hair style, and second by the degree to which he made decisions without their help. The results showed marked differences between the groups. Those who had gone away to college reported that they not only enjoyed better communication with their parents, but also that they and their parents had more affection for each other than did students living at home.

At the same time, a curious thing has been happening in the 1980s. Like birds flying back to the nest, more young adults are moving in with their parents after years of absence from home. The number of individuals 18 years or older living at home increased from 13.7 million in 1970 to 19.1 million in 1982. The increase in "nesters," as some social service workers call them, is partly due to there being more people this age in our society. Yet, much of the increase is the result of economic pressures of the past few years. The economy has made it difficult for young people to maintain their own apartments or homes. Many college guaduates, as well as high school graduates, are having a hard time finding a suitable job. Then too, young women, often with a child or two, who find themselves recently divorced, may feel forced to return home for a while to regroup. As you might expect, there are pros and cons to such an arrangement. On the minus side, the increased food bills are sometimes incredible, though some young people must pay board to offset these expenses. Parents may find it natural to ask "Where were you last night?" forgetting their son or daughter is older now. But there are also pluses to having this additional time at home. Individuals and their parents often find this a satisfying time for sharing and strengthening their ties before a son or daughter leaves home again, usually for good (Shapiro and Lounsberry, 1983).

Do You Have a Mentor?

Some people achieve early success in their careers because they are fortunate enough to have a mentor—someone with greater experience or seniority who takes an active interest in helping them along with their careers.

In a study of young men, Daniel Levinson (1978) found that the presence or absence of such a figure in the early adult years was a significant factor in a man's career development. At the same time, young men usually outgrew their mentors in 2 or 3 years, 10 years at the most.

O. J. Simpson, the well-known football player and TV commentator, was helped along by Willie Mays, the famous baseball player. Simpson, who came from a broken home, ran around with delinquents and had already experienced several brushes with the law before being introduced to Mays through Simpson's school counselor. Mays talked to Simpson about developing his talent and the importance of getting on the right track. In retrospect, Simpson says it was mostly Mays' influence that inspired him to attend college and become a professional football player (Santrock, 1984).

Until recently, women had less mentoring in many fields, probably because a career was not deemed as important for them as men. Also, as Gail Sheehy (1977) points out, women were more likely to have a male mentor, with the added danger that the mentor relationship might be transformed into a romantic or sexual one. In recent years, however, the women's movement has helped to bring about both a more extensive support system for women in the workaday world and freedom from sexual exploitation in "moving up the ladder" of their chosen occupation.

Choosing a Career

A major developmental task during this period is the choice of a career along with the appropriate preparation for it. In choosing a career, people this age must strike a balance between two somewhat contradictory tasks. One task is to explore the possibilities in the adult world, keeping one's options open. The other task is to create a stable life-structure with the aim of making something of one's self (Levinson, 1978). Young adults often agonize over the important decisions they must make at this stage, whether they are making the right choice, and, if not, how difficult it will be to change. As a result, many college-bound youth are delaying their entry into college several years or more; once in school they are less hesitant than youth in the past to drop out of college to return later, or not at all, largely out of a need to clarify their career goals as much as from financial need. Even after graduation from school, early adulthood continues to be a time of change and experimentation for many people, with the typical worker this age holding several brief jobs before settling into a more promising position (Crittenden, 1980).

Young men, who've grown up expecting to work and provide for their families, generally are preoccupied with their careers at this time of life. Women tend to be more ambiguous about the conflicting priorities of marriage and work. Yet, today, more young women are working before marriage, delaying marriage, combining work with marriage, and returning to work after the birth of their children. They are also enrolling in college, graduate, and professional schools in greater numbers than ever before, with college-educated women especially likely to combine career and marriage. Although most women would like to continue working outside the home after marriage, not all husbands agree, as we mentioned earlier in the chapter on marriage. Yet, when the woman works outside the home couples tend to share power more equally and are happier with their marriage than other couples (Blumstein and Schwartz, 1983).

Establishing Close Relationships

A major developmental task during this period is forming close relationships with one's peers, especially someone of the opposite sex. Erikson (1974) contends that young adults' success in this venture depends on how well they have resolved the earlier issue of personal identity in adolescence. Individuals who are unsure of themselves or what they want to be may be so fearful of losing themselves in a close relationship they can only enter into superficial, dependent, or unstable relationships. Those with more self-assurance and clearer life goals are freer to engage in the emotional give and take of a close relationship such as marriage. At least one study has shown that young adults of both sexes with a firm sense of identity enjoy deeper and more committed relationships than those who have not developed a clear identity (Kacerguis and Adams, 1980).

At the same time, women tend to follow a more varied pattern than men in this matter. Traditionally, women have established their identities mostly through their intimate relationships, such as marriage and children. Many women still prefer this pattern. Today, however, women increasingly feel free to adopt a more "male" pattern and concentrate on a career before marriage, or, in some cases, instead of marriage. Still other women follow more of an androgynous pattern, pursuing career and marriage goals simultaneously (Hodgson and Fischer, 1979).

How well two people get along as a couple also depends largely on their emotional involvement and commitment to the relationship. In the majority of couples, there is at least one partner who is primarily committed to the relationship—usually, but not always, the woman. Yet, the person who is more emotionally involved is also the more vulnerable and unhappy partner in the relationship. Furthermore, relationships with uneven emotional involvement are not only less satisfying but also less stable. Not surprisingly, couples in which both partners put their relationship first, before work and the children, are generally the happiest of all (Blumstein and Schwartz, 1983).

Starting a Family

Early adulthood is also the time for starting a family. However, couples are giving more thought to whether they want children, and, if so, when to have them. One result is more voluntary childlessness. Few couples resolve this issue directly. Usually, couples decide to postpone having children until they eventually make the postponement permanent. Those who decide to have children tend to wait longer before doing so than did couples during the 1950s. Today many couples do not have their first child until they are in their late 20s or early 30s. The advantages and disadvantages of each pattern were shown in a series of interviews with couples in three different generations who had their children early (in their 20s) or late (in their late 20s or early 30s). Couples who had their children early pointed to the advantages of growing up with their children and getting free of their children at a relatively early age. A major disadvantage was missing the freedom to do things on their own early in the marriage. Couples who waited to have their children cited the advantages of having a chance to strengthen their marriage, advance their careers, and generally grow up before having children. A common disadvantage was the conflict over balancing the claims of careers and childrearing (Daniels & Weingarten, 1981).

Having children may affect a couple's marriage in several ways. On the positive side, many couples report that having children makes them feel more

From the moment of birth, parents and children alike share significant experiences of growth.
(Laimute E. Druskis)

responsible and adult. They also report increased satisfaction in sharing affection and learning experiences with their children, all of which enhance their sense of purpose in life (Hoffman and Manis, 1979). On the minus side, taking care of small children is an added stress on the marriage, leaving less time for the parents to be alone with each other. This also comes at a time when romance is giving way to the realities of married life. Roger Gould (1978) found that individuals in their late 20s and early 30s characteristically expressed a marked increase in the desire to be accepted "for what I am" by their mate as well as a gradual decrease in agreement that their marriage has been a "good thing." There is often a great deal of restlessness and marital dissatisfaction during this period, leading couples to question their marriage, with some of them ending in divorce.

MIDDLE ADULTHOOD

Some time between the late 30s and the early 40s people must make the transition from early to middle adulthood. Men and women begin to see themselves differently, with new opportunities and tasks as well as limitations. They are going through the *midlife transition.*

Midlife Transition

Essentially, this is a time of personal evaluation that comes with the realization one's life is half over. The individual gradually pays less attention to the "time since birth" and starts thinking more in terms of "time I have left." Although people at this age may hide some of the more obvious changes of age or compensate by trying harder, it is more difficult for them to ignore other fundamental changes that come at this age. For one thing, their parents retire, become ill, and die during these years. More of their friends and acquaintances are also lost through death, with death from all causes rising sharply at this time of life. Children grow up and leave home, and middle-aged parents feel more aware of the mistakes they have made raising their children than in earlier years (Gould, 1978). As a result, the early part of middle adulthood becomes an uncomfortable and unstable time for many people, intensifying the mood of restlessness and self-questioning of the early 30s.

In Erikson's view (1968), the main life task at this stage is achieving a sense of *generativity,* which involves looking beyond one's immediate family and extending life in more meaningful ways into the larger community. The realization that life is half over prompts people this age to ask themselves what they would like to do with the rest of their lives. Such self-questioning may lead to changes in their careers, marriages, or personal relationships. It often leads them to take up new interests or become active in community or national affairs as a way of making their world a better place in which to live. It's a time for becoming aware of the "opposite," unrealized side of one's personality. For example, a hard-driving businessman may take more of an interest in helping others, or a mother may go back to school as a way of developing her skills as a research scientist. In either view, middle age is a time for shifting gears and developing new interests and values. Not to do so may result in undue self-absorption or stagnation.

Physical and Cognitive Changes

The most obvious signs of middle age are certain physical changes in appearance. People tend to gain weight around the waist, especially after 40. Men's hairlines may begin to recede around the temples, with a graying of hair for both sexes. All these changes reflect a gradual slowing down in the overall physical system. There is less physical energy and stamina. People get tired more easily and take more time to bounce back from fatigue or stress.

There is actually some improvement in general health in the sense that middle-aged adults get fewer colds, allergies, or minor illnesses, and they experience fewer accidents. But they become more susceptible to chronic and serious illnesses, such as diabetes, heart attacks, strokes, and cancer. As a result, there is increasing concern over health and more attention paid to keeping fit.

Are We Becoming an Age-irrelevant Society?

It just may be. People are no longer surprised to see a 24-year-old mayor or a 28-year-old university president. Professional football players no longer retire automatically when they turn 30. Actresses no longer quit acting when they reach 40. Nor do actors stop working in front of the cameras when their hair turns gray. While people may still blink when a 55-year-old man marries a 26-year-old woman or a 40-year-old woman marries a 25-year-old man, they are no longer shocked or outraged.

Bernice Neugarten says that the whole internal clock that tells us when we're ready to marry or to retire is no longer as powerful or compelling as it used to be. Instead, age has become a poorer and poorer predictor of the way we live. Greater affluence and higher educational levels are helping us to move toward an age-irrelevant society. Another reason is that men and women are finding that getting older isn't all losses. There are gains as well. Parents with grown children are enjoying middle age as a time for taking on new challenges and personal growth. Older people are finding that they are much younger and more vigorous than their parents were at the same age and are able to do more things. All in all, an age-irrelevant society allows people of all ages to engage in a wider variety of lifestyles without fear of being told "act your age."

Source: B. L. Neugarten and E. Hall, "Acting one's age: New rules for old," *Psychology Today*, April 1980, pp. 66–80. Reprinted with permission from *Psychology Today* Magazine. Copyright © April 1980 American Psychological Association.

Changes in cognitive ability vary somewhat depending on the types of activities involved. Test performances that depend on speed usually decline from this period on, mostly because the central nervous system is slowing down. But performances on tasks that require vocabulary and practical problem-solving skills may remain steady or decline more slowly because these depend more on the person's judgment and learning, which benefit with age. A lot depends on how much people improve and use a given ability. Nancy Denney (1981) compared adults' performance on two types of problem-solving tasks: traditional problem-solving and practical problem-solving most likely faced by three age groups: early, middle, and late adults respectively. She found that the performances on both the traditional problem-solving and early adult practical problem-solving tasks decreased in a linear fashion throughout adulthood. However, performance on the practical problems faced by middle and late adults continued to increase through the 30s and remained relatively stable through the 50s before declining. All of this suggests that the more people continue to learn and use their minds, the more they may slow the decline in cognitive abilities that comes with age.

Career Changes

How people's work is affected by the midlife transition depends on many factors, such as their earlier successes and failures, satisfaction on the job, and unfulfilled aspirations. Men who have been successful run the risk of going stale unless they continue to grow. Sometimes the needed challenge comes from a promotion at work or a more rewarding job. For men who have not realized their ambitions, this may be a time for now-or-never decisions. They may redouble their efforts to achieve their career goals at this age—which ironically increases their stress and susceptibility to heart attacks at this age. Or, if they sense they are in a dead-end job, they may switch jobs or careers.

Brad, a middle-aged banker, began selling cleaning supplies on the side to supplement his income as the kids approached college age. After his long-awaited promotion to a management position was denied, Brad decided to go into business for himself full-time. He worked extra hard to add new customers and expand his line of products. His wife, Ann, supported his decision and helped with the clerical work. "It was rough for the first few years," Brad said. "But now that we've built up the business, I'm happier than ever. There's nothing like being your own boss."

Women react to their midlife transitions somewhat differently than men, depending largely on whether their primary involvement has been in a career or the home. Professional women, who have considered but never had children, may realize the biological clock is running down and decide to have a child at this age. Single-mother adoptions also tend to increase at this age. The most common pattern is seen among women who married in their 20s. Their children are in school, and their husbands are working longer hours. Having spent much of their married lives caring for their husbands and children, these women often feel the need to fulfill themselves in other ways. Many women return to school at this age, take a job outside the home, or do both simultaneously.

Nina married soon after leaving high school and enjoyed being a wife and mother. But as her two children approached college age, she began rethinking what she wanted to do with her life. Initially, she joined a paramedic team and began taking one course each semester at the local community college. She quickly gained confidence in her ability to do the work in school and decided to fulfill her ambition to become a nurse. By the time her youngest son graduated from college, Nina received her 2-year degree and became a registered nurse. "I feel lucky," she said. "My husband has been supportive all the way. And I really enjoy nursing."

The Empty Nest

When the last child leaves home, some parents experience the empty nest syndrome. Fathers become tearful and sad. Mothers, especially those whose lives have been wrapped up in their children, may feel depressed and lost. Yet, such experiences are fast becoming the exception rather than the rule.

A study comparing working and nonworking mothers whose children had just left home or were in the process of doing so showed that almost all of them responded to the departure of their children with a decided sense of relief. While most women experienced temporary feelings of anxiety, disappointment, and sadness, these feelings were quickly superseded by an equally powerful need to turn attention to their own lives. Many women regarded this period as the exciting beginning of a new phase of their lives (Rubin, 1979).

Couples who enjoy a good relationship may find this a time for renewed companionship. Relieved from the economic burden of supporting their children, they may take up new interests, travel, and indulge in long-awaited luxuries. Many couples experience an increased marital happiness rivaling their honeymoon years (Rollins and Feldman, 1981).

Sexual Changes

The biological and psychological changes that accompany the loss of reproductive powers contribute significantly to the midlife transition in both sexes. While these changes pose new anxieties for men and women, they also present new opportunities for personal growth.

The most significant change in women is the menopause, or loss of a woman's child-bearing capacities. The menopause tends to occur in women sometime between 45 and 55 years of age. The physical effects vary from a certain degree of atrophy in the uterus, vagina, and breasts to a variety of bodily and emotional changes. Women vary widely in their experience of menopause. Some women find menopause mostly a negative experience, with adverse effects on their appearance and their phsyical, emotional, and sexual lives. Other women experience little or none of these effects. Some positive changes also occur during this period. The lessened fear of pregnancy often leads to increased sexual responsiveness for many women. Studies of women this age suggest that other events of middle adulthood, such as changes in the marriage relationship, freedom from childcare responsibilities, and return to work outside the home are usually more important to women than menopause itself (Notman, 1979).

Although men are not subject to a menopause, they do go through a male *climacteric*, defined technically as the loss of reproductive powers. There is a gradual reduction in fertile sperm, a diminution of testosterone resulting in less aggressive behavior, and reduced sexual vigor along with increasing impotency in some men. However, men tend to reach their climacteric 5 or 10 years later than women, and do so in a more gradual way, with fewer physiological consequences (Troll, 1975). The most significant effects are psychological. Men tend to feel they are losing their masculinity and react in a variety of ways. Some men feel depressed at the prospect of waning sexual vigor. They may become critical of their wives, wishing they had a younger, more sexually attractive partner. Sometimes men compensate by extra efforts at keeping fit and looking younger.

Couples in the empty nest stage usually experience increased marital happiness. (Laimute E. Druskis)

Perhaps the most common reaction is a last attempt to recapture youthful sexual fantasies by having an extramarital affair or marrying a younger wife, thus attempting to deny the aging process.

Men and women who take these changes in stride often find their lives even more satisfying than before. For one thing, the changes and anxieties of this period may make each individual more aware of their need for a spouse and the security of marriage. Nothing helps a man or woman through the turmoil of this stage as much as an understanding and supportive partner. Actually, there is a rise in marital happiness among many couples at this period, with individuals in their late 40s and 50s reporting levels of marital happiness surpassing couples in their 20s (Gould, 1978). The fact that men and women tend to become more like each other also brings each a new sense of freedom and "settling down" in sex and marriage. As Carl Jung said.

> The other sex has lost its magic power over us, for we have come to know its essential traits in the depths of our own psyche. We shall not easily "fall in love," for we can no longer lose ourselves in someone else, but we shall be capable of a deeper love, a conscious devotion to the other. (Jacobi, 1973, pp. 282-283)

LATE ADULTHOOD

What is it like to be old? For most of us, this may be hard to imagine. In an effort to see for herself, one young woman, with the help of a theatrical makeup artist, transformed herself into an 85-year-old woman. She altered the shape and texture of her face with a mask and makeup and tinted her hair gray. She inserted clouded lens into her eyes, taped her fingers together, and swathed herself in splints, bandages, and corsets to restrict her body movements. Then off and on for the next 3 years she experienced life as an old person. She discovered that old people don't fit into our society. Bottle caps are too hard to get off. The print on medicine labels is so small old people can't read it. During a period of turbulence on an airplane flight, the cabin attendant spilled coffee all over her, but pretended not to notice. Had the cabin attendant spilled coffee on a businessman's pants, it probably would have been a different story, wouldn't it? (Brown, 1985).

As most of us know, the number of people reaching late adulthood is rising rapidly. Today, about 26 million men and women, or 12 percent of the American population, are 65 years of age or older. By the year 2080, the elderly proportion of the population will almost double, making for an older and more diverse society. The "graying of America" will alter every aspect of society—business, education, government spending, housing, medicine, and leisure.

Physical and Cognitive Changes

As individuals get older, there is a progressive slowing down of all bodily processes. As a result, older people eat less, exercise less, and have less zest for life. They also sleep less restfully, though they spend more time in bed compensating for their lack of sleep. Their senses become less efficient, and difficulties in hearing and vision (especially in the dark) are common problems at this age. Older people also have more trouble maintaining their sense of balance. Deaths from falls occur twice as frequently as those from other accidents. Chronic diseases and deaths from all causes increase with age, with the greatest percentage of deaths resulting from heart and circulatory disorders.

Fortunately, with improved understanding of aging and the importance of health care and supportive environments for the elderly, we are discovering that older people can remain in reasonably good health and function better at the same age than their parents and grandparents did. We're also learning that many of the negative changes associated with aging are due to stress and disease rather than to the aging process itself. Senility, which is associated with symptoms such as impaired attention, memory loss, and disorientation in time or place, is actually a disease caused by damage to the brain's cells and affects only a small number of very old people.

Cognitive functions are also affected by the aging process, though rarely to the extent justifying the stereotype of the absent-minded old person. *Fluid intelligence*, which refers to those mental abilities most affected by aging of the ner-

Older adults function better at the same age than their parents and grandparents did. (Ken Karp, Sirovich Senior Center)

vous system, such as the speed of mental reactions and visualizing an old problem in new ways, does decline somewhat in middle age and more sharply in late adulthood. As a result, older people exhibit slower mental reactions and are often less adept in processing new information. But *crystallized intelligence*, which refers to those abilities most affected by learning, such as verbal skills and vocabulary usage, remains the same and in many instances continues to improve with age (Botwinick, 1978).

It is also thought that individuals can maintain their creativity well into late adulthood, depending on their type of work. Artists hit their peak in their 40s, scientists maintain their creativity well into their 60s, while those in the humanities (for example, historians and philosophers) may show a steady increase in creativity through their 70s. For example, Benjamin Franklin invented the bifocal lens at age 78, and Will and Ariel Durant continued working on their story of philosophy series well into their 80s. It just may be that the decreased creativity ordinarily seen among older people is due more to their restricted environments than to aging.

Personal and Social Adjustment

To see how people change with age, Bernice Neugarten (1977) interviewed 700 men and women over a 7-year period. These were people between the ages of 40 and 90 years of age who lived in homes and apartments (not institutions) in the Kansas City area. She found that as these people grew older, they exhibited both continuity and change in their personalities.

Their basic personality traits remained remarkably stable, with an accentuation of these traits increasing with age. For example, an overly dependent adult would probably become even more helpless as an old person. People's adaptive skills also remained stable, with those who were well-adjusted in earlier years continuing to cope more successfully with their surroundings than those who had been poorly adjusted.

There were also some important changes in personality with age. For one thing, men and women saw their respective sex roles reversed. Males were perceived as more submissive and females as more authoritative. A second change was a marked tendency toward a more interior orientation. Older people saw their environments as more complex and dangerous and tended to focus more on their inner feelings and interests. Another related change was a shift in coping style, from active to passive mastery, with individuals conforming rather than attempting to change their environments to meet their needs.

Another area of change has to do with the presence of family and friends. Although the majority of older people in the United States have living children, only about one in eight of them lives with a grown child. The major reason is the mutual desire for independence and privacy among older people and their children. At the same time, many older people live near a grown child and visit frequently. Elderly parents can assist their grown children with child care, while

Alzheimer's Disease

Picture a competent, energetic high school teacher and coach in his late 50s. He's one of the most popular teachers in school. His students as well as his sons have won scholarships at well-known universities. He's a devoted husband who enjoys a well-rounded life, including fishing, skiing, and sailing. Now imagine this same person 4 years later. He's alternately cranky, angry, and jealous. He's constantly misplacing things. He can't remember what he had for breakfast, though he can tell you the batting average of famous baseball players 20 years ago. His incompetency finally costs him his job. His wife and sons feel frustrated and helpless. And his friends now avoid him.

This man has Alzheimer's disease, a form of dementia (mental deterioration) brought on by pathological changes in the brain tissue. Although Alzheimer's disease can begin as early as 40, it is more common after 65 years of age and among women than men. Unfortunately, Alzheimer's disease is incurable with a progressive deterioration of the mind until death. If the onset is after 65, the average duration of symptoms from onset to death is about 5 years. Up to 4 percent of the population of those 65 and older is estimated to have Alzheimer's disease (DSM-III, 1980).

Patients with Alzheimer's disease may be cared for at home during most of the course of the illness, depending on the cooperation of family members and the resources available to them. Such help would include informing family members about the disorder, suggesting how they can deal with this type of patient, and providing counseling and support for the family. Yet, most patients with Alzheimer's disease eventually require custodial care in a nursing home (Bootzin and Acocella, 1984).

the latter can help their parents with finances and emotional support in times of illness.

Because most married women will outlive their husbands, there are more widows than widowers among the elderly. More than half the women in the United States are widowed by their early 60s; 80 percent are widowed by their early 70s. Among those over 65, widows outnumber widowers four to one. Yet women tend to adjust to the loss of their spouse more readily than men. Although widowers are usually better off financially than widows, they tend to have more difficulty coping with routine household tasks, feel lonelier, and are less happy than widows (Barrett, 1978). People who have remained single throughout their lives often feel more satisfied in late adulthood than do widows or widowers the same age, possibly because they have chosen a single lifestyle and become better adjusted to it.

Women often have an easier time making and keeping friends in their old age, partly because of the way they have been socialized and the disproportionate number of older women. Yet, with the reduction of social contacts at this age, friends become even more important to both sexes. People who continue to live in the same neighborhood as they get older, an increasing phenomenon, may keep in touch with their friends from the past. Those who move elsewhere to retire must make new friends. According to several studies, friends play an even more important role than relatives in preventing loneliness among the elderly (Perlman, Gerson, and Spinner, 1978). Perhaps this is why some people, in order to have more friends the same age, prefer to live in a retirement home or community.

Retirement

When Congress extended the retirement age from 65 to 70 in business and industry, some executives worried that corporate mobility would be slowed. But such fears have not materialized. Most workers continue to retire in their mid-sixties, with a trend toward retirement at even earlier ages (Turner and Helms, 1983).

The retirement experience, which varies considerably from one person to another, usually depends on several factors. First and foremost is the person's attitude toward retirement. The more voluntary the retirement, the better the adjustment during retirement. Second, having reasonably good health is also an important predictor for a satisfying retirement, with many retired people's complaints related to poor health (Kimmel, Price, and Walker, 1978). Third, an adequate income is also very important at this age. Yet, it is the "perceived adequacy" of one's income that is the most crucial factor. Although retired people usually have a reduced income, they also have fewer major expenses, such that their income may be sufficient for their present lifestyle. At the same time, people from upper-level careers generally report a more favorable retirement experience, partly because they have ample income (Bengston, Kasschau, and Ragan, 1977).

Being in good health helps to make retirement more enjoyable. (Laimute E. Druskis)

The majority of people grow old and retire in place. Most remain in the same house. Even those who move tend to remain in the same community. Only a small number of retired people move to a warmer climate (Neugarten and Hall, 1980). Furthermore, only a small proportion of the aged, about 5 percent, move into some type of institution. Women are especially likely to be institutionalized because they live longer than men. Also, women who have never married and lack a family may be forced to move into a retirement or nursing home (Palmore, 1976). Because old people who are institutionalized may become more dependent on others, and suffer loss of morale, there is a movement to provide better services for the elderly in the community. Arrangements such as daycare centers, visitation by volunteers, and local retirement communities enable older people to take care of themselves as long as possible.

Phases of Retirement

Robert Atchley views retirement as a process and social role that unfolds through six phases as shown below. Because the retirement experience varies widely among individuals, it's impossible to assign ages to these phases. Also, individuals do not necessarily experience all these phases or in the given order.

The preretirement phase can be subdivided into two substages: a remote phase, in which retirement is seen as a remote event, and a near phase, which emerges as workers become more aware of their approaching retirement. The honeymoon phase, immediately following the retirement event, is frequently a busy, happy time spent in activities such as traveling and visiting family members. Eventually, this period is followed by the disenchantment phase, in which the eagerly anticipated retirement activities may have lost their original appeal. This ushers in the reorientation phase when the retired person develops a more realistic view of retirement, including opportunities of involvement, often with the assistance of community groups. The stability phase does not imply the absence of change as much as the mastery of the retirement role, with individuals realizing what is expected of them as well as their strengths and weaknesses. Although death may occur at any time, the termination phase is often occasioned by the disability that accompanies old age. When people are no longer able to care for themselves, they take on the role of the sick and disabled.

Preretirement phase		Honeymoon phase	Disenchantment phase	Reorientation phase	Stability phase	Termination phase
remote	near					

PRERETIREMENT	RETIREMENT	
RETIREMENT EVENT		END OF RETIREMENT EVENT

Source: R. C. Atchley, *The Sociology of Retirement* (Cambridge, MA: Schenkman Publishing Company, 1976).

As the population of older adults swells, there is increasing concern for a more humane policy toward the elderly. Individuals from a variety of fields—academia, business, government, and medicine—have begun discussing key issues such as the importance of preretirement planning, alternative work patterns for the elderly (such as part-time or slower-paced jobs), and phased-in retirement (Gonda, 1981). There is a growing realization that as more and more older adults view their later years as productive and satisfying, everyone in society will benefit.

Successful Aging

Which person does a better job of growing old gracefully—the individual who continues to work actively as a lawyer and keeps up an active social life, or the person who retires to a rocking chair on the porch? Authorities who favor the activity theory of aging suggest that the more active a person remains, the more satisfied and better adjusted that person is likely to be, regardless of age. Those who adhere to the disengagement theory of aging point out that individuals tend to disengage from society with advancing age, with psychological disengagement usually preceding social withdrawal by about 10 years.

Actually, there is no single way to age successfully, with different people adapting to old age in their own way. Bernice Neugarten (1977) found that each person tends to select a style of aging that best suits his or her personality, needs, and interests. Thus, an energetic, hard-working person will continue to tackle new projects with age, while a more contemplative person will probably do more reading. Yet Neugarten found that some older people tend to benefit from activity more than others. For example, while those with a well-integrated personality generally adjusted better to old age regardless of how active they were, the less well-integrated exhibited better adjustment with higher levels of activity.

It's also important for individuals to have an inner satisfaction with their lives as they grow older. According to Erikson (1968), the developmental task of older people is to establish a sense of integrity—a sense that one's life as a whole has been meaningful and satisfying. Those who have experienced a great deal of frustration and suffering may have more misgivings than satisfactions, experiencing despair and depression. Actually, people ordinarily experience both ego integrity and despair, but the healthier the person, the more self-acceptance and satisfaction will prevail.

Older people get a sense of their lives as a whole through engaging in the *life review*—a naturally occurring process prompted by the realization that life is approaching an end (Butler, 1975). Although such a process potentially leads to wisdom and serenity in the aged, it may also evoke some negative aspects, such as regret, anger, guilt, depression, or obsessional rumination about past events. The process consists of reminiscence, thinking about one's self, reconsideration of past events and their meanings, along with mirror gazing. For example, a passing glance in the mirror may remind old people of the obvious—that they are getting older. Some older people may prefer to review their lives privately, while others may enjoy doing it more externally, such as by making a family tree or telling their children and grandchildren about the significant aspects of their family history. Such reminiscing serves to provide them with a final perspective of their lives, while leaving a record of the past to their family and friends.

Summary

Early Adulthood

1. We began the chapter by noting that the transition to adulthood is more prolonged than ordinarily understood, especially for affluent young people whose lengthy education postpones financial independence.

2. Leaving home has to do with autonomous decision making and differentiation from one's parents as well as moving out of the family home, with going away to college a natural transition for many people this age.

3. Although men tend to be preoccupied with preparing for their career during this period, women tend to follow a more varied pattern in combining work and marriage.

4. Intimate relationships are very important to men and women at this age, with couples in which both partners put their relationship first the happiest of all.

5. Couples are giving more thought to whether they want children, and if so, when to have them. Many couples are waiting until their late 20s or early 30s to have their first child.

Middle Adulthood

6. Sometime between the late 30s and the early 40s, people experience the midlife transition, a time of personal evaluation that comes with the realization one's life is half over.

7. The most obvious signs of middle age are certain physical changes such as graying hair and slower mental reactions, though practical problem-solving skills may remain at a high level, depending on use.

8. This period of life often brings changes in careers for both sexes, with many men changing jobs or careers to fulfill their aspirations, and many women taking a job outside the home or returning to school.

9. The biological and psychological changes that accompany the loss of reproductive powers pose new anxieties and new opportunities for both sexes, with men and women experiencing a new stability in their marriages as they enter their 50s.

Late Adulthood

10. About 26 million men and women, or 12 percent of the American population, are now 65 years of age or older.

11. As people get older, there is a progressive slowing down of all bodily functions. Yet, crystallized intelligence, or those cognitive functions that depend mostly on learning, may continue to improve with age.

12. People's basic adaptive abilities tend to remain remarkably stable throughout adulthood, with an accentuation of one's personal traits increasing with age.

13. Adjustment and satisfaction in retirement depend on a variety of factors, such as one's attitude toward retirement, health, income, and involvement in meaningful activities.

14. There is no single way to age successfully, with each individual adapting to old age in his or her own way.

Self-test

1. The major developmental tasks of early adulthood include:

    a. preparing for a career
    b. leaving home

    c. starting a family
    d. all of the above

2. The young adult's leaving home refers to:

    a. moving out of the family home
    b. becoming financially less dependent on parents

    c. assuming new roles and responsibilities
    d. all of the above.

3. Young adults with a firm sense of identity enjoy more satisfying close relationships with their peers than those whose identity is less developed, according to:

    a. Daniel Levinson
    b. Erik Erikson

    c. Bernice Neugarten
    d. Robert Butler

4. Today, many married couples are:

    a. having more children
    b. having only girl babies

    c. starting their families later
    d. starting their families earlier

5. A time of personal evaluation that comes with the realization one's life is half over is the:

    a. midlife transition
    b. senior citizen's crisis

    c. empty nest syndrome
    d. retirement blues

6. The most obvious signs of middle age are:

    a. declines in vocabulary usage
    b. memory losses

    c. physical changes in appearance
    d. more colds and allergies

7. Couples in the empty nest stage of marriage often find this a time of:

    a. great anxiety
    b. regret

    c. renewed companionship
    d. sadness

8. A disease caused by damage to the brain cells that affects only a small number of very old people is:

    a. senility
    b. depression

    c. advanced old age
    d. aging

9. The majority of people grow old and retire in:

    a. an adult community   **c.** a warmer climate

    b. a nursing home   **d.** their same home

10. A naturally occurring process that comes with the realization one's life is approaching an end is:

    a. midlife crisis   **c.** life review

    b. senile psychosis   **d.** belief in an afterlife

Exercises

1. *How have you grown as an adult?* Write a brief paragraph describing your personal developments since adolescence. In what ways has your personality changed or remained the same? Comment on the factors that have contributed to your personal growth, such as success at school, disappointment in love, or new responsibilities at work.

2. *Leaving home.* Describe your experience in "leaving home." If you're already living on your own, how peaceful or stormy was your departure? If you're still living at home or are away at college part of the year, how well are you coming to terms with this developmental task? How helpful are your parents in this matter?

3. *Mentors.* List all the people who've influenced your career development from your high school years and up. Have any of these people served as your mentor, that is, encouraged or sponsored your career? What effect has this person had on your career?

4. *The midlife transition.* If you're going through the midlife transition or have completed this stage, write a page or so describing your experience. To what extent has this been a stressful time or "crisis" for you? In what ways have you reevaluated your life situation and grown as a person?

5. *Widows and widowers.* Select an older person you know well who has outlived his or her spouse, including yourself if this applies to you, and comment on how well this person has adjusted to living alone. What have been the most difficult adjustments? Has the experience of loss also brought about personal growth?

6. *Successful aging.* Select someone in your family who has reached late adulthood, such as an aunt, uncle, or grandparent. Then comment on how successfully this person has aged. To what extent has the person kept active or become disengaged from his or her environment? Has this person also grown old in his or her own distinctive way? How has your relationship with this person affected your understanding of aging?

Questions for Self-reflection

1. In what ways have you mellowed with age and experience?

2. Would you agree that "leaving home" involves more than moving out of the family home?

3. What were your parents like at your age?

4. At what stage of adulthood are you now?

5. Are you aware that the midlife transition doesn't have to be a crisis?

6. Do you realize that people in middle and late adulthood are more active for their age than in the past?

7. What kind of old people were you familiar with as a child?

8. What would you like to do when you retire?

9. Are you aware that our personal traits become more pronounced with age?

10. What do you think you'll be like at age 70?

Recommended Readings

Aslanian, Carol B., and Henry M. Brickell. *Americans in Transition.* New York: College Entrance Examination Board, 1980. A fresh look at adult education, showing how a variety of life transitions and events triggers learning and development throughout adulthood.

Comfort, Alex A. *A Good Age.* New York: Simon & Schuster, 1978 (paperback). A famous gerontologist provides factual understanding as well as advice for those who wish to lead an active and meaningful life well into late adulthood.

Jones, R. *The Other Generation.* Englewood Cliffs, NJ: Prentice-Hall, 1977. A book about the growing number of older people in the United States and the impact they are likely to have on our society.

Levinson, Daniel J. *The Seasons of a Man's Life.* New York: Ballantine, 1979 (paperback). An overview of adult development, based on the lives of the men in Levinson's longitudinal study of early and middle adulthood.

Rubin, Lillian B. *Women of a Certain Age.* New York: Harper & Row, 1979. A look at how women are meeting the challenges of the middle years in a way that dispels many of the myths associated with this period.

Skinner, B. F., and M. E. Vaughan. *Enjoy Old Age.* New York: W. W. Norton & Company, 1983. A highly readable book full of insights and timely suggestions for enjoying old age.

16 Death and Bereavement

Although children are curious about death, adults often avoid discussing the subject because of their own negative attitudes toward death. One young mother became acutely aware of this while reading a story to her 5-year-old daughter. Turning the page, the mother spotted a passage about a little boy discovering his pet cat dead. Initially she felt panic and thought of protecting her daughter from the words about death. But after a short hesitation, she read aloud, "The cat was dead when John found it. Its eyes were closed, and there was no heart beating. That's how they knew the cat was dead. John became very sad when told he would not have his cat to play with anymore." Surprisingly, the little girl treated the story in a matter-of-fact way and seemed to learn something about life and death. The mother also came to a new realization, namely, how much she herself had been influenced by our society's death-denying attitudes.

DEATH AND DYING

In many ways, our attitudes toward death reflect our attitudes toward life. Where life is hard and short, death becomes a familiar fact of life and is faced openly and directly. In the remote villages of Africa it is not uncommon for mothers to lose as many children to malnutrition and disease as those who survive into adulthood. Daily contact with old people and the presence of dying persons in the home help to prepare the young for the fact of death and how to deal with it. By contrast, in the affluent nations, where infant mortality is low and chronic diseases are postponed into old age, death has become less of a reality. It is not uncommon for people in the United States to reach maturity without ever having seen someone die (Foster and Anderson, 1978). Instead, the prospect of death, like aging itself, seems so remote that it doesn't have much relevance. Death tends to be avoided, glossed over, and joked about—in short, denied.

Fortunately, the taboo against death is lessening, partly because of greater openness toward many aspects of life that were traditionally repressed, like divorce and homosexuality. As a result, there is greater social recognition of death as a natural part of life. Books, classes, seminars, and journals all help to give us a better understanding of death. There's also a new concern for a variety of issues that ensure people may die with dignity, as we'll discuss later in the chapter. But let's begin by taking a look at the awareness of death and the experience of dying in our society.

Awareness of Death

How often do you think about your own death? If your reply is, "once in a while," you've got a lot of company. When 30,000 people, representing a cross-section of all ages, were asked this question, over half of them said, "occasionally." Fewer than one-fourth of them said, "frequently" or "very frequently." An equal number of people claimed they rarely had thoughts about their own death. When asked how they felt about dying, most people said it made them feel glad to be alive and resolved to make the most of life. However, about one-third of the respondents said the idea of their own death made them feel fearful or depressed. People in their late 20s were the most fearful of all (Shneidman, 1973).

As individuals reach late adulthood, they think about death more often and talk more openly about it than young adults (Kalish and Reynolds, 1976). The increase in chronic illnesses and the death of close friends at this age are all reminders that death is the natural end of life. Yet, older people are usually less fearful of death than other age groups. After all, they've already lived a reasonably long life and may have less to look forward to. Also, those with a deep religious faith, including a belief in some kind of afterlife, are generally less fearful of death. The strong association between a positive attitude toward death and belief in the afterlife suggests that such a belief provides an important mechanism for dealing with the anxieties of aging and death (Dempsey, 1975). When an elderly woman was asked if she feared death, she replied, "I'm more worried about ending up in a nursing home and becoming a burden to my children than I am of dying. I've made my peace with death."

The thought of our own death is so frightening we have difficulty facing it realistically. In one study, students were given actuarial tables on life expectancies and asked to estimate how long they expected to live. Most students estimated that they would live 10 to 20 years longer than their projected ages. When asked to explain why, typical remarks were "It won't happen to me," "I'm not like other people," and "I'm unique" (Snyder, 1980). Such a denial of death also results in a great deal of misunderstanding about the actual risks of death from various causes. Generally, we overestimate the frequency of death from sensational causes such as accidents and homicides. At the same time, we tend to underestimate the risk of death from nonspectacular causes that claim one victim at a time, like heart attacks, strokes, and diabetes. Such misjudgment has to do partly with our tendency to judge an event as likely to occur if we can easily imagine or recall it—which is further compounded by the mass media's practice of reporting dramatic events such as accidents and homicides. For example, newspapers carry about three times as many articles about death from homicide as about death from diseases. But the latter take a hundred times more lives than homicide. We also tend to underestimate the risk of death from familiar hazards such as driving a car, smoking, and x-rays. Yet, these are the very things over which each of us has a great deal of control (Slovic, Fischoff, and Lichtenstein, 1980).

Near-death Experiences

Suppose you're knocked unconscious in an automobile accident and taken to the hospital. Critically injured, you're put on a life-support system that keeps you alive. After a couple of days you regain consciousness, only to discover you almost died. There's also a good chance you've had a near-death experience—the distinctive state of recall associated with being brought back to life from the verge of death.

Psychiatrist Raymond Moody (1977) found that various accounts of such experiences show striking similarities. Initially, individuals experience a detachment from their bodies and being pulled through a dark tunnel. Then, they find themselves in another kind of "spiritual body," in which physical objects present no barrier and movement from one place to another is almost instantaneous. While in this state they may experience a reunion with long-lost friends and loved ones. One of the most incredible elements is the appearance of a brilliant light, perceived as a warm, loving "being of light," which fosters a kind of life-review, but in a nonjudgmental way. Finally, people report being drawn back through the dark tunnel and experiencing a rapid reentry into their bod-

Table 16–1.   HOW LONG WILL YOU LIVE?   The life-expectancy quiz below is one of many health questionnaires now being used by medical centers and insurance companies. Such quizzes, while hardly precise, may nevertheless give a more realistic picture of probable longevity than the old-fashioned actuarial tables based on the individual's hereditary patterns and medical history. Current questionnaires try to measure risk in relation to the person's lifestyle, stress, and environment.
Start with the number 73. This is based on an overall average of life spans: 71.6 for white males, 67.1 for black males; 78.8 for white females, 75.3 for black females.

Personal Facts:
If you are male, **subtract 3.**
If female, **add 4.**
If you live in an urban area with a population over 2 million, **subtract 2.**
If you live in a town under 10,000 or on a farm, **add 2.**
If any grandparent lived to 85, **add 2.**
If all four grandparents lived to 80, **add 6.**
If either parent died of a stroke or heart attack before the age of 50, **subtract 4.**
If any parent, brother or sister under 50 has (or had) cancer or a heart condition, or has had diabetes since childhood, **subtract 3.**
Do you earn over $50,000 a year? **Subtract 2.**
If you finished college, **add 1.** If you have a graduate or professional degreee, **add 2 more.**
If you are 65 or over and still working, **add 3.**
If you live with a spouse or friend, **add 5.** If not, **subtract 1** for every ten years alone since age 25.

Running Total ☐

Lifestyle Status:
If you work behind a desk, **subtract 3.**
If your work requires regular, heavy physical labor, **add 3.**
If you exercise strenuously (tennis, running, swimming, etc.) five times a week for at least a half-hour, **add 4.** Two or three times a week, **add 2.**

Do you sleep more than ten hours each night? **Subtract 4.**
Are you intense, aggressive, easily angered? **Subtract 3.**
Are you easygoing and relaxed? **Add 3.**
Are you happy? **Add 1.** Unhappy? **Subtract 2.**
Have you had a speeding ticket in the past year? **Subtract 1.**
Do you smoke more than two packs a day? **Subtract 8.** One to two packs? **Subtract 6.** One-half to one? **Subtract 3.**
Do you drink the equivalent of $1\frac{1}{2}$ oz. of liquor a day? **Subtract 1.**
Are you overweight by 50 lbs or more? **Subtract 8.** By 30 to 50 lbs.? **Subtract 4.** By 10 to 30 pounds? **Subtract 2.**
If you are a man over 40 and have annual checkups, **add 2.**
If you are a woman and see a gynecologist once a year, **add 2.**

Running Total ☐

Age Adjustment:
If you are between 30 and 40, **add 2.**
If you are between 40 and 50, **add 3.**
If you are between 50 and 70, **add 4.**
If you are over 70, **add 5.**

**ADD UP YOUR SCORE
TO GET YOUR LIFE EXPECTANCY.**   ☐

Source: Robert F. Allen and Shirley Linde, *Lifegain* (Morristown, NJ: Human Resources Institute, 1981).

ies. For most people, the near-death experience brings a profound change in attitudes. They not only become less fearful of death, but they are more concerned with learning and loving and valuing the life they have.

Cardiologist Michael Sabom (1981), using a random sample of patients who had suffered near-fatal medical crises, found that 40 percent of them had vivid memories of their brush with death. He too was struck with the uniformity of the patients's accounts. But Sabom found no religious similarities among people who reported such experiences. Atheists and church-goers were equally likely to report them. Nor were there any similarities in regard to education, race, or occupation among people reporting such experiences. Curiously,

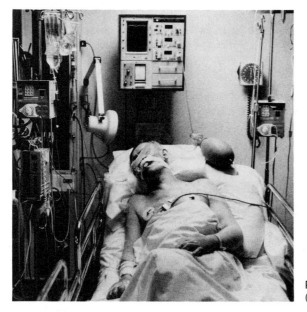

Patient in the intensive care unit.
(Ken Karp)

though, women with near-death experiences were more likely to recall seeing their loved ones.

People have made a variety of claims about such experiences, including that they are mystical or peak experiences or glimpses of the afterlife. Some researchers believe these experiences are little more than hallucinations brought on either by the patient's physical condition or intense emotions aroused by the nearness of death. While Sabom personally believes in life after death, he readily admits his work does not prove it. He does, however, believe that such experiences suggest dying brings about a splitting apart of the non-physical part of our being from our bodies, but feels that we still have much to learn about his.

The Experience of Dying

Now that people are likely to die in a hospital, often sedated and isolated from all but their immediate family and hospital personnel, the experience of death has become something of a mystery for the average person. Many people have never been in the presence of someone who is dying. Even people who have sat with a loved one or friend who is dying have only a limited awareness of the dying person's inner world or how to communicate with that person. For those who are heavily sedated, perhaps the final moments are meaningless, if they are aware at all. But some people with a terminal illness remain alert right up to the end and have expressed their thoughts and feelings about dying, giving us a more accurate understanding of it.

One of the best-known pioneers in this field is Elisabeth Kübler-Ross. She and her colleagues have interviewed more than 500 terminally ill people at the University of Chicago hospital. She also started a course on the dynamics of death and dying. Dr. Kübler-Ross (1975) has found that even when patients were not told of the seriousness of their illness, they usually sensed that fact as well as the approximate time of their death. Hence, there is a growing realization that when persons indicate a willingness to know the truth about their impending death, it may be wiser to share the relevant knowledge than to protect these patients with a conspiracy of concealment. How this knowledge is shared becomes more important than the particular facts communicated. Furthermore, dying people have benefited from the opportunity to face death openly, with the opportunity to talk about it removing much of the fear of death, the sense of isolation, and the mystery of dying.

Dr. Kübler-Ross noted that individuals tend to go through several stages in dying, even though there is considerable overlap between these stages. The first stage consists of a *denial* of death, with people characteristically feeling "No, not me." Such denial protects one against the deep emotions associated with death and provides time to cope with the disturbing facts. Later, individuals tend to show small signs that they are now willing to talk about it. But at this stage a friend or a professional should talk about it only for a few minutes at a time, allowing the dying person time to make the needed adjustment. In the second stage, denial eventually gives way to the emotions of *anger* and *resentment*. "Why me?" people ask. The sight of others enjoying their health evokes the emotions of envy, jealousy, and anger. They often take their feelings out on those closest to them, but mostly because of what these people represent—life and health. Consequently, it is important for those nearby not to take these remarks personally, but rather to help the dying person express his or her feelings.

The third stage characteristically consists of attempts to *bargain* for time. Individuals at this stage often say, "I know I'm dying *but* ..." And then they indulge in a bit of magic, thinking, "If I cooperate with the doctor or my family, maybe God will let me live till my daughter graduates or my son gets married." When individuals tend to drop the "but" and admit "Yes, I'm dying," they enter the fourth stage of *depression*. In a sense this is a natural response to the threat of losing one's life, and it is very important to allow persons to grieve and express their feelings of sadness. One of the worst things a friend can do is deny these feelings and say "Cheer up." This is why it is so important for family and friends as well as professionals to learn to accept their own feelings about death so that they can help dying people accept their own impending death without dwelling on it unduly.

The final stage is the *acceptance* of death, though not all dying persons reach this stage. By this time, most people who are dying have pretty much disengaged themselves from others and ask for fewer visitors. But they don't want to die alone, which is why most people prefer to die at home, though they are more likely to die in a hospital. In fact, much of the pain of dying comes from the mental anguish, especially the fear of being separated from loved ones.

Table 16–2. THE THREE LEADING CAUSES OF DEATH BY AGE GROUP AND SEX IN THE UNITED STATES.   Statistics are for the year 1977.

Age		*1*		*2*		*3*	
All Ages	M	Heart disease	396,431	Cancer	210,459	C-V* disease	77,351
	F	Heart disease	322,294	Cancer	176,227	C-V disease	104,583
1–14	M	Accidents	6,275	Cancer	1,407	Congenital anomalies	902
	F	Accidents	3,327	Cancer	957	Congenital anomalies	840
15–34	M	Accidents	31,881	Suicide	8,826	Homicide	8,358
	F	Accidents	8,331	Cancer	3,454	Suicide	2,566
35–54	M	Heart disease	43,592	Cancer	26,646	Accidents	13,660
	F	Cancer	27,972	Heart disease	13,338	C-V disease	4,759
55–74	M	Heart disease	191,458	Cancer	117,884	C-V disease	28,585
	F	Heart disease	99,105	Cancer	87,555	C-V disease	25,531
75+	M	Heart disease	157,986	Cancer	60,417	C-V disease	43,064
	F	Heart disease	107,990	C-V disease	73,663	Cancer	56,222

*C-V = cardiovascular.

Source: Stanley L. Robbins, M.D., Marcia Angell, M.D., and Vinay Kumar, M.D. (eds). *Basic Pathology*, 3rd ed. (Philadelphia: W. B. Saunders Company, 1981).

Unfortunately, the popularization of Elisabeth Kübler-Ross's views has resulted in a stereotyped view of the experience of dying as a fixed, inevitable process, which it is not. Elisabeth Kübler-Ross was the first to point out that many people do not follow these stages. For some, anger remains the dominant mood throughout, while others are depressed until the end. Furthermore, Robert Kastenbaum (1981) points out that Kübler-Ross's theory does not account for the nature of the various diseases and types of deaths, age and sex differences, personality and cognitive styles, and cultural backgrounds. Accordingly, he has found that individual differences are more prominent in the experience of dying than are any stages.

Dying the Way You Live

You may recall from the chapter on adult life stages that each person's uniqueness becomes accentuated in old age. As a result, there is a tendency for people to die the same way they have lived. For a hostile, belligerent person who has lashed out at others throughout life, the dominant mood in the face of death may be anger and blame. Such a person may blame herself, her spouse, the doctor, or even God. On the other hand, for a passive, long-suffering person who has derived a lot of attention from being sick, the dominant mood in the face of death may be despair and depression, with a drawn-out illness requiring months of special care in a nursing home.

One of the most common reactions to death is seen among those with a strong will to live. Even when they are suffering from a physical illness, such people tend to live without the use of machines longer than predicted by medical diagnosis. Yet, when such people are themselves convinced that their time has come, they face death with equal deliberation. An example would by the 86-year-old widow, who despite her good health felt her time was near, consulted her lawyer, sold her house, and within a week was dead. Another common reaction is seen among those who have always coped with stress by denying it. Such persons tend to give only a passing acknowledgment to their impending death without altering the daily routine. For them, death comes as an annoying interruption in a life they live as long as possible.

Psychiatrist Edwin Shneidman (1973) tells of his investigations among elderly people suffering from terminal illnesses who with unexpected energy have ended their lives in a manner similar to the way in which they have lived. Such patients have succeeded in taking out their tubes and needles, climbing over the bed rails, opening heavy windows, and throwing themselves to the ground below. When their past lives were examined, these people had one thing in common—they had never been fired; they had always quit first.

The author recalls a rugged self-made man who for years had enjoyed his wealth by overindulging himself in food, alcohol, and sex. When informed by his physician that he must eat less and stop smoking, drinking, and running around, this man chose to continue his indulgent way of life. Within 4 years he was dead at the age of 48. In his own words, he had "died with his boots on."

BEREAVEMENT AND GRIEF

To lose a loved one or friend through death is to lose part of ourselves. It's a very painful experience labeled variously as bereavement, grief, or mourning. *Bereavement* ("to be deprived of") is the general term for the overall experience of loss. *Grief* refers to the intense emotional suffering that accompanies our experience of loss, and *mourning* refers to the outward expressions of bereavement and grief.

Because death is one of the universal rites of passage, most societies have mourning customs to facilitate the experience of grief. Until recently, widows dressed in black and widowers wore black armbands. Such dress excused any show of grief on the part of the bereaved and afforded them an opportunity to talk about their loss and to receive the needed sympathy. However, many of these customs have been modified or given up in recent years. Wakes and visitations have been replaced by brief funerals and memorial services. Ordinarily, the bereaved are expected to resume their usual dress and activities as soon as possible.

Grief Work

Our modern customs sometimes get in the way of "grief work"—the healthy process of working through our emotions associated with loss. Grief work consists of freeing ourselves emotionally from the deceased, readjusting to life without that person, resuming ordinary activities, and forming new relationships. The grief process parallels the experience of dying and involves many of the same emotions.

Initially, we react to a person's death with a sense of shock and disbelief, especially when death occurs unexpectedly. When we've been anticipating a person's death, as in the case of someone who is terminally ill, our initial response may be subdued accompanied by a sense of relief. After the initial shock wears off, we're likely to be bothered by memories of the deceased. We may not feel like socializing with our friends, especially in activities that remind us of the deceased. Negative emotions such as anger and guilt are likely to surface at this stage. We may blame God, fate, or those who've been taking care of the deceased. It's not uncommon to blame the deceased person for having abandoned us, especially if that person committed suicide. Also, we may have feelings of guilt because of something we said or did or feel we should have done while the person was still with us. Yet, some of our guilt may be "survivor's guilt," that is, feeling guilty simply because we're still alive and the other person is not.

The emotional intensity of grief often appears in the disguise of physical symptoms, especially among older adults. In the early months of bereavement, the most common symptoms of grief are crying, depressed feelings, lack of appetite, and difficulties concentrating at work or at home. Many people rely on sleeping pills and tranquilizers at some point during their bereavement. However, an understanding family physician may realize that such symptoms are a normal part of the grief process.

In the final stage of grief, we've come to terms with our loss and have resumed ordinary activities. This may occur anytime from a few months to a year or more after the initial loss, depending on how close we were to the person and the circumstances surrounding this person's death. From this time on, we're likely to recall the deceased person with pleasant memories. In some ways we never fully get over the death of a loved one, such as a parent, child, or spouse. But the more fully we work through our grief, the more likely we'll be able to get on with our lives. People who are unable to do so may delay the grief process.

Unresolved Grief

Unresolved grief may assume a variety of forms, from unexplained physical complaints to psychological symptoms. In some instances, the psychological reactions are obviously related to the loss. For example, some people can't bring themselves to return to the house, hospital, or room where a patient has died

Saying Goodbye

The two women were very similar. Both were in their late 50s and had grown children. Also, both of them had recently lost their husbands through death. Yet, they were quite different in one important way. One woman was devastated and felt sorry for herself. The other woman, though sad, began building a new life for herself, filling her days with friends and activities. The second woman had learned how to say goodbye.

Actually, life is a series of separations, with death the most significant goodbye of all. Parents who can comfortably say goodbye when their kids go off to school and college or get married are better prepared to survive the death of a loved one. Those who handle separation best have a firm sense of self-identity and other interests and don't think of themselves solely in terms of their roles as parents or spouse. By the time their children reach their 20s, healthy parents learn how to "let go." Similarly, a healthy spouse is able to say, "I can make it on my own if I have to."

How have you handled separations, such as leaving home or breaking up with a friend or spouse? Have you learned how to say goodbye?

because of unresolved grief. In other cases, unresolved grief may be more disguised. One woman complained that when her father died, she had not really experienced any grief. She recalls that she never cried, nor experienced the usual grief reactions. Much of the reason for this was found to be that she was left out of the family bereavement process. No one in the family had talked to her about her father's death. She had not been allowed to accompany them when they attended the funeral or burial afterwards. Years later, this woman discovered that much of her resentment toward her mother and her apprehensiveness over her husband's traveling were related to unresolved grief over her father's death. As she expressed the pentup tears and anger over her father's death, she gradually worked out her grief, which resulted in more satisfying relationships with her mother and husband.

People who live alone, especially those without close friends, are the most likely to have difficulty working through their grief. Studies have shown that such people are more prone to a variety of illnesses, such as heart disease, strokes, cirrhosis of the liver, hypertension, and cancer, as well as premature death. For example, heart disease, depending on the age of the individual, is anywhere from two to five times higher among the divorced, single, and widowed than among married people (Lynch, 1979). Men are especially likely to die within a few years after the death of their spouse. Yet, women's chances of dying are almost unaffected by their husband's death. Although there is little difference in the death rates between people who have lost a spouse in the past year and married people the same age, in the ensuing years widowed men suffer a much greater mortality rate than their married counterparts. Widowed men between the ages of 55 and 65 die at a 60 percent higher rate than married men the same age. The most likely explanation is that the quality of life changes more drastically for men than women, possibly because of their greater reliance

Widowed men are more apt to die than married men the same age. (Ken Karp, Sirovich Senior Center)

on wives for their emotional and daily needs. Women tend to have a better support system for coping with their grief. Yet, when widowers remarry, they have an even lower mortality rate than their married counterparts who have never lost a spouse (Helsing, Szklo, and Comstock, 1981).

Good Grief

So far, we've seen that it is better to go through the full experience of bereavement, however painful it may be, than to get over it too quickly. But there are also more positive aspects of grief. That is, grief may be a learning experience that helps us grow. It is sometimes said that we don't fully appreciate something until we have lost it, which is especially applicable to human relationships. While people are still with us, we often have ambivalent feelings toward them. One moment we love them, another we don't. In retrospect, however, grief helps us appreciate loved ones and friends more fully despite their shortcomings. Grief also helps us value our relationships with those still living. In short, good grief means that we have learned and grown in our bereavement.

There are several ways to make the experience of bereavement more effective: talking it out, feeling it out, and acting it out. Even though it may be very difficult to talk about the death of a loved one for the first several weeks, this is the time when talking it out can be most helpful. The main thing to remember is that the focus is on the feelings of the bereaved. Some things may sound trivial or hollow, such as "at least he is out of his misery," but whatever it takes, a friend should attempt to listen and help the bereaved person to talk out his or her feelings as much as possible.

Encouraging the bereaved to express their feelings may also be cathartic. People tend to feel less embarrassment when they can do this in the company of a few close friends, especially those who consider themselves "private" people. Men usually have more difficulty expressing feelings of bereavement, largely because society considers a show of emotions by men a sign of weakness. It is also important to realize that each person's characteristic way of expressing his or her emotions differs somewhat from one person to another. For some, moistened eyes and a warm handclasp are about as close as they ever come to expressing grief. Others may cry openly and unashamedly. Still others seem to be inclined toward more dramatic, and at times hysterical, expressions of grief, such as screaming and tearing their hair and clothes.

Another way of resolving grief is to express it in appropriate ways. Sometimes just sheer physical activity helps to alleviate the tension and sadness of bereavement, at least temporarily. Funeral rituals may afford an outlet for grief. Also, taking care of the affairs of the deceased may be therapeutic as well as helpful. As the executor of my father's estate, I found myself faced with a great deal of correspondence and many legal transactions. Initially I regarded it as a burden, but I soon realized it was one of the few tangible things I could do for my father. It became a way of showing my respect for him and helping me express my own grief.

LIFE AND DEATH IN PERSPECTIVE

Now that the average life expectancy is about 70 years, more people are apt to suffer from chronic diseases such as cancer, heart disease, and kidney failure. As a result, death comes more slowly and usually occurs in the hospital. Yet hospitals tend to be large and impersonal institutions, geared more to the treatment of acute illnesses and the prolonging of life. Consequently, the change in the context of death presents us with new ethical issues, such as the use of life-saving machines and the right to die in a dignified way. Examining such issues may help us put life and death in better perspective.

The Right to Die

Marie remembers what her husband Mike was like in the early years of their marriage. He was a fun-loving, hard-working, out-of-doors kind of person. Then, five years ago, Mike was seriously injured in an automobile accident which left him in a coma. Ever since, Mike has been sustained by a feeding tube in a nursing home. At this point, Marie, together with Mike's parents and brothers, wants to have the feeding tube removed. All of them feel that Mike would not want to continue this way.

Patients like Mike—there are about 10,000 such Americans—pose an ethical dilemma for their families and doctors. Family members are torn between their desire to be loyal to their loved one and the emotional, financial realities of supporting someone in a permanent vegetative state. Doctors also face the conflict between their duty to sustain life and their obligation to relieve suffering. Doctors often continue treatment because of their moral commitments or the fear of legal consequences of doing otherwise. In recent years, however, the American Medical Association's Council on Ethical and Judicial Affairs has provided some guidelines for doctors in such situations. After struggling with the issue for two years, the seven-member panel affirmed that it is not unethical for doctors to discontinue all life support systems for patients who are in an irreversible coma, even if death is not imminent. A more controversial provision includes food and water on the list of treatments that might be withheld. In each case, the patient's wishes, as well as can be determined, should be respected, and the patient's dignity maintained. The council's decision reflects growing public support on such issues. According to national surveys, more than 8 out of 10 adults think terminally ill patients ought to be able to tell their doctors to let them die. A similar number support the idea of the doctor withdrawing feeding tubes, if this was the patient's wish. Since the council's decision is not binding, doctors are free to follow their consciences. But such guidelines may make it easier for the doctors to comply with a patient's or family's request to end treatment (Wallis, 1986).

All too often, however, family members and physicians ignore their elderly or ailing patients' desire to be allowed to die. One study (Cohn, 1984) found that while one in three patients would reject any medical intervention if he or she were about to die, patients were seldom asked their wishes in the matter. In a review of 154 cases in which physicians tried to restart a patient's heart, only thirty patients had been asked in advance. Yet, of the twenty-four patients who managed to survive in a mentally competent state, eight said they would have preferred to die. The study suggested that doctors often assumed they knew what their patients wanted, even though they had not asked the patient. Only one doctor in ten had actually discussed resuscitation with his or her patients. And only one in five consulted family members rather than the patient, even when the patient was fully competent. Such evidence suggests an overprotectiveness that is ill-founded. Most patients, whether they are well or seriously ill, wish to be well-informed and to participate in medical decisions.

A President's Commission on this subject, including doctors, lawyers, theo-

Most patients want to participate in the medical decisions affecting their lives. (Visiting Nurse Service of New York)

logians, and others, has concluded that a competent patient who is able to understand treatment choices and their consequences has the all-but-absolute right to decide his or her fate. When a person is incompetent, a surrogate, usually a family member, should be given the authority to make such decisions. Such thinking has led to a growing use of such instruments as the so-called "living will," in which a person instructs doctors and family members to stop using life-sustaining procedures in the event of a terminal condition. Some "right-to-die" laws attempt to make these directives binding on doctors, who may then transfer medical responsibility for the patient if they disagree with the patient's wishes. Since such documents may not cover the precise circumstances that occur, many authorities prefer the powers of attorney, which empower anyone—relative, friend, or adviser—to make any medical decision when the signee becomes incompetent. At least three-fourths of the states already have laws authorizing the powers of attorney in such situations. Both the living will and powers of attorney may be revoked by the rational person, but the powers of attorney are more adaptable (Tifft, 1983).

A Natural Death

One of the dangers of the right-to-die movement is that it may unwittingly program people to die quickly. It is often said that death is more of a problem for the survivors than for those who die. For this reason, sudden death from a heart attack or an automobile accident is more appreciated than death from a drawn-out illness. On the surface, the dying are supposed to have been spared the suffering of a terminal illness. But they have also saved the rest of us the burden of taking care of an invalid or having to watch someone die slowly. Hastening death also helps us to avoid our social responsibilities, such as caring for the lingering convalescent and the aged. Ironically, the revolt against needless prolongation of life may incline us toward an equally "unnatural" hastening of death. Yet a quick, induced death does not answer the key questions: How old is old? How ill is ill? At what point should a person on the heart-lung machine be allowed to die? When does a life cease to have meaning? Perhaps the nearest we come to a natural death is helping people to die at their own pace and style. For example, if a young person has been an active, outdoor type and doesn't have the will to adjust to an invalid state, perhaps that person should be allowed to die a dignified death. Others who may suffer from equally disabling handicaps but who prefer making the adjustment to their diminished capacities should be encouraged and supported in their efforts to go on living.

The hospice movement for the terminally ill represents a giant step toward the kind of humane and supportive community needed for a dignified death. In the Middle Ages the hospice was a shelter for travelers who had nowhere else to go. Today the hospice is a place to take care of those approaching the end of their lives. As we mentioned earlier, much of the suffering of the terminally ill consists of the treatments, the impersonal atmosphere, and the sense of isolation experienced in hospitals. In contrast, the hospice is a community that helps people to *live*, not merely exist, while they are dying.

The term hospice generally refers to a *system* of care that integrates a physical facility for the terminally ill with the patient's family and home. In some cases, patients may spend their final days at home being taken care of by loved ones and trained volunteers. In addition to helping with such practical matters as pain control and preparing meals, hospice personnel also give emotional support and guidance to family members. The aim throughout is to provide a humane and supportive community in which the patient may die with dignity. Begun in England, the hospice movement has since spread to other countries, including several hundred hospice programs in the United States and Canada. The increasing population of elderly people and rising costs of hospitalization are such that the hospice movement is likely to expand during the years ahead (Fulton, et al., 1978).

Funerals

When death finally comes, it is a rite of passage to be recognized by the family and community alike. In most societies, parting with the dead is recognized by some kind of funeral—the ceremonies and rituals associated with the burial or cremation of the dead. Philippe Aries, in his book *The Hour of Our*

While the dead are remembered at funerals, the ceremonies are more for the benefit of the survivors. (Ken Karp)

Death (1981), says that such rites have enabled people to maintain order and defend themselves against the untamed forces of nature.

In earlier eras, when belief in an afterlife was a more dominant influence in human affairs, funerals were held primarily for the benefit of the dead. Death was seen as a passage to heaven or eternal life. Hence, some ancients not only buried the corpse, but included personal items of the deceased to be used on the journey. In today's secularized society, however, the emphasis tends to be humanistic and materialistic. While it is the dead who are remembered at funerals, the ceremony is more for the benefit of the survivors. Funerals have become the occasion for according the dead the recognition and honor they may not have achieved in life. Families get caught in a status game, selecting expensive bronze caskets, ornate headstones, and choice burial sites to maintain their position in society. Consequently, funerals have become increasingly lavish and expensive. While the funeral industry has been criticized for exploiting people in their bereavement, their spokesmen point out that bereaved family members themselves are partly to blame because they choose on the basis of their emotions rather than through reason. Thus, whether out of respect for the dead, guilt, or vanity, many of the expensive funeral practices continue.

According to the Federal Trade Commission, funerals are the third largest consumer purchase, following a home and a car. The average cost of a funeral is now about $2500 (O'Donnell-Cox, 1984). Yet, you can easily pay more than this. One widow was shocked when confronted by a funeral bill of more than $5000. Like many, she didn't think to ask about all those extras, such as the use of the chapel, visitation room, and parking lot. And like many, she paid the bill, feeling she had no other option. However, under the recent "truth-in-funerals" ruling, funeral directors must now send itemized bills and provide information regarding the cost of coffins and other burial procedures. They must also offer embalming as an option where it isn't required by state law. In cases of crema-tion, funeral directors must also notify a customer that a casket is not necessary and present the option of buying a plain wood box or alternate container for use in burial. Most important of all, we need to realize that the decisions made at such a time are our decisions, and to make sure that we are not being pres-sured into anything against our wills.

The movement toward simpler funerals can also be seen in the nonprofit funeral and memorial societies springing up all around the country. Members have access to expert guidance and can specify what they want done with their bodies and what kind of funeral they want. All of this helps people to end their lives in a way that reflects their lifestyle and values, while sparing their relatives the worry of how best to carry out their wishes. For example, Charles Lindbergh requested that he be buried without embalming or eulogies within 8 hours of his death in a tiny church cemetery in Hawaii. The only mourners present were his wife and one son. It was a fitting end for a man who cherished privacy (Dempsey, 1975).

The awareness of death helps to put life in proper perspective. (Marc P. Anderson)

Words To Live By

It is the denial of death that is partially responsible for people living empty, purposeless lives; for when you live as if you'll live forever, it becomes too easy to postpone the things you know that you must do. You live your life in preparation for tomorrow or in remembrance of yesterday, and meanwhile, each day is lost. In contrast, when you fully understand that each day you awaken could be the last you have, you take the time *that day* to grow, to become more of who you really are, to reach out to other human beings.

Source: Elisabeth Kübler-Ross, *Death: The Final Stage of Growth* (Englewood Cliffs, NJ: Prentice-Hall, Inc., 1975), p. 164.

Death and Growth

It may seem strange relating death to growth. Ordinarily, death is seen as the end of growth and existence. Yet, in the larger scheme of things, death is an integral part of life that gives meaning to human existence. It sets a limit on our lives, reminding us to spend our days on the things that matter most. Those who are fortunate enough to have some warning of their end often find it a time of personal growth. Similarly, grieving over the loss of a loved one may help us relate more deeply to those who remain.

Whether you are young or old, if you can begin to see death as an inevitable companion of life, it may help you live your life fully rather than passively. Not that you should rush out and begin doing all those things people fantasize about. Instead, the awareness that you have only so much time to live may help you make the most of your life—the disappointments and pains as well as the joys. As one recent widower told me, "I've begun to take time to smell the roses." Usually, it is those who have not lived their lives fully who are the most reluctant to die. Haunted by broken relationships and unfulfilled dreams, they grow ever more anxious and fearful in the face of death.

Far from being morbid, thinking about your own death may give you a new perspective on life. For instance, if you were told you had only a limited time to live, how would you spend the time? What unfinished business would you be most concerned about? Which people would you most want to be with? Pondering the answers to such questions may help you to clarify what is really important to you. Better plan to do these things before it's too late. As Elisabeth Kübler-Ross reminds us, the greatest lesson we may learn from the dying is simply "LIVE, so you do not have to look back and say, 'God, how I wasted my life'" (1975, p. xix).

Summary

Death and Dying

1. The prospect of one's own death is so frightening that people, young adults in particular, tend to overestimate how long they will live and underestimate the risk of death from familiar hazards such as smoking.

2. Near-death experiences, often associated with the use of life-saving machines, tend to make people less fearful of death and more appreciative of life.

3. Terminally ill people tend to go through several stages of dying, such as denial, anger, bargaining, depression, and acceptance, with considerable overlapping between the stages and individual differences.

4. There's also a tendency for individuals to die in the same way they have lived, such as those with a strong will to live fighting for their lives right up to the end.

Bereavement and Grief

5. It is important for the bereaved to actively engage in grief work, a process that parallels the experience of dying and involves many of the same emotions.

6. Unresolved grief may assume a variety of forms from physical complaints to more persistent psychological symptoms. People who live alone are especially likely to have difficulty working through grief.

7. Healthy grief consists of expressing our feelings of grief and taking part in suitable rituals and activities that may eventually alleviate our grief.

Life and Death in Perspective

8. The growing use of life-saving technology has posed critical questions as to when it's appropriate to prolong or end a person's life, with a growing use of such instruments as the living will and the powers of attorney.

9. The importance of providing terminally ill people with a humane and supportive community has led to the hospice movement, which is likely to expand in the coming years.

10. Criticism of the funeral industry has spurred a movement toward simpler and less expensive funerals in recent years.

11. Far from being morbid, the awareness of death as an inevitable companion of life may help you to put life in better perspective and to live your life more fully.

Self-test

1. We tend to underestimate the risk of death from:

    a. dramatic events such as earthquakes   **c.** familiar hazards such as smoking

    b. airplane accidents   **d.** homicides

2. People who have experienced a near-death experience become:

a. more concerned with learning about life
b. less fearful of death
c. more appreciative of life
d. all of the above

3. According to Elisabeth Kübler-Ross, the first stage of dying usually consists of:

a. resentment
b. a denial of death
c. depression
d. bargaining for time

4. The healthy process of working through our emotions associated with loss is called:

a. grief work
b. bereavement
c. grief
d. mourning

5. The group with a higher than average rate of death compared to others their age is:

a. widows over 55
b. married people
c. widowed men over 55
d. college-educated people

6. Good grief, or becoming more appreciative of life as the result of one's experience of grief, involves:

a. talking out one's grief
b. trying to forget one's loss
c. avoiding thoughts of death
d. repressing one's grief

7. While as many as one in three patients would reject any medical intervention if he or she were about to die, patients:

a. do not have such a legal right
b. seldom express their wishes
c. usually change their minds
d. seldom are asked their wishes

8. A system of care that integrates a physical facility for the terminally ill with the patient's family and home is known as:

a. hospital
b. euthanasia
c. hospice
d. life-support

9. In most societies, death is:

a. recognized by some kind of funeral
b. a rite of passage
c. acknowledged by the community
d. all of the above

10. The realization that death is an inevitable companion of life:

a. is associated with depression
b. may give you a new perspective on life
c. is a morbid idea
d. usually hastens one's death

Exercises

1. *Subjective life expectancy.*[1] *Simply knowing a person's age does not tell you how that person feels about his or her future. To discover this, try the following exercise in subjective life expectancy. You may want your friends or other individuals to try it as well.*

[1] Robert J. Kastenbaum, *Death, Society, and Human Experience*, 2nd. ed. (St. Louis: The C.V. Mosby Co., 1981).

   1. I *expect* to live to age (circle your answer)

   25 30 35 40 45 50 55 60 65 70 75 80 85 90 95 100

   2. I *want* to live to age (circle your answer)

   25 30 35 40 45 50 55 60 65 70 75 80 85 90 95 100

Are there discrepancies between the expressed desire and expectation? If so, what are the possible reasons? Are there differences in desires with increasing age?

Usually findings have shown that those past middle-age expect and wish to live to a later age than younger subjects do. Did you find this to be true? When people expect to live less than the average life expectancy for their age, do they have a good reason? Did you find some people afraid to specify an age for fear this will somehow make death occur at a given age?

2. *Your attitude toward death.* Do a self-analysis of your attitudes toward death. First, write down your actual experiences with death, such as the loss of a friend or loved one, the ages at which this occurred, and so forth. Then describe some of your feelings and attitudes toward death. Include your own responses to the subjective life expectancy exercise as well.[2]

3. *Death as an altered state of consciousness.* Some people have observed a similarity between dying and the marginal state of awareness experienced just before sleep. Try to catch yourself in this state some night and make a mental note of your reactions. Was it a peaceful state? Did you find yourself naturally giving into it? How did you feel after the loss of control or power?[2]

4. *Reflections on the experience of bereavement.* Recall a personal experience of bereavement, whether the loss of a loved one or friend. Then describe your experience in a page or so. To what extend did your experience include the grief work process described in the chapter? In what ways was your experience unique? Finally, how has your experience of grief affected your life? Has it made you more cautious and, perhaps, bitter toward life? Or has it eventually become a "good grief," leading you to make the most of life and reach out to others in a more meaningful way?

5. *Disposing of your body.* If you had a choice, how would you want your body disposed of? Do you want to be embalmed and buried? Or would you rather be cremated? If so, what do you want done with your ashes? While some people ask that their ashes be scattered over water or a favorite spot on land, many people prefer that their ashes be left in a mausoleum or buried in a cemetery. People sometimes write down such preferences and leave them with their families or a memorial society.

Have you thought about donating organs from your body? If so, which ones? Are you interested in leaving your body for use by medical science?

6. *Write your own obituary.* This isn't as strange as it may seem. Major newspapers usually have a file of obituaries written while celebrities and national figures are still alive, and then they update these accounts at the time of death.

Try writing your own obituary in two or three paragraphs. In addition to giving the standard information, such as your name, age, and position at work, point out some of your major accomplishments in life. Which community activities would you mention? Who are your survivors?

[2]From Carol R. Hoffman, Montgomery County Community College, Blue Bell, Pa., 1985. Used by permission.

In addition, list your funeral and burial plans. What day and time do you prefer to be buried? Where is your service being held? Do you have any preferences regarding financial contributions to charities in lieu of flowers? Where do you want to be buried or your ashes deposited?

Questions for Self-Reflection

1. Do you occasionally think about the possibility of your own death?
2. Have you ever had a close brush with death?
3. Are you afraid of dying?
4. How often do you think of someone who is dead?
5. Is there something you would especially like to do before you die?
6. Can you recall your first experience of grief? Whose death was it?
7. Have you ever experienced good grief?
8. Have you made a will?
9. What kind of funeral would you like?
10. What do you believe happens to us after death?

Recommended Readings

Aries, P. *The Hour of Our Death.* New York: Alfred A. Knopf, 1981. An interpretative account of the meaning and customs associated with death in different historical eras.

Kübler-Ross, Elisabeth, and M. Warshaw. *To Live Until We Say Good-Bye.* Englewood Cliffs, NJ: Prentice-Hall, 1978 (paperback). A pictorial account of leave-taking, especially appropriate for patients choosing to die at home.

Kushner, H. *When Bad Things Happen To Good People.* New York: Shocken, 1981 (paperback). A philosophical and religious explanation of the occurrences of misfortune and untimely death.

Ramsay, R. W., and R. Noorbergen. *Living With Loss.* New York: William Morrow, 1980. A guide for coping with bereavement based on a dramatic new breakthrough in grief therapy.

Sabom, M. B. *Recollections of Death.* New York: Harper & Row, 1981. A physician's view of the near-death experience, including the author's own studies.

Veninga, Robert. *A Gift of Hope.* Boston: Little, Brown, 1985. A practical, inspiring book about how people triumph over life's adversities.

References

ALLEN, ROBERT F., and SHIRLEY LINDE. *Lifegain*. Morristown, NJ: Han Resources Institute, 1981.

ALTMAN, I. *The Environment and Social Behavior*. Monterey, CA: Brooks/Cole, 1975.

AMERICAN PSYCHIATRIC ASSOCIATION. *Diagnostic and Statistical Manual of Mental Disorders* (DSM-III), 3rd ed. Washington, DC: APA, 1980.

ANDREASEN, N. C., and S. OLSEN. "Negative Versus Positive Schizophrenia: Definition and Validation," *Archives of General Psychiatry*, 39, 1982: 789–794.

ANTILL, J. K. "Sex-role Complementarity Versus Similarity in Married Couples," *Journal of Personality and Social Psychology*, 45, 1983: 145–155.

ARCHER, D. *How to Expand Your S.I.Q. (Social Intelligence Quotient)*. New York: M. Evans, 1980.

———. "Reading Nonverbal Clues," in Z. Rubin and E. B. McNeil, *The Psychology of Being Human*. New York: Harper & Row, 1979.

———, B. IRITANI, D. D. KIMES, and M. BARRIOS. "Face-ism: Five Studies of Sex Differences in Facial Prominence," *Journal of Personality and Social Psychology* , 45, 1983: 725–735.

ARIES, P. *The Hour of Our Death*. New York: Knopf, 1981.

ARIETI, SILVANO. *Understanding and Helping the Schizophrenic*. New York: Simon & Schuster, 1981.

ARONSON, ELLIOT. *The Social Animal,* 3rd ed. San Francisco: W. H. Freeman, 1980.

ATCHLEY, R.C. *The Sociology of Retirement*. Cambridge, MA: Schenkman Publishing Company, 1976.

BANDURA, ALBERT. "Self-efficacy: Toward a Unifying Theory of Behavior Change," *Psychological Review,* 84, 1977: 191–215.

———. *Social Learning Theory*. Morristown, NJ: General Learning Press, 1971.

BANE, M. J. "Marital Disruption and the Lives of Children," in G. Levinger and O. C. Moles (eds.), *Divorce and Separation*. New York: Basic Books, 1979.

BARON, ROBERT A., DONN BYRNE. *Social Psychology*, 4th ed. Boston: Allyn and Bacon, 1984.

BARRETT, C. J. "Effectiveness of Widows' Groups in Facilitating Change," *Journal of Consulting and Clinical Psychology*, 46, 1978: 20–31.

BECK, A. T. *Cognitive Therapy and Emotional Disorders*. New York: American Library, 1979.

BECK, A. T., and J. E. YOUNG. "College Blues," *Psychology Today*, 80, 1978: 85–86, 89, 92.

BELL, A. P., M. S. WEINBERG, and S. F. HAMMERSMITH. *Sexual Preference.* Bloomington: Indiana University Press, 1981.

BENGSTON, V. L., P. L. KASSCHAU, and P. K. RAGAN. "The Impact of Social Structure on Aging Individuals," in *The Handbook of The Psychology of Aging,* J. E. Birren and K. W. Schaie (eds.). New York: Van Nostrand Reinhold Company, 1977.

BENJAMIN, M., et al. "Test Anxiety Deficits in Information Processing," *Journal of Educational Psychology,* 73, 1981: 816–24.

BERNARD, JESSIE. Quoted in "Psychology for the Taking," *Psychology,* April 1977.

BERSCHEID, ELLEN, and ELAINE H. WALSTER. *Interpersonal Attraction,* 2nd ed. Reading, MA: Addison-Wesley Publishing Company, 1978.

BLEULER, M. E. "The Long-Term Course of Schizophrenic Psychoses," in L. C. Wynne, R. L. Cromwell, and S. Matthyse, *The Nature of Schizophrenia: New Approaches To Research and Treatment.* New York: John Wiley, 1978.

BLUMSTEIN, PHILIP, and PEPPER SCHWARTZ. *American Couples.* New York: William Morrow and Company, 1983.

BOHANNAN, PAUL. "The Six Stations of Divorce," in Ruth E. Albrecht and Wilbur Bock, *Encounter: Love, Marriage, and Family.* Boston: Holbrook Press, 1975.

BOLLES, RICHARD N. *What Color Is Your Parachute?* Berkeley, CA: Ten Speed Press, 1985.

BOOTZIN, RICHARD R., and JOAN ROSS ACOCELLA. *Abnormal Psychology,* 4th ed. New York: Random House, 1984.

BOTWINICK, J. *Aging and Behavior,* 2nd ed. New York: Springer, 1978.

BOYAR, JAY. "The 'Cute Meet' of Lovers-to-be Generally Occurs Only in Films," *The Philadelphia Inquirer,* Dec. 13, 1984: 7-C.

BROWN, PATRICIA L. "Disguised to Learn the Troubles of Age," *The Philadelphia Inquirer,* May 15, 1985: 1.

BURNS, DAVID. *Feeling Good.* New York: William Morrow and Company, 1980.

BUTLER, R. N. *Why Survive? Being Old in America.* New York: Harper & Row, 1975.

CAMPBELL, DAVID. *If You Don't Know Where You're Going, You'll Probably End Up Somewhere Else.* Allen, TX: Argus Communications, 1974.

Cancer Facts and Figures. New York: American Cancer Society, 1985.

CARTWRIGHT, R.D. "Happy Endings for our Dreams," *Psychology Today,* December 1978: 66–76.

CASH, THOMAS F., BARBARA A. WINSTEAD, and LOUIS H. JANDA. "The Great American Shape-up," *Psychology Today,* April 1986, 30–37.

CASSILETH, B. R., E. J. LUSK, D. S. MILLER, L. L. BROWN, and C. MILLER. "Psychosocial Correlates of Survival in Advanced Malignant Disease?" *New England Journal of Medicine,* 312, 24, 1985: 1551–1555.

CHERLIN, ANDREW, and JAMES MCCARTHY. "Remarried Couple Households: Data from the June 1980 Current Population Survey," *Journal of Marriage and the Family,* 47, February 1985: 23–30.

CLORE, G. L. and D. BYRNE. "A Reinforcement-affect Model of Attraction," in T. Huston (ed.), *Foundations of Interpersonal Attraction.* New York: Academic Press, 1974.

COHN, N. B., and D. S. STRASSBERG. "Self-disclosure Reciprocity Among Preadolescents," *Personality and Social Psychology Bulletin*, 9, 1983: 97–102.

COHN, VICTOR. "Last Wish: Some Patients Would Choose to Die If Asked, Studies Find," *The Philadelphia Inquirer*, April 26, 1984: 11-A.

COLE, S. "Send Our Children to Work?" *Psychology Today*, July 1980: 44–68.

COONS, P. M. "Multiple Personality: Diagnostic Considerations," *Journal of Clinical Psychology*, 41, 1980: 330–336.

CORBIN, CHARLES B., and RUTH LINDSEY. *Concepts of Physical Fitness With Laboratories*, 5th ed. Dubuque, IA: Wm C. Brown, 1985.

COSTA, P. T., and R. R. MCCRAE. "Hypochondriasis, Neuroticism, and Aging," *American Psychologist*, 40, January 1985: 19–28.

CRAIGHEAD, L. W., A. J. STUNKARD, and R. M. O'BRIEN. "Behavior Therapy and Pharmacotherapy for Obesity," *Archives of General Psychiatry*, 38, 1981: 763–768.

CRITTENDEN, A. "One Life, 10 Jobs," *The New York Times*, Nov. 23, 1980.

CROOKS, ROBERT, and KARLA BAUR. *Our Sexuality*, 2nd ed. Menlo Park, CA: The Benjamin/Cummings Publishing Company, 1983.

CSIKSZENTMIHALYI, M., and R. GRAEF. "Feeling Free," *Psychology Today*, December 1979.

CUNNINGHAM, M. R. "Sociobiology as a Supplementary Paradigm for Social Psychological Research," in L. Wheeler (ed.), *Review of Personality and Social Psychology*, vol. 2. Beverly Hills, CA: Sage, 1981.

DANIELS, P., and K. WEINGARTEN. *Sooner or Later*. New York: W. W. Norton, 1981.

DAVID, KEITH E. "Near and Dear: Friendship and Love Compared," *Psychology Today*, February 1985, 22–30.

DAVISON, G. C., and J. M. NEALE. *Abnormal Psychology*, 3rd ed. New York: John Wiley, 1982.

DECI, E. L., and R. M. RYAN. "The Empirical Explorations of Intrinsic Motivational Processes," in L. Berkowitz (ed.) *Advances in Experimental Social Psychology*, vol. 13. New York: Academic Press, 1980.

DEMENT, W. C., and V. ZARCONE. "Pharmacological Treatment of Sleep Disorders," in J. D. Barchas, et al. (eds.), *Psychopharmacology: From Theory to Practice*. New York: Oxford University Press, 1977.

DEMPSEY, D. *The Way We Die*. New York: Macmillan Publishing Company, 1975.

DENNEY, NANCY. "A Model of Cognitive Development Across the Lifespan," paper presented at the meeting of the American Psychological Association, Los Angeles, California, August 1981, in John W. Santrock, *Life-span Development*. Dubuque, IA: Wm. C. Brown, 1983.

DEPAULO, BELLA M., MIRON ZUCKERMAN, and ROBERT ROSENTHAL. "Human Lies," *The Journal of Communication*, 30, 1980: 129–139.

DIAMOND, E. L. "The Role of Anger and Hostility in Essential Hypertension and Coronary Heart Disease," *Psychological Bulletin*, 92, 1982: 410–433.

DINKLAGE, L. B. *Adolescent Choice and Decision-making*. Cambridge, MA: Harvard University Press, 1966.

DOANE, J., K. WEST, M. J. GOLDSTEIN, E. RODNICK, and J. JONES. "Parental Communication Deviance and Affective Style as Predictors of Subsequent Schizophrenia Spectrum Disorders in Vulnerable Adolescents," *Archives of General Psychiatry,* 38, 1981: 679–685.

EGELAND, J. A., and A. M. HOSTETTER. "Amish Study: I. Affective Disorders Among the Amish," *American Journal of Psychiatry,* 140, 1983: 56–61.

EKMAN, P. "Expression and the Nature of Emotion," in K. R. Sherer and P. Ekman (eds.), *Approaches to Emotion.* Hillsdale, NJ: Erlbaum, 1984.

———. "The Universal Smile: Face Muscles Talk Every Language," *Psychology Today,* September 1975.

ELLIS, A. "Rational-emotive Therapy," in R. J. Corsini (ed.), *Current Psychotherapies,* 2nd ed. Itasca, IL: F. E. Peacock, 1979.

———, and ROBERT A. HARPER. *A New Guide to Rational Living.* Englewood Cliffs, NJ: Prentice-Hall, 1975.

ERIKSON, ERIK H. *Childhood and Society,* 2nd ed. New York: W. W. Norton, 1963.

———. *Dimensions of a New Identity.* New York: W. W. Norton, 1974.

———. *Identity: Youth and Crisis.* New York: W. W. Norton, 1968.

FALLOON, I. R., J. L. BOYD, C. W. MCGILL, et al. "Family Management in Prevention of Exacerbation of Schizophrenia: A Controlled Study," *New England Journal of Medicine,* 306, 24: 1437–1440.

FEATHER, N. T. "Reactions to Male and Female Success and Failure in Sex-linked Occupations: Impressions of Personality, Causal Attributions, and Perceived Likelihood of Different Consequences," *Journal of Personality and Social Psychology,* 31, 1975: 20–31.

FEIST, JESS. *Theories of Personality.* New York: Holt, Rinehart & Winston, 1985.

FOLKES, V. S. "Forming Relationships and the Matching Hypothesis," *Personality and Social Psychology Bulletin,* 82, 1982: 631–636.

FORREST, J. D., and S. K. HENSHAW. "What U.S. Women Think and Do about Contraception," *Family Planning Perspective,* 15, 4, July/August 1983.

FOSTER, G. M., and B. G. ANDERSON. *Medical Anthropology.* New York: John Wiley, 1978.

FOXMAN, SHERRI. *Classified Love.* New York: McGraw-Hill, 1982.

FREUD, SIGMUND. *An Outline of Psychoanalysis.* Trans., James Strachey. New York: W. W. Norton, 1949.

———. *New Introductory Lectures of Psychoanalysis.* Trans., James Strachey. New York: W. W. Norton, 1965.

FREY, W. H., et. al. "Crying Behavior in the Human Adult," *Integrative Psychiatry,* 1, 1983: 94–98.

FRIEDMAN, H. S., L. M. PRINCE, R. E. RIGGIO, and M. R. DIMATTEO. "Understanding and Assessing Nonverbal Expressiveness: The Affective Communication Test," *Journal of Personality and Social Psychology,* 39, 1980: 333–351.

FRIEDMAN, M., and R. F. ROSENMAN. *Type A Behavior and Your Heart.* New York: Knopf, 1974.

FULTON, R., E. MARKUSEN, G. OWEN, and J. L. SCHEIBER (eds.). *Death and Dying: Challenge and Change.* Reading, MA: Addison-Wesley Publishing Company, 1978.

GALLUP, G. *Public Opinion 1972–1977,* vol. 1. Wilmington, DE: Scholarly Resources, 1978.

GARFINKEL, B. C., A. FROESE, and J. HOOD. "Suicide Attempts in Children and Adolescents," *American Journal of Psychiatry,* 139, 1982: 1257–1261.

GELATT, H. B., V. VARENHORST, and R. CAREY. *Deciding*. New York: College Entrance Examination Board, 1972.

GERGEN, KENNETH. "The Healthy, Happy Human Being Wears Many Masks," in Abe Arkoff (ed.), *Psychology and Personal Growth*, 2nd ed. Boston: Allyn and Bacon, 1980.

GLENN, NORVAL D., and CHARLES N. WEAVER. "Education's Effects on Psychological Well-being," *Public Opinion Quarterly*, 45, 1, 1981: 22–39.

GLICK, P. C. "Marriage, Divorce, and Living Arrangements: Prospective Changes," *Journal of Family Issues*, 5, 1984: 7–26.

———. "Updating the Life Cycle of the Family," *Journal of Marriage and the Family*, February 1977.

GOLEMAN, DANIEL. "Can You Tell When Someone Is Lying to You?" *Psychology Today*, August 1982: 14–23.

———. "Staying Up: The Rebellion Against Sleep's Gentle Tyranny," *Psychology Today*, March 1982: 24–35.

GONDA, J. "Convocation on Work, Aging, and Retirement: A Review," *Human Development*, 24, 1981: 286–292.

GONZALES, M. H., J. M. DAVIS, G. L. LONEY, C. K. LUKENS, and C. M. JUNGHANS. "Interactional Approach to Interpersonal Attraction," *Journal of Personality and Social Psychology*, 4, 1983: 1192–1197.

GOODHART, ROBERT S., and MAURICE E. SHILS. *Modern Nutrition in Health and Disease*. Philadelphia, PA.: Lea and Febiger, 1980.

GORDON, THOMAS, and JUDITH S. SANDS. *P.E.T. in Action*. New York: Bantam, 1978.

GOTTESMAN, I. I. "Schizophrenia and Genetics: Where Are We? Are You Sure?," in L. C. Wynne, R. L. Cromwell, and S. Matthysee (eds.), *The Nature of Schizophrenia: New Approaches to Research and Treatment*. New York: John Wiley, 1978.

GOULD, ROGER. *Transformations*. New York: Simon & Schuster, 1978.

GREELEY, A. M. "The State of the Nation's Happiness," *Psychology Today*, January 1981.

GREENBERG, J. "Suicide Linked to Brain Chemical Deficit," *Science News*, 121, 1982: 355.

GREENBERG, R. P., and S. FISHER. *The Scientific Credibility of Freud's Theories and Therapy*. New York: Basic Books, 1977.

GREENWALD, HAROLD. *Direct Decision Therapy*. San Diego, CA: Edits Publishers, 1973.

———, and ELIZABETH RICH. *The Happy Person*. New York: Avon Books, 1984.

GROVER, K. J., C. S. RUSSELL, W. R. SCHUMM, and L. A. PAFF-BERGEN. "Mate Selection Processes and Marital Satisfaction," *Family Relations*, July 1985: 383–386.

HACKER, ANDREW (ed.). *U/S: A Statistical Portrait of The American People*. New York: The Viking Press, 1983.

HALEY, JAY. *Leaving Home*. New York: McGraw-Hill, 1980.

HALL, J. "Decisions, Decisions, Decisions," *Psychology Today*, November 1971.

HALLORAN, J. *Applied Human Relations*, 2nd ed. Englewood Cliffs, NJ: Prentice-Hall, 1983.

HARRELL, J. P. "Psychological Factors and Hypertension: A Status Report," *Psychological Bulletin*, 87, 1980: 482–501.

HARRIS, SYDNEY J. "Age Is in the Mind of the Individual," *The Philadelphia Inquirer,* June 8, 1984: 21-A.

Harvard Medical School Health Letter, April 1981: 2.

Harvard Medical School Health Letter, "AIDS: Update (Part I)," November 1985a: 1–4.

Harvard Medical School Health Letter, "AIDS Update (Part II)," December 1985b: 2–5.

HARVEY, J. H., B. HARRIS, and R. D. BARNES. "Actor-Observer Differences in the Perceptions of Responsibility and Freedom," *Journal of Personality and Social Psychology,* 32, 1975: 22–28.

——, and J. M. JELLISON. "Determinants of the Perception of Choice: Number of Options and Perceived Time in Making a Selection," *Memory and Cognition,* 1974: 539–544.

HATCHER, ROBERT, M.D., et al. *Contraceptive Technology 1984–1985,* 12th rev. ed. New York: Irvington Publishers, 1984.

HELSING, K. J., M. SZKLO, and G. W. COMSTOCK. "Factors Associated with Mortality After Widowhood," *American Journal of Public Health,* 71, August 1981: 802–809.

HERMAN, C. P., M. P. OLMSTED, and J. POLIVY. "Obesity, Externality, and Susceptibility to Social Influences: An Integrated Analysis," *Journal of Personality and Social Psychology,* 45, 1983: 926–934.

HETHERINGTON, E. M., M. COX, and R. COX. "Play and Social Interaction in Children Following Divorce," *Journal of Social Issues,* 35, 4, 1979: 26–46.

HILL, C. T., Z. RUBIN, and L. A. PEPLAU. "Breakups before Marriage: The End of 103 Affairs," *Journal of Social Issues,* 32, 1, 1976: 147–168.

HIRSCHFELD, R. M. A. and C. K. CROSS. "Epidemiology of Affective Disorders: Psychosocial Risk Factors," *Archives of General Psychiatry,* 39, 1982: 35–46.

HITE, SHERE. *The Hite Report.* New York: Macmillan, 1976.

HODGSON, J. W., and J. L. FISCHER. "Sex Differences in Identity and Intimacy Development in College Youth," *Journal of Youth and Adolescence,* 8, 1979: 37–50.

HOFFMAN, L. W., and J. D. MANIS. "The Value of Children in the United States: A New Approach to the Study of Fertility," *Journal of Marriage and the Family,* 41, 1979: 583–596.

HOLMES, T. H., and M. MASUDA. "Life Change and Illness Susceptibility." In B. Dohrenwend and B. Dohrenwend (eds.), *Stressful Life Events: Their Nature and Effects.* New York: John Wiley, 1974.

——, and R. H. RAHE. "The Social Readjustment Rating Scale," *Journal of Psychosomatic Research,* 11, 1967: 213–217.

HORNER, M. S. "Toward an Understanding of Achievement-related Conflicts in Women," *Journal of Social Issues,* 28, 1972: 157–175.

HOWARD, KENNETH, S. MARK KOPTA, MERTON S. KRAUSE, and DAVID E. ORLINSKY. "The Dose-effect Relationship in Psychotherapy," *American Psychologist,* Feb. 1986: 159–164.

HUNT, MORTON. *Sexual Behavior in the 1970s.* Chicago, IL: Playboy Press, 1974.

———, and B. HUNT. *The Divorce Experience.* New York: McGraw-Hill, 1977.

IZARD, C. E., et al. "The Young Infant's Ability to Produce Discrete Emotional Expressions," *Developmental Psychology,* 16, 1980: 132–140.

JACOBI, JOLANDE. *The Psychology of C. G. Jung.* New Haven: Yale University Press, 1973 edition.

JANIS, I. L. "Decision Making Under Stress," in L. Goldberger and S. Breznitz (eds.), *Handbook of Stress.* New York: Free Press, 1982, pp. 69–87.

———, and L. MANN. *Decision Making.* New York: Free Press, 1977.

———, and D. WHEELER. "Thinking Clearly about Career Choices," *Psychology Today,* May 1978: 66–76, 121–122.

JENKS, V. O. *The Success Triad.* Englewood Cliffs, NJ: Prentice-Hall, 1983.

JOHNSON, MARCINE MCDONALD. "Psychotherapy as a Precipitant of High Level Discontent," unpublished dissertation, Saybrook Institute, 1980. In Carl Rogers, "Toward a More Human Science of the Person," paper delivered at the conference on "A Quarter Century of Humanistic Psychologies," March 7, 1985, San Francisco.

KABANOFF, B., and G. E. O'BRIEN. "Work and Leisure: A Task Attributes Analysis," *Journal of Applied Psychology,* 65, 1980: 596–609.

KACERGUIS, M. A., and G. R. ADAMS. "Erikson Stage and Resolution: The Relationships between Identity and Intimacy," *Journal of Youth and Adolescence,* 9, 1980: 117–126.

KALISH, R. A., and D. K. REYNOLDS. *Death and Ethnicity: A Psychocultural Study.* Los Angeles: University of Southern California Press, 1976.

KAPLAN, HELEN SINGER. *Disorders of Sexual Desire.* New York: Brunner/Mazel, 1979.

———. *The Illustrated Manual of Sex Therapy.* New York: Quadrangle/The New York Times Book Company, 1975.

KASTENBAUM, R. J. *Death, Society and Human Experience,* 2nd ed. St. Louis: The C. V. Mosby Company, 1981.

KAUFMANN, WALTER. *Without Guilt and Justice.* New York: Dell Publishing Company, 1975.

KELLEY, H. H., et al. *Close Relationships.* San Francisco: W. H. Freeman, 1983.

KIESLER, C. A. "Mental Hospitals and Alternative Care," *American Psychologist,* 37, 1982: 1323–1339.

KIMMEL, D. C., K. F. PRICE, and J. W. WALKER. "Retirement Choice and Retirement Satisfaction," *Journal of Gerontology,* 33, 3, 1978: 575–585.

KIPNIS, DAVID, and STUART SCHMIDT. "The Language of Persuasion," *Psychology Today,* April 1985: 40–46.

KLEINGINNA, P. R., and A. M. KLEINGINNA. "A Categorized List of Motivation Definitions with a Suggestion for a Consensual Definition," *Motivation and Emotions,* 5, 1981: 263–291.

KLEINKE, CHRIS L. *First Impressions.* Englewood Cliffs, NJ: Prentice-Hall, 1975.

———, and M. L. KAHN. "Perceptions of Self-Disclosers: Effects of Sex and Physical Attractiveness," *Journal of Personality,* 48, 1980: 190–205.

KNOEPFLER, PETER, M.D. "Transition: A Prephase of the Human Sexual Response Cycle," *Journal of Sex Education and Therapy,* 7, 1, 1981.

KÜBLER-ROSS, E. *Death*. Englewood Cliffs, NJ: Prentice-Hall, 1975.

KUKLA, R. A., and H. WEINGARTEN. "The Long-term Effects of Parental Divorce in Childhood on Adult Adjustment," *Journal of Social Issues*, 33, 4, 1979: 50–78.

KUNZ, JEFFREY R. M. (ed.). *The American Medical Association Family Medical Guide*. New York: Random House, 1982.

LA FARGE, P. "The New Woman," *Parents*, October 1983.

LANDERS, ANN. "The U. S. Conscience Fund: A Way for Gyppers to Ease Their Souls," *Philadelphia Inquirer*, October 23, 1981: 9-B.

———. *The Philadelphia Inquirer*, November 1, 1978.

LANDY, FRANK. "Industrial and Organizational Psychology," in *Psychology: The Science of People*. Englewood Cliffs, NJ: Prentice-Hall, 1984.

LAUER, JEANETTE, and ROBERT LAUER. "Marriages Made to Last," *Psychology Today*, June 1985, 22–26.

LAZARUS, A. S. *The Practice of Multimodel Therapy*. New York: McGraw-Hill, 1981.

LAZARUS, R. S. "Little Hassles Can Be Hazardous to Health," *Psychology Today*, July 1981: 58–62.

LAZARUS, R. S., and A. DELONGIS. "Psychological Stress and Coping in Aging," *American Psychology*, 38, 1983: 245–254.

LEO, JOHN. "The Revolution Is Over," *Time*, April 9, 1984.

LEONARD, GEORGE. *The End of Sex*. Los Angeles, CA: J. P. Tarcher, 1983.

LERNER, BARBARA. "Self-esteem and Excellence: The Choice and the Paradox," *American Educator*. Winter 1985: 10–16.

LEVENTHAL, HOWARD. "Wrongheaded Ideas about Illness," *Psychology Today*, January 1982: 48–55, 73.

LEVIN, ROBERT J. "The Redbook Report on Premarital and Extramarital Sex," *Redbook Magazine*, October 1975: 38–44, 190–192.

LEVINSON, DANIEL J., et al. *The Seasons of a Man's Life*. New York: Knopf, 1978.

LEWIN, T. "A New Push to Raise Women's Pay," *The New York Times*, January 1, 1984.

LEWINE, R.R.J. "Sex Differences in Schizophrenia: Timing or Subtypes?" *Psychological Bulletin*, 90, 1981: 432–444.

LICHTENBERG, JAMES W. "Psychotherapeutic Processes, Guilt, Expectations, Counseling," *Journal of Counseling and Development*, 63, 2, 1984: 101–102.

LICHTENSTEIN, E. "The Smoking Problem: A Behavioral Perspective," *Journal of Consulting and Clinical Psychology*, 50, 1982: 804–819.

LOWRY, R. (ed.). *Dominance, Self-esteem, Self-actualization: Germinal Papers of A. H. Maslow*. Monterey, CA: Brooks/Cole, 1973.

LYNCH, J. J. *Broken Heart*. New York: Basic Books, 1979.

MACE, DAVID, and VERA MACE. *How To Have a Happy Marriage*. Nashville, TN: Abington Press, 1977.

MACKLIN, ELEANOR D. "Cohabitation in College: Going Very Steady," *Psychology Today*, November 1974: 53–59.

MAIER, STEVEN F., and MARK LAUDEN-SLAGER. "Stress and Health:

Exploring the Links," *Psychology Today*, August 1985: 44–49.

MARX, M. B., GRANT W. SOMES, THOMAS F. GARRITY, ARVIL C. REEB, JR., and PATRICIA A. MAFFEO. "The Influence of a Supportive, Problem-solving, Group Intervention on the Health Status of Students with Great Recent Life Change," *Journal of Psychosomatic Research*, 28, 4, 1984: 275–278.

MASLOW, ABRAHAM H. *The Farther Reaches of Human Nature.* New York: Viking, 1971.

———. *Motivation and Personality*, 2nd ed. New York: Harper & Row, 1970.

———. *Toward a Psychology of Being*, 2nd ed. New York: Van Nostrand Reinhold Company, 1968.

MASTERS, ROBERT, and JEAN HOUSTON. *Listening to the Body.* New York: Dell Publishing Company, 1978.

MASTERS, W. H., and V. E. JOHNSON. *Human Sexual Inadequacy.* Boston: Little, Brown, 1970.

———, and V. E. JOHNSON. *Human Sexual Response.* Boston: Little, Brown, 1966.

———, V. E. JOHNSON, and R. C. KOLODNY. *Human Sexuality*, 2nd ed. Boston: Little, Brown, 1985.

MAY, P.R.A., A. H. TUMA, and W. J. DIXON. "Schizophrenia: A Follow-up Study of the Results of Five Forms of Treatment," *Archives of General Psychiatry*, 38, 1981: 776–784.

MAY, ROLLO. "Will, Decision and Responsibility: Summary Remarks," in Raymond Van Over (ed.), *The Psychology of Freedom.* Greenwich, CT: Fawcett Publications, 1974.

McCORMACK, NORMA. "Plain Talk about Mutual Help Groups," *National Institute of Mental Health.* DHHS Publication No. (ADM) 81-1138; Washington, DC: U.S. Government Printing Office, 1981.

MEDNICK, S., T. MOFFIT, V. POLLACK, S. TALOVIC, and W. GABRIELLI. "The Inheritance of Human Deviance," paper presented at Conference on Human Development from the Perspective of Person-Environment Interaction, Stockholm, Sweden, June 1982. In I. G. Sarason and B. R. Sarason, *Abnormal Behavior*, 4th ed. Englewood Cliffs, NJ: Prentice-Hall, 1984.

MEICHENBAUM, D. H. *Cognitive-behavior Modification.* New York: Plenum, 1977.

MELTZER, H. Y. "Biochemical Studies in Schizophrenia," in L. Bellak (ed.), *Disorders of the Schizophrenia Syndrome.* New York: Basic Books, 1979.

MIDDLEBROOK, PATRICIA NILES. *Social Psychology and Modern Life*, 2nd ed. New York: Knopf, 1980.

MISCHEL, WALTER. *Introduction to Personality*, 4th ed. New York: Holt, Rinehart & Winston, 1986.

———. "On the Interface of Cognition and Personality," *American Psychologist*, 34, 1979: 740–754.

MOODY, R. A., JR. *Reflections on Life After Life.* Atlanta, GA: Mockingbird, 1977.

MOOR, R. *Evaluating Educational Environments.* San Francisco: Jossey-Bass, 1979.

MORROW, LANCE. "Advertisements for Oneself," *Time*, September 2, 1985: 74

NAGY, I., and B. KRASNER. *Between Give and Take.* New York: Bruner-Mazel, 1986.

NARDONE, TOM. "The Job Outlook in Brief," *Occupational Outlook Quarterly.* Washington, DC: U.S. Department of Labor, Bureau of Labor Statistics; Government Printing Office, Spring 1984.

NATIONAL CENTER FOR HEALTH STATISTICS. *Health: United States, 1984.* DHHS Pub. No. (PHS) 85-1232; Washington, DC: Public Health Service, U.S. Government Printing Office, 1984.

NEUGARTEN, B. L., and E. HALL. "Acting One's Age: New Rules for Old," *Psychology Today,* April 1980: 66–80.

———. "Personality and Aging," in J. E. Birren and K. W. Schaie (eds.), *Handbook of the Psychology of Aging,* New York: Van Nostrand Reinhold, 1977.

NIAID STUDY GROUP. *Sexually Transmitted Diseases: 1980 Status Report.* NIH Pub. No. 81-2213; Washington, DC: U.S. Government Printing Office, 1981.

NIELSEN, ROBERT. "Will Colleges Change as Jobs Change?" *On Campus,* 3, 3, November 1983: 16.

NISBETT, R., and LEE ROSS. *Human Inference.* Englewood Cliffs, NJ: Prentice-Hall, 1980.

NOTMAN, M. "Midlife Concerns of Women: Implications of the Menopause," *American Journal of Psychiatry,* 136, 1979: 1270–1274.

Occupational Outlook Handbook: 1984–85 Edition. Washington, DC: U.S. Department of Labor, Bureau of Labor Statistics; Government Printing Office, 1984.

O'DONNELL-COX, DALE. "Think Ahead About Funeral Expenses," *The Philadelphia Inquirer,* November 17, 1984: 5-C.

On Campus, "Teen Suicide: The Alarming Statistics," February 1985, 4–7.

PALMORE, E. "Total Chance of Institutionalization Among the Aged," *The Gerontologist,* 16, 1976: 504–507.

PARLEE, MARY BROWN, and the editors of *Psychology Today.* "The Friendship Bond," *Psychology Today,* October 1979: 43–54, 113.

PENNEBAKER, J. W., and D. Y. SANDERS. "American Graffiti: Effects of Authority and Reactance Arousal," *Personality and Social Psychology Bulletin,* 2, 1976: 264–267.

PEPLAU, L., Z. RUBIN, and C. HILL. "Sexual Intimacy in Dating Relationships," *Journal of Social Issues,* 33, 1977: 86–109.

PERLMAN, D., A. C. GERSON, and B. SPINNER. "Loneliness Among Senior Citizens: An Empirical Report," *Essence,* 2, 1978: 239–248.

PLUTCHIK, ROBERT. *Emotion: A Psycho-evolutionary Synthesis.* New York: Harper & Row, 1980.

POPE, H., and C. W. MUELLER. "The Intergenerational Transmission of Marital Instability," in G. Levinger and O. C. Moles (eds.), *Divorce and Separation.* New York: Basic Books, 1979.

PRICE, R. A., and S. G. VANDENBERG. "Matching for Physical Attractiveness in Married Couples," *Personality and Social Psychology Bulletin,* 5, 1979: 398–400.

PUTNAM, F. "Traces of Eve's Faces," *Psychology Today,* October 1982.

RACHMAN, S. J., and R. J. HODGSON. *Obsessions and Compulsions.* Englewood Cliffs, NJ: Prentice-Hall, 1980.

RAVEN, BERTRAM H., and JEFFREY Z. RUBIN. *Social Psychology,* 2nd edition. New York: John Wiley, 1983.

REEDY, M. N., J. E. BIRREN, and K. W. SCHAIE. "Age and Sex Differences in Satisfying Love Relationships Across the Adult Life Span," *Human Development,* 24, 1981: 52–66.

REIS, H. T., L. WHEELER, N. SPIEGEL, M. H. KERNIS, J. NEZLEK, and M. PERRI. "Physical Attractiveness in Social Interaction: Why Does Appearance Affect Social Experience?" *Journal of Personality and Social Psychology,* 43, 1982: 979–996.

RENWICK, PATRICIA A., and EDWARD E. LAWLER. "What You Really Want from Your Job," *Psychology Today,* May 1978.

RISMAN, B., C. T. HILL, Z. RUBIN, and L. A. PEPLAU. "Living Together in College: Implications for Courtship," *Journal of Marriage and the Family,* 43, 1, 1981: 77–83.

ROBBINS, M., and G. JENSEN. "Multiple Orgasm in Males," *Journal of Sex Research,* 14, 1978: 21–26.

ROBINS, L. N., J. E. HELZER, M. M. WEISSMAN, H. ORVASCHEL, E. GRUENBERG, J. D. BURKE, JR., and D. A. REGIER. "Lifetime Prevalence of Specific Psychiatric Disorders in Three Sites," *Archives of General Psychiatry,* 41, 1984: 949–958.

RODIN, J. "Current Status of the Internal-External Hypothesis for Obesity: What Went Wrong?" *American Psychologist,* 36, 1981: 361–372.

ROGERS, CARL R. *A Way of Being.* Boston: Houghton Mifflin, 1980.

———. "In Retrospect: Forty-six Years," *American Psychologist,* 29, 1974: 115–123.

———. "Toward a More Human Science of the Person," paper delivered at the conference, "A Quarter Century of Humanistic Psychologies," March 7, 1985, San Francisco.

———, B. STEVENS, et al. *Person to Person.* Lafayette, CA: Real People Press, 1971.

ROLLINS, B. C., and H. FELDMAN. "Marital Satisfaction Over the Family Life Cycle," in L. D. Steinberg (ed.), *The Life Cycle: Readings in Human Development.* New York: Columbia University Press, 1981.

ROMBERGER, BEVERLY. Unpublished doctoral dissertation, Pennsylvania State University, in Darrell Sifford, "What Women Think They Should Think About Men," *The Philadelphia Inquirer,* August 26, 1985.

ROSSI, A. S. "Aging and Parenthood in the Middle Years," in P. B. Baltes and O. G. Brim, Jr. (eds.), *Life-span Development and Behavior,* vol. 3. New York: Academic Press, 1980.

ROUNSAVILLE, B. J., G. L. KLERMAN, and M. M. WEISSMAN. "Do Psychotherapy and Pharmacotherapy for Depression Conflict?" *Archives of General Psychiatry,* 38, 1981: 24–29.

RUBIN, L. B. *Women of a Certain Age.* New York: Harper & Row, 1979.

RUBINSTEIN, CARIN. "Survey Report: How Americans View Vacations," *Psychology Today,* May 1980.

———. "Survey Report: Money and Self-esteem, Relationships, Secrecy, Envy, Satisfaction," *Psychology Today,* May 1981: 29–44.

———. "Who Calls In? It's Not the Lonely Crowd," *Psychology Today,* December 1981.

———. "Wellness Is All," *Psychology Today,* October 1982: 28–37.

——, P. SHAVER, and L. A. PEPLAU. "Loneliness," in N. Jackson (ed.), *Personal Growth and Behavior, 82/83.* Guilford, CT: The Dushkin Publishing Company, 1982.

SABOM, M. *Recollections of Death.* New York: Harper & Row, 1981.

SANDERS, J. S., and W. L. ROBINSON. "Talking and Not Talking About Sex: Male and Female Vocabularies," *Journal of Communication,* 29, 2, 1979: 22–20.

SANTROCK, JOHN W. *Life-span Development.* Dubuque, IA: Wm C. Brown, 1984.

——, R. A. WARSHAK, and G. ELIOT. "Social Development and Parent-Child Interactions in Father Custody and Stepmother Families," in M. E. Lamb (ed.), *Nontraditional Families.* Hillsdale, NJ: Erlbaum, 1982.

SARASON, I. G. "The Test Anxiety Scale: Concepts and Research," in C. D. Spielberger and I. G. Sarason (eds.), *Stress and Anxiety,* vol. 5. Washington, DC: Hemisphere, 1978.

——, and B. R. SARASON. *Abnormal Psychology,* 4th ed. Englewood Cliffs, NJ: Prentice-Hall, 1984.

SAXE, JAMES GODFREY. *The Blind Men and The Elephant.* New York: McGraw-Hill, 1963.

SCHACHTER, STANLEY. "Recidivism and Self-cure of Smoking and Obesity," *American Psychologist,* 37, 1982: 436–444.

SCHREIBER, F. R. *Sybil.* Chicago: Henry Regnery, 1973.

SCHWARTZ, G. E. "Psychosomatic Disorders and Biofeedback: A Psychobiological Model of Disregulation," in J. D. Maser and M.E.P. Seligman (eds.), *Psychopathology: Experimental Models.* San Francisco: W. H. Freeman, 1977.

——. "Testing the Biopsychosocial Model: The Ultimate Challenge Facing Behavioral Medicine," *Journal of Consulting and Clinical Psychology,* 50, 1982: 1040–1053.

SELIGMAN, MARTIN E. P. *Helplessness.* San Francisco: W. H. Freeman, 1975.

SELYE, HANS, M.D. *Stress Without Distress.* Philadelphia: J. B. Lippincott, 1974.

——. "The Stress Concept Today," in I. L. Kutash, et al. (eds.), *Handbook on Stress and Anxiety: Contemporary Knowledge, Theory, and Treatment.* San Francisco: Jossey-Bass, 1980.

SHAPIRO, HOWARD S., and EMILIE LOUNSBERRY. "Nesting: Young Adults Flock Back to Their Parents' Homes," *The Philadelphia Inquirer,* February 22, 1983: 1-D

SHNEIDMAN, E. S. *Deaths of Man.* New York: Quadrangle Books, 1973.

——. *Voices of Death.* New York: Harper & Row, 1980.

SIFFORD, DARRELL. "For Young People, 'A Heavy Burden,'" *The Philadelphia Inquirer,* November 4, 1985: 5-D.

SLOVIC, P., B. FISCHHOFF, and S. LICHTENSTEIN. "Risky Assumptions," *Psychology Today,* June 1980: 44–48.

SMITH, D. "Trends in Counseling and Psychotherapy," *American Psychologist,* 37, 1982: 802–809.

SMITH, M. L., G. V. GLASS, and T. J. MILLER. *The Benefits of Psychotherapy.* Baltimore: Johns Hopkins, 1980.

SMITH, R. J. *The Psychopath in Society.* New York: Academic Press, 1978.

SNYDER, M. "Self-monitoring Processes," in L. Berkowitz (ed.), *Advances in Experimental Social Psychology,* vol.

12. New York: Academic Press, 1979.

SPAIN, D., and M. S. BIANCHI. "How Women Have Changed," *American Demographics,* May 1983.

SPENCE, J., and R. HELMREICH. *Masculinity and Femininity.* Austin, TX: University of Texas Press, 1978.

SPITZER, R. L., A. E. SKODOL, M. GIBBON, and J.B.W. WILLIAMS. *Psychopathology; A Case Book.* New York: McGraw-Hill, 1983.

STARK, ELIZABETH. "Preeetty Scary, huh?" *Psychology Today,* February 1985: 16.

SULLIVAN, K., and A. SULLIVAN. "Adolescent-Parent Separation," *Developmental Psychology,* 16, 2, 1980: 93–99.

SWENSEN, C. H., R. W. ESKEW, and K. A. KOHLEPP. "Stage of Family Cycle, Ego Development, and the Marriage Relationship," *Journal of Marriage and the Family,* 43, 4, 1981: 841–853.

TAVRIS, CAROL. *Anger: The Misunderstood Emotion.* New York: Simon & Schuster, 1983.

———. "Masculinity," *Psychology Today,* January 1977: 34.

———, and T. E. JAYARATNE. "How Happy Is Your Marriage? What 75,000 Wives Say About Their Most Intimate Relationships," *Redbook,* June 1976: 90–92, 132.

TAYLOR, C. B. "Behavioral Approaches to Hypertension," in J. M. Ferguson and C. B. Taylor (eds.), *The Comprehensive Handbook of Behavioral Medicine,* vol. 1. New York: S. P. Medical and Scientific Books, 1980: 55–88.

TIFFT, SUSAN. "Debate on the Boundary of Life," *Time,* April 11, 1983: 68–70.

TOFFLER, ALVIN. *The Third Wave.* New York: William Morrow, 1980.

TROLL, LILLIAN. *Early and Middle Adulthood.* Monterey, CA: Brooks/Cole, 1975.

TROWELL, I. "Telephone Services," in L. D. Hankoff and B. Einsidler (eds.), *Suicide: Theory and Clinical Aspects.* Littleton, MA: PSG Publishing, 1979.

TURNER, JEFFREY S., and DONALD B. HELMS. *Lifespan Development,* 2nd ed. New York: Holt, Rinehart & Winston, 1983.

U.S. BUREAU OF THE CENSUS. *Social Indicators III.* Washington, DC: U.S. Government Printing Office, 1980.

———. *The Statistical Abstract of the United States 1984,* 105th ed. Washington, DC: Government Printing Office, 1984.

U.S. DEPARTMENT OF HEALTH AND HUMAN SERVICES. *Schizophrenia: Is There an Answer?* Rockville, MD: U.S. Department of Health and Human Services, 1981.

———. *Special Report to Congress on Alcohol and Health.* DHHS Pub. No. ADM 81-1080, d; Washington, DC: U.S. Government Printing Office, 1981.

U.S. DEPARTMENT OF LABOR, BUREAU OF LABOR STATISTICS. *Monthly Labor Review,* November 1985. Washington, D.C.: U.S. Government Printing Office, 1985.

VAILLANT, G. E., and E. S. MILOFSKY. "Natural History of Male Alcoholism IV: Paths to Recovery," *Archives of General Psychiatry,* 39, 1982: 127–133.

VAN ATTA, BURR. "F. W. Demara, Jr., 60, 'The Great Impostor,'" *The Philadelphia Inquirer*, June 9, 1982: 3-F.

VEROFF, J., E. DOUVAN, and R. A. KULKA. *The Inner American.* New York: Basic Books, 1981.

WALKER, J. INGRAM, M.D. *Everybody's Guide to Emotional Well-being.* San Francisco: Harbor Publishing, 1982.

WALLERSTEIN, J. S., and J. B. KELLEY. *Surviving the Break-up.* New York: Basic Books, 1980.

WALLIS, CLAUDIA. "AIDS: A growing threat," *Time,* August 12, 1985: 40–47.

———. "To Feed or Not to Feed?" *Time,* March 31, 1986: 60.

WALLSTON, KENNETH A., ROBERTA A. SMITH, JOAN E. KING, PATRICIA R. FORSBERG, BARBARA STRUDLER WALLSTON, and VIVIAN TONG NAGY. "Expectations About Control Over Health: Relationship to Desire for Control of Health Care," *Personality and Social Psychology Bulletin,* September 1983: 377–385.

WALSTER, E., and G. W. WALSTER. *A New Look at Love;* Reading, MA: Addison-Wesley, 1978. In Sandra Scarr and James Vander Zanden, *Understanding Psychology,* 4th ed; New York: Random House, 1984.

WEGNER, DANIEL M., and ROBIN R. VALLACHER. *Implicit Psychology.* New York: Oxford University Press, 1977.

WEISINGER, HENDRIE, and NORMAN M. LOBSENZ. *Nobody's Perfect.* New York: Warner Books, 1981.

WEIST, W. "Semantic Differential Profiles of Orgasm and Other Experiences Among Men and Women," *Sex Roles,* 3, 1977: 399–403.

WHELAN, ELIZABETH. *Preventing Cancer.* New York: W. W. Norton & Company, 1978.

WHITE, G. L. "Jealousy and Partner's Perceived Motives for Attraction to a Rival," *Social Psychology Quarterly,* 44, 1, 1981: 24–30.

WOLF, S. "Cardiovascular Disease," in E. D. Wittkower and H. Warnes (eds.), *Psychosomatic Medicine: Its Clinical Applications.* New York: Harper & Row, 1977.

WOLPE, J. *The Practice of Behavior Therapy.* New York: Pergamon Press, 1973.

YANKELOVICH, DANIEL. *New Rules.* New York: Bantam Books, 1981.

———. "The Work Ethic Is Underemployed," *Psychology Today,* May 1982: 5–8.

———, SKELLY, and WHITE, INC. "A Study of Women's Attitudes Toward Contraceptive Alternatives," report prepared for the Upjohn Company, December 1982. In *Family Planning Perspectives,* 16, 1, January/February 1984: 41–42.

ZILBERGELD, B. *Male Sexuality.* Boston: Little, Brown, 1978.

ZIMBARDO, PHILIP G. *Psychology and Life,* 11th ed. Glenview, IL: Scott, Foresman, 1985.

———. *Shyness.* Reading, MA: Addison-Wesley.

ZUBIN, J. "Chronic Schizophrenia from the Standpoint of Vulnerability," in C. Baxter and T. Melnechuk (eds.), *Perspectives in Schizophrenia Research.* New York: Raven Press, 1980: 269–294.

ZUCKERMAN, M. *Sensation Seeking.* New York: Halstead Press, 1979.

———, R. S. DEFRANK, N. H. SPIEGEL, and D. T. LARRANCE. "Masculinity-Femininity and Encoding of Nonverbal Cues," *Journal of Personality and Social Psychology,* 42, 1982: 548–556.

——, BELLA M. DEPAULO, and ROBERT ROSENTHAL. "Verbal and Nonverbal Communication of Deception,"

in Leonard Berkowitz (ed.), *Advances in Experimental Social Psychology,* vol. 14. New York: Academic Press, 1981.

ZURCHER, LOUIS A., JR. *The Mutable Self.* Beverly Hills, CA: Sage Publications, 1977.

Glossary

acting out: The unconscious mechanism by which we relieve anxiety or unpleasant tensions through expressing them in overt behavior.

activity theory of aging: The view that the more active people remain as they grow older, the more satisfied they will be.

actualization therapy: An approach that stresses self-actualization as the goal of psychotherapy.

adaptation: Biologically, the changes in an organism's structure or function that facilitate the survival of the species. (See *cultural adaptation*.)

addictive relationships: Love relationships that are characterized by undue dependency or the need for approval.

adjustment: The changes in ourselves and our environment that enable us to achieve satisfying relationships with others and our surroundings.

adulthood: The period of life from physical maturity on, including the continuing sequence of psychosocial changes throughout early, middle, and late adulthood.

aging: A decline in the biological processes that comes with advancing years, usually accompanied by appropriate psychosocial changes and the increasing risk of illness and death.

AIDS (Acquired Immune Deficiency Syndrome): a sexually transmitted disease that is communicated through blood products and is ultimately fatal.

Alzheimer's disease: A brain disorder that usually occurs after 60 years of age, characterized by progressive deterioration of the mind which continues until death.

anal stage: According to Freud, the second stage of psychosexual development in which the child's mastery of bowel and sphincter movements becomes the major source of physical pleasure.

anger: The feeling of extreme displeasure, usually brought about by frustration of our needs or desires.

antisocial personality disorder: A personality disorder characterized by long-standing habits of thought and behavior that cause less stress to the individuals themselves than to those involved with them.

anxiety: A vague, unpleasant feeling warning of impending danger.

anxiety disorder: A disorder characterized by symptoms of inappropriate or excessive anxiety or by attempts to escape from such anxiety.

assertiveness: The act of expressing one's own thoughts, feelings, or rights, but in a way that respects those of others.

assertiveness training: A therapeutic strategy aimed at helping individuals express their personal desires and rights more effectively through developing their assertiveness skills.

attraction, law of: The view that people are attracted to others according to the proportion of similar attitudes shared.

autonomy versus shame and doubt: According to Erikson, the second stage of psychosocial development in which the child gains an initial sense of autonomy.

balance sheet: A helpful strategy of weighing one's potential gains and losses in making an important decision.

behavior therapy: A group of therapies aimed at helping the client change specific behaviors through such action-oriented techniques as assertiveness training.

bereavement: The process of adjusting to the experience of loss, especially the death of one's friends or loved ones.

bipolar disorder: An affective disorder characterized by both manic and depressive episodes.

body ideal: The part of the self-concept pertaining to the idealized appearance of one's body, which is also influenced by the standards of beauty in one's culture.

body image: The part of the self-concept that is based on the individual's perception of his or her own body and satisfaction with it.

career: The purposeful life pattern of work, as seen in the sequence of jobs held throughout one's life.

chlamydia infections: Inflammation of the urethra tube.

climacteric: Physiological changes in reproductive ability that accompany the aging process, as seen in menopause in women and the more gradual reduction of fertile sperm in older men.

cognition: A general term for information processing, including attention, perception, thinking, and memory.

cognitive restructuring: A behavioral therapy procedure aimed at altering clients' way of perceiving their lives in order to change their behavior.

cohabitation: Unmarried couples living together, sharing bed and board.

commitment: The pledge or promise to make something work, as in committing ourselves to a relationship with someone.

community mental health center: A center designed to provide a variety of psychological services for people living within a specified area.

complementary needs theory of attraction: The view that individuals tend to select friends and love partners with traits or needs that complement their own.

conflict: The felt pressure to respond simultaneously to two or more incompatible forces.

conformity: Change in one's behavior because of real or imagined pressure from others.

contextual therapy: According to Nagy, an intergenerational approach to family therapy that emphasizes each person's search for fair treatment.

coping devices for minor stress: A variety of spontaneous mechanisms for reducing emotional stress, such as crying, laughing, or cursing.

cultural adaptation: A process by which humans achieve a beneficial adjustment to their environment through the use of their intelligence, language, and problem-solving skills. Also, the result of this process.

death: The cessation of biological life, as measured by the absence of breathing, heartbeat, and electrical activity of the brain.

decidophobia: The fear of making the more important decisions in our lives.

decision making: The process of gathering information about relevant alternatives and making an appropriate choice.

decision-making strategies: The variety of ways individuals go about making decisions, such as the impulsive and intuitive strategies.

defense mechanisms: Automatic, unconscious mechanisms that protect us from the awareness of anxiety, thereby helping us to maintain a sense of self-worth in the face of threat.

delusion: An irrational belief that an individual defends with great fervor despite overwhelming evidence that such a belief has no basis in reality.

denial: The unconscious mechanism by which we protect ourselves from unpleasant aspects of reality by refusing to perceive them.

depersonalization: The sense of not being intimately attached to one's body.

depression: An emotional state characterized by intense and unrealistic sadness that may assume a variety of forms, some more severe and chronic than others.

desensitization: A method of controlling anxiety through learning to associate an incompatible response, such as relaxation, with the fear-provoking stimulus.

direct decision therapy: The view that therapy is best aimed at helping clients see their problems in terms of previous decisions and choosing a more satisfying alternative.

disengagement theory of aging: The view that aging is normally accompanied by the individual's decreasing psychological and social involvement in society.

distress: Stress that has an unpleasant or harmful effect.

divorce: The legal dissolution of marriage, usually accompanied by psychological, social, and financial adjustments.

drive-reduction model of motivation: The view that organisms act mostly to reduce the tension of unmet needs.

ego: According to Freud, the executive agency of the psyche that manages the personality according to the reality principle.

electroconvulsive therapy: The administration of an electrical current to the client's brain in order to produce a convulsion, sometimes used in the treatment of severe depression.

emotion: A complex state of awareness, including physiological changes, subjective experience, and outward expressions and reactions to events.

erectile inhibition: The difficulty of having or maintaining an erect penis in response to sexual stimulation.

euthanasia: A merciful, painless death as a way of ending a person's suffering, especially someone who is terminally ill.

existential therapy: A therapeutic approach that emphasizes the capacity of clients for growth and transcendence through affirmation of their personal values and free choice.

family therapy: A therapeutic approach that counsels the entire family on the assumption that the disturbance of one member of a family reflects problems in the whole family's interactions.

friendship: The affectionate attachment between friends of either sex.

general adaptation syndrome: According to Selye, the reaction to stress includes three progressive stages—an alarm reaction, resistance, and exhaustion.

generativity versus stagnation: The psychosocial crisis in Erikson's seventh stage of development, in which middle-aged adults extend their concern beyond themselves and their families to the welfare of others, including the younger generation.

genital herpes: A sexually transmitted disease that, in addition to the discomfort of the symptoms, may lead to serious medical complications.

genital stage: According to Freud, the final adult stage of psychosexual development in which childhood sexual conflicts are resolved and a stable sexual identity is achieved.

gestalt therapy: A therapy approach that uses behavior in the here and now to facilitate the client's integration of self.

giving/getting contract: The unwritten rules governing what we give in our personal relationships, work, and community, and what we expect in return.

gonorrhea: A sexually transmitted disease characterized by inflammation of the mucous membrane of the genitourinary tract.

good grief: The positive benefits that may result when grief becomes a learning experience.

grief: The intense emotional suffering that accompanies our experience of loss.

grief work: The healthy process of working through our emotions associated with loss.

group therapy: All those forms of therapy in which a leader meets with a group of clients, including preexisting groups such as families and those consisting of strangers.

groupthink: The tendency for group members to suppress critical thinking because of the pressure for consensus and conformity.

growth model of motivation: According

to Maslow, the view that once our basic needs are relatively satisfied, we become increasingly aware of our growth needs.

guilt: The emotion that follows the violation of our conscience or our moral principles, involving self-reproach and apprehension over the fear of punishment.

hallucination: A sensory perception that occurs in the absence of an appropriate external stimulus.

health hazard: Anything that poses a potential hazard to our health, such as food additives.

hierarchy of needs: According to Maslow, the hierarchical manner in which needs and motives function in relation to each other so that the lowest level of unmet needs remains the most urgent.

hospice: A system of care that integrates a physical facility for the terminally ill with the patient's family and home, allowing the patient to have a dignified death.

humanistic psychology: The group of related theories and therapies that emphasizes the values of the individual and personal freedom.

hyperstress: Excessive stress.

hypertension: Chronically high blood pressure.

hypochondriac: A person who habitually complains of unfounded ailments or exhibits an undue fear of illness.

hypostress: A state in which too little stress leaves us bored and unchallenged.

"I" message: The expression of your feelings about another person's behavior in a nonjudgmental way.

id: According to Freud, the unconscious reservoir of psychic energy that drives the personality.

ideal self: The self a person would like to

be, including one's aspirations, moral ideals, and values.

identity achievement versus identity confusion: The developmental crisis of adolescence in which the individual normally revises his or her identity in light of self-chosen values.

incentive: Any external influence that stimulates us to take action or work harder, usually through anticipation of receiving the incentive.

industry versus inferiority: According to Erikson, the fourth stage of psychosocial development in which the school-aged child's sense of self-esteem depends largely on the acquisition of age-appropriate competencies.

inhibited sexual desire: The lack of sexual desire or a low level of such desire.

inhibited vaginal lubrication: Insufficient lubrication in the vagina during sexual activity.

initiative versus guilt: According to Erikson, the third stage of psychosocial development in which it is desirable for children to have greater freedom within limits for exercising their autonomy.

integrity versus despair: The psychosocial crisis in Erikson's final stage of development in which it is desirable for older adults to reflect upon their life with a deep sense of satisfaction.

intimacy: Interpersonal closeness between two or more people that may or may not include sexual intimacy.

intimacy versus isolation: The psychosocial crisis in Erikson's sixth stage of development in which young adults put special emphasis on establishing close relationships with their peers.

job: A position of employment; the set of work activities and responsibilities associated with a given position.

job satisfaction: How well you like a given job, depending on such factors as the people you work with as well as your pay.

latency stage: According to Freud, the fourth stage of psychosexual development in which the childhood sexual conflicts are repressed.

learned helplessness: The subjective realization that one's actions have little or no effect on the environment, frequently leading to passivity and depression.

leisure: Time free from work or duty that may be spent in recreative acivities.

life review: A process of self-reflection among aged persons, prompted by the realization that their life is approaching an end.

lifestyle: The overall way individuals express themselves in their distinctive attitudes, behaviors, and values.

living will: An instrument a person writes instructing doctors and family members to stop using life-sustaining procedures in the event the person has a terminal condition.

logotherapy: According to Victor Frankl, the process by which clients are confronted with the responsibility for their existence and pursuing the values inherent in life.

loneliness: Feelings of emptiness and isolation resulting from the absence of satisfying relationships.

love: A complex emotional state accompanying a person's needs for attachment as well as the satisfaction of those needs. Also, an intimate relationship including such emotion.

maladaptive behavior: The inability of a person to meet the practical demands of life adequately, such as holding down a job and dealing with family and friends.

marital adjustment: The changes and adjustments in a couple's relationship during the course of married life.

marriage relationship: The personal relationship or companionship aspects of marriage, as distinguished from marriage as a functional, role relationship.

menopause: Cessation of the menstrual cycle in a woman's life.

mentor: A person with greater experience or seniority who takes an active interest in helping you along with your career.

midlife transition: The period of self-assessment accompanying the realization that your life is half over, beginning about 40 years of age.

mind-body unity: The concept that holds that the mind and body are so closely interwoven that any mental event may affect our bodily processes and *vice versa.*

motivation: The tendency to act to achieve a particular goal or end-state.

motive: A specific goal-directed activity, such as the hunger motive to satisfy the need for food.

motive targets: The people toward whom our motives are directed.

mourning: The outward expressions of bereavement and grief, such as wearing black.

multiple personality: One of the dissociative disorders in which the individual alternates between two or more distinct personalities.

multiple selves: The idea that the overall self-concept includes hundreds of self-perceptions of varying degrees of clarity and intensity.

mutual help groups: Groups of people who share a common problem or concern and meet regularly to discuss their problems without the guidance of professionals.

near-death experience: The distinctive state of recall associated with being brought back to life from the verge of death.

need: A state of tension or deprivation that arouses us to seek appropriate gratification.

negative feedback: The process in which information is returned to a system in order to regulate that system.

negotiation: A cooperative approach to bargaining, synonymous with cooperative problem-solving.

neurotransmitter: A chemical substance involved in the transmission of neural impulses between neurons.

nonverbal cues: All those expressions of emotions that rely on nonverbal behavior such as facial expressions and hand gestures.

obesity: Excessive amount of body fat, usually defined as exceeding the desirable weight for one's height, build, and age by 20 percent or more.

observational learning: The process by which people learn by observing other people and events without necessarily receiving any direct reward or reinforcement.

obsessive-compulsive disorder: The condition characterized by an involuntary dwelling on an unwelcome thought and/or involuntary repetition of an unnecessary action.

oral stage: According to Freud, the first stage of psychosexual development in which the infant's mouth becomes the primary means of physical pleasure.

orgasm: An extremely pleasurable peak of sexual activity involving the release of tensions from sexual excitement and usually accompanied by ejaculation in the male.

panic attack: A state of almost unbearable anxiety and its related symptoms, lasting for a few minutes or several hours.

perceived freedom: The subjective sense of freedom one feels in a given situation.

person-centered approach to therapy: According to Carl Rogers, the view that the therapist's acceptance and empathetic understanding of the client are necessary to facilitate the latter's personal growth.

personal growth: Change or development in a desired direction, including the fulfillment of one's inborn potential.

phallic stage: According to Freud, the third stage of psychosexual development in which the child's genital area becomes the primary source of physical pleasure.

phenomenal self: The individual's overall self-concept, which is available to awareness, though not necessarily in awareness.

phobic disorder: The condition characterized by persistent and irrational fear of a specific object or activity.

pleasure principle: According to Freud, the principle by which the desires of the id automatically seek pleasurable gratification.

powers of attorney: A document that empowers anyone to make medical decisions when the signee becomes incompetent.

psychoanalysis: A form of psychotherapy developed by Freud, aimed at helping the client gain insight and mastery over unconscious desires and conflicts.

psychodynamic theory: The view that human behavior is based on the dynamics of interaction or the driving forces of personality, such as desires, anxiety, conflicts, and defenses.

psychological disorder: The condition characterized by painful symptoms or personal distress and significant impairment in one or more areas of functioning.

psychological hardiness: A set of attitudes toward life that includes an openness to change, personal involvement in whatever one is doing, and a sense of personal control over events.

psychosurgery: A surgical procedure involving the destruction or disconnection of brain tissue in an attempt to regulate abnormal behavior.

psychotherapy: A helping process in which a trained, socially sanctioned therapist performs certain activities that will facilitate a change in the client's attitudes and behaviors.

rational-emotive therapy: A form of psychotherapy developed by Albert Ellis, in which the client is encouraged to replace irrational ideals with a more rational, problem-solving approach to life.

rationalization: The unconscious mechanism by which we attempt to justify our unacceptable behavior through "good" reasons.

reactance: The psychological response of asserting our personal freedom all the more in the face of external threats against it.

reaction-formation: The unconscious attempt to control unacceptable desires by adopting the opposite feelings and behaviors.

reality principle: According to Freud, the rational orientation that guides the ego in its attemps to put a person's well-being above the pleasure seeking of the id and restrictive control of the superego.

REM sleep: The rapid eye movement stage of sleep in which most dreaming occurs.

remarriage: The act of marriage when one or both partners has been divorced.

repression: The automatic, unconscious act of putting a threatening idea or feeling out of awareness.

retirement: Withdrawal from one's regular career activity and status, usually because of changes in one's age or health.

romantic love: The state of emotional and physical attraction to a person of the opposite sex, often involving a marked tendency to idealize one's partner.

schizophrenia: A group of related psychotic disorders characterized by severe disorganization of thought, perception, emotions, bizarre behavior, and social withdrawal.

self-actualization: The process of fulfilling your inborn potential, involving an inherent actualizing tendency as well as self-conscious efforts at growth.

self-assessment in career choice: Taking stock of your interests, abilities, and personal traits as a means of choosing a compatible career.

self-concept: The overall pattern of perceptions of "I" and "me," together with the feelings, beliefs, and values associated with them.

self-consistency: The tendency to perceive your experiences in a manner that is consistent with your self-concept, such that experiences that are not consistent with the self are distorted or denied to awareness.

self-disclosure: The voluntary disclosure of your deeper thoughts or feelings to others.

self-efficacy: The belief that you can perform adequately in a particular situation.

self-esteem: The sense of personal worth we associate with our self-concept.

self-fulfillment: The fulfillment of your potential as in self-actualization or personal growth.

sexual dysfunction: A persistent problem that prevents a person from engaging in or enjoying sexual intercourse.

sexual intercourse: Sexual activity involving the penetration of the female vagina by the male penis, characteristically accompanied by pelvic thrusting and orgasm for one or both partners.

sexual response cycle: The basic sexual response patterns of men and women as in sexual intercourse.

sexual stereotypes: Widely held generalizations about the characteristics of men and women that exaggerate the differences between the sexes.

sexually transmitted disease: An infection transmitted primarily by sexual intercourse.

shyness: The tendency to avoid contact or familiarity with others.

single-parent families: Families headed by only one parent, more often a woman.

social change: Changes in the structure of society, its institutions, and social patterns.

social learning theory: The view that emphasizes the primary role of learning and the environment in behavior.

social norms: The rules governing what is acceptable and unacceptable behavior in a given society.

social selves: All those self-perceptions derived from your social roles and your interactions with others.

somatic therapy: A group of therapies that relieve the symptoms of psychological disorders by direct intervention in a person's physiological makeup, through drugs, electroconvulsive therapy, or psychosurgery.

stereotypes: Widespread generalizations about people that have little, if any, basis in fact.

stress: The pattern of specific and nonspecific responses we make to stimulus events that disturb our equilibrium and tax our ability to cope.

stress tolerance: The degree and duration of stress we can tolerate without becoming irrational and disorganized.

stressors: The collective label for the variety of external and internal stimuli that evoke stress.

subjective self: The way you see yourself; the self you think you are.

suicide: The act of taking one's own life intentionally.

superego: According to Freud, that part of the psyche that has been shaped by the moral standards of society as transmitted by the parents.

syphilis: An infectious disease transmitted by sexual intercourse, which if left untreated may lead to the degeneration of bones, heart, and nerve tissue.

tardive dyskinesia: A muscle disorder characterized by abnormal movements of the face, tongue, and neck, caused by some antipsychotic drug.

therapy: The process in which a trained, socially sanctioned healer treats people with a physical or psychological disorder.

trust versus mistrust: According to Erikson, the first stage of psychosocial development in which children need to establish a sense of trust in their caretakers.

unresolved grief: A psychological state in which a person's reaction to loss remains repressed, often being manifested in unexplained physical or psychological symptoms.

values: The sense of worth associated with the various aspects of life.

wellness: The positive ideal of health in which you strive to maintain and improve your health.

withdrawal: A potentially constructive approach to stress, especially when used as a temporary strategy in the face of an overwhelming situation.

Name Index

Subject Index

Answers to Self-tests

CHAPTERS			QUESTIONS							
	1	2	3	4	5	6	7	8	9	10
1.	d	c	a	b	c	d	b	b	b	d
2.	b	c	d	a	c	d	a	a	c	b
3.	b	c	d	b	d	d	b	a	c	a
4.	b	d	a	c	b	d	d	d	b	b
5.	a	d	b	b	c	a	c	d	c	b
6.	d	c	b	c	b	d	a	d	c	b
7.	b	a	c	d	c	b	a	c	b	d
8.	b	c	b	c	d	a	c	d	a	c
9.	d	a	b	c	d	c	a	c	b	d
10.	c	d	a	b	b	c	a	b	d	a
11.	c	b	d	c	b	c	c	a	d	a
12.	c	b	a	d	c	b	a	d	c	b
13.	d	b	b	c	a	c	a	b	a	c
14.	a	c	d	b	d	b	a	c	b	c
15.	d	d	b	c	a	c	c	a	d	c
16.	c	d	b	a	c	a	d	c	d	b

ABOUT THE AUTHOR

Eastwood Atwater is professor of psychology at Montgomery County Community College in the greater Philadelphia area. He is also lecturer in psychology at Gwynedd-Mercy College, and conducts a private practice, primarily with couples. His Ph.D. from the University of Chicago included the year-long practicum in counseling under the supervision of Carl Rogers. Dr. Atwater belongs to the American Psychological Association, Pennsylvania Psychological Association, National Register for Health Service Providers in Psychology, and The Philadelphia Society of Clinical Psychologists. He is the author of several books, including two other textbooks: *Adolescence*, and *Human Relations*. He is married and has two grown daughters.